Lithophanes

Margaret Carney, Ph.D.

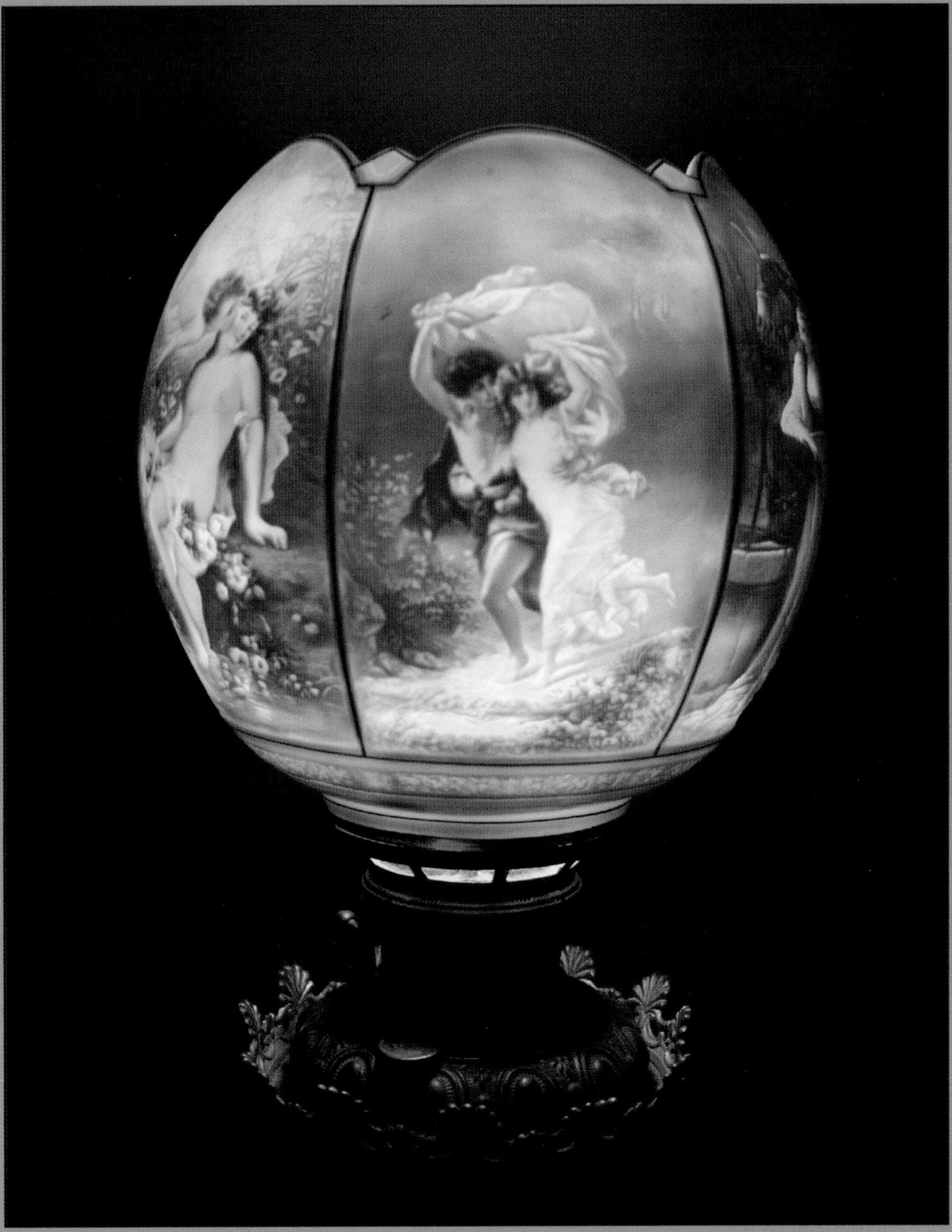

Schiffer Publishing Ltd
4880 Lower Valley Road Atglen, Pennsylvania 19310

Dedicated to Bob Huebner

Library of Congress Control Number: 2008923709

Designed by "Sue"
Type set in Lydian BT/Adobe Jenson Pro

ISBN: 978-0-7643-3019-3
Printed in China

Schiffer Books are available at special discounts for bulk purchases for sales promotions or premiums. Special editions, including personalized covers, corporate imprints, and excerpts can be created in large quantities for special needs. For more information contact the publisher:

Published by Schiffer Publishing Ltd.
4880 Lower Valley Road
Atglen, PA 19310
Phone: (610) 593-1777; Fax: (610) 593-2002
E-mail: Info@schifferbooks.com

For the largest selection of fine reference books on this and related subjects, please visit our web site at **www.schifferbooks.com**
We are always looking for people to write books on new and related subjects. If you have an idea for a book please contact us at the above address.

This book may be purchased from the publisher.
Include $5.00 for shipping.
Please try your bookstore first.
You may write for a free catalog.

In Europe, Schiffer books are distributed by
Bushwood Books
6 Marksbury Ave.
Kew Gardens
Surrey TW9 4JF England
Phone: 44 (0) 20 8392-8585; Fax: 44 (0) 20 8392-9876
E-mail: info@bushwoodbooks.co.uk
Website: www.bushwoodbooks.co.uk
Free postage in the U.K., Europe; air mail at cost.

Contents

Acknowledgments

There are many people to thank for making this project a reality. Foremost would be Laurel Blair, the man who had the vision to begin collecting lithophanes and never stop until he had gathered together the largest collection in the world in his hometown of Toledo, Ohio. That story is revealed in this book. He often promised but never wrote the book on lithophanes himself, leaving behind just a few pages on various lithophane-related topics written with a typewriter that had a cursive script. Dr. Beroud, from whom Mr. Blair bought more than 1,500 lithophanes, also mentioned but never wrote *his* book about lithophanes either. Others, such as Robert Elder and Bernard Rushton threatened to write the book, too. In many ways I wish they'd all written their books, since they were the authorities in their day and because they had purchased all the lithophanes so they were very well acquainted with the available lithophanes and, in some cases, the literature. Through this book they are all contributing, via correspondence and research notes left behind for posterity.

Laurel's brother, Banana George (Blair), made his own contribution by first shopping with his brother for lithophanes in New York City in the early 1960s and then by encouraging him in his quest for domination of the lithophane world. The Blair Museum of Lithophanes original Advisory Board members, including Robert Huebner, Greg Knott, Peggy Grant, and Sandra Wiseley all were active in getting the Museum physically set up during the decade that followed Laurel Blair's death in 1993. None was as active as Bob Huebner who took on the City and its baffling bureaucracy and succeeded in every instance, albeit at a frustrating pace. It was Bob to whom I pitched the lithophane book idea in a letter in late 2003, and after a meeting with Bob and Posy Huebner and Peggy Grant, I was hired as curator and future lithophane book author. Posy was Laurel's cousin and she has admirably filled the void left by Bob's untimely death in May 2004. She has spearheaded the docent program and remains committed to fulfilling the dreams of her cousin, husband, and the greater Toledo community. A staunch supporter of the arts in Toledo, she has not snubbed this decorative art form of the 19th century, but has rallied others to join in supporting this unique feature of Toledo. Our docent program would not exist without Posy Huebner and her endless energy and loads of friends. Banana George has continued to be a supporter of the Museum as he has financed the curatorial position since its inception in 2004. His daughter Georgia (Gee Gee) is a Board member and active supporter of the Museum, as are some of her siblings.

Several of Laurel Blair's friends, colleagues and associates have been instrumental in this project. Chief among those is Greg Knott, who once served as Mr. Blair's curatorial assistant, but was always his friend; Greg with his lithophane knowledge and marvelous stories about the life and times of Laurel Blair has been an asset to the Museum and this book project. Marilyn Kehl and Kurt Hanushek have assisted in so many ways with the Museum and this project that it is impossible to begin to thank them for their time, ideas and generosity in every way.

The current Blair Advisory Board, including Posy Huebner, Heide Klein, Greg Knott, Peggy Grant, Jim Larrow, Bill Mies, Sandra Wiseley, Brad Huebner, Dennis Seffernick, and Gee Gee Blair, remain committed to the lithophane book project, while balancing other responsibilities. While each helped in his or her own way, heartfelt thanks go to Heide Klein, an extraordinary friend and colleague who spent hour after hour translating lithophane articles from German or French to English, knowing that my rudimentary language skills in these areas were frighteningly wanting. She patiently explained puns to me, while we shared glee in the cleverness of those who provided German titles to some of the lithophanes. For all her assistance and patience with my questions, Heide deserves the title Saint Heide. Other translation assistance was provided by Elizabeth Gulacsy in Alfred, New York, who taught me that "litofan ablak" in Hungarian means "lithophane window." Now you know two words in Hungarian, too.

Who is more knowledgeable about lithophanes than the collectors themselves? The United Kingdom has important private collections, and those collectors contributed significantly to this project. Not only have they shared their knowledge, but also their collections, and their love of lithophanes. Andy Cook was generous in agreeing to read the many chapters of this book before it was presented to Peter Schiffer for publishing. Without complaint, he gave weeks of his life over to this project. If the book is any good, it is thanks to his gentle but thorough comments and suggestions. If there are errors, they are all mine. In addition to Andy, I heartily thank the other U.K. collectors I have gotten to know — John and Eve Coleman, Barry Steadman, and Darren King for their friendship and generosity with knowledge. Bernard Rushton, also from the U.K. and now deceased, was an important collector and lithophane researcher. Three members of his extended family, Margaret Rushton and Ian and Emma Seath have supported this project by sharing precious archival materials gathered by Mr. Rushton through the years. His collection included some of the most interesting lithophanes ever produced, several of which are illustrated in this book. Those who own pieces from his collection, know they have won the lithophane lottery.

Other private collectors were generous in sharing images of the pieces in their collection for both research purposes and for book illustrations. This list includes Sandy Melnikoff, Connie and John Scott, Nan Gole, the McWrights, and Graham and Helen Pullen.

There are friends who aren't Blair board members and fellow curators who have been immensely supportive of this book project. Chief amongst those is sculptor Mary Jo Bole, who has contagious energy and novel approaches to problem solving. Above all, she's a great listener and friend and loves lithophanes, too. Canadian ceramist Léopold Foulem was an inspiration early on – supplying ideas and references whenever he came across them, long before I was prepared to understand their significance. The co-author of my last book on Flint Faience tiles, Ken Galvas, was the best book co-conspirator ever, and influenced the outcome of this book in immeasurable ways. Steve Arrasmith has been a great friend and colleague in supporting my research and this project.

Regarding buildings in the United States with lithophanes as architectural features, there were several individuals and institutions that made the "lithophanes *in situ*" chapter a viable concern. Sincere thanks are extended to Ulf Hedberg, archivist at Gallaudet University in Washington, D.C., who promised and produced wonderful images of the President's home, the lithophanes, and even the original blueprints. Jim and Sharon Larrow also assisted with the contacting of Gallaudet University. Brian Scriven who works at Letchworth State Park, a New York State historic site located in Castile, New York, was of stellar assistance with investigating and photographing the lithophanes located at the Glen Iris. The employees of the Glen Iris Inn were welcoming on both visits to the Inn where we tried not to interfere with guests and wedding parties. The current owners of the Surry House Bed & Breakfast, Mary Anne Bonafair and Eileen Duffy, were most gracious in their assistance, answering pestering questions and obtaining professional photographs of their marvelous lithophane of Mount Vesuvius. Information about Samuel Colt was first brought to my attention by Posy Huebner, cousin of Mr. Blair and a member of the Blair Museum of Lithophanes Advisory Board. I thank her for this lead on the fascinating article that appeared in *The Magazine Antiques*, which resulted in locating the book about Samuel Colt by Herbert Houze and subsequent email correspondence with Adria Patterson at the Wadsworth Atheneum as well as Herb Houze. Both were generous in sharing their knowledge and expertise. Though a personal visit by this author to the Campbell House Museum in St. Louis has not yet happened, the incredible photographs from the 1800s and information provided by their director, Andy Hahn, was an excellent substitute. It is on my "next time I'm even near St. Louis to-do list." And their website makes one want to book a direct flight. Antje Sauerteig at Louisa's Place in Berlin was helpful in sending photographs of their stairway. Many leads on lithophanes *in situ* were provided by Andy Cook, a dedicated lithophane collector, researcher and friend.

There are libraries and librarians who I thank for their assistance in so many ways. These would include the librarians at Scholes Library of Ceramics at the New York State College of Ceramics at Alfred University, Mercedes Hanbach, Elizabeth Gulacsy, and Pat LaCourse. While in the United Kingdom, there were several librarians who excelled at enriching my bibliographic resources, including Ann Pace at CERAM in Stoke-on-Trent and the librarians in the Hanley Archives, also in Stoke. The Interlibrary Loan librarian at the Toledo Public Library, Rita, has a gift for obtaining obscure treasures direct from the Library of Congress, and Mary Jane Horn at the University of Toledo's Carlson Library has been of wonderful assistance.

Museum curators, my colleagues at home and abroad, have been extremely generous in sharing information, images, and access to collections. In the United Kingdom, Neil Hyman, Keeper of Decorative Art for the Hampshire County Council Museums and Archives Service, was gracious to share their beautiful lithophane collection one afternoon in July 2007. Neil saved the day when our light table transformer burned out and did not get visibly upset when smoke starting coming from the ill-fated electronic device. He cheerfully made his own light box available for our photography. I wish I worked with Neil on a daily basis.

Museum professionals in the United States, United Kingdom, France, Germany, Italy and Portugal, all were extremely helpful with this project. Klaus-Jochen Wahl and Helga Scheidt at the Schloßmuseum Arnstadt were wonderful to send their catalogue on von Schierholz along with a copy of the 1865-70 PPM/C.G. Schierholz *Preis-Courant I* and several later versions. Helga was the soul of patience answering endless questions and provided some of the most interesting documentation relating to lithophanes. In Portugal, Filipa Quatorze of the Vista Alegre Museum, was extremely helpful in supplying images of veilleuses and backstamps in a timely manner. Oliva Rucellai, Director of the Doccia Museum was a marvel when it came to sleuthing out elusive facts from their archives and the factory, too. Jessie McNab, curator at the Metropolitan Museum of Art, was a delight and fount of information during a dreary day in October. Just a brief list of the many other experts who assisted would include Aasmund Beier at the Porsgunnsmuseene in Norway, Deborah Harding at the Carnegie Museum of Natural History in Pittsburgh, Ann Dorsett at the Carmarthenshire Museums Service, and Isotta Poggi at the Getty Research Institute, part of the J. Paul Getty Museum.

Along the same vein, collectors John and Eve Coleman loaned us a tripod and photo backdrop box to use during our fourteen days in the UK, and then met us at Gatwick to retrieve these loans. We hope the quality of our photographs was enhanced by this kind gesture. The Colemans, Andy Cook, and Darren King have been true collaborators on this project, sharing information, their collections, and their ceaseless enthusiasm. Andy Cook, collector and lithophane researcher, took a look at and critiqued every chapter for my benefit and his many valuable ideas are reflected positively in this publication. As for other collectors, all roads seemed to lead to legendary lithophane connoisseur Bernard Rushton. Through Darren King and John Coleman and Barry Steadman all the pieces came together and contact was made with his descendents who shared his archival papers.

There were also those in related ceramic industry positions who assisted enthusiastically with this project. That would include Paul Farmer, managing director of Wade Ceramics, Ltd. in Stoke-on-Trent, who met with us and attempted to put us in contact with a former employee of Wade Pottery. Most incredibly helpful was Johannes Kraus, with Seltmann USA, who provided amazing current information about Plaue and its current managers and owners, Royal Tettau and Seltman Weiden. Constantin v. Schierholz, related to the von Schierholz porcelain legacy, was extremely helpful also and I gratefully thank him for his assistance.

There are many individuals, too numerous to mention, who I would like to thank. I appreciate Steve Mattison alerting me about the Herend Church windows in Herend, Hungary, and also providing the photograph. And Dr. Karl-Heinz Steckelings was kind to share ideas with me before I was even prepared to have a salient discussion and later sent me a copy of the PPM *Preis-Courant* I had not seen previously, in exchange for an article he needed for *his* book on lithophanes. Researcher and scholar Dr. Baerbel Kovalevski was so kind to share a Meissen *Preis-Courant* that added valuable information. Sandy Shroth, Walter Ford's daughter, was a great supporter in terms of sharing documents and ceramic materials.

There were also people who are specialists in various areas who were willing to take look at small sections of the book. These generous experts include Peggy and Jon Kerner, Paul and Zena Thomas, and James Sapp.

Saving the best for last, isn't really my style, but my most loving thanks are for my husband, Bill Walker, who lived this project with me for the past several years. Not only did he assist with a myriad of Museum duties too numerous to list, but he took precious photographs for the book, and read and reread chapter after scintillating chapter and shared his sense of humor throughout. His artistic and technical knowledge made insurmountable tasks and information almost enjoyable. Overall he made the project more fun that it should have been.

While attempting to thank all the people who have made the lithophane book project a reality, there is one more to thank. The one more entity is not a person, but a cat who has served as my muse for manuscripts dating back to 1986. Libby was just a kitten when she sat perched on my shoulders as I wrote my doctoral dissertation in Eugene, Oregon. She sat on my husband's shoulders as he wrote his doctoral dissertation a decade later, and back on mine again for other book scribing. This year, in 2007, Libby once again assisted in my writing of one of the chapters for this book. She was over 20 years old, and no longer wanting to dangle on my shoulders, but she sat by my side and offered periodic comments in her insightful way. She passed away not long after that one chapter was drafted – the chapter about lithophanes *in situ*, when she herself was *in situ*. Absent but not forgotten, her spirit guided the rest of the project as I wrote these thousands of words in the room where she chose to spend her final few months and where she ultimately passed on. Every time I see a cat or kitten in a 19th century lithophane, I think of Libby.

Introduction

Probably every person who has ever encountered a lithophane for the first time believes that he or she has discovered a lost Victorian art form. While they were made in Europe by the hundreds of thousands in the 19th century and they were wildly popular for decades, they seem rare today. And while they may be found in the permanent collections of the grandest of museums, such as the Metropolitan Museum of Art in New York, the Victoria & Albert Museum in London, and the Smithsonian Institution's National Museum of American History in Washington, D.C., they are seldom on public display. Perhaps they were not "lost" but rather went out of fashion. Their heyday was nearly two hundred years ago, during times when electricity was non-existent, and building interiors were illuminated by candles and oil lamps, and heated by fireplaces. When electricity became common, lithophanes became less common. The incandescent light bulb was invented in 1879, and the waning of lithophane popularity had already begun. Not too long after, the word lithophane disappeared from common usage, as the lithophanes were stored away in dresser drawers and closets. Sometimes memories seem not just short, but fickle. Lithophanes have been described as "greatly prized at the time..." but are now seen in museums "among other bric-à-brac of the period."[1]

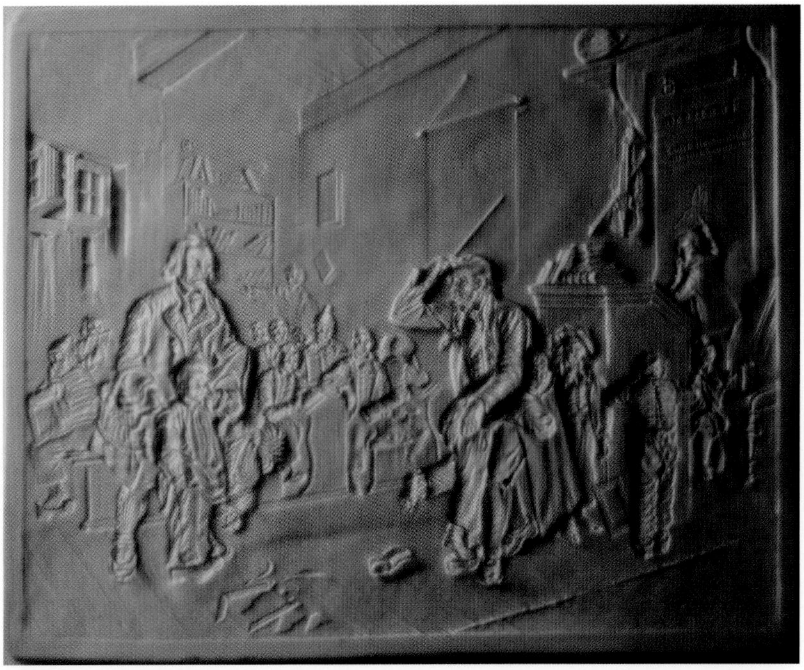

Lithophane, *Der neue Schüler* (*The New Student*), unlit, German, 19th century, PPM 624, Blair Museum acc. no. 1003, 6" x 7.5". *Courtesy of the Blair Museum of Lithophanes.*

To appreciate the beauty of lithophanes they need to be viewed in person. Photographs of lithophanes simply do not adequately convey the three-dimensional quality of the porcelain surface that magically appears in stunning detail when the piece is backlit. The best 19th century lithophane plaques made by KPM or Meissen in Germany or the large single cast shades marked Lithophanie Francaise rival the finest engravings of the day. In fact they were porcelain copies or reproductions of the finest engravings of the day, which were, in turn, often based on popular paintings.

Porcelain is the key to this magical phenomenon known as lithophanes. One could be a scholar of porcelain, understand the subtle technical nuances of working with specialized high temperature materials, kilns, and the like, but who amongst us can fully grasp how the rays of light coming through the window, that appear in the backlit lithophane, were translated from copying an engraving, carving a wax model, making a plaster mold from the model, and molding a porcelain plaque? How were those light rays captured and translated in porcelain? The finished product is porcelain and nothing but porcelain – yet it is as detailed and beautiful as any mezzotint.

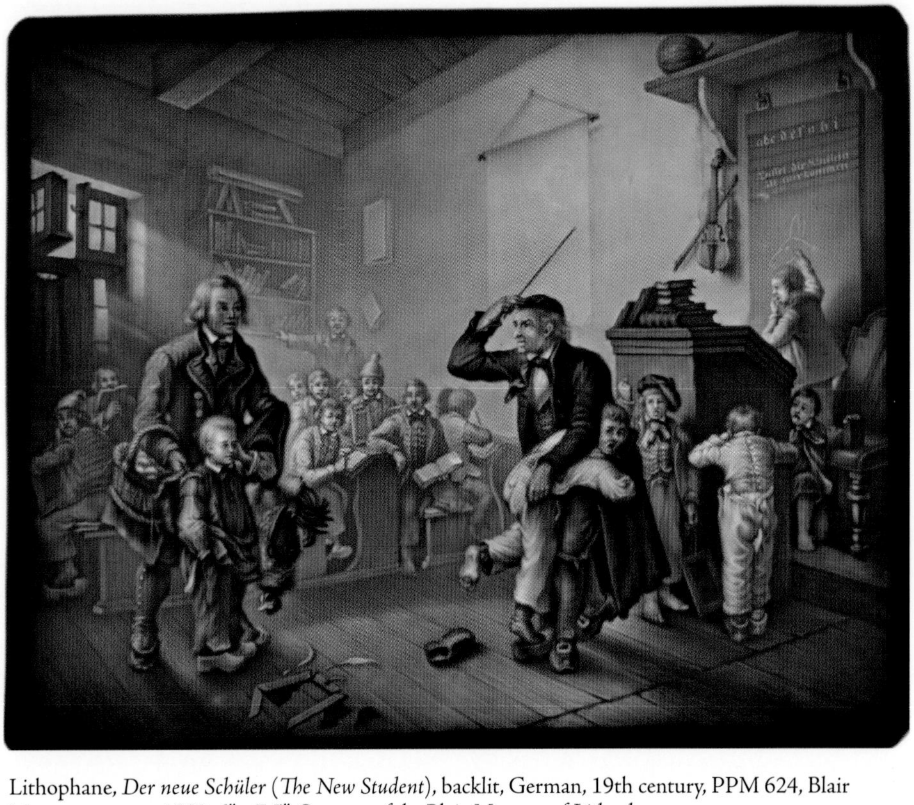

Lithophane, *Der neue Schüler* (*The New Student*), backlit, German, 19th century, PPM 624, Blair Museum acc. no. 1003, 6" x 7.5". *Courtesy of the Blair Museum of Lithophanes.*

It isn't that people have not been fascinated by lithophanes. The fascination is both evident and paramount in every article, now numbering in the hundreds, which mentions lithophanes and their origins. In recent decades there have been several scholars or authorities on the subject, most of whom were continually threatening to publish a book on the topic. Chief amongst these were Harold Newman, Bernard Rushton, Robert A. Elder, Jr., Dr. Edmond Beroud, and Laurel Blair. Harold Newman (1899-1993) published extensively about veilleuses and also wrote one of the best articles about lithophanes.[2] Thomas Bernard Rushton (1923-1993) was a respected authority on lighting and porcelain who collected rare and beautiful lithophane specimens and gathered together significant historical sources on lithophanes in the 1960s and 1970s, clearly with a book in mind. Robert A. Elder, Jr. was a Smithsonian Institution curator, who wrote to a colleague in 1959, "I am the one who is writing the history of lithophanes in book form and developed the idea of such a possibility through contact with Dr. Beroud's very comprehensive collection now of some 1,775 specimens, and our continuous collaboration since."[3] Dr. Edmond Beroud (died 1993) amassed the largest collection of lithophanes in the world beginning in 1947 and conducted much scholarly research with institutions and manufacturers and was planning on writing *the* book as early as 1953. He wrote in correspondence in 1954, "...but piece by piece I am getting the information that I desire, and some day in a near future I will write a book on 'LITHOPHANE.'"[4] Laurel Blair, of Toledo, Ohio, collected hundreds and hundreds of lithophanes before purchasing Dr. Beroud's collection, and traveled worldwide, to collect and meet with other interested parties. He established a museum, formed a collectors' club and published a newsletter six times a year. He bought and sold lithophanes and helped organize, rally and excite the interested public in this "lost Victorian art form." Among all those who were planning to write a book, he never wrote the book for the longest period of time, even though his correspondence to everyone is laced with the notion that he "now had time to write the book." In 1965 Mr. Blair responded to a query from the United Kingdom seeking information about lithophanes. He wrote, "It will take me most of this year to write the book and then to have it published will take another year or so, but hope that I can announce in the not too distant future that one will be ready, and will keep your name on file for that eventuality."[5] In 1967 he wrote, "Right after I return from Europe I will start writing my book and hope that it will be finished by the beginning of next year on the whole subject of lithophanes."[6]

There was even a bit of a rivalry amongst several who were anticipating the joy of writing *the* book on lithophanes. Robert Elder wrote to Laurel Blair in a detailed letter dated August 14, 1964, "In a letter from Beroud he mentioned in passing, something about your planning to do a book on lithophanes, which I hope to hear was not a really serious idea, because I am sure that I told you when we began corresponding that this was exactly what I have been working on for 15 years. I have been gathering all the data and records of anything of this type that I could hear of, with the plan to write a fully comprehensive History of Lithophanes. I have spent a great deal of time on this project, and though I know there is a lot to go yet (for this reason we are not ready to rush into print on it) I would surely hope that you would have enough to do with your collection and its display in a Museum, if that is what you have in mind, and would let me go ahead with the book angle??"[7] All these plans to write the book, and it never happening in sixty years, makes one wonder if the field is jinxed. That truly is not the case, it just turns out that writing *the* book is far more complicated than a simple porcelain plaque might lead one to believe.

The following twelve chapters will convey the simple and complex connections involving definition of terms and description; the creation of lithophanes from carving beeswax models, making plaster molds, and molding porcelain; the history of porcelain and how it relates to the invention of lithophanes and related patent issues; major European factories, as well as U.S. production by companies and individual artists; examples of backstamps and factory markings; locations to visit where the 19th century lithophanes remain *in situ*; the relationship between lithophanes and photography; lithophanous inspiration in terms of engravings, masterpiece paintings, books such as the Bible and popular literature; Asian inspiration; the uses of lithophanes in portraits, candle shields, veilleuses, lanterns, erotica, doll house miniatures, fairy lamps, beer steins, and more; innovations in lithophanic art such as coloring the pieces; Victorian humor as viewed through a backlit lithophane plaque; the history of the Blair Museum of Lithophanes and its origins; other museum collections worldwide; and lithophanes made of plastic, edible chocolate and more.

In terms of hierarchies of art materials studied by art historians, ceramics have always ranked well below paintings and sculpture. There aren't many ceramic art historians, nor are there many art history courses, be it ancient, medieval, or modern, that weave the history of world ceramics through any particular era's masterpiece paintings, architectural edifices, or monumental bronzes. And within the hierarchy of ceramics, porcelain could be viewed as most "highly evolved" in relationship to earthenware and stoneware, but in books about the porcelain production at KPM, Meissen, or Worcester, lithophanes are relegated to lesser art form status among the creative output of those esteemed manufacturers. This is why the topic is so long overdue.

Why lithophanes should have disappeared from everyday life and everyday vocabulary is not really a mystery. When found in a grandmother's attic, they would have been discarded because with reflected light there is nothing to see. One might wonder, "why did grandma keep this?" In Europe, where they were originally made, they were either destroyed by wars that impacted homes, museums, and repositories for related archival materials,[8] or they were discarded as being out of style. New items came on the market in the 1870s that caused the lithophanes to seem out-of-date. By the turn of the 20th century they were relegated to attics or trash piles or, in the case of museums, sometimes deaccessioned. The word "lithophane" itself disappeared from dictionaries and encyclopedias about this same time and it did not reappear until about 1982, thanks to Mr. Blair.

While there is some trepidation that the publication of this manuscript might raise more questions than it answers, it is certain to be a journey taken with many friends. These friends may be of the human variety, collectors and artists and researchers of 19th century phenomena, or these may be the new friends -- those sitters identified in the lithophane plaques, such as Goethe, Napoleon, Jenny Lind, or Abélard. It is this act of discovery that is revealed in each magical lithophane when back lit – depicting a special place, a memorial event, a captivating story, or a person of interest. Lithophanes truly captured an era that will not be forgotten, but was rather recorded in bisque porcelain in the 19th century for one to rediscover light by light.

Chapter One
Lithophanes: Definition and Description

A Google™ search will lead the novice "lithophane" investigator to websites with either scintillating images of moths with a distinctive white and charcoal camouflage coloring or information about three-dimensional translucent porcelain plaques which when backlit reveal detailed magical images. An investigation of the latter, involves the 19th century phenomenon known as lithophanes, derived from the Greek *litho* meaning *stone* and *phainen* meaning *to cause to appear*. This Greek derivation has proven confusing to people who might know some basic Greek, but do not know that lithophanes have nothing to do with stone or a stone product, but are made of porcelain.

They are known as *Lithophanien* in Germany; *lithophanies* in France; *litofan* in Hungary; *litofanie* in Italy; *litofaanit* in Finnish, *litofanier* in Norwegian, and *litofanias* in Spain and Portugal. English speakers sometimes refer to lithophanes as lithopanes. Most literature about lithophanes is in German and a little is in French. During the 19th century they were additionally referred to as lithophanous pictures, photophanic pictures, bisque or parian pictures, Berlin transparencies, Bijou transparencies, bisque intaglios, translucent embossments, tableaux lithophaniques, lithophanic translucids, and transparencies. No matter what they were called, all were made of porcelain at that time, utilizing a procedure first patented in France and produced in France and Germany in the late 1820s.

Lithophanes are porcelain plaques formed in a mold cast from a model made in wax, which when back lit have the appearance of being painted in grisaille (a style of monochromatic painting in shades of gray, used especially for the representation of relief sculpture). They appear as strange bumpy white objects when viewed with reflected light. Yet when illuminated from behind, the delicate image magically appears, with all the gradations of light and shadow, with the resulting image as clear as a mezzotint. Where the porcelain is thicker, less light can penetrate and a dark effect is created; and where the porcelain is thinner, more light is transmitted and that area of the lithophane appears bright. The front surface has a three-dimensional picture in low relief, while the back is flat and smooth. The exquisite detail of the carving apparent in 19th century lithophanes and their remarkable translucency compared to those produced in the 20th century makes differentiating the lithophanes of these two centuries relatively easy.

A more general definition of lithophanes in recent years encompasses a thin translucent plaque which could be comprised of any number of materials created by molding or computer-assisted carving, which must be illuminated from behind for the detailed three-dimensional image to be revealed. These various translucent materials include porcelain, plastic, other composites, or even chocolate. Details about Lithoplastics, Epix, and Chocpix chocolate photographic lithophanes are provided in Chapter Eleven.

And finally, lithophanes have been described in this computer age, as images that can be created by limiting the amount of light that passes through a material. By changing the thickness of the material the amount of light passing through creates a contrast.

Montage of lithophanes from the Blair Museum collection, backlit. *Courtesy of the Blair Museum of Lithophanes.*

Large KPM lithophane, *Der Fischerknabe, nach Goethe*, German, 19th century, KPM 302 B, Blair Museum acc. no. 154, 13.75" x 11". *Courtesy of the Blair Museum of Lithophanes.*

Chapter Two
Creation of Lithophanes

Most lithophane collectors will view their treasures as the result of industrial magic. They were popular well into the Victorian era, and were the rage in Europe between 1840 and 1870. This Victorian craze was invented, patented, perfected, and marketed almost simultaneously by individuals and factories in France, Germany and England circa 1827-28. While these delicate porcelain panels and plaques do not reveal their secrets until held before a strong light, unlike paintings, etchings and prints, they are three-dimensional pictures.

During the 19th century lithophanes were made in a factory setting by skilled, primarily anonymous craftspeople. The process involved using precision hand tools to model an image in wax on a backlit glass panel. The tools would have been similar to those used by a dentist, though they could have been made of metal, wood or ivory. A small amount of white lead may have been mixed with the wax.[1] Where the wax was thinnest more light would shine through; and where it was thickest, less light is transmitted. This skillful modeling is what allowed all the subtle nuances of the engraving to be translated ultimately into the finished porcelain lithophane. The carving of the wax model would have taken several weeks and depending on the size and complexity of the piece, it could have taken two months or more. The wax carving served as the model and it was used to create a plaster mold, which in turn was used to mold lithophanes in porcelain. The important fact about the use of molds was that it allowed for the production of multiples and, indeed, tens of thousands of lithophanes were produced in the 19th century.

Carved wax model for a lithophane titled *Maria Magdalena, nach Battoni*, German, 19th century, Blair Museum acc. no. 2598, 6.5" x 9.25", frame 8" x 10.75". *Courtesy of the Blair Museum of Lithophanes.*

Carved wax model for a lithophane titled *Spring*, German, 19th century, Blair Museum acc. no. 379, 4.125" x 3.5", frame 5.625" x 4.625". *Courtesy of the Blair Museum of Lithophanes.*

Lithophane, *Spring*, PPM 423, German, 19th century, Blair Museum acc. no. 630, 3.5" x 2.875". *Courtesy of the Blair Museum of Lithophanes.*

Original 19th century wax carvings are extremely fragile, and therefore very rare. The Blair Museum collection has only five original wax carvings, and none are in pristine condition. Mr. Blair noted that he saw many original waxes during his visit to the von Schierholz factory in Plaue in 1965. Because a plaster mold would have a limited lifespan when used to mold porcelain, a master mold (called a case in English and American factories) would have been utilized, too. One type of master mold, created from a plaster mold, would have been made of pewter, tin or type-metal allowing for the ease of manufacture of multiple plaster molds.[2]

Carved wax model for the PPM 258 lithophane, *Champagnertrinker*, German, 19th century, Blair Museum acc. no. 663, 7.375" x 5.5". *Courtesy of the Blair Museum of Lithophanes.*

Carved wax model for a lithophane, woman and child with deer in the background, German, 19th century, Blair Museum acc. no. 1, 7.125" x 5.5". *Courtesy of the Blair Museum of Lithophanes.*

One or two-piece plaster molds were used for the pressing or slipcasting of porcelain multiples. Until around 1890, all of the molds used would have been press molds, as slipcasting was not prevalent until the last decade of the 19th century. Few original 19th century plaster molds have survived.

The porcelain recipe would have been guarded with some secrecy in the plant, as the quality of materials in the formula would have determined the end quality of the product. A typical porcelain body formula may have included 66% kaolin, 30% feldspar, and 4% soapstone.[3] The porcelain paste was then pressed into the mold and after the plaster had absorbed the appropriate amount of moisture from the porcelain, the hardened porcelains were removed from the molds. After drying, they were then fired to about 2300° Fahrenheit (approximately 1300° Celsius). At that temperature, a large percentage, perhaps up to 60% of these fragile porcelains, warped, slumped or cracked in the kiln and was lost. Predictable shrinkage occurs from the time the porcelain is formed in the mold to after it is fired – between 12-20%. Comparing an original wax carving model with the finished porcelain lithophane makes this shrinkage easy to detect. The finished lithophane is about 1/8th of an inch thick.

Because the ceramic body of choice for lithophanes needed to be translucent porcelain or a Parian[4] body, often it was not until individual factories invented, discovered or introduced a suitable material into the company repertoire, that lithophanes would be produced.

The original lithophane patent by Baron Paul (Charles-Amable) de Bourgoing (1791-1864) dated 1827, gives a good description of the process, including many details that have been somewhat confusing in more recent descriptions. The patent accordingly describes three embodiments of the invention called lithophany, and provides for the invention to be made from any number of materials. The first embodiment is what we commonly think of as a lithophane, and the others have never really been practiced.

The second known patent is an English patent granted to Robert Griffith Jones in 1828, and might be more accurately described as a license to practice the invention of lithophany in England. It closely matches the description of the first embodiment of the French patent. When considering the patents relating to lithophanes in both France and England, the question often arises as to whether or not there was a German patent. Mr. Blair made a considerable effort to find a German patent to no avail. At the time lithophanes were created there was no central patent office in Germany as it consisted of many smaller states. The central patent office did not come into existence until after Bismarck unified Germany in 1871.[5] If patents were granted in Prussia or Thuringia, they have not been found. Additionally in the 1870s there was a new law regarding copyrights and the payment of royalties which impacted all reproduction of images, including lithophanes.

Above right:
Two-piece plaster mold for the lithophane *Maria Stuart* (Mary Queen of Scots), German, date unknown, Blair Museum acc. no. 2732, 8.125" x 7.125" x 2.875". *Courtesy of the Blair Museum of Lithophanes.*

Right:
Plaster mold for the lithophane *Imogen*, German, date unknown, Blair Museum acc. no. 177, 6" x 5.5" x 0.375". *Courtesy of the Blair Museum of Lithophanes.*

The process, as described in the French patent is as follows:

1. melted wax is poured onto a piece of glass;

2. the wax is manipulated into the desired image, by a variety of techniques, including building up multiple layers of wax, adding wax cutouts and carving the wax. The finished wax model is called by Bourgoing an *Aperçu* (meaning "outline"), abbreviated A;

3. a plaster cast or mold is made from the wax. This cast is called a *Base* ("foundation"), abbreviated B;

4. a second plaster cast called a *Contra-éprevue* ("counter-proof" or "check-against"), or C, is made of the *Base*. This might be made from a colored plaster so it can easily be distinguished from the *Base* or from the *Définitif* described in the next step;

5. the *Définitif* ("final"), or D, is cast on the *Contra-éprevue* and used as the mold to form many copies of the lithophane. The D can be made from copper, tin, or plaster.

6. the final products are called *Exemplieres* ("copies"), or E.

The patent goes on to explain other methods that might be used during the modeling. Liquid wax might be blown upon to create the effect of clouds. Figures made from copper might be pressed into the wax to mold the surface, or the copper figures might even be embedded into the wax. The patent also notes that some elements of the picture are more easily carved into the *Base* than modeled in wax in the *Aperçu*. For example, dark tree branches against a light sky, and fine details might be added with a graveur to a metal *Définitif*.

In de Bourgoing's 1827 patent, this first process is described as "translucid lithophany." While one is familiar with porcelain lithophanes, the patent states that they may also be made from glass, enamel, wax, or gum. The patent goes on to describe two other embodiments of the invention, which he also calls lithophany. These are both opaque, and form images that are visible in normal reflected lighting.

The first type of opaque lithophane, described as the "clear-fading" or "*clairs-ternis*" (meaning "tarnished light") variety, consists of an opaque white base with a relief surface. It is covered with a layer of a transparent colored material, which may be wax, resin, enamel or even glass. The front surface is flat, so the thickness of this transparent colored layer varies depending on the relief of the opaque base. Because it is colored, thick regions of this transparent layer form dark areas representing shadows and thin regions form light highlights. If a mold used to form a translucent porcelain lithophane were to be filled with a colored transparent resin, and the resin was left in place after it had hardened, an opaque lithophane of this first type would be formed.

The third embodiment of the 1827 patent is a second type of opaque lithophane, described as "lithophany with soft shadows." It is similar to the first type of opaque lithophane, with the light and dark layers reversed. It consists of a dark opaque relief that is coated with a thin coating of a white enamel or opal glass. The front surface is flat, so in this case, the thickness of the white layer varies and creates the image. Because the white enamel is somewhat opaque, the image is more diffuse, creating the effect of soft shadows. The lithophane relief used for this second type of opaque lithophane process is similar to that used for translucent lithophanes, but it is formed in a dark opaque material. The light regions corresponding to the thin portions of the transparent lithophane would be light due to the pooling of the white enamel. Likewise, the thicker dark portions of the translucent lithophane would be dark because of the thinner layer of enamel over the underlying dark material.

In 1842 de Bourgoing was granted a patent for another invention, which he also called "lithophany", but is better known as *émail ombrant*. It is a variation on the two types of opaque lithophanes described in the 1827 patent. A thin layer of colored transparent glaze is applied over an opaque white lithophanic relief. During firing, the glaze pools in the recessed areas to form the dark regions of the image, while the thinner glaze on the raised portions reveals the light body underneath to form the light highlights of the image. The relief is similar to that of a mold used to form a transparent lithophane. In the case of *émail ombrant* the surface has a slight relief due to the underlying relief.

The Blair archives contain a typed copy of the 1827 patent in French and a typed translation in English, which was presumably commissioned by Mr. Blair.

For a complete English translation of the original Bourgoing French patent no. 5117, see Appendix A. The English patent granted to Jones is included in Appendix B.

The creation of lithophanes involves processes that have fascinated artists, engineers, collectors, and ceramophiles for nearly two centuries. One can picture skilled wax modelers with delicate tools, toiling in 19th century factories over intricate carvings of beeswax over a backlit piece of glass. These mental images only tell part of the story. Nearly simultaneously, photography was being developed which eventually lead to a portion, albeit a relatively small portion, of the 19th century lithophanes being created by the use of photomechanical processes on ceramics in some of these same factories.

While the relationship between photography and lithophane production will be detailed in this chapter, it has long been noted in the literature, by even the novice collector. Frequently in introductory presentations in newspaper articles and journal articles, the author will describe how some people perceive that the lithophane is formed by sandwiching a photograph between two thin sheets of porcelain. This is not the case. Examining a lithophane with ones own hands and eyes, reveals the three-dimensional sculptural quality of the work.

In 1965, Mintons sent Laurel Blair a Minton lithophane and the corresponding press mold. The one-piece plaster mold was made in 1965 from an old plaster case in the factory. D.H. Henson, the Minton designer, sent Mr. Blair a photostatic copy of the 1890 Woodbury article (see following paragraphs) that explained how a photographic technique was probably used to produce the molds for lithophanes, such as the cathedral or church image he sent. The designer wrote that "instead of taking lead impressions from the gelatine (as described by Woodbury) we probably cast a plaster mold."[6] Mintons is a clear example of how the debate of hand-carved wax models vs. photo process on ceramics is unsolvable.

A variety of photo processes have been described in the literature from the 19th century onward and the proof of the usage of such techniques in the factory setting can be seen in the existence of 19th century lithophanes that possess photographic images on porcelain.

Lithophane portraits and city scenes were popular in the heyday of lithophanes during the 19th century. It has been noted that the popularity of lithophanes declined when photography became more commonplace and also when inexpensive postcards were made available. The concept of *Carte-de-visité* was introduced around 1859. The relationship between photography and porcelain plaques was, at times, more a collaboration than adversarial.

Both lithophanes and photography had their origins in the 1820s. The first permanent photo was taken in 1822 when Joseph Niépce invented what he called heliography and created a "photo" of an engraving of Pope Pius VII. In 1826, this same gentleman focused a camera onto a sunny scene outside the third-floor window of his home in France for some eight hours and captured the first photo of nature by means of taking a pewter plate and coating it with bitumen of judea. The first daguerreotypes emerged towards the end of the 1830s, when Louis Daguerre (1787-1851) utilized a copper plate that had been cleaned and sensitized by exposure to iodine vapors, exposed the plate in the camera for ten minutes, and then developed it using mercury vapors, fixed and dried. Meanwhile, in England, Henry Fox Talbot produced his own photographic negative in 1835, now referred to as the Calotype.

It has been recorded that a photograph had successfully been printed on a ceramic surface by Pierre-Michel Lafon de Camarsac (1821-1905) in France in 1854, who published this information in 1855. This feat has also been credited to Bulot and Cattin, who patented the process in England on December 13, 1854. Camarsac used a gum bichromate system[7] similar to others used successfully up to the present day. Basic pottery books describe some of these methods of decorating porcelain with photographs.[8] The lithophanes and ceramic tiles made in the latter half of the 19th century likely utilized a related bichromate[9] process with gelatin in the photographic production of relief molds.[10] Information about photo ceramics is available, one of the best being a thesis prepared by Graham B. Meeson in the United Kingdom, an unpublished, circa 1970s version of which Mr. Blair had in his possession. Its subject matter dealt not only with photo ceramics but also the tile portraiture of George Cartlidge and even the debate of whether Cartlidge used photographic processes in his *émail ombrant* creations.

Walter Woodbury is credited with using a chemical process to produce photographic relief surfaces as early as 1865. It is likely that a process such as this was used to create lithophanes. Excerpts from *The Encyclopedia of Photography*, published in 1890, clarify the process:

> Photo Reliefs.—Images in relief produced by photography, and largely employed in photo-mechanical printing processes. The simplest method of making a relief is based on the peculiar property of dichromatised gelatine to become insoluble when acted upon by light. If we take a glass or a sheet of paper coated with a thick film of dichromatised gelatine and expose it beneath a negative, those parts situated beneath the transparent parts of the negative image lose their solubility, while the parts not affected retain it. The remaining parts of half-tones of the negative allow it to be affected in different degrees, according to the amount of their transparency. If the exposed gelatine film be laid in cold water, only the soluble or unaffected parts will swell up, the insoluble portions remain the same. By this means we get a true relief. From this a casting may be made, and electrotype printing blocks produced.
>
> If the exposed film be laid in hot water, however, we have already explained that the unaffected parts will dissolve away ... If this be placed in cold water the unexposed portions will swell up above the others ... If, however, it be laid in warm water the soluble parts will then dissolve ... It will be noted here the half-tones are lost; they have no support, and consequently are easily detached and torn away ... To prevent this, however, a new support is given to the gelatine, or the film may be coated on a collodion or other transparent film, and exposed on the reverse side under the negative.
>
> If we compare (the two) we shall see that by the two processes, i.e., the application of cold and hot water, we get two opposite kinds of reliefs; the first the unexposed parts stand out in relief, but in the latter case it is those which have been exposed to the light.[11]

As contemporary ceramic artist and lithophane creator Curtis Benzle has observed, "Clearly the photo process is much more efficient and it is easy to understand why this process has long been the process of choice among lithophane producers. It is also fairly easy to understand why the carved wax concept became so widely assumed to have been the primary production method, in that it sounds much more interesting."[12] Benzle has himself used both methods in creating his own original lithophanes (see Chapter Twelve). The romantic view of the skilled wax carver is probably responsible for the belief held by some that the earliest lithophanes were carved entirely by hand, creating one-of-a-kind porcelain masterpieces (as opposed to multiples created by the use of molds).

Contemporary lithophane artists are not in agreement about the frequency of use of the photo-mechanical process in creating lithophanes in the 19th century (see Chapter Twelve), yet contemporary makers are extremely familiar with the investigations by Woodbury in the 19th century and Walter Ford in the 1930s.

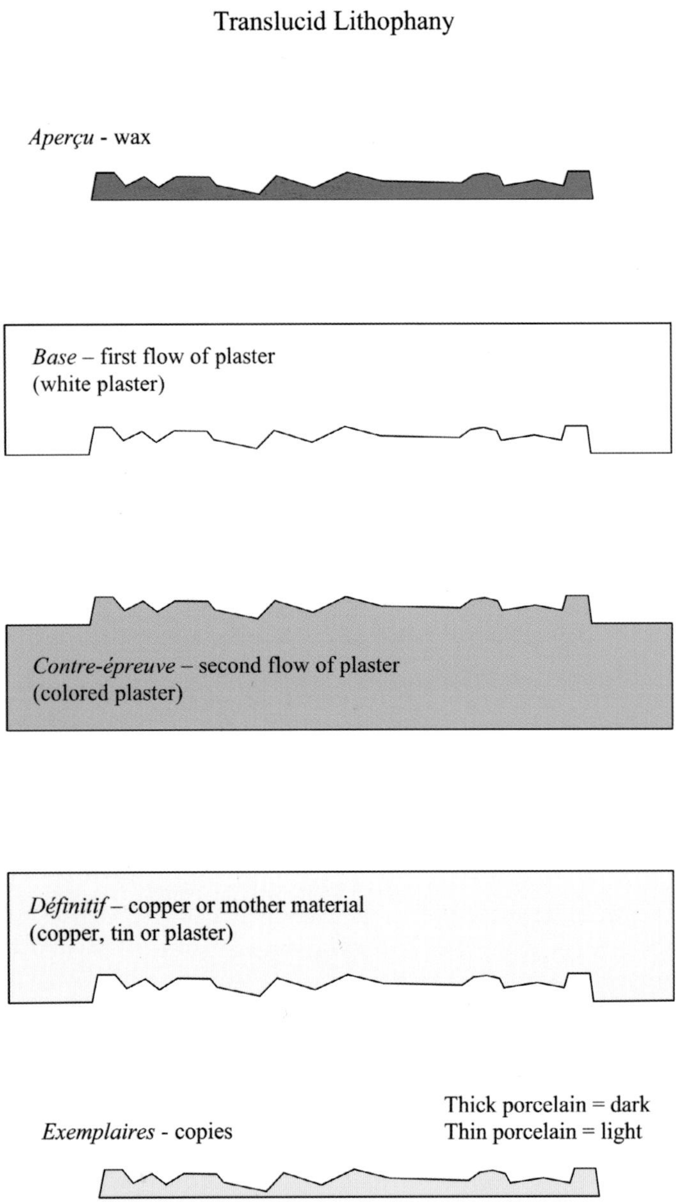

Diagrammatic drawings illustrating the process for making translucent porcelain lithophanes from Patent No. 5117. *Courtesy of William J. Walker, Jr.*

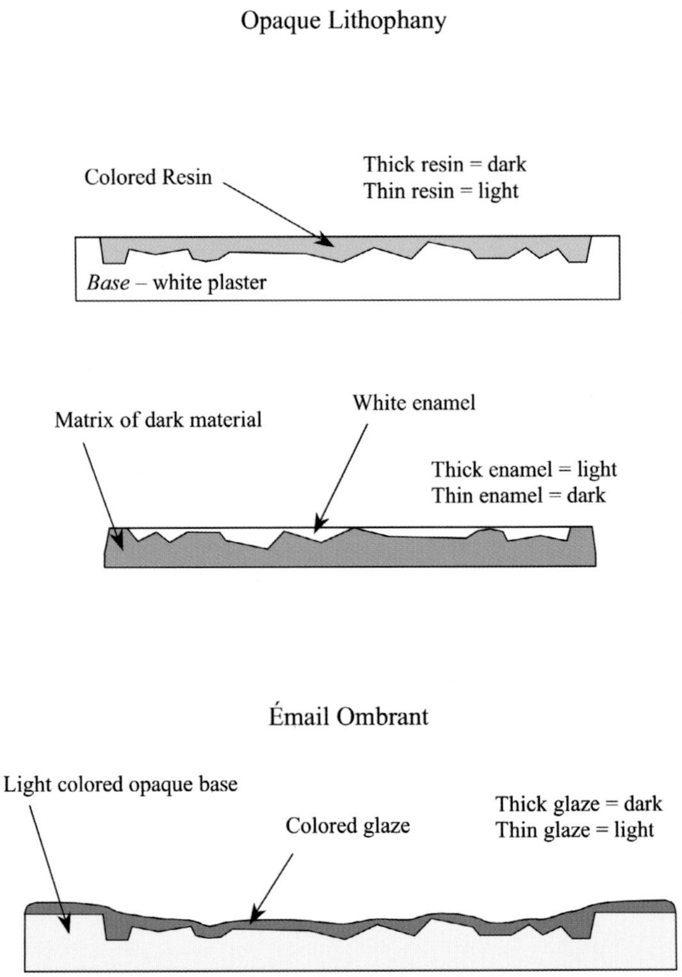

Diagrammatic drawings illustrating opaque lithophanes from Patent No. 5117, and *émail ombrant* from the later 1842 patent also titled "Lithophanie." *Courtesy of William J. Walker, Jr.*

There are quite a few lithophanes in the Blair Museum collection that are conspicuously photographic-type images on the porcelain. One example is the lithophane that pictures *Mannequin Pis*, a bronze statue located in Brussels, Belgium. The statue was cast in bronze after a model by Jerome Duquesnoy in 1619. It depicts a child that allegedly was lost in Brussels in the 17th century. The frantic father supposedly found his child at the corner of Rue du Cheme and Rue de L'Etuve. He was so overjoyed that he had a statue of his lost child erected at the very site upon which he was found, even showing the child's pose when he was discovered. Mounted in blue stained glass with red corners, the porcelain image was clearly produced via photo process on the porcelain, and not through carving beeswax.

Lithophane, *Mannequin Pis*, marked 1922, framed in stained glass, 19th century, Blair Museum acc. no. 917, 5" x 4.25", stained glass 7.25" x 8". *Courtesy of the Blair Museum of Lithophanes.*

There are other lithophanes in the Blair Museum that appear clearly to have been produced with the aid of photography. Included would be several German lithophanes, the view of Versailles, *Les Eaux du Parc de Versailles*, and *Obelisque de Louqsor* (Blair Museum acc. no. 10, marked PPM 853), and a lithophane marked 1461, featuring a monument to Germany as a statue of a goddess. Plaue lithophanes utilizing photo process probably date after 1880.

An examination of the Blair Museum collection suggests that Plaue was the only German company to embrace photo process on ceramics. This is a logical occurrence, since KPM was making lithophanes between 1828 and 1865, and Meissen between 1828 and 1860 (and then again after World War II), and Plaue between 1849 (or possibly as early as 1842) and 1914 (and then again in the 1970s onward). The use of photography on ceramics had its beginnings circa 1854, when KPM and Meissen were gradually reducing lithophanes from their inventories.

Lithophane, *Les Eaux du Parc de Versailles*, with stained glass frame, PPM 854, German, 19th century, Blair Museum acc. no. 425, 6.5" x 8.25", stained glass 10.875" x 9". *Courtesy of the Blair Museum of Lithophanes.*

Lithophane, German monument, with stained glass frame, marked 1461, 19th century, German, Blair Museum acc. no. 918, 5" x 4.25", stained glass 7.25" x 8". *Courtesy of the Blair Museum of Lithophanes.*

Often cited is the work of Walter D. Ford, who researched and created lithophanes and other ceramics by means of photo process. Ford (1906-1988) was a graduate of the Ohio State University, receiving his degree in Ceramic Engineering in 1930, his Master of Science degree in 1931, and finally his Professional Degree of Ceramic Engineering in 1940. He founded Ford Ceramic Arts in 1936 in Columbus with some assistance from Paul Bogatay. His company specialized in placing photographic images on tiles and dinnerware in relief or counter relief (intaglio).[13] It closed in 1941 when he assumed the position of Senior Ceramic Engineer in the Research Laboratory of the Pittsburgh Corning Corporation, where he stayed for 30 years until his retirement in 1971.

What is of the greatest interest of all of Ford's ceramic explorations and experiments, is the subject matter of his dissertation which involved his work on "application of photography in ceramics" including "relief process" which involves the "translucent type" which he never refers to as lithophanes. His dissertation was reprinted in its entirety in *The Bulletin of the American Ceramic Society*, vol. 20, no. 1, January, 1941. As he stated in the introduction of his thesis, its purpose was to present a summary of all the known information about photography on ceramics. Of all the processes he describes, it is only his description of the various relief processes, including the translucent type of relief process, which directly relate to 19th century lithophanes and the patents that created such treasures. He describes the preparation of the gelatin, sugar, potassium bichromate and water solution, heating and drying, exposing the dried plate under a negative, soaking the exposed plate in distilled water and finally taking a plaster cast of the relief that was formed. The variables then used in producing replicas from the mold are described as colored glaze, porcelain cameo type, and translucent type. The latter he described as follows:

> Make a plaster cast from a gelatin relief, and from this cast, make a plaster mold having the same relief as the original gelatin. Form a porcelain piece on this mold by any method desired, and dry and fire to complete vitrification. When it is removed from the kiln, there is no interesting photographic likeness visible to the eye. There is only a relief, which is the reverse of that on the original gelatin, but when a light is placed back of the piece, a perfect photographic likeness of high quality is reproduced. This results from the variable thickness of porcelain, which allows a variable intensity of light to shine through this translucent porcelain piece. Such translucent application so far is limited and is applicable only to porcelain lamp shades and similar wares.

Ford held U.S. patents on a number of related processes, including nos. 2,180,002, 2,147,770, and 2,181,452. Examples of his lithophanes are in the permanent collection of Baggs Memorial Library, the Ohio State University; the Lightner Museum in St. Augustine, Florida; and the Blair Museum of Lithophanes. Interestingly, three images in the three separate collections include lithophane portraits of Franklin Delano Roosevelt.

One expert and lithophane artist, David Jefferson, has offered a third and highly plausible explanation concerning the creation of lithophanes from metal dies. Rather than working directly in wax, the artisans carved the images in metal using similar methods as used in the production of mezzotints, but with much deeper relief. This would account for the crisp mezzotint-like detail observable

Lithophane, portrait of Franklin Delano Roosevelt, by Walter Ford, c. 1939-40, Baggs Memorial Library acc. no. 1997.364, 4.375" x 3.5". *Courtesy of the Baggs Memorial Library Collection, The Ohio State University.*

in lithophanes such as *Goldschmidts Töchterlein, La Sainte Vierge, and Der neue Schüler*. Waxes were cast from the metal dies or carvings in order to check the progress. Jefferson also believes that the porcelain was pressed into metal rather than plaster dies, possibly using mechanical pressing machinery. He also believes that plaster dies may have been coated to make them resistant to wear so they would last longer. Supporting this theory is the difficulty in carving waxes with the necessary precision and detail and that plaster molds wear out rather quickly. Thousands of lithophanes were produced in Germany in a span of less than half a century. Indeed, Jefferson himself used metal dies to produce his lithophanes beginning in the 1970s. This method was probably utilized later in 19th century lithophane production, at factories such as Plaue in Thuringia.

There exists a fourth method of producing porcelain lithophanes, in addition to carving waxes, photo process on ceramic, and the carving of metal dies, and that is by means of computer-generated mechanical processes. The first individuals attempting this process using their home computers and CADCAM date to the 1990s. Contemporary artist Nicolai Klimaszewski has documented his investigation with using computers to carve photographic surfaces beginning in 1990, with a prototype machine in operation in 1994. His method involves the use of "homemade machines (that) run on homemade software that translates the grey scale contained in a photograph into a carved surface." He uses these carved surfaces to make lithophanes, *émaux ombrants* tiles, and more. More details are included in Chapter Twelve and at his website www.klimko.com.

There are several companies producing porcelain lithophanes today using computer processes, including The Porcelain Garden. This company is detailed in Chapter Twelve. Computer generated and photo processed lithophanes made of plastic and other composites are detailed in Chapter Eleven. A general search of the Internet finds information such as the "Lithophane Tutorial" at one site that uses Denford Quick CAM and a CNC Machine to make lithophanes from various materials including 3mm (1/8") thick Cast Plexiglas and Corien. Others advocate the use of the ArtCAM Pro and a 3 axis milling or engraving machine. Translucency is the only requirement for machining lithophanes.

The inventor of lithophanes described carving wax in his patent in 1827. The first lithophanes were clearly created from carved wax models. From all evidence it would not have been possible to create lithophanes using photo process on ceramics until after the mid-1850s. And even then, this innovation in technology was not likely to have been put into practice in the factory to any extent until sometime later. Even so, this new method had little impact on lithophanes. Relatively few have a photographic-like quality. Clearly most 19th century lithophanes look like old engravings, not old photographs.

Although it is tempting to debate the pros and cons of the various methods used to produce lithophanes in the past 180 years, it is more remarkable to ponder the endless boundaries of the mind that have created such innovative methods of enhancing our environment with three-dimensional porcelain pictures.

Lithophane, *La Sainte Vierge*, after a painting by Raphael, German, 19th century, PPM 271, Blair Museum acc. no. 446, 8.625" x 6.625". *Courtesy of the Blair Museum of Lithophanes.*

Chapter Three
Lithophane Production History

Archaeological evidence indicates that true porcelain, comprised of a refractory white clay known as kaolin, and a feldspathic rock also known as petuntse existed as early as the Tang dynasty (618-907 A.D.) in China. This high-fired (about 1450° C) ceramic ware has a ringing tone when struck and it is translucent where it is the thinnest. Porcelain is shaped by throwing on the wheel, molding, and modeling. Due to early porcelain exports from China and early visitors into China, all points west marveled at this rare and exotic porcelain. It was considered suitable material for gifts between princes. Porcelain fever struck Europe and attempts were made to invent true porcelain, with the only early success being the mimicking of the qualities of porcelain by creating tin-glazed earthenware that had a white surface that could be decorated. These tin-glazed earthenwares were known as faience in France and Germany, majolica in Italy and Delftware in the Netherlands. Even these imitation porcelain wares were not available until the beginning of the 15th century, hundreds of years after the invention of true (hard paste) porcelain in China. Even in the 17th century, porcelain was so little understood that it was referred to in the famous Florentine dictionary compiled by the Accademia della Crusca as "precious clay."

Nearly one thousand years after the creation of true Chinese porcelain, Europe invented its own hard porcelain. In 1709, an alchemist named Johann Friedrich Böttger (1682-1719), developed Böttger Porzellan at the Meissen factory in Dresden, Germany. It was not nearly as translucent as Chinese porcelain nor did it originally have the white body of its Chinese counterpart. More of that story is contained in the section in this chapter about Meissen porcelain.

Given the history of porcelain in China and Europe, it is not surprising that the inspiration for lithophanes came from China. The countries and companies in Europe that imported and copied Chinese porcelains to the greatest extent in the 17th and 18th centuries, were the same that invented and produced the first lithophanes in the early 19th century. Developed and manufactured almost simultaneously in France and Germany, the French held the first lithophane patent, while the Germans had the best porcelain knowledge to develop this art form to its fullest potential. Ironically France is credited with the earliest patent, but overall they appear to have produced few lithophanes compared to Germany.

The story of the patenting of lithophanes appears at first glance to be confusing. This is acknowledged in a letter from Laurel Blair to a Mr. de Clairmont in 1967, where he wrote, "When I was in Paris I went to the town of Rubelles, and there we located two very old books which were of great value as they revealed the difficulties in assigning the invention of lithophanes to the Baron (Bourgoing) instead of a German. We found that he had used the word for his own purposes rather than for what he really was making, but used the word in obtaining the patent, which has confused the subject for many years."[1] However, it is not so confusing when one realizes that the misunderstanding revolves around the later 1842 patent registered by Baron Charles de Bourgoing in association with Baron Alexis du Tremblay, which refers to the *émail ombrant* technique utilized at the Rubelles factory. This faience decorating method involved the use of transparent shaded enamels viewed by reflected light. It is, in essence, a process related to that of lithophane production. However, *émail ombrant* utilizes the thickness of the glaze, pooled in the recesses of the intaglio to create light and shadow on an opaque ceramic body. The original lithophane process was developed at Sèvres and a patent was issued in 1827 to Baron Charles Paul de Bourgoing of France.[2] In order to protect the invention in France, the French government had issued Bourgoing a "Brevet d'Invention," a patent valid for fifteen years. Patent No. 5117 was issued January 12, 1827, "Brevet 5117, Brevet D'Invention de 15 ans en date du 12 Janvier 1827, Au Sieur De Bourgoing, A Paris Pour le Procedes de Lithophanie." Details concerning this patent are presented in Chapter Two, and a translation from the original French patent appears in Appendix A. The original French patent is believed to have been initially licensed to factories in England and Germany. Production at Meissen commenced in 1828, and was employed nearly simultaneously at Berlin and later at other factories in Germany and Bohemia. The process of manufacturing lithophanes was patented in England on March 13th, 1828, by Robert Griffith Jones (Patent no. 5626),[3] who had acquired the rights from the French inventor. As a result, the English factory, Grainger, Lee & Co. of Worcester also made lithophanes in the early 19th century. The Jones patent is presented, in full, in Appendix B.

Bourgoing transmitted his knowledge and physical evidence to his colleague Alexandre Brongniart who was the director at Sèvres, and to Georg Friedrich Christoph Frick (1781-1848) the director at the Königlichen Porzellan-Manufactur (KPM) in Berlin between 1832 and 1848.[4]

There is documentation that lithophane production was attempted at KPM in 1828, but not perfected until Frick invented a more translucent porcelain body containing soapstone (steatite) that he obtained from Bavaria near the Czechoslovakian border.[5] Frick also noted in his writings about KPM, that 136,730 lithophanes were produced between 1834 and 1843.[6]

An alphabetical listing of countries that made lithophanes in the 19th century, are alleged to have produced lithophanes, or are currently manufacturing them would include: Austria, Belgium, Bohemia/Czechoslovakia, Denmark, England, France, Germany, Hungary, Ireland, Italy, Japan, Norway, Portugal, Russia, Sweden, the United States, and Wales.

One might believe it to be a simple matter to look at a lithophane and its markings and know when and where it was manufactured. This is not the case. Few lithophanes are signed by individual artists and those were made after the 19th century. Some lithophanes are clearly marked with the manufacturer's initials, others only with the plaque number (corresponding to the manufacturer's price list). However, quite often a lithophane plaque must be judged on the nature of the ceramic body and the quality of the overall finished piece. These particulars will be reviewed as each manufacturer is summarized. In general, it must be acknowledged that there are many variations of each factory backstamp. The illustrated factory marks throughout the book may be considered the most common.

Backstamps

In addition to the factory marks presented with the entries for each of the manufacturers there are many backstamps or marks that can not at this time be 100% confidently attributed to a known manufacturer. Lithophanes made by the later manufacturers – Bernardaud, Haviland, Porsgrund, Rörstrand and others, include the manufacturer's full name within the factory mark. A listing of the backstamps, based largely on the Blair Museum inventory records, includes, alphabetically:

AdT in cursive script and sometimes a number (Alexis du Tremblay, France)
Adderley and Lawson, Provo Patent (England)
Avramov (Spain)
beehive or **shield symbol** with 3 numbers indicating date (Vienna, Austria)
Belleek or Belleek Co. Fermanagh (Ireland)
BERNARDAUD (France)
Blue (Alpha Gene Blue, Native American, 20th century only)
BPM (usually in Old German script) with numbers (Buckau Porzellan Manufaktur, Madgeburg, Germany)
CMH (possibly CM Hutschenreuther Porzellanfabriken, Hohenberg, Germany)
(cross hatch in underglaze cobalt on stein or night light body, not lithophane – Plaue, Germany)
EGZ with numbers (E.G. Zimmerman, Germany)
E.D.S. with numbers
E.D.S. & C with numbers
F
F.W. Roberts
Failing or **David Failling** (United States)
G
Gamarius
G.A.S. Philad a/. (Meissen, manufactured for American company)
GMP
Grainger, Lee & Co. (Worcester, England)
H
H & L with numbers
Haviland Limoges (French)
Herend and **Hungary** under a symbol (Hungary)
Herrmann et Laurent ... France (lampshades)
Holly © Bow
HPF
HPM with numbers and frequently letters (Hennebergsche Porzellan Manufactur, Germany)
Japan (Japan)
Jefferson Art (David Jefferson, United States)
JP (veilleuse only, underglaze cobalt on veilleuse, not lithophane) (Jacob Petit, France)
JTS
KPM handwritten incised numbers very early; later with sceptre and numbers and frequently letters (Königlichen Porzellan-Manufactur, Germany)
Limoges (France)
Lithocérame (cup and saucer in Limoges collection)
Lithophanie Francaise (France)
LH (designer László Horváth initials, Herend Porcelain, Hungary)
L.H. and a number (Lippert & Haas, Bohemia/Czechoslovakia)
MDS and number
Meissen (handwritten incised or stamped numbers, and often a second smaller stamped number, and 20th century with blue crossed swords on the front, Germany)
MINTON CHINA (England)
MINTONS (England)
Nakajima and sometimes number (Japan)
shield symbol with "P" (Nymphenburg, Munich, Germany)
numbers without letters (Plaue, Germany and Meissen, Germany, see illustrations under individual entries)
PD
Petit (veilleuse only, incised under glaze, Jacob Petit, France)
Phoenix Pottery (Phoenixville, Pennsylvania, United States)
PMP with or without von Schierholz (Plaue, Germany)
PPM usually with numbers (Plaue Porzellan-Manufaktur, Germany)
Porsgrund (Norway)
P.R. (sickle) sometimes with numbers (France)
Rörstrand Sweden with three crown symbols (Sweden)
Royal Copenhagen (Denmark)
RPM and number
S
Société Ceramique, Brevetée, Mons (Belgique) (Belgium)
SOUTH WALES POTTERY (Wales)
StP M and number
T.K. (Klásterec Factory, Bohemia)
VA (Vista Alegre, Portugal)
Venitienne L. S and red ink oval stamp (France)
Von Schierholz
WEDGWOOD in tiny overglaze print sometimes with the addition of "**ENGLAND**" (England)

Information will first be presented on the 19th century manufacturers in Germany and France.

Germany

While it is known that Germany began production of lithophanes nearly simultaneously with the French around 1828, there is still much unknown about several of the German lithophane factories. The highest quality European lithophanes are German. They are also the most abundant.

The three major German companies that produced lithophanes are the Königliche Porzellan-Manufaktur in Berlin, which after about 1836 usually marked their lithophanes with the scepter and "KPM" backstamp with a number corresponding to the factory's price list and an additional letter code; Meissen, located near Dresden in Meissen, with 19th century pieces simply marked with (usually) hand-incised or stamped numbers, one corresponding to the factory's price list; and Plauesche Porzellanmanufactur, founded in 1817, located in Plaue-on-Havel, Thuringia, with pieces backstamped PPM with a number corresponding to the factory's price list. These will be discussed in detail after a brief discussion of other German manufacturers.

Among collections of lithophane plaques are some believed to be of German manufacture with backstamps about which virtually nothing is known. Those lithophanes marked with the backstamp "BPM" have been hypothetically described as the initials of Buckau Porzellan Manufaktur in Madgeburg.[7] The Blair Museum has at least nine lithophanes bearing the "BPM" backstamp, including eight plaques and one single cast shade. The backstamp is in old German script and is accompanied by numbers.

Those marked with the backstamp "HPM" have been credited to Hennebergsche Porzellan Manufaktur in Gotha, Thuringia. The Blair Museum owns at least sixty-eight lithophanes with the HPM backstamp. A portion of the HPM-marked lithophanes also have a single letter in addition to the numbers that accompany the HPM mark. In addition to rectangular flat plaques, there are HPM-marked trapezoids, single cast shades, and curved rectangular examples.

Lithophane, Sherlock Holmes, German, 19th century, BPM 512, Blair Museum acc. no. 70, 6.75" x 5.875". *Courtesy of the Blair Museum of Lithophanes.*

Lithophane, Girl with Apple, German, 19th century, HPM 114, Blair Museum acc. no. 49, 5.75" x 5". *Courtesy of the Blair Museum of Lithophanes.*

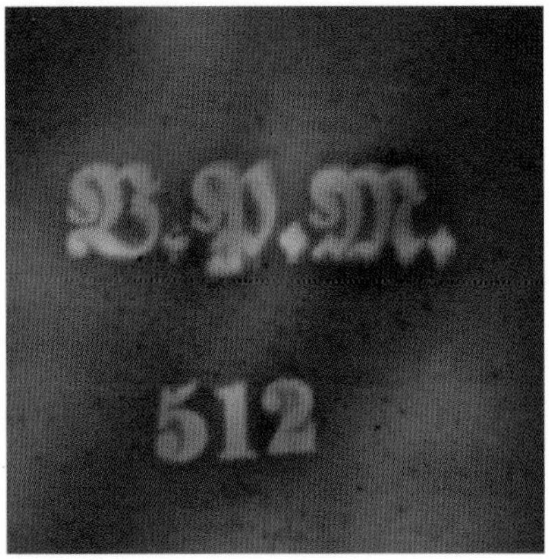

Detail of backstamp for BPM 512, Sherlock Holmes lithophane, Blair Museum acc. no. 70. *Courtesy of the Blair Museum of Lithophanes.*

Detail of HPM 114 lithophane backstamp, Girl with Apple, Blair Museum acc. no. 49. *Courtesy of the Blair Museum of Lithophanes.*

Lithophane, Girl with Dog and Cat, in stained glass frame, German, 19th century, HPM 111, Blair Museum acc. no. 64, lithophane 7.75" x 6.25", stained glass 12.25" x 12.5". *Courtesy of the Blair Museum of Lithophanes.*

Lithophane, untitled, German, 19th century, HPM 29, Hampshire County Council Museums and Archives Services acc. no. 1980.22.2, 4.375" x 5.5". *Courtesy of the Hampshire County Council Museums and Archives Services.*

The Blair Museum collection has four lithophanes marked with the "EGZ" backstamp. Additionally, the "fancy shop" excavation in Pittsburgh, Pennsylvania, dating from 1855-1858, turned up an "EGZ 10" backstamped lithophane.[8] Consensus is that it is German in origin. One possible origin for the EGZ marked lithophanes would be the initials of the E.G. Zimmermann company of Hanau, Germany, which manufactured cast iron stands for lithophanes in the 19th century. In a 1975 letter from the E.G. Zimmermann company to lithophane researcher Bernard Rushton, it was noted that, "We remember very well that these [cast iron lithophane stands] have been manufactured about 80 years ago, however we regret very much to inform you that we do not know the name of the supplier of the lithophanes. Since our company was completely destroyed during World War II, there are no old files available which might help us in finding out the supplier of the lithophanes."[9] Their letterhead has the initials "EGZ" inside a sun emblem and under it "since 1842." Logically they could have commissioned these lithophanes and perhaps had their own backstamps added to the production at another plant such as Plaue. The EGZ mark is accompanied by numbers and the Blair examples include small plaques and a trapezoid panel.

Lithophane, Wine Tasting, German, 19th century, EGZ 4, Blair Museum acc. no. 1343, 6.5" x 5.25". Note the 1834 date on the wine cask. *Courtesy of the Blair Museum of Lithophanes.*

Detail of backstamp for EGZ 4 lithophane, Wine Tasting, Blair Museum acc. no. 1343. *Courtesy of the Blair Museum of Lithophanes.*

Another well-known German company that has been mentioned in lithophane literature is Nymphenburg, in Munich, which is still producing lithophanes. The Nymphenburg Porcelain Company was founded in 1747. While there exists substantial information about the company itself and its other products, its lithophane history is not well known. 19th century lithophanes produced at the Nymphenburg Porcelain Company could be considered very rare.

Several other German companies have manufactured lithophanes. Porzelanfabrik Gerold & Co., in Tettau, produced steins with lithophane bottoms. Fürstenberg Porzellan Manufaktur in Hannover, Germany, established in 1747, produced lithophanes in the late 19th and early 20th centuries. Correspondence between Mr. Blair and Dr. Otto Weise of the manufactory in the 1960s did not provide any elaboration on specific motifs or numbers. CM Hutschenreuther Porzellanfabriken, established in 1814, and located in Hohenberg, produced lithophanes beginning in the mid-19th century. They were still producing lithophane lampshades with Victorian themes in 1974, when there was correspondence between a factory representative and researcher and collector Bernard Rushton. At that time they sent Mr. Rushton a fact sheet about their lithophanes, including excerpts from a January 5, 1855 contract with CM Hutschenreuther modeler and painter Balduin Haag, that recorded his monthly monetary compensation.

Detail of a Nymphenburg lithophane backstamp.

Detail of two KPM (with scepter) backstamps. *Courtesy of the Blair Museum of Lithophanes.*

Königliche Porzellan-Manufaktur

The first porcelain manufactory in Berlin was established in 1751, but closed in 1757. The second factory, established by Johann Ernst Gotzkowsky in 1761, ceased production in 1763, and was taken over by Frederick the Great for the state of Prussia in 1763. Thus was the beginning of the Königliche Porzellan-Manufaktur (KPM) also known as the King's Porcelain Manufactory, or the Royal Porcelain Manufactory in Berlin, which, from about 1836, usually marked their lithophanes with the sceptre and "KPM" backstamp. They produced lithophanes between 1828 and 1865 and they have become the quality standard by which all other lithophane plaques are judged. Note that this KPM mark that came into use in 1825 in Berlin, should not be confused with the earlier Meissen porcelains (not lithophanes) that were also marked with the KPM backstamp between 1723 and 1727 and again in 1875.

Bourgoing received his patent for the lithophane in 1827 in Paris, and by 1828 Georg Friedrich Christoph Frick (1781-1848) was already conducting experiments at KPM to formulate a new translucent porcelain body for producing these plaques in Berlin. Frick, who became the director of the Königliche Porzellan Manufaktur in 1832, created a new porcelain body that had a high soapstone content which when fired at a lower temperature, guaranteed excellent translucency. It is not entirely clear whether this KPM lithophane development occurred independently of the French invention.

In 1844, at the Industrial Exhibition in Berlin, there was a display of 68 lithophanes by KPM, including the four largest ever produced. KPM lithophanes were exhibited in other major exhibitions, as the *Official Descriptive and Illustrated Catalogue* of the 1851 Great Exhibition in the Crystal Palace in London notes on page 1060 that the Royal Prussian Porcelain Manufactory, Berlin exhibited lithophanes.[10] In fact it has been recorded that KPM was then first to exhibit colored lithophanes at that same London exhibition.[11] They may have been the first to exhibit colored lithophanes, but Meissen was the first to create colored lithophanes as early as 1834.[12]

Lithophane, *First Lie*, German, 19th century, HPM 98, Blair Museum acc. no. 1594, 6.5" x 5.5". *Courtesy of the Blair Museum of Lithophanes.*

There were 580 separate plaque numbers issued between 1828 and 1865. Only the Plaue factory surpassed this number much later in the 19th century. It has been recorded and widely published that KPM sold 136,730 lithophanes between 1834 and 1845. KPM *Preis-Courant* lists are available and it is useful to note the dates of first production of the various plaque numbers given in the *Preis-Courant*:

KPM mark
1-156 (1828-1836)
157-190 (1836-1837)
191-248 (1837-1840)
249-262 (1840-1841)
263-315 (1842-1846)
316-351 (1846-1847)
352-376 (1847-1848)
377-410 (1848-1850)
411-516 (1850-1859)
517-535 (1859-1860)
536-555 (1861-1862)
556-580 (1862-1865)

The significance of the letter code which often appears on KPM lithophane plaques has not yet been determined. Through a comparison of plaques in the Blair Museum and elsewhere it can be deduced that the letter code does not signify the initial of the artist (wax carver), the dimensions of the plaque, or the price. It may signify the year of production. It is even more plausible that the letter code refers to the person who made the lithophane from the mold. This person was the one who actually pressed the plastic clay into the mold, scraped off the back to flatten it, etc., and would have been the one to incise or impress the backstamp(s). The reasoning for this addition of a letter code (signifying the maker) would have been that the person was paid by the piece (common practice in ceramic factories) and they could count his completed work at the end of the day. Additionally, after the firing, the pieces that survived the kiln could be counted. If the ones with "N" broke more often there might be some quality control issues. Perhaps "St" was gifted, so "St" was given the larger pieces to make. Of the approximately 197 KPM-marked lithophanes in the Blair collection, 150 have the additional letter code. Those codes, followed by the number of pieces in the Blair collection with those codes are as follows:

A (4)
B (34)
G (18)
L (1)
M (1)
N (36)
O (4)
S (2)
St (13)
Z (37)

Half (34) of the 68 lithophanes in the Blair collection marked HPM, also have a similar letter code following the backstamp and number.

Large KPM lithophane, *L'Algerienne*, German, 19th century, KPM 268 St., Blair Museum acc. no. 1047, 10.75" x 14". *Courtesy of the Blair Museum of Lithophanes.*

KPM produced the largest lithophane plaques ever produced, with several designs including:

KPM 20 and KPM 34, both *Eine Ansicht des Vesuvs (A View of Vesuvius)*, 19.5" x 18"

KPM 112, *Das Innere der Cathedrale zu Worcester (The Interior of Worcester Cathedral)*, 19.5" x 18"

KPM 127, *Peristil aus dem Vatican (Peristyle of the Vatican)*, 19.5" x 18"

KPM 408, *Undine, oben halbrund*, 15.5" x 11"

There is no evidence of KPM producing ceramic lithophane objects other than plaques and very small circular shades. A small shade with a KPM backstamp was sold at the Mellors & Kirk auction in Nottingham, United Kingdom, February 2007.

Four KPM lithophanes mounted together in one panel with cased glass frame, German, 19th century, beginning at the top, KPM 45 *Landschaft, mit Rindvich im Vordergrunde*, KPM 46 Z *Landschaft, mit Meeresküste und Schiffen*, KPM 42 Z *Landschaft, im Vordergrunde eine grosse Windmühle*, 43 (no KPM) *Der Geiser auf Island*, Blair Museum acc. nos. 1660, 1659, 1662, 1661, overall 10.375" x 7.75". *Courtesy of the Blair Museum of Lithophanes.*

KPM lithophanes featured a variety of subjects, including paintings by Carl Begas, Peter von Cornelius, Wilhelm V. Kaulbach, Ludwig Richter, Julius Schnorr v. Carolsfeld, Josef Stieler, as well as well-known works by Rembrandt, Rubens, and Ruisdel. It has been noted that the inclusion of representations of famous or popular paintings coincided with the establishment of the first major public museums in Germany.[13] Popular KPM portrait subjects included key political figures of the time, such as Prussian Kings and Queens, nobility in Germany or elsewhere in Europe, as well as those of Pope Pius IX, and Americans Samuel Colt and Henry Clay. KPM produced lithophanes featuring historic figures, like Goethe, or celebrities such as Jenny Lind. Scenes of Berlin, Austria, and Italy were also produced in lithophane format.

Records show that there were patterns for KPM lithophanes created in sepia watercolor, postcard format.[14] Several grisaille on paper lithophane patterns, one dated 1834, by Carl Daniel Freydanck (1811-1887) have been published, including the image of *The Royal Guardhouse in Berlin.*[15] The corresponding lithophane, marked with the sceptre and KPM 120 Z has also been located and is titled *Die neue Wache in Berlin. Also illustrated in Along the Royal Road: Berlin and Potsdam in KPM Porcelain and Painting 1815-1848*, is an 1838 oil on canvas painting by Freydanck titled *The Palace of Prince Wilhelm at Babelberg (Schloß Babelberg)*, which became a grisaille on paper pattern for a lithophane in 1839,[16] and then the lithophane KPM 535.

While much has been written about Berlin or KPM lithophanes, the master's thesis and doctorial dissertation by Kirsten Dorothée Rather remain the most thorough on the topic. KPM became the Staatliche Porzellan Manufaktur in 1918. The company is still in operation today, however, all production of lithophane plaques by KPM ceased in 1865.

Lithophane, *Faust und Gretchen*, mounted in cased glass, German, 19th century, KPM 151 St., Blair Museum acc. no. 506, lithophane 6.125" x 7.125", cased glass 13.5" x 16.875". *Courtesy Blair Museum of Lithophanes.*

Meissen

The Meissen factory was founded in 1710 by Augustus the Strong (1670-1733), which coincides with the 1709 discovery of hard paste porcelain by the alchemist Johann Friedrich Böttger (1682-1719). Böttger had been held prisoner by Augustus the Strong who was fanatically interested in manufacturing gold from base metals. In his respected book on Meissen porcelain, *The Book of Meissen*, author Robert E. Röntgen covers the topic of Meissen lithophanes in the chapter titled "Medals and Coins, Lithopanes, Tiles, Knick-Knack and Technical Porcelain." Meissen lithophanes are amongst the most highly sought collectible of all lithophane production worldwide. Meissen began the production of lithophanes in 1828, after lithophane examples were brought from France and it was recommended to King Anton that Meissen could copy and sell a similar product. After some resistance by the Meissen manufactory officials, the ing's authority prevailed and lithophane production began.

Although the market for lithophanes was highly competitive, especially from the Royal Porcelain Manufactory (KPM) in Berlin, and factories in Paris, the Meissen lithophanes were commercially successful. Comparisons are frequently made between the whiter porcelain body of the Berlin transparencies, compared to the slightly brownish-yellow of the Meissen factory. Records show that demand for lithophanes produced by the Meissen factory peaked in around 1840, and although they were more greatly appreciated in North America in the mid-1840s, overall demand was down.[17] Meissen exhibited lithophanes in 1851 at the Crystal Palace exhibition in London and again in Leipzig in 1857 at the Easter Fair.[18] It has been estimated that up to 12 percent of the Meissen porcelain products presented at Leipzig fairs were their translucent plaques. Apparently part of the 1851 exhibition included lithophane lampshades.[19] With declining sales, in 1851 thirty percent of the 220 lithophanes then in production were eliminated and after 1860 all lithophanes were removed from the listing of Meissen wares being produced.[20] One could still special order pieces after that date and lithophanes were again regularly produced after World War II. There is a price list from 1970, which shows the thirteen lithophanes that were again available.[21] Meissen made plaques, lampshades and hanging lamps. The lithophane plaques from the 19th century simply had numbers incised or stamped on the back. A comparison of plaques with the numbers, titles, or descriptions, and dimensions given in the factory price list confirms attribution to Meissen. The Meissen *Preis-Courant* lists plaque numbers up to 251. Meissen did not use the blue crossed swords on 19th century plaques. Some 20th century Meissen plaques were marked with the blue crossed swords.

Lithophane, *Madonna mit schlafendem Christus-Kinde*, German, 19th century, Meissen 134, 7.625" x 6.125". *Courtesy of Andy Cook.*

Lithophane, *Landscape with Knight*, German, 19th century, Meissen 191 (hand-incised) with 67, Blair Museum acc. no. 1948, 6.5" x 8.125". *Courtesy of the Blair Museum of Lithophanes.*

The records at Meissen give detailed information about the individuals involved in the creation of their lithophanes. Georg Friedrich Kersting (1785-1847) was the manager of the decorating department from 1818 to 1845 and was significantly involved in the production of lithophanes, as was Carl Gottfried Habenicht (active mid-19th century), who as the head of the art department created 130 models. Kersting is well known as the painter of the image of the two children in a window surrounded by grape vines, which was also produced as an engraving by W.E. Tucker exclusively for *Godey's Lady's Book* in 1851, and produced as lithophanes at Meissen, KPM, and the South Wales Pottery. These are illustrated in Chapter Five. Habenicht was highly regarded as a wax modeler at Meissen, along with Johann Gottlieb Scheibel (active mid-19th century).

Lithophane, *Dresden After Midnight*, German, 19th century, Meissen 206 (stamped) with 50, with "K" lightly stamped on front center bottom border, Blair Museum acc. no. 1949, 8.375" x 6.5". *Courtesy of the Blair Museum of Lithophanes.*

Meissen produced many of the same images on their lithophanes as the Royal Porcelain Manufactory (KPM) in Berlin. While they "borrowed" images from each other, they appear to have independently had waxes carved of popular images, surprisingly not exactly replicating the other factory's product through piracy (taking molds from finished porcelain plaques). Between 1830 and 1850 they manufactured tens of thousands of lithophanes. Meissen later became the Staatliche Porzellan-Manufaktur Meissen. The Meissen officials sent Mr. Blair a note dated June 23, 1965, which listed twelve lithophanes and their accompanying numbers: girl at the draw-well, no. 13; mother with child and storm-clouds, no. 74; girl with dog, no. 85; girl in arbour, no. 135 x; Venus, sleeping, no. 136 x; the children of Kersting, no. 139 x; 2 girls in landscape, no. 145; trader under a gateway, no. 146; girl under trees, no. 151 x; the punished curiosity, no. 167; *Esmeralda*, no. 181; and country woman with child in cradle, no. 183. This typed list, proves that their lithophanes were back in production prior to 1970.

Lithophane, *Mädchen am Ziehbrunnen* (*Girl at the Draw Well*), German, 19th century, Meissen 13 (hand-incised), Blair Museum acc. no. 979, 8.25" x 5.5". *Courtesy of the Blair Museum of Lithophanes.*

Lithophane, colored, *Juden vor Babylon*, German, 19th century, Meissen 127, 7" x 10.5". *Courtesy of Andy Cook.*

Although it will be elaborated on at the conclusion of this chapter, KPM and Meissen were in competition from the very beginning. While KPM had a superior porcelain body, Meissen was the first to create colored lithophanes as early as 1834, according to Meissen scholar Baerbel Kovalevski who discovered this information in the Meissen Manufacture Annual Reports.

Regarding Meissen backstamps on lithophanes, there is some clarity. The numbers were incised by hand on the earliest pieces, with a few later 19th century lithophanes having stamped numbers. 20th century pieces all possess stamped numbers and any with the Meissen crossed swords backstamp are from the 20th century.

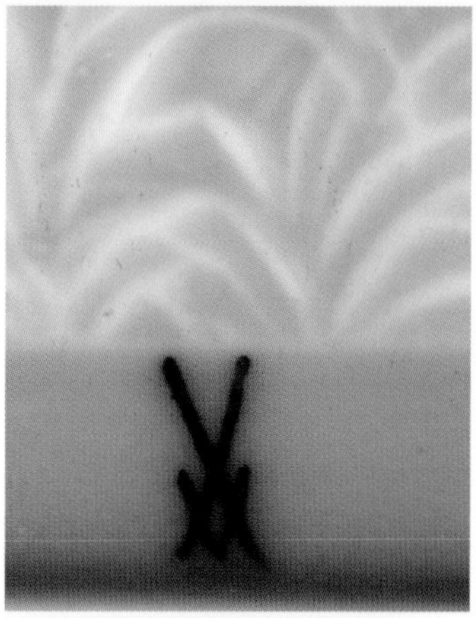

Detail of 20th century Meissen blue double crossed swords mark on the front bottom center of Meissen 151, issued originally in 1838 as *Christ as a Boy*, and in 1970 as *Girl Under a Tree*, Blair Museum acc. no. 546. Meissen 151 hand-incised on back. *Courtesy of the Blair Museum of Lithophanes.*

Detail of Meissen 139 hand-incised backstamp. *Courtesy of the Blair Museum of Lithophanes.*

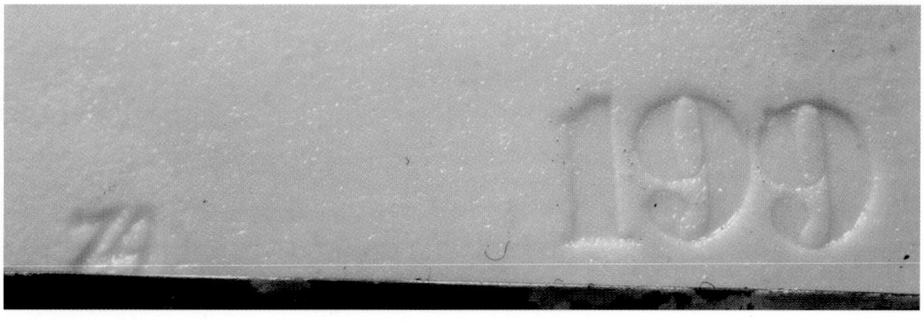

Detail of Meissen 199 impressed backstamp. *Courtesy of the Blair Museum of Lithophanes.*

Lithophane plaque mounted in stained glass frame, featuring a father and mother with a crying baby, German, 19th century, PPM 869, Blair Museum acc. no. 79, lithophane 6.25" x 5.5", stained glass 11.75" x 11". *Courtesy of the Blair Museum of Lithophanes.*

Plauesche Porzellanmanufactur

The factory located at Plaue-on-Havel in Thuringia produced approximately 2,000 separate plaque numbers during their long history, more than twice as many as were produced in Berlin at KPM. Plauesche Porzellanmanufactur or Manufactur Schierholz Plaue, established in 1817, was owned by the Schierholz family until 1945, then administered as a trust from 1945 until 1972, at which time it was nationalized. In 1992 the company was returned to the family. This company was the biggest competitor to KPM in Berlin between 1849 and 1865 and has been fortunate to retain their original plaster molds and waxes for use up to the present, although many were destroyed during the War. Plaue began making lithophanes around 1849 (although it could have been as early as 1842 that they began carving waxes), and by 1875 they had a huge range of motifs and featured popular images in different sizes and shapes. It does not appear that Plaue produced single cast lampshades. In 1972 the company started making lithophanes again and these are marked PMP. These later lithophanes were produced from the original 19th century molds but with a newly developed clay body.[22]

There are three distinct Schierholz *Preis-Courants* from the 1800s. Version one, *Preis-Courant über transparente Licht-schirme von C.G. Schierholz & Sohn in Plaue bei Arnstadt*, obtained from the Schloßmuseum Arnstadt archives, dates circa 1865-70, and lists lithophane subject numbers up to number 716, with a few gaps. An attached appendix lists lithophane nos. 717-755. This version is reproduced in Appendix E. Version two, of the same title, lists subject numbers up to 782, with additional numbers and themes recorded by hand, nos. 783-819. Version three, is also similar to *Preis-Courant I*, except it has numbers up to 871 added by hand. These lists include nothing but rectangular plaques, no trapezoids or lampshades. Certain motifs are repeated on the lists under different numbers and with different dimensions. Additionally, there exist several pages from undated *Preis-Courants*, that list, in handwritten German script, some trapezoid lithophanes (nos. 1-70), some lithophanes framed in glass, and outline drawings of some of the shapes and sizes of available rectangular and trapezoid plaques. There are even a few engravings showing examples of utilizing lithophanes as part of veilleuses, etc.

According to several sources, there exists a fragment of a photo catalogue that dates to around 1900 with illustrations of lithophanes manufactured by Plaue, with illustrations of no. 23 through no. 1746.[23] Interest in lithophanes waned towards the close of the 19th century and it was not until the 1960s that von Schierholz began making lithophanes again from the old molds, and a few new images, too.

What is most noticeable about PPM lithophanes is that the images they originally used were the same as those selected by KPM and Meissen. In 1865 Plauesche Porzellanmanufactur first began the use of their regular backstamp so all PPM marked lithophanes date no earlier than 1865. Prior to this time the lithophane plaques were marked with only plate numbers that match the *Preis-Courants*. This makes the earliest pieces difficult to date. Apparently the marking of PPM followed by a number was first used in 1880, and after 1890, some lithophanes from Plaue were marked with only numerals, and no alphabetical backstamp. It has been hypothesized that Plaue didn't need a more elaborate backstamp at that time because they were the only major manufacturer still making lithophanes. It has also been suggested that the use of the PPM mark was discontinued due to a change in intellectual property laws in Prussia beginning in the 1870s, which restricted the reproduction of images. Prior to this there had been no protection of intellectual property rights. Following the adoption of new laws, there were lawsuits connected to the production of lithophanes at Schierholz and this may have been a cause for Plaue to produce and market lithophanes in France in the 19th century.

While Plaue did not use the # (crosshatch mark) on its lithophane plaques, Schierholz did use this mark in underglaze cobalt on the bases of some of their porcelains, including at least one night light containing lithophane panels (illustrated in Chapter Two) which also bears the backstamp "Germany," indicating its manufacture after 1891.

It can be hypothesized that there may be a direct connection between these German PPM-marked lithophanes and those marked Lithophanie Francaise and P.R. (sickle) manufactured between 1899 and World War I. In 1899 Arthur von Schierholz died and his company became a limited liability corporation with one of the principals being affiliated with a porcelain manufacturer using the backstamp P.R. (sickle). Just as Meissen marketed lithophanes in the United States with "G.A.S." marks, it is likely that Plaue skirted around intellectual property laws in Prussia by manufacturing and/or marketing lithophanes in France, marked with "French" backstamps [Lithophanie Francaise and P.R. (sickle)] not PPM. There is no evidence of any site of manufacturing for Lithophanie Francaise or P.R. (sickle) in France, only showrooms in Paris. And Plaue opened showrooms in Paris and Berlin in 1890. Further evidence can be seen by the similarity between the Plaue and P.R. (sickle) lithophanes. Some lithophanes are marked with both backstamps on the same plaque. An illustration is provided under "Lithophanie Francaise and P.R. (sickle)." This would indicate that a PPM mark might signify the manufacturer and the P.R. (sickle) or Lithophanie Francaise mark might signify the retailer or distributor in France.

A stack of three lithophanes with PPM backstamps. *Courtesy of the Blair Museum of Lithophanes.*

A stack of three lithophanes with only numbers and no "PPM" or other marks. *Courtesy of John Coleman.* Photo by John Coleman.

While lithophane production in Plaue was reduced after 1900 due to lack of demand, it was never completely abandoned. Gert Leib was hired as the artistic director, and served from 1953 to 1992. Plaue continued to reissue lithophanes, utilizing the original molds. Newer lithophanes, beginning around 1972, bear the backstamp PMP with or without a crown and the name "von Schierholz". This coincided with Plaue becoming a State owned industry. According to an October 26, 2007 email from Constantin von Schierholz, a descendent of the original Plaue company founders, the first lithophane carved by Gert Leib after the resumption of production, bears the number 1007. Beginning in 1995, the Plaue factory has been operated by Royal Tettau, a wholly owned subsidiary of Seltmann Weiden.

For those who need a hands-on experience, as of July 2007, an Internet site, www.sitzendorf-porzellan.com, advertises week-long courses on Thuringian Porcelain, which include three hours of "modelling, installing, casting of forms, engraving lithophanies, ... right before dinner is served."

Lithophane, *Sinkendes Segelschiff*, German, 20th century, PMP 2054, 9.5" x 7.875". *Courtesy of Andy Cook.*

Detail of PMP modern backstamp from PMP 2054 lithophane. *Courtesy of Andy Cook.*

France

Alexis du Tremblay AdT

Some of the most interesting lithophanes of the 19th century were marked with the "AdT" mark, which, atypically for lithophane plaques, was molded on the front or face of the lithophane. Over the years, some have interpreted the "AdT" mark on a portion of the lithophanes as reading "AdC," because the cursive script "T" resembles a "C." Sometimes there is a number in addition to the AdT mark. Quite frequently the AdT mark is almost camouflaged by the scenery in which it is placed, e.g. rocks and shrubbery. Some marks are so well concealed that the pieces have gone unattributed for decades. Sometimes there is a number or a letter on the reverse of the plaque. AdT stands for the initials of the Paris factory's founder and owner, Alexis du Tremblay, who also owned the Rubelles factory located in nearby Melun, that manufactured embossed earthenware known as *émail ombrant*.

Detail of an AdT mark from a 19th century French lithophane plaque. *Courtesy of the Blair Museum of Lithophanes.*

There are many very interesting examples of AdT lithophanes, including the charming lithophane depicting the cat looking in a hand mirror having his or her whiskers trimmed by monkeys with goat feet (illustrated in Chapter Eight). A pair of handscreens in a private collection that are both marked AdT are illustrated in Chapter Six. Marvelous composition can be seen in the very three-dimensional lithophane portrait of the sentinel standing guard. A true masterpiece can be seen in the Gothic nightlight with four AdT panels which is owned by the Blair Museum and was loaned to the Getty Museum in 2000 for a special exhibition (illustrated in Chapter Six).

The catalogue that accompanied the exhibition at Britz Castle in 2001, *Lithophanien: Die Welt des Biedermeier im Porzellanbild*, noted that the exhibition included a copy of an early *Preis-Courant* dating to 1827-28, from a small Parisian manufacturer referred to as "Manufacture de Lithophanie" located at no. 767 Rue de Richelieu.[24] Dr. Kirsten Rather connects this small manufacturer with Baron Charles P. de Bourgoing. A handwritten note in the

Lithophane plaque featuring a sentry standing guard, French, 19th century, AdT, Blair Museum acc. no. 896, 6" x 4.125". *Courtesy of the Blair Museum of Lithophanes.*

Blair/Beroud Archives in Toledo, records this same address and company name with the addition of "1830 – Manufacture à Montreuil Sens-Boise (Seine); Agency Paris Rue de Richelieu, #89." In 1967, an official at the Staatliche Porzellan-Manufaktur Berlin sent Mr. Blair typed excerpts from Frick's history of KPM book, that implied that French lithophanes were being manufactured in 1830 at Montreuil-Sens-Bois (Seine), and sold through an agency in Paris located at Rue de Richelieu No. 89. Handwritten translations of French documents (origins unclear) in Mr. Blair's archives repeat similar addresses up to 1839.

Interestingly, Mr. Blair corresponded with Comte Le Moyne de Martigny in the mid-1960s concerning Rubelles earthenwares and lithophanes. She was a descendent of Baron du Tremblay, her mother being born Mademoiselle du Tremblay, Alexis du Tremblay being her great grandfather. It is not clear what contribution she made to Mr. Blair's knowledge of lithophanes. He kept some secrets "for his book."

Du Tremblay is listed as showing specimens of "Lithopony" on page 1xxv of the *Official Descriptive and Illustrated Catalogue of the Great Exhibition of the Works of Industry of all Nations 1851* in London. Some believe the AdT lithophanes inferior to those manufactured elsewhere, describing a coarser granular texture, a thicker cast body, and less detailed designs. Others find them the most unique and artistically outstanding. Additional information on M. du Tremblay may be found under the entry on "Rubelles."

Lithophane plaque featuring a sentry standing guard, unlit, French, 19th century, AdT, Blair Museum acc. no. 896, 6" x 4.125". *Courtesy of the Blair Museum of Lithophanes.*

Bernardaud

The porcelain factory known as Bernardaud was established in 1863 at Limoges, and today produces table services and giftware, such as lithophane candle lamps which they refer to as VotiveLight™ candles, VotiveLight™ lamps, and VotiveSphere™ candles. In general these 20th and 21st century products can be described as porcelain dishes in which one places the lit candle, and the hemispherical lid is placed on top, and the carved porcelain is thereby backlit from within revealing scenes of ice skaters, cityscapes, the Louvre, and more. The bisque porcelain is beautiful even when unlit, but captivating with its dancing flame when backlit. They hold a modern patent on their dome-shaped votive.

Domed lithophane votive light featuring ice skaters, French, 20th century, Bernardaud, Height 2.5", Diam. 4.5". *Courtesy of Margaret Carney and Bill Walker.*

Lithophane dome and saucer, French, 20th century, Haviland, Height 3.625". *Courtesy of John and Eve Coleman.*

Haviland

Haviland Porcelain Company, located in Limoges, France, was founded in 1842 and apparently only produced lithophanes beginning in the 20th century. In correspondence on Haviland letterhead dated April 27, 1951, to Lieutenant Harold B. Feldman stationed in Paris, Mr. Harold Haviland states that he has sent four lithophane samples in three sizes. Mr. Blair wrote to Mr. Haviland in 1965, not knowing he was deceased. In a handwritten reply on Haviland letterhead, dated April 1, 1965, Mr. Jean d'Albis, who claimed "a very thorough knowledge of the output of our factory for the last 100 years," said he did "not remember our ever having made any lithophanes."[25] Mr. d'Albis claimed also that the curator of the Limoges Museum said they had none in the Museum. He further stated that to the best of his knowledge, "lithophanes were not the product of factories but that of artisans."[26] What is evident is that there are fairy lamps of the dome and saucer variety, that Haviland has produced, as they bear the Haviland backstamp.

Detail of backstamp on Haviland, Limoges, lithophane dome and saucer. *Courtesy of John and Eve Coleman.*

Four-sided veilleuse théière in two pieces with elaborate gilding, featuring religious themes of the Madonna and child, Jesus on the cross, Jesus at the Last Supper, and a cathedral interior, designed by Jacob Petit, unlit view, French, 19th century, signed "JP" in underglaze cobalt on the base, missing lid, Blair Museum acc. no. 2502, 12.25" x 6.375" x 5.5". *Courtesy of the Blair Museum of Lithophanes.*

Jacob Petit

Jacob Petit (1796-1868) established his factory in Paris in 1830, survived bankruptcy in 1848, and sold his company to an employee in 1862. He then began afresh in Paris, with the purchasers of his old factory continuing to use his old models and marks. All of his signed work has a certain flamboyance that is in stark contrast to traditional classical or Empire style Parisian porcelains that were popular at the time. According to Godden, by 1840, "he had a warehouse or retail premises on the Rue de Bondy and he was employing over 200 work-people."[27] According to the authority on veilleuses, Harold Newman, those pieces with the "JP" (Jacob Petit) mark are extremely rare, and he only knew of signed Jacob Petit veilleuses with lithophanes in the Broulard Collection and the Freed Collection. The Blair Museum of Lithophanes owns an enchanting veilleuse théière with gilding and double dog head pouring spouts on the teapot. It is signed "JP" in underglaze cobalt on the base. It was purchased for Mr. Blair by his brother George in 1965, in Paris. The lid is missing.

Detail of lithophane from the signed Jacob Petit veilleuse théière, Blair Museum acc. no. 2502. *Courtesy of the Blair Museum of Lithophanes.*

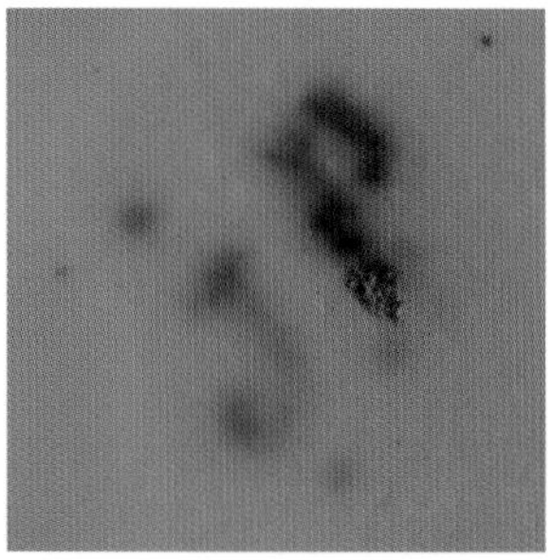

Detail of the Jacob Petit signature "JP" from the base of the veilleuse théière, Blair Museum acc. no. 2502. *Courtesy of the Blair Museum of Lithophanes.*

A second signed veilleuse théière has recently been discovered in the Blair collection. This five-sided piece, featuring *Faust und Gretchen,* is marked with an unusual incised "Petit" under the glaze on the bottom. This has tentatively been attributed to Jacob Petit and needs further investigation.

Jacob Petit manufactured more than veilleuses, in terms of ornamental and decorative work, including clock cases and scent bottles. He was a painter by training and this is reflected in his approach to porcelain forms and decoration. It has been noted that he has been recognized as "the leader of the Romantic School of French porcelain which commenced about 1830. Reacting vigorously against the severity of the Empire Period, it deliberately broke all restraints, creating capricious lines and rococo decoration, as well as using vivid colors and much gilt."[28] His work was popular in England and North America during its heyday and remains extremely collectible to this day. He won a "Special Mention" award at the 1851 Crystal Palace Exhibition in London. Although the production of Jacob Petit's factory was on a grand scale, his signed veilleuses with lithophanes remain rare and precious. There is no evidence of production of plaques or single cast lampshades.

Limoges

The factory at Limoges has its origins in the 18th century, being established in 1771, not far from newly discovered deposits of kaolin, the chief ingredient in hard-paste porcelain. In the 1992 catalogue *La Lithophanie et Limoges,* from the Musée National Adrien Dubouché, curator Chantal Meslin-Perrier writes that it is rather paradoxical that France created so few lithophanes compared to Germany, when the origin of lithophanes was in France. In fact, she notes that Limoges itself rarely produced lithophanes because the French public was not very interested in this type of product.[29]

Located in Limoges, the Musée National Adrien Dubouché, was established in 1845, and was named after the first curator of the Museum who was appointed in 1865. Originally it was located in a former lunatic asylum. Their collection includes a selection of lithophanes, including examples created at Plaue in the 19th century. According to correspondence from the early 1960s, this museum owns a teacup with handle and a saucer with twelve scallops. Both the cup and the saucer have lithophane images of a woman holding a child.[30] The piece is inscribed "Lithocérame." A curator at the Louvre first alerted Mr. Blair about this rare Limoges lithophane. However, it is uncertain if this cup and saucer were a product of the Limoges factory.

The porcelain industry has thrived in the Limoges region due to excellent supplies of the raw material kaolin, plentiful water for processing the raw materials and for the production of slurries and pastes, and wood for furnace fuel. Today, Limoges is highly regarded for its current production of small lithophane shades of fine, matt, translucent porcelain at Bernardaud. 19th century lithophane production in Limoges is more difficult to verify. A lithophane with "C O" and "Limoges" incised on the bottom right corner of the face of the lithophane is in a private collection in Switzerland. There is no mark or number on the back and the hunting scene is similar to pieces produced at factories such as Plaue. The owner notes that the quality of the lithophane is poor.

Five-sided veilleuse théière featuring Faust and Gretchen, attributed to Jacob Petit, French, 19th century, incised "Petit" under glaze on base, Blair Museum acc. no. 2512, 7.75" x 6.5" x 6.125", overall height 11.5". *Courtesy of the Blair Museum of Lithophanes.*

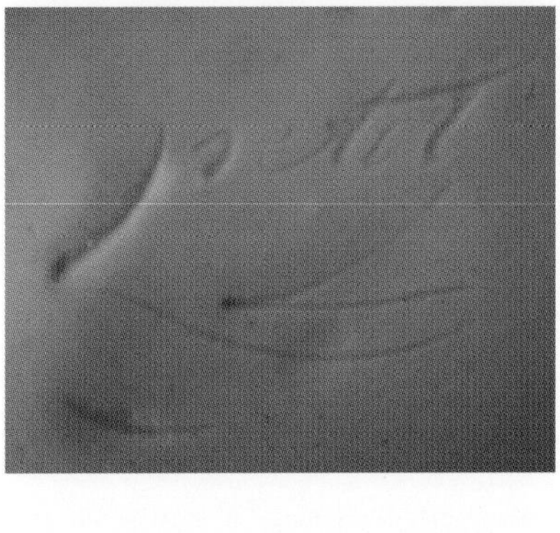

Detail of incised "Petit" signature under the glaze on the base of a five-sided veilleuse théière attributed to Jacob Petit in the collection of the Blair Museum, Blair Museum acc. no. 2512. *Courtesy of the Blair Museum of Lithophanes.*

Lithophanie Francaise and P.R. (sickle)

Lithophanes marked with the "Lithophanie Francaise" backstamp or "P.R." with a sickle, appear to have been made at the same factory and sold in showrooms in Paris. In fact, the circular Lithophanie Francaise backstamp includes a "PR" in its logo. Little is known about this company other than the location of showrooms in Paris. A specific factory site in France has never been identified. Notes by a researcher commissioned by Mr. Blair to research sources in French libraries state, "the mark P.R. – little probability that it applies to Rubelles porcelains ... Would it not more logically be a German trademark?" As mentioned in the entry under Plaue (PPM), it is quite possible that lithophanes marked either Lithophanie Francaise or P.R. (sickle) were manufactured in either Germany or France, by Plaue, for a French audience.

Detail of Lithophanie Francaise circular backstamp from a lithophane lampshade. *Courtesy of the Blair Museum of Lithophanes*

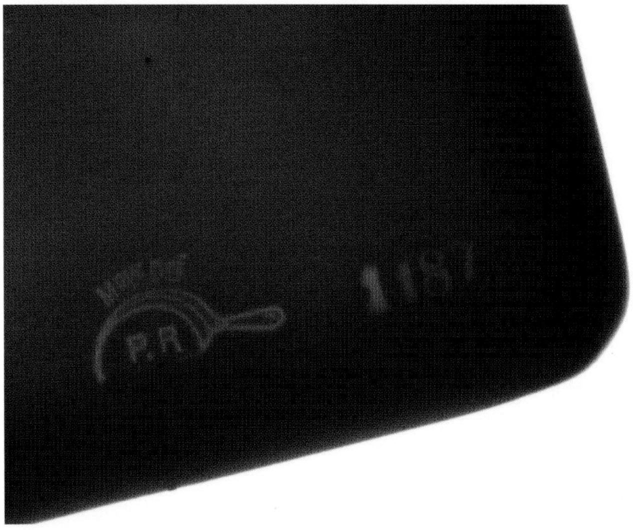

Detail of a P.R. (sickle) 1187 backstamp from a plaque. *Courtesy of the Blair Museum of Lithophanes.*

The small lithophane plaques marked "P.R." often have two small holes in the top for fitting a brass hanging hook. When present, the hanger is marked "Lithophanie Francaise." There exist quite a few lithophanes that are simply marked with impressed numbers and no letters or other alphabetical backstamps. Some can be attributed to the P.R. production and others to the German manufacturer at Plaue. Usually the numbered backstamp contains four numerals beginning with the number one, in other words, "1xxx." A few lithophanes bear multiple backstamps, including those with the P.R. (sickle) backstamp as well as a PPM backstamp.

Whereas PPM is best known for its flat plaques in rectangular and trapezoid form, Lithophanie Francaise is best known for single cast lampshades and P.R. (sickle) is responsible for the creation of many interesting novelties, in the form of night lights.

There further exists evidence to support the theory that there is a direct connection between the manufacturers of lithophanes marked P.R. (sickle) and those produced at Plaue. After the death of Arthur von Schierholz in 1899 and until World War I, one of the controlling principals at Plaue may have been connected with a porcelain manufacturer in Limoges.[31]

Metal hanger marked "Lithophanie Francaise, Paris," and "Paris depose" from a P.R. (sickle) 1407 plaque, Blair Museum acc. no. 2557. *Courtesy of the Blair Museum of Lithophanes.*

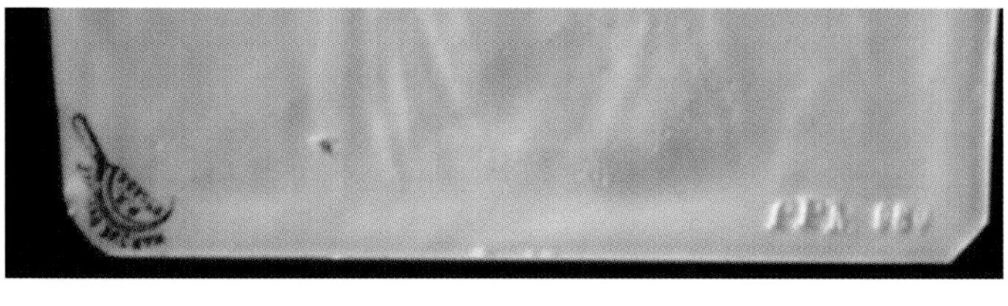

Lithophane plaque bearing two backstamps, both the P.R. (sickle) and PPM marks on one piece. *Courtesy of Ray Burnside.*

Model of the Eiffel Tower with four lithophane panels, 19th century, marked with an impressed P.R. (sickle) mark and an upside down "50", Height 11.25", base 4.75" square. *Courtesy of Barry Steadman.* Photo by John Coleman.

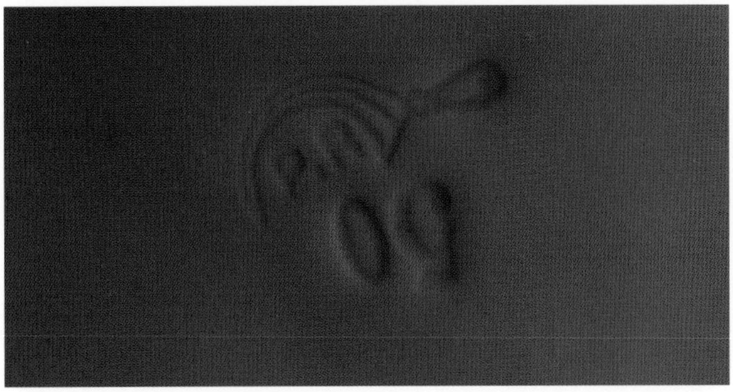

Detail of the impressed P.R. (sickle) backstamp on the base of the Eiffel Tower model. *Courtesy of Barry Steadman.*

In addition to the simple plaques and fine single cast lamp shades the factory with the backstamp "P.R." produced, there was also a range of novelty items, illustrated in the contemporary 19th century "Bijou Novelties" advertisement (see entry in Chapter Six under "Fairy Lamps"). These lithophane novelties include a sedan chair, a Victorian bathing cart fairy lamp/night light, and a model of the Eiffel Tower. The unique 11.25" high three-dimensional porcelain model of the Eiffel Tower contains four lithophanes inside the arches. Bearing the "P.R" beneath a sickle backstamp and an inverted "50" on its 4.75" square base, this rare piece is owned by United Kingdom collector Barry Steadman, who purchased it in 1986 from Mr. Bernard Rushton at an antique fair. The lithophanes include reproductions of Cot's paintings *The Storm* and *Springtime*, and one scene of the ubiquitous courting lovers.

There are two known examples of the largest single cast lampshade in the world, both marked with the Lithophanie Francaise backstamp, with one in the Blair Museum of Lithophanes (acc. no. 1878). It features the popular depiction of a pair of hunters in the Alps, shooting a large bird in a tree, with deer nearby. The bird, which looks a bit like a turkey, is called a capercaille. The lampshade measures 17.5" in diameter and is 12" high and is illustrated in Chapter Six.

There are also a few lithophane plaques marked with the Lithophanie Francaise backstamp as well as at least one small colored globe lampshade and a veilleuse théière which bear this mark.

Lithophane plaque featuring a romantic couple outdoors, framed in stained glass, 19th century, marked with a Lithophanie Francaise oval backstamp, Blair Museum acc. no. 528, lithophane 6.5" x 5", stained glass 12" x 10". *Courtesy of the Blair Museum of Lithophanes.*

Detail of oval Lithophanie Francaise backstamp from lithophane plaque, Blair Museum acc. no. 528. *Courtesy of the Blair Museum of Lithophanes.*

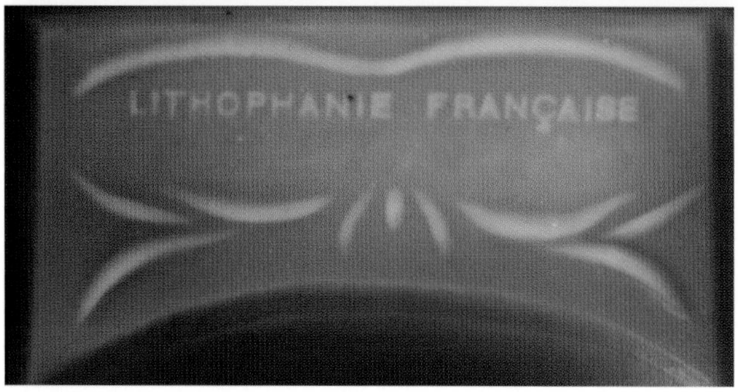

Veilleuse théière with three lithophane pictures, one featuring the Madonna and child, 19th century, marked "Lithophanie Francaise" above the candle door opening (see illustration), teapot marked "BRASSAC" impressed on base, Blair Museum acc. no. 1887, overall height 10.25". *Courtesy of the Blair Museum of Lithophanes.*

Detail of "Lithophanie Francaise" mark above the candle door opening on a veilleuse théière, Blair Museum acc. no. 1887. *Courtesy of the Blair Museum of Lithophanes.*

Besides the three-dimensional model of the Eiffel Tower, there is an equally rare lithophane plaque of the Eiffel Tower commemorating its opening in 1889, now in the collection of the Blair Museum, which bears the P.R. (sickle) backstamp and the number 1614. It has been damaged and repaired. No other examples depicting the Eiffel Tower in plaque format are known.

Lithophane plaque featuring the Eiffel Tower, 19th century, marked P.R. (sickle) 1614, Blair Museum acc. no. 920, 7.125" x 5.75". *Courtesy of the Blair Museum of Lithophanes.*

Detail of P.R. (sickle) 1614 backstamp on the Eiffel Tower plaque, Blair Museum acc. no. 920. *Courtesy of the Blair Museum of Lithophanes.*

Fluted plate decorated with embossed enamels known as *émail ombrant*, French, 19th century, Rubelles, with oval backstamp, Blair Museum acc. no. Plate 3, Diam. 8.25". *Courtesy of the Blair Museum of Lithophanes.*

Rubelles

The patent issued in 1842 for "lithophanes" has confused collectors and researchers for decades, if not more than a century. The factory located in the quiet village of Rubelles in Seine-et-Marne, near Paris, not far from Melun produced only embossed enamels known as *émail ombrant* or *émaux ombrants* (plural), a type of faience ware, but not porcelain lithophanes, despite the inference in the infamous 1842 Bourgoing patent. In addition to the confusion caused by the terminology in the 1842 patent for "lithophanes," both the AdT and Rubelles factories were owned by the same person, Alexis du Tremblay, and both used the AdT initials, although not identically. This Rubelles factory apparently began operation in 1839 or 1840, and M. du Tremblay directed production until 1854, when his son-in-law, M. Hocédé du Tremblay, succeeded him. The factory closed in 1858, with its molds being sold to Wedgwood in 1873, after first being declined by Minton. Interestingly, some of these molds were used by Wedgwood in 1863 before they had obtained the legal rights to use them.

The term *émail ombrant* is a French term that literally means "shaded enamel." This type of ware, according to an unpublished type-script sent for consultation by Harold Newman to Laurel Blair, could be described as "Earthenware impressed with an intaglio picture or design, then, completely covered with a translucent coloured glaze to produce a smooth surface, thus creating an effect of light and shade due to the varying depths of the glaze. The process, sometimes referred to as a 'counterpart of lithophane,' (where the design is similarly in intaglio), was invented c. 1842 by Baron A. du Tremblay who made such ware at an earthenware factory at Rubelles, near Melun (France), and some pieces are marked AdT."[32] This explanation is not quite accurate. He shared the success of this invention with Bourgoing who was granted the original 1827 patent for lithophanes. The joint patent dated April 29, 1842 was issued to du Tremblay and de Bourgoing for *émail ombrant* and the process was used at the Rubelles factory for 15 years. Some backstamps on the earthenware pieces include in a circular seal "Brevet d'invention A.D.T."

In summary, there is a connection between the processes used in making lithophanes and the embossed enamel earthenware known as *émail ombrant* as noted in the detailed description under the "Wedgwood" category. The "confusion" that Mr. Blair described was only due to a lack of understanding of the processes that linked lithophanes and embossed enamel earthenwares, and that the second Bourgoing patent was, indeed, a modification of his initial 1827 invention. Rubelles won awards for their faience products and a great deal has been written about the history of this factory.

Sèvres

The history of porcelain manufacturing at Sèvres is far too complicated to summarize adequately. In 1756 the Vincennes porcelain factory was moved to Sèvres. The King took over the factory in 1759, and directors and modelers of merit came and went over the next several decades. The production of hard-paste porcelain began in 1768, but it was not used exclusively until 1804. Alexandre Brongniart (1770-1847) had become the manager in 1800 and the company flourished under his guidance.

It is significant and no coincidence that Brongniart was the director at Sèvres at the same time that Bourgoing was conducting his first experiments regarding lithophanes and firing his first specimens in the kilns at Sèvres.[33] Brongniart, noted in 1845, that the first attempts in making lithophanes by M. Baron de Bourgoing were made at Sèvres in the royal work rooms.[34]

In his tome published in London in 1850, *Collections Towards A History of Pottery and Porcelain in the 15th, 16th, 17th, and 18th Centuries*, and then again in 1857, in *A History of Pottery and Porcelain, Medieval and Modern*, Joseph Marryat notes that Lithophanie or Tableaux Lithophaniques "are made in great perfection at the royal manufactories of Berlin and Sèvres."[35] This statement was published while lithophanes were wildly popular and less than 25 years after their invention by Bourgoing, which he also mentions. Both these factors lend credibility to what Marryat wrote, however there is no other evidence to support his assertion that France was commercially producing lithophanes at Sèvres.

It has been recorded in several publications, including the Brongniart and Riocreaux 1845 publication, that the Museum at Sèvres had possession of a lithophane depicting a church interior with the largest dimensions known, measuring 21 inches (52 cm) by 19 inches (48 cm) and presumably manufactured at the Berlin factory during the 19th century.[36] It has been hypothesized that the large lithophane is KPM 112, *Das Innere der Cathedrale zu Worcester*. Its whereabouts is presently unknown. They currently have three German lithophanes, including one KPM (the exceptionally large no. 408, 15.75" x 11" *Undine*), a Meissen shade and a Meissen plaque (the *Marriage Proposal*, illustrated in the Kunze article).

Despite the historical treatises linking Sèvres and lithophanes, there is no hard evidence today that lithophanes were ever produced commercially at Sèvres.

Detail of Rubelles backstamp from *émail ombrant* round plate no. 3, Blair Museum. *Courtesy of the Blair Museum of Lithophanes.*

Detail of Rubelles backstamp from *émail ombrant* oval plate no. 4, 11" x 7.25". *Courtesy of the Blair Museum of Lithophanes.*

Austria

Wiener Porzellan-Manufaktur

Information about lithophanes produced in Vienna is scant. Two items with Viennese (K.K. Wiener Porzellan-Manufaktur or Kaiserliche und Königliche Porzellan-Manufaktur) backstamps were sold at auction at Mellors & Kirk in Nottingham, England in February 2007, which confirmed their existence. A rare parian ware model, identified by the auction house as the Parthenon, in fact is a model of the Theseus Temple, measuring 3.5" in height and 8" in length and 5.125" in width, and was purchased by the Blair Museum of Lithophanes, gift of Posy Huebner in memory of her husband Robert Huebner. This unusual piece has the impressed beehive shield backstamp, along with the numbers 847 and 15, and dates to 1847, according to the backstamp. One observes a clear image of the interior lithophane by looking through the open door. The scene, as identified by the auction

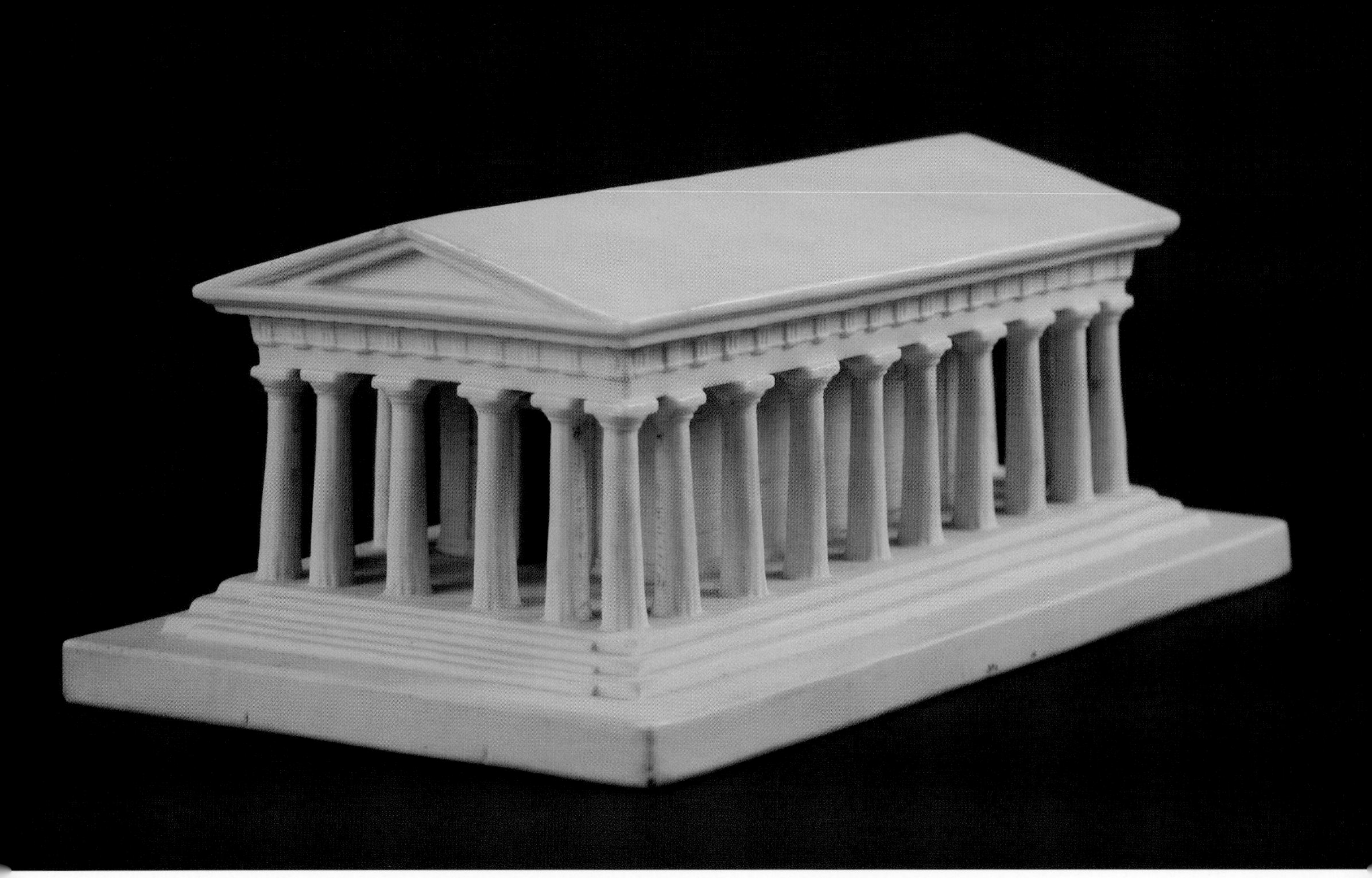

Porcelain model of the Theseus Temple, Viennese, 1847, beehive shield with 847 and 15, Blair Museum acc. no. 2007.1, 3.5" x 8" x 5.125". *Courtesy of the Blair Museum of Lithophanes*. Gift of Posy Huebner in memory of Robert Huebner.

house, is that of Herakles slaying the centaur Nessus.

In Austria there is a similar architectural model of the Theseus Temple from the Vienna Volksgarten. It has an interior lithophane of Theseus in battle with a Minotaur and has identical dimensions to the Blair temple model. It is owned by the MAK – Österreichisches Museum für angewandte Kunst in Vienna. Their Museum records on this object indicate it is Viennese porcelain dating from 1847. The MAK Theseus Temple model is apparently currently on view at the MAK Branch Geymüllerschlössel located outside Vienna. The MAK in Vienna also owns a lithophane plaque with a portrait of Baron Jellacic (1801-1859), who was a Croatian general and administrator (Viennese banded shield backstamp and numbers 849 and 15), and also a portrait plaque of Kaiser Franz Joseph (Viennese banded shield backstamp and numbers 850 and 38). These last two were donated to the MAK in 1895.

Interior lithophane as seen through the front door of the model of the Theseus Temple, depicting Herakles slaying the centaur Nessus, Blair Museum acc. no. 2007.1. *Courtesy of the Blair Museum of Lithophanes*. Gift of Posy Huebner in memory of Robert Huebner.

Another rare Viennese lithophane, a nightlight, datable to 1838, was sold at the Mellors and Kirk auction. This three-sided piece has images of a woman at a window, a cat and kittens, and a landscape. It is 7" in height and also has the impressed shield, and the markings F, 838, an incised 2 and the number 18 in gilt. It is similar to a Viennese veilleuses théière illustrated in the catalogue of the Freed collection now in Trenton, Tennessee.

The Vienna factory opened in 1717, it being only the second porcelain factory in Europe. In 1718, the founder, Claudius Innocentius du Paquier, secured the services of the arcanist Samuel Stölzel, who had previously worked for Meissen. According to some sources, Claudius Innocentius du Paquier was an arms-supplier, who obtained the secret of Meissen porcelain through bribery.[37] While the story is too complex to retell in a few paragraphs, like many porcelain manufacturers, the company endured its hard times. The factory was sold in 1744 to the Austrian Empress Maria Theresa. This is the period when the shield mark or backstamp was introduced. After more successes and failures, in 1784, the company was again for sale. Between 1784 and 1805, the factory added an additional year mark besides the shield. After 1800, the last three figures of the year were added to the backstamp. Thus it can be concluded that the temple model in the Blair Museum collection must have been created in 1847 and the three-sided lithophanic nightlight in 1838. In 1827, when Dr. Benjamn Scholz was director of the factory, there were more experiments to improve the clay body. It is at this same time, that they also changed their backstamp to make it more difficult to copy and to distinguish the new products made from the new clay body.[38] The factory mark was no longer painted in blue, but rather impressed in the raw porcelain. This marked a new era. The factory eventually closed in 1864. It should be noted that there are numerous imitations of the Viennese backstamp utilized on porcelain that originated from Germany and France.

There are at least two other Viennese lithophanes in the Blair Museum collection. One is an 8.5" x 6.75" lithophane plaque mounted in stained glass (12.5" x 10.5"), depicting *St. Stephens Cathedral* in Vienna. It is not only marked with the Austrian factory backstamp shield but also the number "840" which indicates it was produced in 1840. The second, also mounted in stained glass, depicts *St. Justina – A. Bonvicino* (a man, woman, and unicorn) – copied from a tapestry by Bonvicino, the lithophane marked with the shield backstamp and "I5" and number "842" indicating it was produced in 1842.

Three-sided nightlight with three gilt framed lithophanes, Viennese, 1838, marked F, 838, an incised "2" and the number 18 in gilt, height 7". *Courtesy of Andy Cook.*

Lithophane, *St. Stephens Cathedral in Vienna,* mounted in stained glass, Viennese, 1840, marked with the beehive shield and "840", Blair Museum acc. no. 453, lithophane 8.5" x 6.75", stained glass 12.5" x 10.5". *Courtesy of the Blair Museum of Lithophanes.*

Lithophane, *St. Justina*, mounted in stained glass, Viennese, 1842, marked with the beehive shield and "842" with "15", Blair Museum acc. no. 77, lithophane 7.375" x 6.25", stained glass 12.5" x 10.5". *Courtesy of the Blair Museum of Lithophanes.*

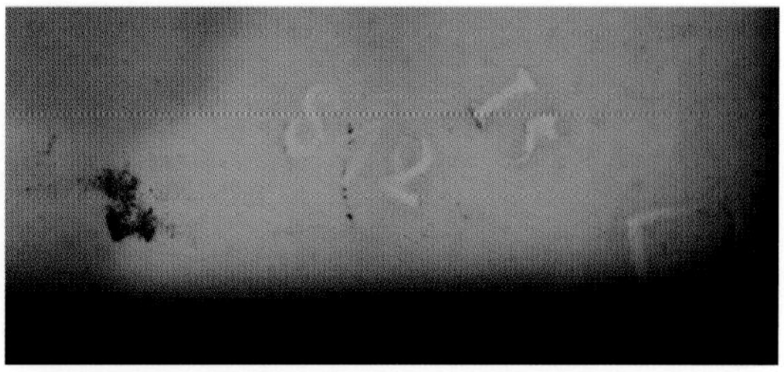

Detail of Viennese backstamp from *St. Justina* lithophane, Blair Museum acc. no. 77. *Courtesy of the Blair Museum of Lithophanes.*

Single cast lithophane lampshade with five scenes including that of a haircut, Belgian, 19th century, marked "Société Ceramique, Brevetée, Mons (Belgique) 26," Blair Museum acc. no. 216, Height: 4.25" Diam: 7.125". *Courtesy of the Blair Museum of Lithophanes.*

Belgium

Regarding lithophanes made in Belgium, there are several fine lithophane single cast lamp shades in the collection of the Blair Museum that have the impressed backstamp that reads, "Société Ceramique, Brevetée, Mons (Belgique) 26." According to correspondence between Mr. Blair and various individuals in the 1960s, there was also a factory, Hermann et Laurent, Berevate, located in Avergnon or Quaregnon. All Mr. Blair learned from his research was that the factory had been working perhaps until 1940, but had since disappeared.[39] Correspondence in 1983, between Mr. Blair and lithophane and veilleuse authority Harold Newman contains information about a veilleuse that Mr. Newman acquired which was marked "Herrm..........ent" and then "...Quaregnon, Belgium."[40] Correspondence from the curator at the Musées du Centenaire, Céramique, in the village of Mons, notes that they own a dozen lithophanes made early in the period when the porcelain factory Pêtre in Baudour (near Mons) was producing between 1900 and 1939, but they knew nothing of the factories that Mr. Blair was researching.[41] Harold Newman wrote several books on veilleuses which include only brief entries about Belgium, and none of his descriptions mention lithophanes incorporated into the design of these Belgian veilleuses.[42] Belgium lithophanes remain somewhat of a mystery.

Detail of backstamp from 19th century Belgian lampshade, Blair Museum acc. no. 216. *Courtesy of the Blair Museum of Lithophanes.*

Bohemia

Bohemia, now part of the Czech Republic, had a number of porcelain companies that made lithophanes in the early to mid-19th century. Some small companies were involved in lithophane production in a minor way, but several others are worth describing. The Bohemian porcelain factories were aided by the fact that valuable kaolin deposits were discovered in Northwest Bohemia, near the Karlovy Vary (Karlsbad) region.

Elbogen

The factory founded in 1815 in Elbogen was known as Springer & Co. and they are known to have made veilleuses.[43] Whether or not they made lithophanes is a mystery.

Hüttner & Dietl

Hüttner & Dietl was a factory located in Chodau, near Karlsbad that reportedly began producing lithophanes in 1835.[44] The factory mark on these lithophanes plaques and lampshades is unknown and production ceased in 1847.[45]

Klásterec Factory

The Klásterec Factory was begun in the 1790s, and operated under Karl Venier's management beginning in 1848. According to Geoffrey Godden's English translation of Emanual Poche's *Bohemian Porcelain*, the Klásterec factory produced lithophane shades with figure compositions, including genre themes, scenes from mythology, historical scenes from Napoleonic times, and more.[46] Godden states that the factory mark at the time was the impressed initials "T.K."[47] There are no known lithophanes with the backstamp "T.K." Godden further states that other Bohemian lithophanes were made at Schlaggenwald, which is corroborated by Rüdiger van Dyck (see the following entry). The authority on veilleuses and related matters, Harold Newman, wrote to Mr. Blair about a window panel with five or six lithophanes in it that he saw in a castle called Klásterec, near Karlsbad (Karlovy-Vary) in Bohemia, Czechoslovakia, in early 1967.[48]

Lippert & Haas

The factory of Lippert & Haas was located in Schlaggenwald, where production of lithophanes was begun in 1831, and they are marked with the factory backstamp "LH."[49] They were apparently known for producing large lampshades. The impressed backstamp was usually accompanied by a number. There are at least four examples of lithophanes with this backstamp in the collection of the Blair Museum of Lithophanes. One is a plate (Blair acc. no. 1822, marked LH138), one a round plaque (Blair acc. no. 383, marked LH126), and two are single cast shades. The backlit shades reveal school house scenes on one (Blair acc. no. 1913, marked LH52) and scenes of Versailles and Obelisk on the other (Blair acc. no. 1877, marked LH3). There is a lithophane panel of a man with a walking staff, a gun slung over his shoulder, standing on a mountain ledge, that is in the large collection at the Wichita Center for the Arts. It is marked on the lower left corner "838" with a numeral "1" underneath, and also printed in the lower right corner "Lippert & Haas Schlagggenwald." It is described as "very thick" and "non transparent."

Circular lithophane depicting a woman spinning yarn, with her cat nearby, Bohemian, 19th century, Lippert & Haas, marked L.H. 128, Blair Museum acc. no. 1822, Diam. 6.75". *Courtesy of the Blair Museum of Lithophanes.*

Detail of L.H. 128 backstamp on Lippert & Haas lithophane, Blair Museum acc. no. 1822. *Courtesy of the Blair Museum of Lithophanes.*

There are three lithophanes produced in Schlaggenwald that were illustrated in the 1927 Hans Meyer book *Böhmisches Porzellan und Steingut*. These include two *Wundertasssen*, or wonder cups, that have lithophane bottoms with scenes of a girl with her dog and a copy of a painting by Ramberg and a pastoral landscape plaque. Lippert & Haas are also known to have exhibited lithophanes at the 1844 Industrial Exhibition in Berlin. Apparently after 1845, production of lithophanes at Lippert & Haas was almost completely halted.[50]

Denmark

Royal Copenhagen Porcelain Manufactory Ltd.

Lithophanes from Denmark were produced only at the Royal Copenhagen Porcelain Manufactory Ltd., in Copenhagen. They briefly made only two different plaques beginning in 1848 in very limited annual numbers. Their records indicate that in 1848 they produced 118; in 1849 they produced only 82; in 1851 still only 82; and in 1855, the final number of 80.[51] The two subject matters are well-known. One is Horace Vernet's (1758-1836) portrait of the sculptor Bertel Thorvaldsen (1770-1844) working on a portrait bust of the artist, based on the 1835 oil painting now in the Thorvaldsens Museum in Copenhagen and a copy at the Metropolitan Museum of Art in New York. The other is a 6.5" diameter circular lithophane profile portrait of King Frederick VII of Denmark.

An article published in 1951 in the *Pottery Gazette and Glass Trade Review*, presented detailed information about the wax modeling method used in Copenhagen. It additionally noted that Royal Copenhagen exhibited lithophane panels at the Crystal Palace Exhibition in London in 1851.[52] The article was, at some levels, refuting a popular belief that lithophanes were made strictly by photographic means. An article on the relationship between lithophane production and photography had appeared in an earlier edition of the *Pottery Gazette and Glass Trade Review*.

England

England is highly regarded world wide for its ceramics and perhaps best known for its transferware decorated in factories at Worcester, Bow, Chelsea, and even Derby, some dating as early as the 18th century. Lithophanes were made at or reputed to have been made at Adderley & Lawson; W H Goss; Grainger, Lee & Co. of Worcester; Mintons; and Wedgwood. Apparently lithophanes were made at Grainger, Lee & Co. "working under license from Robert Griffith Jones of London who had acquired the method from the French inventor."[53]

Lithophane portrait of Bertel Thorvaldsen based on a 1835 painting by Horace Vernet, depicting the sculptor Bertel Thorvaldsen working on a portrait bust of the artist. This version is a Meissen copy, virtually identical to the rare Royal Copenhagen example, German, 19th century, Meissen 203, Blair Museum acc. no. 2005.4, lithophane 6.75" x 5.25". *Courtesy of the Blair Museum of Lithophanes.* Gift of Greg Knott.

Adderley & Lawson

Several British authorities have claimed that Adderley & Lawson of Burslem made lithophanes.[54] According to Bernard Hughes, it was when the patent expired in 1842, that a few English companies, including Adderley & Lawson in addition to Grainger, Lee & Co. of Worcester, made a few lithophanes.[55] An auction in Nottingham, United Kingdom, in February 2007, offered by Mellors & Kirk, included an Adderley & Lawson small domed lithophanic lampshade with the mark "ADDERLEY AND LAWSON" and also imprinted on the interior "Provo Patent."[56] The rare dome is 3.25" in height and has a base diameter of 4.25". Another example of a similar Adderley & Lawson-marked domed fairy lamp is illustrated in the Ruf book, *Fairy Lamps*.

Detail of Adderley & Lawson backstamp on small domed lampshade. *Courtesy of John and Eve Coleman.*

Small domed lithophanic lampshade, English, 19th century, Adderley & Lawson, H: 3.25" Diam: 4.25". *Courtesy of John and Eve Coleman.*

Coalport

Coalport China, located in Shropshire, has been in production, in one form or another, since 1795, when it was established by John Rose. He had been an apprentice at Caughley until 1785 when he started his own pottery which he left to move to Coalport. He acquired Caughley in 1799 and absorbed it in 1814. Improvements were made to Coalport China in the 1820s when they began producing the firm's feldspar porcelain. They copied lavish works of Sèvres, Meissen and Chelsea at that time. They won awards for successfully replicating some of these famous wares in the mid-1800s. Parian ware was produced in small quantities after the late 1840s, but there is no record of lithophane production until recently. Laurel Blair visited Coalport China in 1965, but he apparently did not see anything directly related to lithophane manufacture. Earlier correspondence from the sales manager at Coalport noted that they had "no records of porcelain transparencies being made in the early days of Coalport but a few samples were made around 1955."[57] Subsequent correspondence implies that while there were no lithophane samples remaining from those made at the factory around 1955, there was a fairly large collection of earlier models of the cameo type from which it might have been possible to develop lithophanes.[58] This same correspondence noted that the 1955 samples "were not put on the market," and apparently even the models had disappeared before Mr. Blair's visit.

The mystery of the Coalport lithophanes is somewhat clarified by the discovery of an article about one item in the collection of the Coalport chairman, Mr. Stanley Harrison, and an interview with the firm's modeler and designer, Mr. S.R. Sanders. The article published in December 1955 by the *Pottery Gazette and Glass Trade Review*, features a Coalport tankard designed by Mr. Sanders, which has a lithophane in the base. The article clearly notes that "the tankard illustrated was not made for sale commercially, but to add to Mr. Harrison's personal collection of special pieces."[59]

Copelands

Over the years there has been speculation as to whether Copelands produced any lithophanes. Interesting correspondence between Laurel Blair and Dr. Leonard Rakow from 1983 centered around the same question. Dr. Rakow mentioned in one letter that Robert Copeland of Spode was writing a book on Copeland production and although he "has found frequent references to Copeland production of lithophanes by other authors, he has never seen a marked Copeland (or Spode) lithophane."[60] He cited Laurel Blair as the world's authority on lithophanes and inquired as to whether there were any appropriately marked lithophanes in his collection. Blair replied that there were none marked "Copeland" or "Spode." He invited Mr. Copeland to visit the collection and see if he could identify such unmarked pieces based on the qualities of the porcelain.

Earlier 1963 correspondence from the City of Stoke-on-Trent City Museum and Art Gallery to Mr. Blair, seemed to perpetuate the idea that Copeland produced lithophanes. Although this correspondence from the curator, A.R. Mountford, notes that "none of our specimens bear factory marks of any description," he does retell the story that "the panel with reproduction of Old Master painting has been identified as Copeland as the donor acquired it from a man who worked at Copelands and remembers it being made there around 1900"[61] (acc. no. 82.P.48). However, in 1965, Mr. Blair received rather definitive correspondence from W. Duckers at Spode/W.T. Copeland & Sons, LTD., that after much discussion with their Art Director it could be concluded that they "have at no time produced lithophanes."[62]

W H Goss, Stoke-on-Trent

W H Goss (Ltd), founded by William Henry Goss (1833-1906), can be described as a manufacturer of porcelain, parian and earthenware, all produced at Falcon Pottery, Stoke-on-Trent, between 1855-1944. Impressed and printed marks include "W H GOSS," "W H G," and a crest mark with a goshawk bird insignia located above the "W.H. GOSS." The company is best known for its production of ceramic souvenirs and mementos. The small porcelain replicas and souvenirs frequently bear the crests of locations and names of visitor attractions and such.

There exists only one documented example of an appropriately marked Goss piece with a lithophane that has been published and illustrated in at least two sources. It is a small circular piece, with a diameter of 3.5", which appears to be of the type used in the interior base of a small cup. The Art Nouveau style female with a star in her hair was signed and dated "J.A. 1888," and also includes the impressed mark of W. H. Goss. The modeling was by Joseph Astley who worked as the chief modeler at the Falcon Works of W. H. Goss at Stoke-on-Trent and also at the Belleek factory in Ireland.[63]

There are two pieces in the Blair Museum collection that Mr. Blair attributed to the William H. Goss factory. This was probably wishful thinking. Mr. Blair referred to William H. Goss as the "father of the 'Take-Home-a Memento-of-Your-Holiday.'"[64]

Grainger, Lee & Co., Worcester

The name Grainger is associated with Worcester beginning in 1801. That is the year that Thomas Grainger (1783-1839), who had been an apprentice at Robert Chamberlain's Worcester factory with his partner John Wood, had established a rival porcelain company in Worcester. It is this company, known between 1814-1839 as Grainger, Lee & Co., owned by partners Thomas Grainger and James Lee, that produced lithophane cottages, also known as pastille burners or candleholders comprised of soft-paste porcelain.[65] The scenes include Napoleon with the sentry and Belisarius. Some sources state that Grainger, Lee & Co. "bought the British patent to make lithophanes taken out by Robert Griffith Jones of Middlesex in 1828."[66] The Blair Museum owns four pastille burners of this type, but only one of them has the impressed stamp.

A pair of unsigned Grainger, Lee & Co. pastille burners was purchased at the Mellors & Kirk auction in February 2007 and is now in the private collection of Graham and Nancy Pullen in the United Kingdom (illustrated in Chapter Six). These exhibit some production flaws in the porcelain and have been dated to circa 1830-35.[67]

In a letter from Worcester curator Henry Sandon to researcher and collector Bernard Rushton dated May 14, 1968, Sandon wrote regarding lithophanes produced by Grainger, Lee & Company, "...a large quantity must have been made by us, as Graingers of Worcester had the British patent." In fact, there are less than a dozen known Grainger, Lee & Co. lithophanes. There are no plaques known to be of 19th century origin, with all attributable examples in the form of pastille burners or nightlights. Few are signed.

Pastille burner and nightlight with a lithophane of Napoleon with a sentry, English, 19th century, marked Grainger, Lee & Co., Worcester, Blair Museum acc. no. 302, 6.5" x 4.5" x 3.375". *Courtesy of the Blair Museum of Lithophanes.*

Detail of a rare backstamp from a Grainger, Lee & Co. pastille burner night light, Blair Museum acc. no. 302. *Courtesy of the Blair Museum of Lithophanes.*

At the present time there are four molds for the production of lithophane plaques in the Worcester Porcelain Museum. Two are plaster press molds and two are plaster cases. Correspondence from 1963 to 1965 between Laurel Blair and Worcester curator C. Schingler acknowledges that two molds dating from the Grainger, Lee & Co. period had been located. Schingler believed they were of Continental origin. One depicts "a lady undressing and struggling with her corsets, the other is a portrait of a gentleman who might be William IV."[68] In the 1970s Worcester experimented making new lithophanes using the old molds. At the same time it was proposed that they develop some new lithophanes, but this idea was quickly abandoned.

The Worcester experimentation involved using the 19th century molds to make new cases. They also took a broken 19th century KPM lithophane of Mendelssohn Bartholdy and made a plaster mold of it (there is evidence of the crack in the mold) and produced at least one lithophane. The fourth mold, possibly dating from the 19th century, depicts the popular character Belisarius, shown blind and ravaged by time. The back of the mold is marked "pattern 183 (or 1830?) Belisarius." The dimensions of the plaque are close to that of Meissen 48, depicting the blind Belisarius. This image appears in several extant examples of Grainger, Lee & Co. pastille burners. It is important to note that all Grainger, Lee & Co. pastille burners and nightlights, marked or attributed, exhibit flaws suggesting firing issues.

Plaster mold featuring *Belisarius*, English, possibly 19th century, Grainger, Lee & Co., of Worcester, marked "pattern 183" or "1830" and "Belisarius" in cursive writing, exterior 9.875" x 8" x 1.25", interior 8.25" x 6.5" with tapering spare. *Courtesy of the Worcester Porcelain Museum.*

Lithophane plaque featuring *Belisarius*, English, possibly 20th century (made from the original mold), no marks, parian ware body, 7.375" x 5.75". *Courtesy of the Worcester Porcelain Museum.*

Mintons

Mintons, Stoke-on-Trent, has a long history, having been established in 1789. Mintons has been famous through the years, largely for blue transfer-printed cream-colored earthenware, pearl ware, and bone china, many with wildly popular decorative patterns of exotic birds and flowers. The patterns were ever changing along with the fashions of the day. The demand for the table services was ever present. One favorite was the scarce reproductions of Palissy ware and Della Robbia during the 1870s. Another favorite was the Pâte-sur-Pâte which Marc Louis Solon perfected at Mintons. In other words, the history of Mintons is well-documented. However, the history of Minton and its relationship with lithophanes is a bit more complicated. The short version is that Mintons did make lithophanes, with the question being "when."

Dr. Edmond Beroud, the lithophane collector who ultimately sold his massive collection to Laurel Blair, was endeavoring to write his own book about lithophanes in the early 1950s. In 1953, he wrote to Mintons with this goal in mind, stating that he had discovered that "about 1860, the Mintons Pottery...made 'lithophanes.'"[69] In his letter he asked numerous questions about when they first manufactured them, what the sizes and subjects were, and how they were marked. The October 1953 response from J. Steel at Mintons summarizes the photographic process vs. carving waxes debate that had been the subject of a 1950 article in the *Pottery Gazette and Glass Trade Review*.[70] He supplies no definitive answers.

There is a listing of Minton lithophanes or "Berlin transparencies" which was noted in a letter from the curator of the City of Stoke-on-Trent City Museum and Art Gallery, in Hanley, Stoke-on-Trent. The curator notes in his 1963 correspondence that their subjects include "copies of Old Masters, portraits, and landscapes," including the titles: *The Penitent, Naomi and her daughters in law, Mother and Child, Guardian Angel, Quentin Durward, Mother and dying child, The Agony in the Garden, The Jolly Good Fellow,* and *The Offering*.[71] His information was no doubt obtained from the same source that Geoffrey A. Godden utilized in the writing of his 1968 book *Minton Pottery & Porcelain of the First Period 1793-1850*. Godden had perused the archival Minton correspondence in great detail and noted in his book a letter dated January 3rd, 1848, addressed to a Miss Halcomb where "Transparencies" are mentioned in the following context, "...We beg to inform you that the Transparencies you require are in stock, and shall be forwarded by the Carrier on Friday next."[72] The listing of the Minton lithophanes in their archives (the same as listed above) was dated February 1850.[73] From Godden's earlier book *Antique China and Glass Under £5* (page 5) Laurel Blair interprets the materials in the archives at Mintons to mean that the listing of lithophanes (noted earlier) were ones purchased from the Berlin factory to copy at Mintons.[74] Mintons sent Mr. Blair a copy of that Berlin invoice in question, dated February 20th 1850.

In 1966, the designer D.H. Henson from Mintons wrote to Mr. Blair about the four molds that had been discovered in the factory. He listed the lithophane molds as: a cow with a calf by a pond; a woman kneeling before the Virgin Mary; a cathedral in a square; and water wheel and mill.[75] An identical list was sent by Minton Ltd. to Bernard Rushton in 1969.[76] Godden also notes in his 1968 book, that four lithophane molds were recently discovered at the Minton factory. His list varies slightly, stating the molds were those depicting a cathedral and town square; a mountain view; cow and calf at a pool; and a female kneeling at an altar, which he speculates might be *The Penitent* listed on the 1850 Minton lithophane listing.[77]

In 1965 Laurel Blair visited Mintons. Subsequent to his visit, Mintons promised and shipped a plaster lithophane mold and lithophane. The recipe they sent for their Bone China body which was pressed into the Plaster of Paris mold in its plastic state was 25% Cornish stone, 25% China clay and 50% calcined animal bones.[78] The Minton designer, D.H. Henson noted that the mold that Mr. Blair was sent (the Cathedral) was made from an old case mold, which "in order to cut down the weight ..." (for mailing purposes) they "cut about the same thickness away at the back, as the mould is thick now."[79] He elaborated, "In other words, moulds that would be used for producing a lithophane would be about twice as thick as the one we are sending to you, as they have to stand quite a bit of pressure during the making process, when the clay is pressed into them."[80] He also commented on one possible method that Mintons used to produce lithophane molds – utilizing casting a plaster mold rather than taking lead impressions from the gelatine.[81]

In summary, it seems likely that Minton purchased some German lithophanes in 1850 with the intention of manufacturing a similar product. In the early 20th century Mintons experimented with utilizing a photographic process to produce lithophanes, including an image of Lord Baden-Powell, founder of the Boy Scout movement. None of these early examples have been identified, only two marked Mintons lithophanes and a plaster mold are in collections today. The mold was made from an old case mold and the lithophanes may date no earlier than 1965.

Wade Potteries

No one in the field of lithophane research has ever mentioned Wade Potteries in Burslem, Stoke-on-Trent as a possible link with lithophane history. However, a 1976 letter from Anthony J. Wade, Chairman of Wade Potteries, to Laurel Blair inquired about general lithophane information, including particulars about lithophanes that belonged to Mr. Wade's father. In his letter marked "CONFIDENTIAL," Mr. Wade noted "Over recent years we have developed a highly translucent but exceptionally strong body, which would, I think, be ideally suited to the production of lithophanes."[82] After he listed the usually cited English lithophane manufacturers such as Mintons, Adderley & Lawson, Copelands and Graingers of Worcester, Wade wrote, "Possibly you may surprise me by mentioning someone who makes them even today, but my impression is that they almost come into the category of a lost art."[83] He continues, "If we were to reintroduce them, naturally we want to ensure that they are tastefully done and that the marketing treatment is in line with a quality product."[84] There is no proof that Wade Potteries Ltd. followed through with this line of interest in producing new lithophanes. Perhaps Mr. Wade was startled by Mr. Blair's reply the following month, that there were factories in Germany (von Schierholz), Hungary (Herend), and Portugal (Vista Alegre) producing lithophanes.[85]

The May 15th 1978 Blair Museum *Bulletin* elaborated in a couple of paragraphs about Wade Potteries Limited and lithophane production. Mr. Blair had recently visited the factory and noted that Mr. Wade had "put his men to work on reproducing them in a very special porcelain formula which he has developed for his electrical items, and this porcelain will not break and yet gives excellent translucency." Mr. Wade promised Mr. Blair that the lithophanes

Plaster mold featuring a cathedral, English, 20th century, made from a 19th century case mold in 1965, Minton, Blair Museum acc. no. 2729, 5.625" x 7.375" x 0.875". *Courtesy of the Blair Museum of Lithophanes.*

Lithophane, cathedral, English, 1965, Minton, Blair Museum acc. no. 2730, 3.875" x 5.625". *Courtesy of the Blair Museum of Lithophanes.*

Detail of backstamp on Minton cathedral lithophane, marked "Minton's China 6-65," Blair Museum 2730. *Courtesy of the Blair Museum of Lithophanes.*

"will be original works and also that they will be marked so that there will not be any possibility of anyone thinking that they are 'antique.'" Yet there is still no evidence that any were produced based on recent contact with the company.

Wedgwood

Josiah Wedgwood first began experimenting with earthenware circa 1750, and it was only a few years later he was in partnership with Thomas Wheildon and soon Thomas Bentley. When one thinks of Queen's Ware, Jasper, and the Portland Vase, one immediately thinks of Wedgwood. It remains a highly priced and recognizable ceramic to this day.

There has been a long-standing debate among lithophane researchers as to whether or not Wedgwood manufactured lithophanes or whether they created beautiful "impressed intaglios" that some (mistakenly) refer to as lithophanes. The most authoritative article on the subject of Wedgwood and lithophanes was titled "Wedgwood Lithophanes," written by Wedgwood scholar, Leonard S. Rakow, and published in 1985, in the journal *Ars Ceramica* by the Wedgwood Society of New York. The title says it all. Whether or not one believes these are true lithophanes, everyone agrees that they are rare.

Wedgwood lithophanes feature classical figures and motifs on a plain background, similar to those found on the well known Jasperware and Black Basalt ware. The difference is that in the lithophanes, the normally raised figures are recessed into the body, causing the porcelain to be thinner so it transmits more light, creating a lithophane effect. These are argued by some to not be true lithophanes because they do not create the image by manipulating dark and light as in a mezzotint with dark and light representing light and shadow along with the shades of objects with different colors, but rather form the image in the way that light would fall on a white marble sculpture.

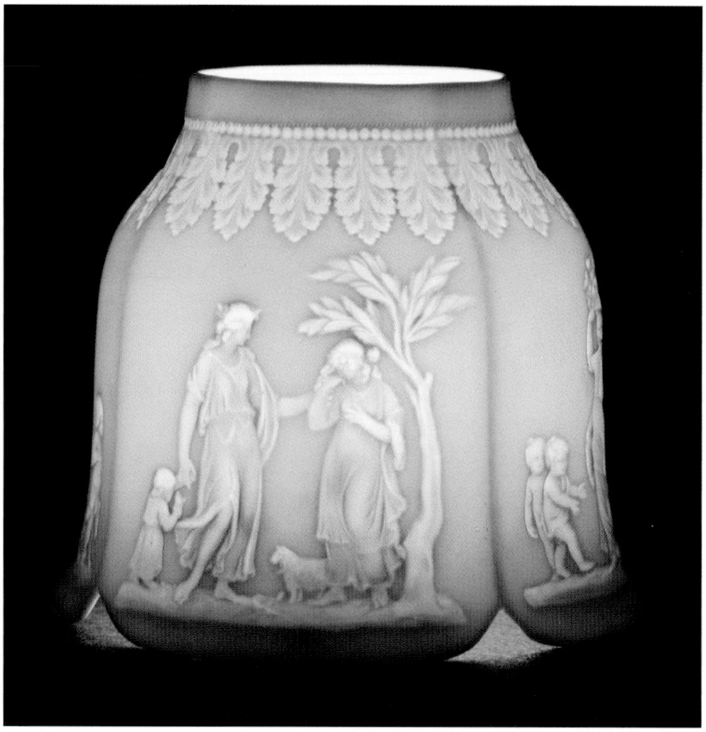

Lampshade with intaglio designs, English, 20th century, Wedgwood, tiny printed "WEDGWOOD" mark under glaze, Blair Museum acc. no. 1944, Height 3.75" Diam. 4.5". *Courtesy of the Blair Museum of Lithophanes.*

According to Dr. Rakow, Wedgwood did not begin manufacturing lithophanes until the early 20th century. This is based on the imprinted backstamps "WEDGWOOD" and "ENGLAND," which indicate manufacture after 1891, but probably prior to 1910.[86] It has also been noted that Wedgwood did not produce bone china until 1878 (although there is some Regency style dinner ware with bone china body that they produced from 1812 to 1822), so any lithophanes would have been manufactured after that date. Wedgwood bone china is made from a mixture of 47% calcined bone, 22% china clay, 26% china stone, 3% ball clay, and 2% flint. There are examples of oval wall sconces, circular hanging lamps and small lampshades, all with classical and neo-classical figures, typical of Wedgwood production. These exist not only as Wedgwood lithophanes, but also appear illustrated in their "Shape Book 1906-1913," as shape nos. 2001-2642. There are no background designs behind the central figures on the Wedgwood lithophanes, but border designs of acanthus, anthemion or other Wedgwood motifs are prevalent. It seems obvious that Wedgwood lithophanes were intended to function as translucent shades for electric fixtures and that the transmitted light is a defining feature. Although these Wedgwood examples could be appreciated with reflected light, their true beauty is revealed only when backlit. In the 1960s the Buten Museum of Wedgwood attempted to reproduce

Wedgwood wall sconces, Blair Museum acc. nos. 1795 and 1798, oval 3.75" x 2.75", overall 27" x 10" x 5". *Courtesy of the Archives of the Blair Museum of Lithophanes.*

Hanging lamp, *Dancing Hours*, English, 20th century, c. 1953, Wedgwood, Blair Museum acc. no. 1907, Diam. 13.5". *Courtesy of the Blair Museum of Lithophanes.*

one of the original Wedgwood catalogues of lithophanes – rather poor quality photographs that had been pasted on cardboard and bound loosely with shoelaces.

To complicate matters for the argument lithophane vs. impressed intaglios, Wedgwood purchased the *émail ombrant* process from the du Tremblay heirs in 1873. Copious archival materials, including correspondence from 1863 from du Tremblay to those associated with Wedgwood supports this fact. These materials, from the Wedgwood research files in New York City, note that the "purchase of the molds ... described by Baron Hocédé (Tremblay, nephew of the inventor, Alexis du Tremblay) as Lithophanie, they were never produced as such by this firm. I mean by that, that they were not produced in Bone China to give the effect of light and shade. The articles were made in our ordinary Queen's Ware, with effect of light and shade produced by colored glazes, the chief color being green. Here I would make it clear that we have produced Lithophanes, but not from the molds above mentioned, they were made in our Bone China body as lamp shades for electric lights which were cast in one piece and with the classical figures such as 'The Dancing Hours,' etc., counter-sunk to give the effect of Lithophane."[87]

Mr. Blair seemed to have had a eureka moment when he learned that the "confusing" patent regarding "lithophanes" made at the Rubelles factory, was nothing more than a patent for a completely different process, *émail ombrant* or *émaux ombrants*, but unfortunately titled "lithophanies." Wedgwood completed the purchase of this patent relating to *émail ombrant* in 1873 even though they were first offered these rights by Baron Hocédé du Tremblay in 1863 and Wedgwood manufactured some of these in 1864 with the molds they had acquired. All of this had earlier been offered to Minton, who had declined. Wedgwood archival materials specifically note that they have a copy of the original Brevet d'invention granted to M. M. de Bourgoing and du Tremblay in Paris in 1842, in addition to the transfer of patent rights from Baron Hocédé du Tremblay to Josiah Wedgwood & Sons. Robert A. Elder, Jr., who was assistant curator of ethnology at the Smithsonian Institution in the 1950s believed that the molds made from the original 1842-patented invention could have been used to produce lithophanes or *émaux ombrants*, as the intaglio design would have been the final product. For the former, a translucent porcelain body would have allowed the design to be viewed by transmitted light, and for the latter an opaque pottery body used and the design brought out by colored glazes shown in reflected light.[88] This belief is corroborated by the written words of Alexandre Brongniart in 1877, "L'émail ombrant n'est qu'une modification de l'invention nommée *lithophanie*, due à M. de Bourgoing, et mentionée surtout avec les travaux de la manufacture de porcelaine de Munich. M. du Tremblay, propriétaire de la fabrique de Rubelles, près Melun (Seine-et-Marne), en a tiré le parti le plus avantageux en créant une fabrication nouvelle qui peut un jour prendre une grande extension (The *émail ombrant* is only a modification of the invention called lithophane created by M. Bourgoing and mentioned mainly with the production of porcelain manufacture in Munich. Mr. du Tremblay, the owner of the company of Rubelles near Melun [Seine and Marne], used from that the most advantageous part by creating an entire new fabrication of production that could one day play a very important part)."[89] As with lithophanes, the term "magical" has been applied to describe *émail ombrant*, also, noting that the surface is smooth and almost flat, but the image is crisp and has great depth.

Correspondence between Robert Elder and Laurel Blair in 1964, implies that the stunning Wedgwood *Dancing Hours* ceiling bowl shade in the Blair collection, was cast in 1953 by Wedgwood from the original plaster mold specifically for research purposes as a gift to Robert Elder and Edmond Beroud.[90] The original *Dancing Hours* is illustrated as no. 2400 in the *1906-1913 Shape Book* from the Wedgwood factory. It is adapted from a design by John Flaxman (1755-1826), who worked with Josiah Wedgwood. There seem to be two other examples of this *Dancing Hours* lithophane shade. It is likely that the others were made early in the 20th century, unlike the Blair example that was made mid-century. Mr. Blair offered one for sale (not the one belonging to the Museum) in *Blair Bulletin* no. 12, January 20, 1978, p. 7, item no. 280. The asking price was $950.

Hungary

Herend Porcelain

The Herend Porcelain factory, located in northwest Hungary not far from Budapest, was founded by Vince Stingl in 1826. Móric Fischer purchased the company in 1839. Herend Porcelain made their fame and fortune manufacturing artistic imitations of old Meissen, Sèvres and Chinese table sets. Many of these copies replaced the missing pieces of table sets for the aristocracy of Europe. Additionally under Fischer's guidance, Herend designed new shapes in addition to their excellent copies which were greatly appreciated at the various international fairs such as the Vienna Exhibition of Industrial Art in 1845 and the Crystal Palace exhibition in London in 1851. England's Queen Victoria ordered a large table service for Windsor Castle, decorated with a Chinese motif of butterflies and flowers.[91] This type of success was contagious, and other significant orders followed. Herend Porcelain was prized at subsequent international expositions in Vienna and also became valued souvenirs for royalty throughout Europe. The Herend factory witnessed fires, bankruptcy crises, and even the closing of the factory in the late 1890s. After reopening and enduring artistic success amidst financial difficulties, the factory became Hungarian state property in 1948.

Herend is best known and highly acclaimed for its imitations of European and Chinese ware, so it is not too surprising that they began making lithophanes at some point in their long history. They apparently made some lithophanes during the 19th century, but these are extremely rare.[92] It has been recorded that they exhibited their first lithophane plaques at an industrial exhibition in Pest in 1842.[93] Factory inventory records further indicate that they were making other lithophane novelty items in 1843, such as panels for lampshades.[94] Herend's business ledgers verify that they continued to make lithophanes through the decades, but on a scale that paled in comparison to their production of dinnerware. However, when they later made lithophanes in the 20th century, they did not copy the motifs of other factories, but rather used a pleasingly white porcelain body and their own designs. Lithophanes produced at Herend after 1948 reflect the marketability of objects of curiosity, for collectors and museums.[95]

Plate with lithophane featuring American President John F. Kennedy, Hungarian, 20th century, Herend Porcelain, Blair Museum acc. no. 156, Diam. 7.5". *Courtesy of the Blair Museum of Lithophanes.*

Detail of Herend Porcelain backstamp on J. F. Kennedy plate, Blair Museum acc. no. 156. *Courtesy of the Blair Museum of Lithophanes.*

While many of the Herend lithophanes are eight-inch-diameter round portrait plates of famous individuals such as Albert Einstein, Albert Schweitzer, Michelangelo, and Bela Bartok, they did create others such as a *View of Budapest* (Herend No. 8078, 7.5" diameter), the *Emperor's Cathedral Castle* (7.5" diameter), a *Bouquet of Daisies* (Herend No. 8071, 6" diameter) and *Seated Man Throwing a Very Large Pot* (Herend No. 8068, 6" diameter). The Blair Museum of Lithophanes owns several fine Herend lithophanes that apparently date from the 1960s and 1970s, including a portrait of John F. Kennedy (acc. no. 156). A gift from the president of Herend Porcelain was acquired by Blair in 1976. It is a plate with a portrait of Albert Schweitzer as its central motif and a diameter of 7.75". The sculptor was László Horváth who has been a designer at the Herend Porcelain Manufactory for several decades. According to 1978 correspondence between Laurel Blair and Robert Grimm, U.S. representative for Herend Porcelain, their lithophanes were "not available for commercial production."[96] But by 1985, Mr. Blair was offering Herend lithophanes to the members of his lithophane collectors club.

Each factory seems to create its own masterpieces, and Herend Porcelain is no exception. In 1935 they created an impressive porcelain lithophane window, comprised of fifty-four smaller panels, for the Herend church (illustrated in Chapter Seven). It was damaged in World War II, but since they had originally created a pair, they were able to replace the damaged portions of the window with the sections that had been safely stored away.[97]

Circular lithophane of Albert Schweitzer, designed by László Horváth and signed "LH" by the artist on the front, Hungarian, c. 1976, Herend Porcelain, Blair Museum acc. no. 158, Diam. 7.75". *Courtesy of the Blair Museum of Lithophanes.*

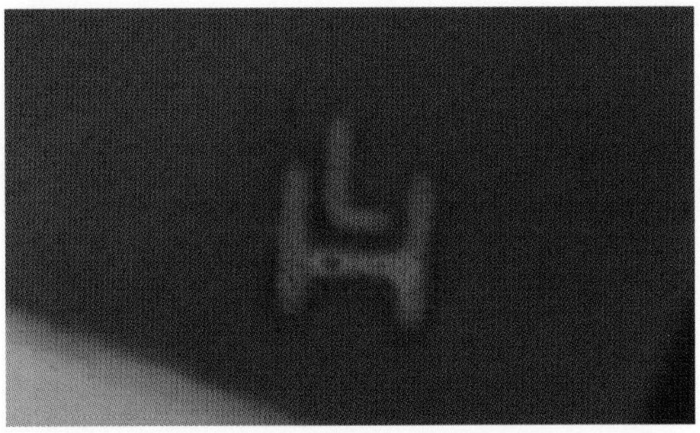

Detail of the artist's mark, "LH" for László Horváth, on the front of the circular lithophane of Albert Schweitzer, Blair Museum acc. no. 158. *Courtesy of the Blair Museum of Lithophanes.*

Ireland

Belleek

Ireland is known for its production of Belleek ware which was first manufactured in 1863 in County Fermanagh, and continues to this day. The nacreous lustre in the glaze of these eggshell thin porcelains is derived from bismuth. While this lustre is an attribute of these highly prized ceramics, many believe that in the case of lithophanes, it impedes the best viewing of the three dimensional images.

There are twelve or thirteen lithophanes that can be identified as part of the Belleek inventory beginning in 1863. Unlike so many other manufacturers, the production of lithophanes at Belleek has been well-documented by Degenhardt and others. All are based on 19th century German examples. Belleek retained the 19th century molds and twelve were reissued as recently as the 1990s. While Belleek lithophanes are highly prized by some collectors, Mr. Blair was not fond of them, noting in one of his Blair Museum of Lithophane newsletters, "their clays are dark sepia tone and highly glazed so that much of the detail is lost."[98] Mr. Blair referred to the reissued lithophanes as "reproductions,"[99] to which he was opposed as he felt this confused the collectors.

Quite often Belleek lithophanes are described as being expensive, new or old. In 1987, Mr. Blair published in his newsletter, that he had passed up the opportunity to be "robbed" by a dealer who wanted $2,000 for the Belleek lithophane depicting *The Priest and the Acolyte*, and $1,800 for *Lovers at Table*.[100] As Mr. Blair noted, "He'll get rich, but not by me!"[101]

Lithophane, *St. Patrick's Cathedral*, New York, Irish, probably 20th century, unmarked, Belleek, Blair Museum acc. no. 1465, dimensions 7.75" x 6.625". *Courtesy of the Blair Museum of Lithophanes.*

Italy

Doccia/Ginori

The Ginori Porcelain Factory was established in Doccia, near Florence, in 1737, by the Tuscan Marquis Carlo Ginori (1702-1757). Ginori porcelain is often referred to as Doccia, for this selected location. For five years, experiments were conducted by Ginori along with the two Viennese painters and the Italian modeler, Gaspero Bruschi, that he had hired. Around 1742, Ginori began to sell the products of the factory to the general public.

At the time that Carlo Ginori founded his factory, there were only two other hard-paste porcelain factories operating in Europe, Meissen in Germany, and Du Paquier, in Austria. This pioneering effort lasted for five generations of Ginori ownership and leadership, followed by the acquisition of the factory by Richard in 1896. The Richard-Ginori double name reflects the harmonious relationship between the artistic manufactory and the industrial aspect that still exists in the factory today.

There seems to have been some debate as to whether or not Ginori ever produced lithophanes. It has been stated that Ginori purchased some lithophane plaques from the von Schierholz factory in Plaue and incorporated these panels into some veilleuses and other items produced by Ginori.[102] However reliable sources, including the director of the Doccia Porcelain Museum and the person in the factory in charge of "artistic casting" state that Ginori had obtained plaster models from outside Italy to produce a few lithophanes, and probably only made them for exhibitions, therefore, neither being for sale nor marketed, they had no backstamps.[103] Furthermore, there is no evidence that any lithophanes were manufactured in the 19th century. It can be concluded that Ginori only produced one original lithophane, and that was in the year 2000 for the Jubilaeum in Rome, where Richard-Ginori created a lamp with a lithophane lampshade depicting Raphael's *Madonna della seggiola*.

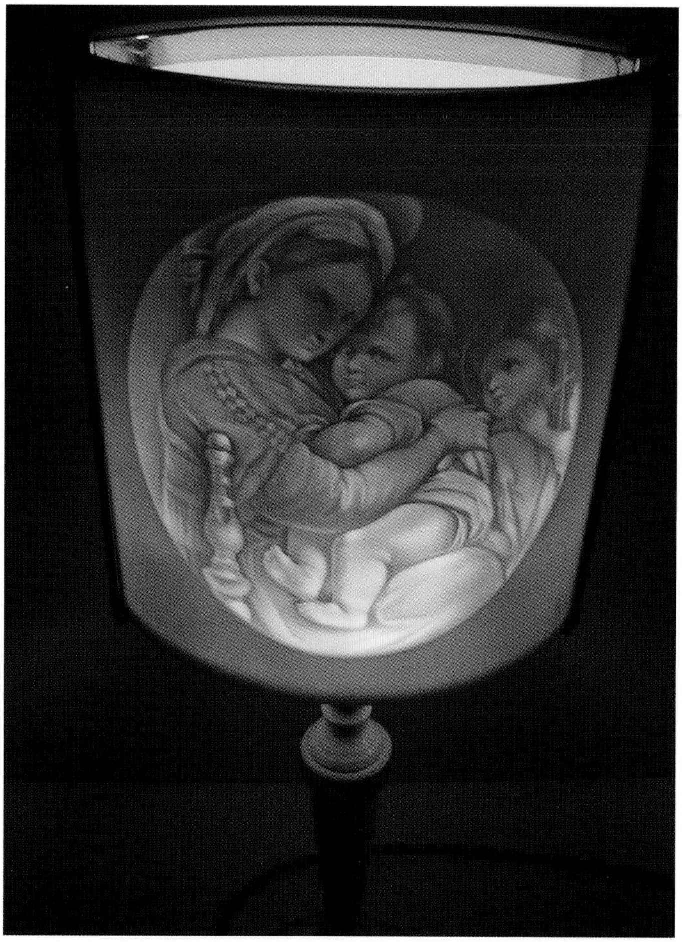

Lithophane lamp shade depicting Raphael's *Madonna della seggiola* (*Madonna della Sedia*) created by Richard-Ginori in the year 2000 for the Jubilaeum in Rome, Italian, lithophane shade 7.25" x 6.25", overall lamp Height 17.5", Diam. 4.375". *Courtesy of Museo Richard-Ginori della Manifattura di Doccia.*

Japan

Japan did not produce lithophanes in the 19th century, but various companies were prolific in the early to mid-20th century. Japanese lithophanes appeared in the bottoms of tea cups, coffee cups, saki cups, as well as souvenir cups, generally in the form of geisha heads. Also popular were full body nudes. These lithophanes were popular in the 1930s and then again after World War II and into the 1950s. In the 1980s there was even a collectors club in New Jersey, Geisha Girl Porcelain, devoted to this seemingly related collectible entity. Geisha Girl Porcelain, actually refers to a particular type of hand painted porcelain, made at Kutani and other Japanese factories, and is not equivalent to Geisha girl lithophanes, although some Geisha Girl Porcelain cups did have lithophanes in the interior. While the earliest Kutani ware was created in Japan in the 17th century, those with lithophanes date from the 20th century. A few other factories that have been identified include Maruku China, and Hayasi Fine China. There are two objects in the Blair Museum collection, a three-dimensional candle shield and a single cast night light that bear the mark "Nakajima." Geishas are the themes on both pieces.

Lithophane of a geisha's head in the bottom of a tea cup, Japanese, 20th century, marked "Japan" in overglaze cobalt on base, Blair Museum acc. no. 542, Height 1.875", Diam. 2.5". *Courtesy of the Blair Museum of Lithophanes.*

Some cups with lithophanes, manufactured in Japan, bear the Kutani backstamp, but many other lesser known factories produced vast quantities of cups with lithophanes in the interior. Most tea cups were parts of sets of around seventeen pieces, 4 cups and saucers, 4 cake plates, one teapot with lid, and a creamer and sugar with lid.

Over 27 different Geisha heads and seven nudes on the interiors of their cups have been identified. They appear frequently on what is referred to as Dragonware, whether it be gold or gilt, moriage, coralene or glass bead, or enamel-decorated. These could be regarded as the most available of all lithophanes collected today. These lithophanes are frequently compared to those that appeared in the bottom of German beer steins beginning in the 19th century. Some differentiate between the two, because the lithophanes in the bottoms of beer steins often had scenes and portraits with the background developed in fine detail, while the Japanese Geishas appear with no background, more like intaglio rather than a true lithophane.

Norway

Porsgrund Porselænsfabrik

The Porsgrund Porselænsfabrik, established in 1885, located in Porsgrunn, produced lithophanes beginning with the first factory production in 1887 until approximately 1900. There are examples located in the Town Museum in Porsgrunn. Unlike many museums, one will find theirs on exhibition, not tucked away in storage. All of the twenty-three subjects found in the illustrated price catalogue from 1887 appear to have been based on German 19th century lithophanes. German factory workers came to Porsgrunn to work in the factory and might have brought original molds with them from the Plaue factory. Only one original lithophane was unique to Porsgrunn. The subject is a female figure clasping her knees in a pastoral setting. A series of lithophanes was made from the original models in 1982 for the exhibit at the Town Museum. The factory has been in operation for 120 years. In addition to producing porcelain flatware and products for the Royal family, they have been producing fireproof goods for professional kitchens as well as exquisite porcelain for the home.

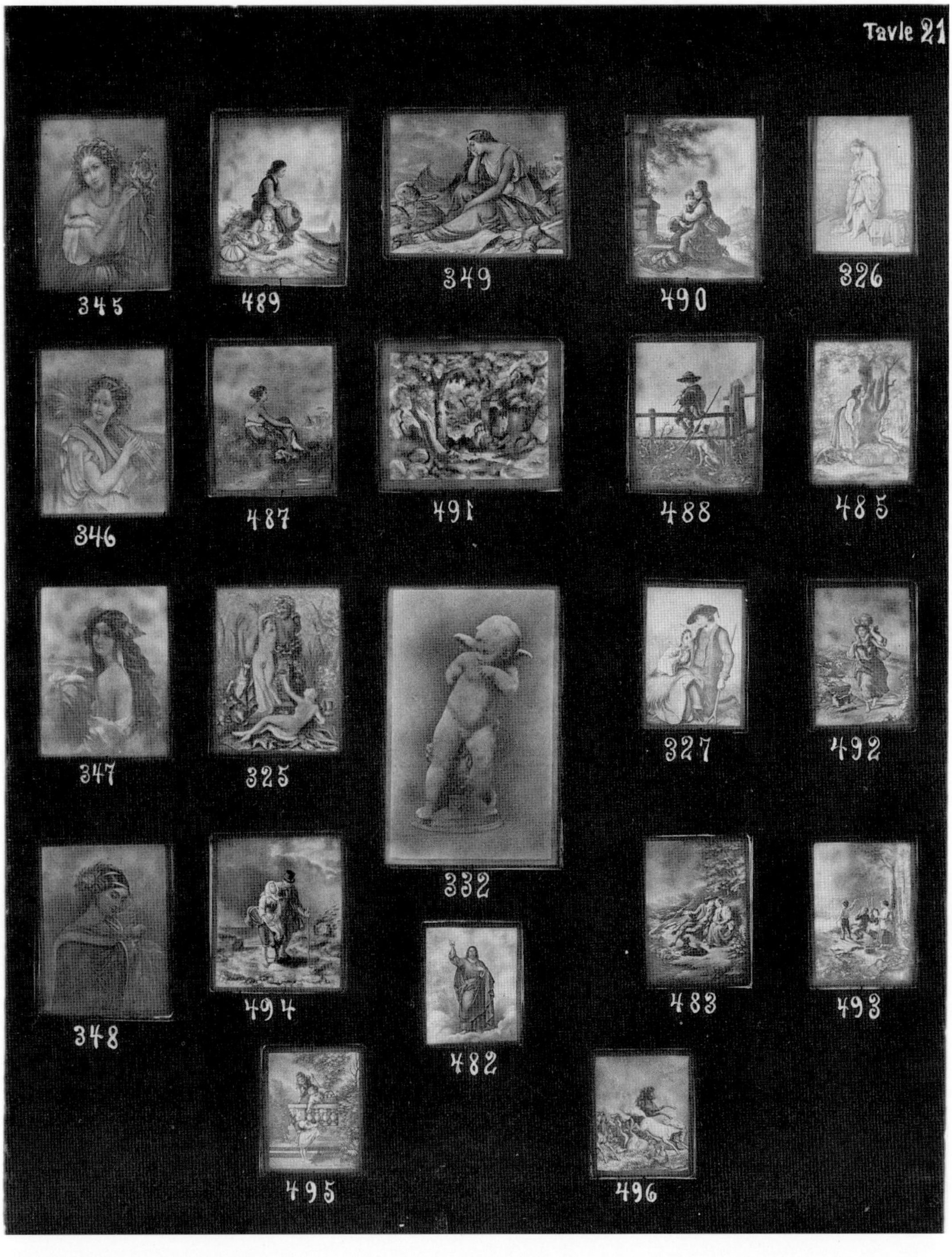

One page from the Porsgrund Porselænsfabrik illustrated *Preis-Courant* published in 1887. *Courtesy of the Town Museum in Porsgrunn.*

Portugal

Vista Alegre Porcelain Factory

Vista Alegre Fabrica de Porcelana, located in the city of Ilhova in the district of Aveiro, Portugal, was founded in 1824, by José Ferreira Pinto-Basto. They produced their first lithophanes circa 1850 and they continued production until the end of the 20th century.[104] This company is well known among lithophane collectors for their veilleuses with lithophane panels. Most appear to be themes based on European models from the 19th century. The backstamps on the veilleuses are "VA" frequently with the additional "Portugal," although there are some other variations. Correspondence between Mr. Blair and Mr. Joaquim Pinto Basto at Vista Alegre from 1967 indicated that Mr. Blair had visited the company, and the company had promised a price listing of their past lithophane production as well as "samples of the items in lithophane which you are making at the present time."[105]

Mr. Blair bought several Vista Alegre veilleuses at antique shops while in Lisbon and he wrote Mr. Pinto Basto that the bases were identical to the ones they had recently cast from an old mold. During his visit to Lisbon, Mr. Blair also discovered other veilleuses for sale in antique shops that were made by Vista Alegre, but did not contain lithophanes. They apparently rarely if ever produced their own lithophane images, but made their molds from existing lithophanes produced by other manufacturers. The Vista Alegre Museum has twenty-one objects with lithophanes, including nine veilleuses, some with just one lithophane and others with three or four on the sides, and the rest plaques. Several lithophanes in their collection claim to be the work of a Portuguese sculptor and one is a portrait of José Estevão de Magalhães, a prominent journalist and political activist, presumably produced as an original product in the 20th century by Vista Alegre, and not copied from a European original.

Veilleuse théière featuring the lithophane *Das Wunder der Rose*, Portuguese, 19th century, Vista Alegre, mark of "VA" on teapot base, Blair Museum acc. no. 2500, overall height 11.625". *Courtesy of the Blair Museum of Lithophanes.*

Lithophane plaque featuring Russian Czarina Alexandra Feodorovna, German, 19th century, KPM 154 St, from one of three 19th century Woburn Abbey panels, 7" x 6.5". *Courtesy of Andy Cook.*

Russia

Although there isn't much evidence that substantial quantities of lithophanes were produced in Russia during the 19th century, the Russian leaders were certainly popular subjects for lithophanes. Two lithophane plaques with Russian themes adorn one of the panels that came from Woburn Abbey in the United Kingdom. One features a portrait of Czar Nicholas I, and the other his wife the Czarina Alexandra Feodorovna. The original portraits were painted by Franz Kruger and are located in the Hermitage Museum in St. Petersburg. Other lithophanes appear to commemorate the engagement or marriage of the Czar and Czarina.

Imperial Porcelain Factory

The Imperial Porcelain Factory was founded in St. Petersburg in 1744, and is believed to have produced lithophanes in the 19th century. Circumstantial evidence of this can be seen in an exquisite example now in the Hermitage Museum in St. Petersburg. Attributed to the Imperial Porcelain Factory, c. 1835, is an unmarked bisquit porcelain lithophane mounted in a wooden candle shield (Hermitage Museum acc. no. ERF 5556).[106] The image on the porcelain is that of the family of Czar Nicholas I on a sea voyage and includes the Czar, his wife, Alexandra Feodorovna, who was the daughter of King Friedrich Wilhelm III, and their second son. The lithophane image is a reproduction of a painting by George Dawe (1781-1829). Apparently lithographs were created based on this painting, and were featured in magazines and on other decorative objects. This is now a state factory.

A.G. Popow'sche Porzellanfabrik

The A. Popov Porcelain Factory was located in Gorbunovo near Moscow, and was in business between 1806 and 1872. They manufactured a good hard-paste porcelain and are reputed to have made lithophanes in the 19th century.

Sweden

Rörstrand

The Rörstrand factory is currently producing lithophanes as cup-shaped votive night light holders. The factory was established in 1726, in Stora Rörstrand in the Delft. Originally they produced a faience type ware, painted in cobalt blue designs. Porcelain was introduced in 1857. In the 19th century, at the same time they were imitating Sèvres porcelain, they produced ironstone china, opaque china, lead-glazed majolica and parian ware. It was probably at this time that they had a porcelain body that was suitable for the production of lithophanes. The factory's 20th century production includes one-piece votive nightlights with the Rörstrand Sweden backstamp amidst three crown-type symbols.

Lithophane votive night light holder, Town Hall, Swedish, 20th century, Rörstrand, Height 3", Diam. at top 3.25". *Courtesy of John and Eve Coleman.*

Detail of Rörstrand backstamp on votive night light holder. *Courtesy of John and Eve Coleman.*

Switzerland

One company is mentioned in relation to Switzerland, although there is no evidence to support the theory. Lithophanes with the backstamp "EDS&C" were identified to have been of Swiss origin, according to Dr. Edmond Beroud[107], while other Swiss sources state that lithophanes were never manufactured in Switzerland. In fact the director of the Musee National Suisse, Dr. Rudolph Schnyder wrote to Mr. Blair, "As much as I know in Switzerland no lithophanes were produced."[108]

United States of America

The facts surrounding the production of lithophanes in the United States are interesting in both historical context involving the ceramic industry in the U.S. and additionally the ongoing production of lithophanes by independent companies and individual artists today. First there is the fascinating situation of lithophane production at the Phoenix Pottery in Phoenixville, Pennsylvania in the late 19th century. Even more rare are the examples of globes and plaque forms marked with the "G.A.S." backstamp which have probably incorrectly been attributed to a yet-unidentified company in Philadelphia during the mid-19th century. For a description of contemporary makers who either made or continue to produce lithophanes, see Chapter Twelve.

Phoenix Pottery
Phoenixville, Pennsylvania

Occasionally the legends or mystique surrounding the production of lithophanes by a particular company garners more attention than is probably due. That is likely the case with the Phoenix Pottery in Phoenixville, Pennsylvania. This company, well-known and thoroughly documented in terms of the Etruscan majolica ware it produced in the last quarter of the 19th century, briefly manufactured lithophanes. Because there was virtually no lithophane production in the United States in the 19th century, Phoenixville has received quite a bit of attention over the years, probably far exceeding what is merited.

One of the earliest documentations of this Phoenix Pottery production was published in the August 1897 issue of *The Clay Worker* and was written by no less of a ceramics historian than Edwin Atlee Barber. In his "Historical Sketch of the Phoenixville (PA.) Pottery," Barber presented the history of the pottery which began operation in 1867, and included the production of lithophanes some time beginning around 1872 when W.A. H. Schreiber was first connected with the pottery and was experimenting with parian ware. According to Barber, Mr. Schreiber had purchased some molds and Barber further noted, "Those made at Phoenixville do not seem to reveal any originality of conception or workmanship. They appear to be copies of foreign designs, probably reproduced by simply making plaster molds from the imported pieces, which were quite common thirty years ago."[109] Barber had learned from Mr. Schreiber, first hand, that he had some "subjects prepared for lithophanes" including the Madonna, Christ crucified, Marguerite and Faust, and Penn's treaty with the Indians.[110] Edwin Barber compared some of the Phoenix Pottery lithophanes with those of known European manufacture and declared them identical except for the words "Phoenix Pottery" stamped on those produced at this Pennsylvania pottery. Additionally, he noted that the quality of the Phoenix Pottery examples was inferior, demonstrating warping and other defects from firing and less stellar clay body recipes. Claims were made of potential modelers and designers in Pennsylvania, but Barber concluded, "neither could have been the designer or original modeler ... Work of this high degree of artistic merit had, perhaps, never been done in this country before the Centennial Exposition."[111]

Barber believed that these were "interesting relics of the early days of this important American pottery. There was probably no intention to deceive in thus reproducing foreign work. There was a demand for such things, and the moldmaker took the best that was

Lithophane plaque featuring *Christ and the Adulteress*, American, 19th century, Phoenix Pottery, marked "Phoenix Pottery" on front top center, 7.875" x 6.25". *Courtesy of the Smithsonian Institution's National Museum of American History.*

at hand, and prepared the molds for the manufacturers in much less time than would have been required to model something entirely new."[112] Barber actually visited the mold room at Phoenix Pottery and noted that he saw the plaster casts of *Christ and the Adulteress, The Descent from the Cross, head of female, Romeo and Juliet, Storm at Sea, Forest Scene, The Nativity,* and the *Fireside Scene*. Many of these lithophanes are illustrated in his article.

Not only did Edwin A. Barber know workers from Phoenixville when he published his article in 1897 (the factory had closed only five years before), but there were interviews conducted by interested researchers in the 1940s and 1950s. These investigations were not fruitful.

Phoenix Pottery closed in 1892 due to a disastrous fire. There are few lithophanes in public collections that are marked with the "Phoenix Pottery" backstamp on the face of the lithophane panel. There are some in private collections that are unmarked, but have either a creamish or gray color that are slightly warped and are somewhat roughly finished that are believed to have been produced at Phoenix Pottery.[113] These include depictions of *Romeo and Juliet* and *Christ and the Adulteress*. In addition to the marked piece at the Smithsonian Institution's National Museum of American History, the Philadelphia Museum of Art owns Phoenix Pottery examples of *Marguerite and Faust* and Correggio's *The Nativity* (also known as *Holy Night*). Both are appropriately marked on the front, "Phoenix POttery," (with the uppercase "O") and both were donated in 1896-97 to the Museum by a trustee who donated objects that Edwin Atlee Barber purchased from factories at the time.

G.A.S., Philadelphia, Pennsylvania

There exists quite a mystery concerning the manufacturer of the rare lithophanes that are marked "G.A.S." or "GAS." and often accompanied by other marks. One antique dealer and author, Thomas U. Schock, believed that G.A.S. stood for the initials of Griffen and Smith who were one of the many, many owners of Phoenix Pottery in the late 19th century.[114] In the 1940s, Schock owned a lithophane copy of "Penn's Treaty with the Indians" with a "GAS." backstamp mounted as a candle shield and he believed it was created in Phoenixville, copied from the German original. He thought the poor quality of the materials confirmed that it was not made in Berlin.

There are few examples of the G.A.S.-marked *William Penn's Treaty with the Indians*. According to archival records and hearsay, the Blair Museum of Lithophanes used to own one of these. Unfortunately it now only has a few copies of this lithophane in plastic – Lithoplastics created by Dr. Beroud from the original. The Wyck, a National Historic Landmark house and garden in Germantown in Philadelphia owns a similar version of this lithophane mounted as a candle shield. Other details about the Wyck and their collections is presented in Chapter Ten. The Wyck owns a wrought iron Gothic-style candle shield measuring 16.75" x 10.5" with a rare lithophane, 8.25" wide and 6.6" tall, that depicts *William Penn's Treaty with the Indians* (Wyck acc. no. 78.24). This title is included at the bottom of the lithophane, so that it is visible when backlit. This panel is based on the John Boydell engraving of June 12, 1775, which in turn was based on the Benjamin West (1738-1820) painting of the same subject, signed and dated 1771. Apparently an original Boydell engraving of this scene once hung in the right wall of the main entrance vestibule at Wyck. The significance of this lithophane, is that it is one of just two known examples of *William Penn's Treaty with the Indians*, that are marked with the rare backstamp "GAS." and "35." According to *Blair Bulletin* No. 22 another one may be marked GAS 50. It is also a mirror image of the original painting. Another lithophane with the same subject, also with a "G.A.S." backstamp but no number, is located in the State Museum of Pennsylvania in Harrisburg.

The Blair Bulletins reflect the confusion around the issue of there being a G.A.S. –marked lithophane of *Penn's Treaty with the Indians* in the Blair collection. In *Blair Bulletin No. 64*, Mr. Blair offered to sell to his Collector's Club members, a G.A.S.-marked candle shield of *Penn's Treaty With the Indians*, 6.5" x 8.25" (lithophane alone) and cast bronze ornate frame, 8" x 10", with an overall height of 16" for $495.[115] A few months later, in the next *Blair Bulletin* (no. 65), he noted, "as far as I know, there is only one other lithophane of the *Penn's Treaty with the Indians* and that is in the Museum Collection."[116] There exist many plastic copies of the *William Penn's Treaty With the Indians* lithophane, which were created in the late 1970s from bronze molds as Lithoplastics[117], and distributed by Laurel Blair as Christmas gifts to his Lithophane Collectors Club members. For more on Lithoplastics, see Chapter Thirteen.

Detail of "GAS." backstamp from *William Penn's Treaty with the Indians*, Wyck acc. no. 78.24. *Courtesy of the Wyck.* Photo by Will Brown.

Detail of the "35" backstamp from *William Penn's Treaty with the Indians*. Wyck acc. no. 78.24. *Courtesy of the Wyck.* Photo by Will Brown.

Opposite page:
Lithophane installed as part of a candle shield, *William Penn's Treaty with the Indians*, German, 19th century, Meissen, marked "GAS." and "35", the Wyck acc. no. 78.24, lithophane 8.25" x 6.6", candle shield frame 16.75" x 10.5". *Courtesy of the Wyck.* Photo by Will Brown.

A globe lampshade marked on the exterior "G.A.S. Philad a/." and "Z 6 8 75" is located in the Blair Museum of Lithophanes. The large globe measures 11.5" high, has an opening at the top of 5.75" and the diameter at the center is 10.5". The ornamented brass base has two marble tables and it is quite elaborate. Mr. Blair purchased this rare lamp from the widow of a dealer in Philadelphia in 1979. After pursuing this trophy for five years, she finally relented.

A similar shade was offered for sale in 2007 in the United States. It was identified by the seller as of German origin, and is marked like the Blair Museum example, "G.A.S. Philad a/." and has identical images. The globe is 11" high with a diameter of 11" and has a 6.25" base. Although an old repair has been made to the shade with five staples, the asking price was $4,800.

Laurel Blair once wrote, "If it can be proven that these were made in Philadelphia, it will change the history of lithophanes considerably."[118] There is no proof of a manufacturer in Philadelphia that matches the "G.A.S." abbreviation, nor is there any proof that a United States manufacturer could produce such a beautiful, high quality lithophane globe. There is every indication by the quality and "Z" backstamp (these were published in Röntgen's book about Meissen) that the lithophanes may have come from Meissen in Germany. A similar globe was purchased in Philadelphia in the mid-1800s and has been *in situ* at Campbell House in St. Louis ever since (see Chapter Seven). It is marked "2626" and "Z 72" and "75." It appears to be Meissen, also, based on quality and the "Z" backstamp. Probably the lithophane manufacturer added the backstamps including the "Philad a/." to indicate the retailer in Philadelphia.

Lithophane globe featuring four scenes with women, German, 19th century, Meissen, marked "G.A.S. Philad a/." and "Z 6 8 75," Blair Museum acc. no. 1794, Height 11.5" Top opening diam. 5.75", overall diam. 10.5". *Courtesy of the Blair Museum of Lithophanes.*

Detail of "G.A.S." and "Z 6 8 75" backstamps on large lithophane globe, Blair Museum acc. no. 1794. *Courtesy of the Blair Museum of Lithophanes.*

Wales

South Wales Pottery, Llanelly

It was only in the past ninety years that it was discovered that Swansea, Nantgarw, *and* Llanelly made porcelain in Wales. Up until around 1921, it was believed that there were only two porcelain manufacturers in Wales and that Llanelly made a respectable earthenware pottery marked with its "South Wales Pottery" backstamp. When the discovery of the lithophane plaques manufactured at Llanelly was announced by an antique dealer, Mr. Kyrle Fletcher, it was also revealed that they had been previously owned by a man who had been foreman in the Llanelly Pottery. In fact, very little porcelain was manufactured in Llanelly, and the porcelain used in the lithophane production was of poor quality. Only fifteen attributed examples have been recorded, and of those, less than ten are known to have been marked with the "South Wales Pottery" backstamp in two lines.

Detail of South Wales Pottery backstamp, Welsh, 19th century, from Blair Museum acc. no. 548. *Courtesy of the Blair Museum of Lithophanes.*

South Wales Pottery was in operation between 1839 and 1922. The pottery was founded by William Chambers and at its peak the factory employed several hundred workers and manufactured two thousand dozen pieces a week.[119] Exports were recorded in 1840, "amounting to 115,712 tons."[120] They started producing parian ware about 1880. It has been said that the workmen from the factory in Llanelly left Wales to establish the factory at Belleek in Ireland.[121] This would have occurred during one of the management changes at Llanelly Pottery.

The recipe for the ceramic composition of lithophanes made at South Wales Pottery in Llanelly was provided in the 1931 book on Welsh porcelain by Isaac Williams. The recipe is as follows: 26 pounds of Bone, powdered and sifted; 14 pounds of Lynn Sand; 2 pounds of Potash. This recipe originally appeared in an 1847 publication by John Taylor, *The Practical Potter*. It noted that the ingredients should be mixed well together with water, then "mould them into lumps the size of a brick, and Fritt them in a hard part of the Biscuit Oven; then pound it and grind for use," with "40 lb of the above Fritt" and "10 lb of China Clay."[122] The lithophanes were allegedly manufactured at Llanelly from a dry powder Nantgraw body, prepared at Bristol.[123]

The best proof of lithophanes being produced at South Wales Pottery in Llanelly is the existence of the actual lithophanes with "South Wales Pottery" backstamps in the collection of the National Museum of Wales, the Blair Museum of Lithophanes, and in private collections. An 1854 publication, *The Cambrian Journal*, in an article titled "The Industrial Capacities of South Wales," noted, "The produce of this pottery is rapidly attaining celebrity. Beautiful dinner services of crockery, jugs, etc., and transparent tableaux of imitation Parian ware are beautifully executed at trifling cost."[124] This 1854 quote predates when they allegedly introduced Parian ware into production in Llanelly, in 1880. Dilys Jenkins explains, "It is interesting to note that the tableaux are described as 'imitation' Parian ware because true Parian is a hard paste porcelain closely akin to the Chinese and containing kaolin and Feldspar but no bone ash. The addition of bone ash as a flux to clay would cut the firing costs by lowering the temperature and the resultant economies would enable the factory to undercut its rivals in the field."[125] Jenkins states that the Llanelly lithophanes were true porcelain.

The South Wales Pottery, at the junction of Murray Street and Pottery Street.

Historic photograph of the South Wales Pottery Factory in Llanelly, c. 1920s.

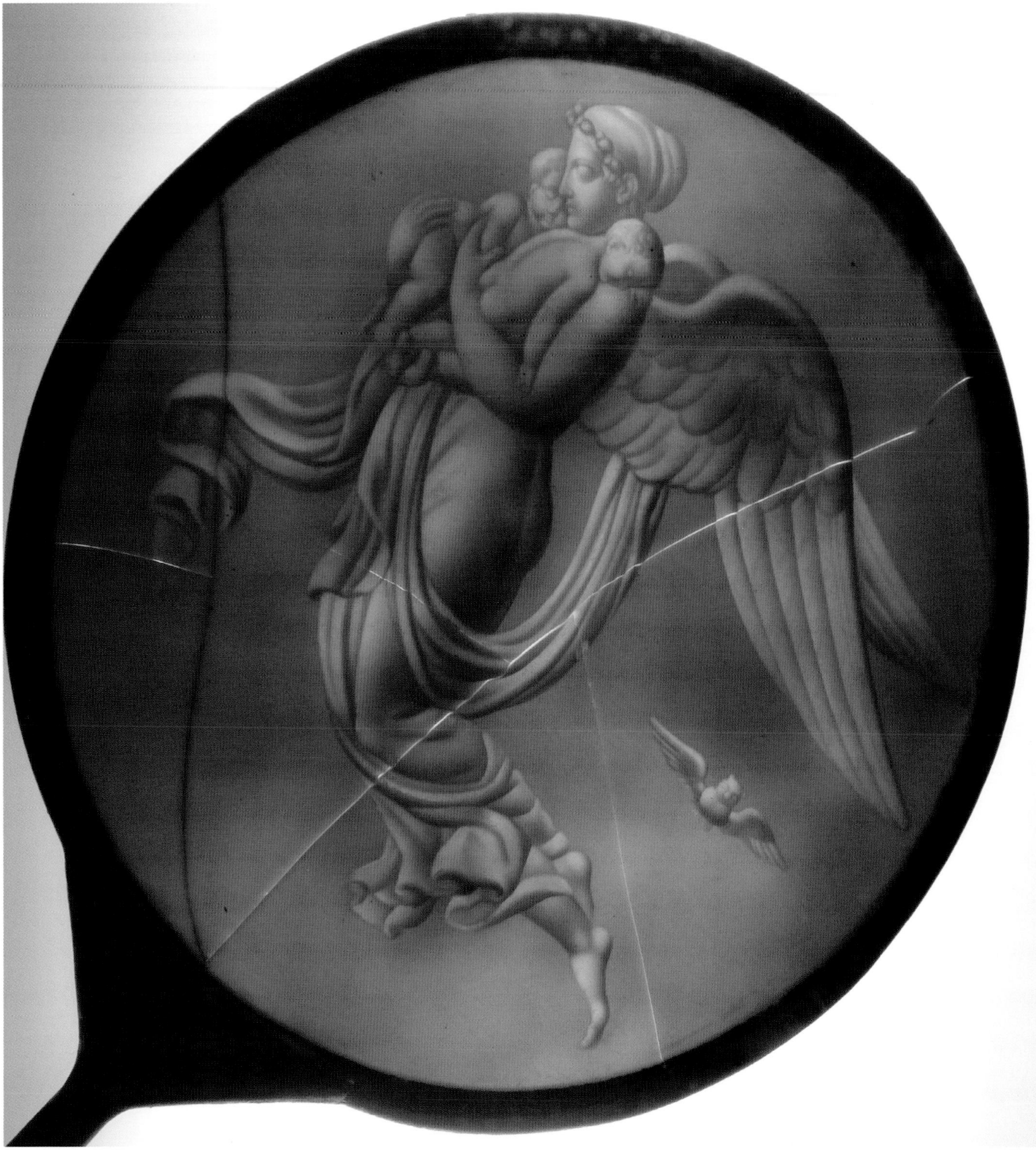

Hand screen with round lithophane, *Night* with a woman carrying a child, Welsh, 19th century, Llanelly, marked "South Wales Pottery," Parc Howard Museum and Art Gallery, Llanelly, acc. no. 1997.0921, Diam. 8.125", Length 16.625". *Courtesy of the Carmarthenshire Museums Service.*

The subject matter of the South Wales Pottery lithophanes includes a *Woman in Profile*, portrait of a woman in an evening dress and furs, and it bears the appropriate "South Wales Pottery" impressed backstamp in two lines; *Children at Play*, which depicts a boy seated on a bench and young girls preparing to play the game of blind man's bluff, also with the Llanelly "South Wales Pottery" impressed backstamp; *The Woodsman*, 5.125" x 4.25", based on a painting by Thomas Barker (National Museum of Wales, acc. no. 1328); *Bunch of Grapes*, "South Wales Pottery" impressed in two lines; and *Boy and Girl*, measuring 5.75" x 4.5", depicting a background of palm trees with a boy, girl and dog. In this lithophane the girl's head rests on the boy's shoulder, and is also marked with the appropriate backstamp. Other lithophanes include *Old Lady Reading*, measuring 5.125" x 3.575", not marked; a round hand screen of *Night* with a woman carrying a child, Parc Howard Museum and Art Gallery, acc. no. 1997.0921, marked; and a boy and dog, marked "South Wales Pottery," Parc Howard Museum and Art Gallery, acc. no. 1997.0914.

The lithophane *Girls and Window with Vine*, with two-line "South Wales Pottery" backstamp is located in the Blair Museum (acc. no. 548) and is illustrated in Chapter Five. This same subject was captured in lithophanes produced in Dresden at the Meissen factory, marked nos. 139 and 144, each referring to the same theme, but different sizes. The original painting was by Georg Friedrich Kersting (1785-1847), who was the manager of the porcelain painting department at Meissen from 1818 to 1845. The Meissen version would predate the Llanelly plaque. Museum records reveal that Mr. Blair paid $16.00 for the South Wales Pottery lithophane in 1963. A comparison of the South Wales Pottery lithophanes with those made in Germany in Berlin (KPM) and Dresden (Meissen) suggests that the Welsh factory copied German lithophanes, either from molds or casting directly from the imported lithophanes. *The Woodsman*, as it is commonly, and incorrectly known, was earlier produced as KPM 183 R (*Der verliebte Alte* or *The Old Man in Love*).

However there appear to be some Llanelly lithophane pictures that are unique to the company. The largest collection can be seen at the Parc Howard Museum and Art Gallery, Llanelly. Some of these lithophanes are marked, and others are not, but the porcelain body on the unmarked has lead to the attribution to South Wales Pottery. The Carmarthenshire County Museum has a rectangular South Wales Pottery lithophane depicting a parrot on a fruiting branch or vine with the appropriate backstamp (Carmarthenshire County Museum acc. no. 1975.0947). There is one final interesting observation about the lithophanes produced at South Wales Pottery in the 19th century – in the ones that appear to be copied from German originals, the picture is in relief, while in the two or three that are apparently unique to Llanelly (the vine with grapes and the pyramid of fruit with a ribbon), the design is in intaglio.

Innovation

Legend and KPM records have reported that around the time of the Crystal Palace Great Exhibition in London in 1851, some lithophanes had additional colored glazes applied to the relief or front surface of the white porcelain. These pieces were fired a second time, at a lower temperature, to render the colors permanent. The pieces with the color added to the relief have a soft attractive quality even when not backlit. However, later pieces (all are single cast lampshades) have the color added to the interior or back of the porcelain, and cannot be detected as tinted except when backlit. It has been stated that KPM was the first factory to exhibit a sampling of these colored lithophanes.[126]

In 1962, officials at the Staatliche Porzellan-Manufaktur Berlin (formerly KPM) sent Laurel Blair copies of index cards from the 1800s. One of these cards had information pertaining to the painted transparencies, "In der Eingabe der Manufaktur-Direktion an das Ministerium für Handel u. Gewerbe vom 16. Januar 1850 wird geschrieben: 'Es sind in neurer Zeit die bemalten Lichtschirmplatten bei dem Publikum sehr beliebt geworden und für das Meßlager in Leipzig so bedeutende Bestellungen eingegangen, dass die vorhandenen Kräfte nicht ausreichen, die sämtlichen Auftrage rechtzeitig zu vollenden.'"[127] There was an attached translation of the German, "In the presentation of the management of Manufacture to the governmental offices for commerce and profession on January 16th, 1850, it says: 'Recently painted transparencies have become very popular, and for the fair-stock in Leipzig so many orders have been made that the means available are not sufficient to carry out all the orders on time.'"

In another attachment from the Berlin factory on the same date in 1962, they quoted an excerpt from the official report from Berlin on the Industrial Exhibition of All Nations in London in 1851. It read, "Die bekannten und in ziemlicher Anzahl in das Ausland, besonders nach Nordamerika, ausgeführten Lithophanien waren in schönen Exemplaren ausgestellt. Eine zum ersten Male zur Anschauung gebrachte neue Methode der Dekoration der Lithophanien durch Anwendung der Malerei hat allgemein gefallen."[128] This has been translated as "The well-known lithophanes which have been exported in large numbers especially into North America were exhibited in fine samples. A newly-introduced method of decorating the lithophanes by the use of painting was universally liked."

Despite KPM generally being considered the first presenter of lithophanes with colored images in London at the Crystal Palace, there is factual evidence that Meissen, their strongest competitor, created colored lithophanes in 1834.[129] KPM had a superior porcelain body, and Meissen may have compensated by being first in creative innovations (which would have covered up their inferior, by comparison, porcelain body.) Early Meissen production is corroborated by existing 1840s *Preis-Courants* that list colored lithophanes.

Lithophane globe with three wilderness scenes, including hunters shooting at a bird in a tree, colored on the interior, part of a piano lamp, unmarked, 19th century, Blair Museum acc. no. 331, Height 11.25", Diam. 10.5", overall lamp height 59". *Courtesy of the Blair Museum of Lithophanes.*

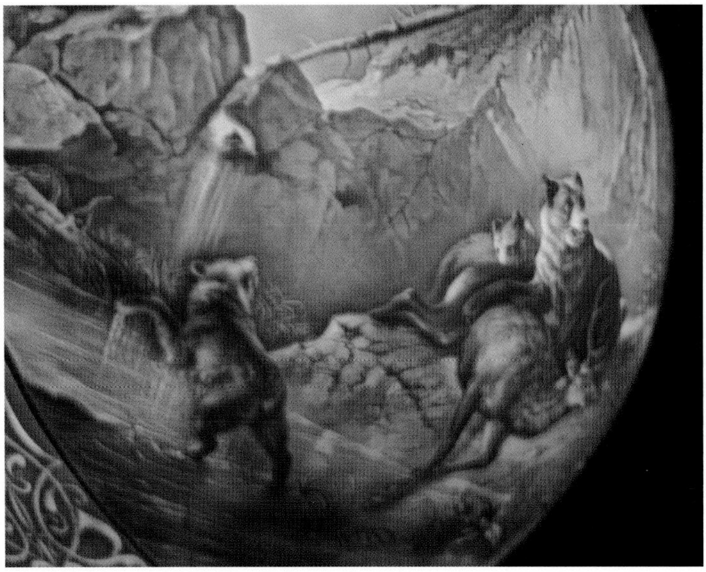

Detail of colored lithophane globe, Blair Museum acc. no. 331. *Courtesy of the Blair Museum of Lithophanes.*

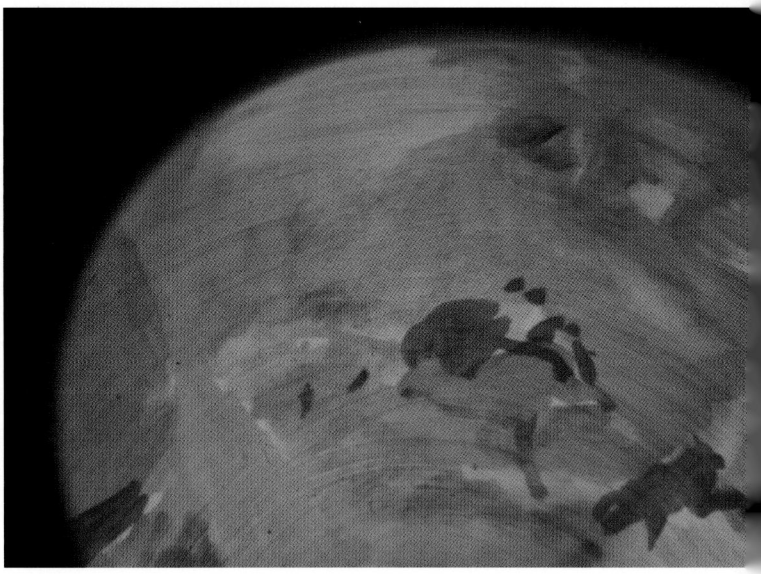

Detail of the interior of the colored lithophane globe, Blair Museum acc. no. 331. *Courtesy of the Blair Museum of Lithophanes.*

There are far fewer colored KPM and Meissen lithophanes compared to those marked PPM, Lithophanie Francaise, or P.R. (sickle). Lithophane sales at Meissen were already declining by the time colored lithophanes were widely introduced and by 1860 they were not advertising that any lithophanes were in production and available. Therefore the somewhat rare colored Meissen lithophane no. 202 (stamped) with a tiny stamped "35," depicting a *Bedouin Abducting a Girl*, is all the more dramatic for its use of blood-red details. Known examples of very rare colored Meissen lithophanes in collections worldwide include: no. 35 *Venus in Wolken* (*Venus in the Clouds*), no. 111 *Kosaken Ueberfall nach Peter Hefs* (*Cossack Raid*), no. 127 *Juden vor Babylon* (*The Jews Before Babylon*), no. 151 *Christ as a boy*, no. 154 *Odalisque*, and no. 187 *Scheherezade*.

Lithophane plaque featuring *Bedouin Abducting a Girl*, colored, German, 19th century, Meissen 202 (stamped) + 35 (tiny and stamped), Blair Museum acc. no. 972, 10.25" x 8.25". *Courtesy of the Blair Museum of Lithophanes.*

In addition to the rare colored lithophane plaques manufactured by Meissen and KPM and the more common examples marked PPM, Lithophanie Francaise, and P.R. (sickle), there are some single cast lampshades colored on the interior surface of the shade that bear the backstamp RPM.

The Blair Museum collection contains 108 colored lithophanes out of approximately 2,340 lithophanes – about 5% of the total collection. The relatively high number of colored lithophanes in the Blair Museum collection probably does not accurately portray the rarity of these items worldwide.

Lithophane plaque featuring a domestic interior, colored, German, 19th century, PPM 1071, acc. no. DA 1980.22.14, 6.875" x 5.75". *Courtesy of the Hampshire County Museums and Archives Services.*

Chapter Four
Asian Inspiration

Investigating the Asian inspirations for lithophanes must logically start with the Chinese discovery of true hard-paste porcelain as early as the Tang dynasty in China, c. 618-907 A.D. This was during a remarkable flourishing of Chinese civilization, when ceramic innovations were abundant, and China was indeed the center of the universe. Merchants and travelers were busy along the Silk Route which encouraged the exchange of goods and services from the Tang capitol in Changan (present day Xian) and all points West. This Chinese quest for a white ware with a kaolinic clay body was not new, but had been one line of investigation since the earliest Chinese ceramics were created during Neolithic times in the Dawenkou Culture (ca. 4500-2500 B.C.) and the subsequent Shang dynasty (1523-1028 B.C.). These kaolinic pieces, including animal-form tripods and jars mimicking bronzes, were created with a kaolinic clay body that was discovered near Anyang, an early capitol city and Great Bronze Age activity center.

It was a thousand years later when the Europeans at the Meissen Porcelain factory created their first hard-paste porcelain. This discovery is specifically credited to the years 1709-1710 when alchemist Johann Friedrich Böttger worked at this illustrious company in Dresden. The search for porcelain in Germany, France, Holland, England, Spain and Italy and the Middle East, had led first to the creation of the tin-glazed earthenwares which mimicked Chinese porcelain in whiteness and surface treatment, known as faience in France, maijolica in Italy, and Delftware in Holland. These wares were immensely successful. Some of these types of tin-glazed earthenwares or soft-paste porcelains (first made in Italy at the end of the 16th century) were continued on even after hard-paste porcelain became commonplace in the 18th century.

China created the first true porcelain during the Tang dynasty and subsequently during the Song (960-1279 A.D.) and Ming (1368-1644) dynasties, mastered the art of manufacturing marvelous translucent porcelain bodies, glazed and unglazed, with mold-made, carved and incised designs that were revealed when held against the light. Although no discoveries of exact Chinese precursor lithophanes have been discovered to date, the relationship between Chinese ceramics, jade, glass, and European lithophanes from the 19th century is undeniable.

One obvious lithophane-Europe-and-Asia connection is evident in the Chinoiserie ceramics of the time. By the mid-1700s all of Europe was enamored of Oriental objects largely seen through imports. Gardens, buildings, furniture, silver, porcelains and such were all embellished with pagodas, Chinoiserie fantasies and the like. European factories such as Meissen in Dresden and the Delftware produced in Holland reflect this obsession – largely expressed through mimicking Chinese blue and white porcelains. There are even several porcelain rooms located within Europe's borders with an Oriental flavor, including the one created in Naples around 1757 – made of Capodimonte soft-paste porcelain. This room may be the ultimate masterpiece of the Chinoiserie genre, with Oriental figures in an Asian setting. Another magnificent 18th century porcelain room can be seen in the Österreichisches Museum für angewandte Kunst, Vienna. Smaller Chinoiserie masterpieces can be seen in the form of 19th century nightlights, one in the form of a Chinese pagoda, now on view at the Blair Museum of Lithophanes. This single cast nightlight, made in Germany, has hunting as the central theme, with popular 19th century scenes of hunters, deer, and a wolf. A more dramatic nightlight is in the Graham and Helen Pullen collection – resplendent with its pagoda shape *and* Chinese figures within the backlit scenes.

Single cast cylindrical lithophane nightlight in the form of a Chinese pagoda, with hunting scenes, German, marked with "#" in underglaze cobalt (Plaue) and "Germany" and nos. 53 and 29 on the base, after 1891, Blair Museum acc. no. 297, H: 9" Diam: 5.5". *Courtesy of the Blair Museum of Lithophanes.*

Two-piece lithophane night light decorated in gilt and blue, with Oriental scenes, 19th century, no marks, H: 7.75" Diam: 5.5". *Courtesy of Graham and Helen Pullen.* Photo by Graham Pullen.

Many Shades of Green on Spring Hills (from a set of *Four Seasons*), Chinese, Qing Dynasty (1644-1911). Dali marble, 20.5" x 27". *Courtesy the Nelson-Atkins Museum of Art, Kansas City, Missouri.* Purchase: Nelson Trust, 59-76/4. Photograph by Jamison Miller.

One rather innovative idea relating to the origins of the word "lithophane" and its Asian precursors, came from a museum curator in the mid-1950s. He questioned the Greek derivation of "litho" or "stone" for lithophanes made from porcelain (not stone) that suggested that this name may have originally been derived from Chinese marble panels. He had traveled widely in China (prior to 1954) and had seen the "Figured Marbles" of Yunnan Province, that have "the most beautiful designs in black lines, traced by nature, on white backgrounds. These, when sawn very thin, make beautiful transparencies."[1] He concluded, "Perhaps, originally, in Europe, that was the source of the English designation of these fascinating 'objet d'art.'" Examples of these Yunnan marbles may be seen today in the permanent collections of the Victoria & Albert Museum in London and the Nelson-Atkins Museum of Art in Kansas City, Missouri.

There are similar ideas relating to European origins for the concept of lithophanes. In 1968 a European researcher hired by Mr. Blair, interviewed a Herr Schütz from the Staatliche Porzellanmanufaktur Berlin (KPM). This porcelain expert was of the opinion that the idea of lithophanes dated back to 18th century ornamental carvings in alabaster. The connection links the derivation of the term "lithophane" (to appear in stone) to a type of stone, "since the word 'lithos' would be inexplicable in connection with porcelain." Translucent works in alabaster were known from the French court of Louis XIV, Italy and even ancient Egypt and Rome. Herr Schütz believed that lithophanes were never truly "invented" in the full sense of the word, but rather a concept that had been known long before was applied to porcelain, and what had been pure ornament became real pictures.

Just as the Europeans were not the first to create porcelain, it is equally unlikely that they were the first to come up with the concept of a three-dimensional design made of a porcelain body that becomes visible only when light is transmitted through the piece. There are numerous Chinese inspirations or precursors that would have been known in Europe and mimicked from the standpoint of aesthetics and technical details. The 1700s and 1800s are rich in translucent ceramic and jade objects in the form of table screens, bowls, and lamps. Even in the earlier Song dynasty (960-1279) ceramics, especially the finely potted Qingbai wares, flaunted the translucency of these pale blue glazed wares with incised, carved and molded designs of flowers, fish and birds. Early writers described the "ideal wares of a classic period" as "thin as paper."[2] Chinese ceramics scholar R.L. Hobson thought this might be a bit of an exaggeration, but he did acknowledge that "many of the white Ting wares are thin enough to be translucent."[3] One Yongle (1403-1424) Ming dynasty bowl described as being "thin as paper" was illustrated in Hobson's tome, volume II, titled *Chinese Pottery and Porcelain*, published originally in 1915. He described the *an hua* or "secret decorated" bowl which is now in the collection of the British Museum, as being "so thin and transparent that it seems to consist of glaze alone, as though the body had been pared away to vanishing point before the glaze was applied – in short, it is *t'o t'ai* or 'bodiless.'"[4] His description continues, "when held to the light it has a greenish transparency and the colour of melting snow, and there is revealed on the sides a delicate but exquisitely drawn figure of five-clawed Imperial dragons in white slip, showing up like the water-mark in paper."[5]

Suffice it to say, that museum collections hold stunning examples of porcelains with this *an hua* or "secret decoration" that one can witness in person, but not a single high resolution photograph can capture it, hence the "secret" designation for the designs. Thus the often-mentioned but never successfully photographed secret decoration of the Ming and Qing dynasties bears a striking similarity to the concept of lithophanes in that the subtle designs are visible only with carefully manipulated light sources. Although the descriptions vary, frequently these pieces are described as white enamel on white porcelain biscuit with finely incised decorations, a concept that was perfected during the Ming and Qing dynasties.

A fine Ming dynasty piece, attributed to the Yongle era (1403-1424), is a bowl with such a hidden decoration located in the Asia Society collection, which comes from the Mr. and Mrs. John D. Rockefeller III collection. The bowl is 4" high and has a diameter of 8.25". The *an hua* design is of two dragons among three clouds. Although unmarked, it is similar to other rare eggshell porcelain bowls of this type that have the Yongle reign mark in archaic characters incorporated in their designs. It must be viewed in person to see the secret decoration.

Lithophane investigators in the past have occasionally mentioned the connection between Chinese ceramics and the lithophanes of the 19th century. Robert Elder, who in 1953 was serving as assistant curator of ethnology at what was then known as the U.S. National Museum in Washington, D.C., wrote, "the rather rare Chinese porcelains with floral patterns cut entirely through the unfired (greenware) body so the designs were only covered with two layers of clear glaze were known in Europe."[6] He notes that these were "usually in globe form for suspension with a candle light like a lantern," and he suggested that these might have been the inspiration for the European inventors of lithophanes.[7]

Yet a vague and sketchy connection was noted much earlier by Mrs. Willoughby Hodgson in her tome *How to Identify Old Chinese Porcelain*, published in London in 1905. She wrote, "The white 'biscuit' porcelain, which is rare and valuable, is generally carved and pierced with fretwork. It is exceedingly thin, and has the appearance of having been pared down by the lathe. Some pieces are decorated entirely in open fretwork, and in other glazed pieces the fretwork is divided by raised medallions ornamented with figures in biscuit in high relief and with sprays of flowers."[8] She continued, "Sometimes this white biscuit porcelain was decorated by a simple design of lines incised in the paste. Boxes were made of it for the vermillion used by the Chinese in writing, and small biscuit porcelain receptacles which were designed to carry about fighting crickets, also pencil-holders, and little screens with landscapes in relief; these latter somewhat resembling those white glass or porcelain pictures which can be bought in Switzerland, and which we sometimes see hanging in windows, or used as lampshades and candle screens, the landscape showing up when the light shines through them."[9]

Not coincidentally, in her next paragraph, Mrs. Hodgson write about the satiny glazes of the white porcelain Blanc de Chine made in China, and how these pieces were exactly copied in factories in Dresden. She further mentions the history of porcelain in China dating back to the Tang dynasty and during the subsequent Song dynasty, the "Ting porcelain was thin as eggshell, and was generally engraved with designs incised in the body under the glaze, which could hardly be seen till held up to the light."[10] She specifically mentions two Ming dynasty Yongle white porcelain bowls with their interiors decorated with "two five-clawed dragons, very faintly engraved in the paste and glazed over."[11] This brings one full circle back to the concept of *an hua* or secret decoration on porcelain, as she was likely describing the same British Museum bowl as Hobson. Pure white porcelain was particularly prized during the early Ming periods, especially during the reign of Yongle. Some of these highly prized white wares were decorated only with molded, carved, engraved or designs painted in white slip under the glaze. These, too, had designs that could only be viewed when held against the light or obliquely to it. The bodiless white wares of the Yongle period are often referred to as being comprised of white eggshell porcelain.

Mrs. Hodgson was likely correct in her comparisons of Chinese porcelain and European lithophanes. The Chinese Blanc de Chine wares do have perhaps the closest connection to lithophanes and may be considered the true inspiration. There is some debate as to the precise beginnings of Dehua porcelain in China. The term Blanc de Chine is an 18th century French term used to designate a highly translucent Chinese porcelain made in Dehua in Fujian Province from the latter part of the Ming dynasty to the present day. However, porcelains were being made in Dehua as early as the

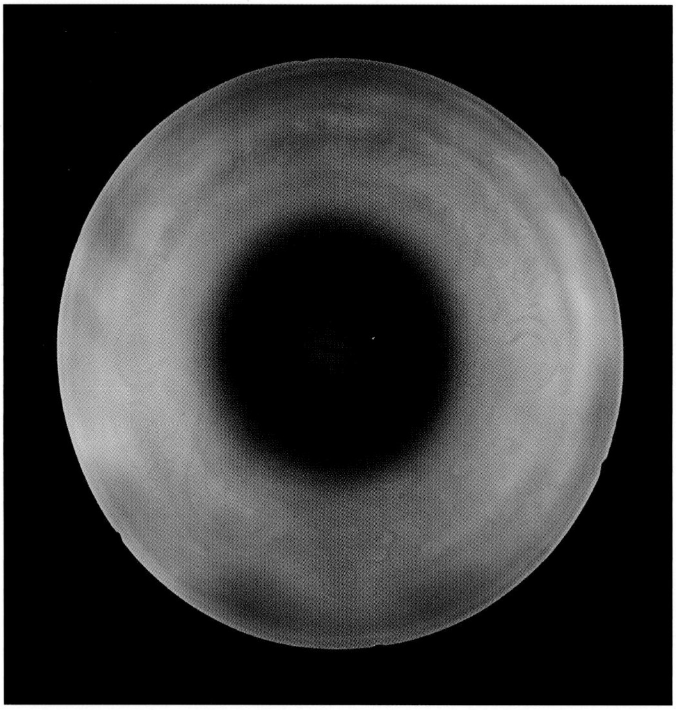

Chinese porcelain bowl, Ming dynasty, mark of Yongle period (1403-1424) with *an hua* decoration of five-clawed Imperial dragons, diam. 8.75". © *Copyright the Trustees of The British Museum.*

Song dynasty (960-1279). The color of these wares varies from a chalk-white to ivory in tone and the glaze is thick, rich and unctuous. Many are small Guanyin figures and cups, bottles, and dishes. These were heavily imported to Europe in the late 17th and 18th centuries. Meissen loved "things Chinese" – always subject to their own interpretation. Not only is there proof that the Chinese Blanc de Chine wares were known in Dresden, but it involves no stretch of the imagination to see how the Oriental cups and bowls would have inspired the Europeans. Meissen made Dehua-type cups and teapots with a Chinese Blanc de Chine flair. Additionally influenced by the Chinese, were the English with their "A" marked ware, and the Chelsea factory, too, as well as the French at their Chantilly factory. The Blanc de Chine ware with its lustrous velvet-soft glaze with white to light-yellowish tone was imitated in the European porcelain factories with great success. The factory at St. Cloud in France produced fine Blanc de Chine wares ornamented with sprays of prunus and also some charming statuettes of "Chinamen" during the 1730s. Lithophanes, of course, were created at some of these same European factories in the early 19th century.

Most of the Chinese Blanc de Chine cups that would have been seen in Europe date between 1650 and 1800, the largest being approximately 5" tall. There additionally were lamps with stands dating between 1650 and 1700. There was a well-known Blanc de Chine incense burner that was exported from China to Europe and could be seen in many collections around 1725. Meissen made reticulated wares, too, similar to some of the Chinese Blanc de Chine examples.

Among the most impressive of all the Blanc de Chine wares are several small cups in the permanent collection of the Asian Civilisations Museum in Singapore. One octagonal ornamental cup has the incised theme of the *Eight Horses of Mu Wang*, and dates to the 17th century. It is a mere 2.36 inches in height. Unlit, it is ostensibly nothing more than a nice white cup with an octagonal form. When backlit, like a lithophane, the *an hua* or secret decoration of the scene of eight horses is magically revealed. The cup was mold-made of porcelain, like a lithophane. Among the most impressive of all the Blanc de Chine wares are several small cups in the permanent collection of the Asian Civilisations Museum in Singapore. One octagonal ornamental cup has the incised theme of the Eight Horses of Mu Wang, and dates to the 17th century. It is a mere 2.36 inches in height. Unlit, it is ostensibly nothing more than a nice white cup with an octagonal form. When backlit, like a lithophane, the an hua or secret decoration of the scene of eight horses is magically revealed. The cup was mold-made of porcelain, like a lithophane.

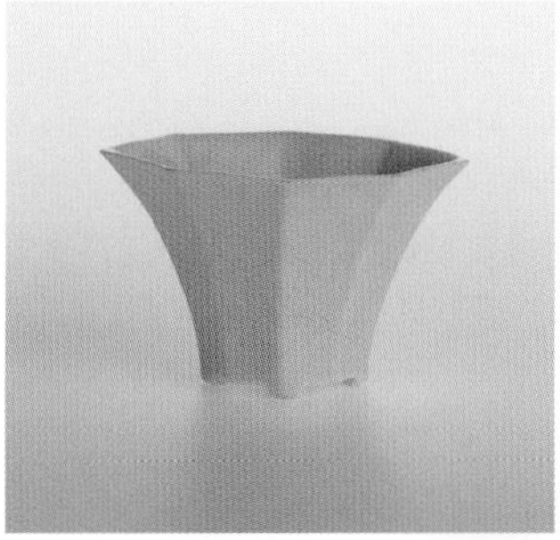

Chinese Blanc de Chine octagonal ornamental cup, molded, with incised *an hua* theme of the *Eight Horses of Mu Wang*, 17th century, H: 2.36". © *Asian Civilisations Museum, Singapore, acc. no. 2000.3382.* Gift of Frank and Pamela Hickley.

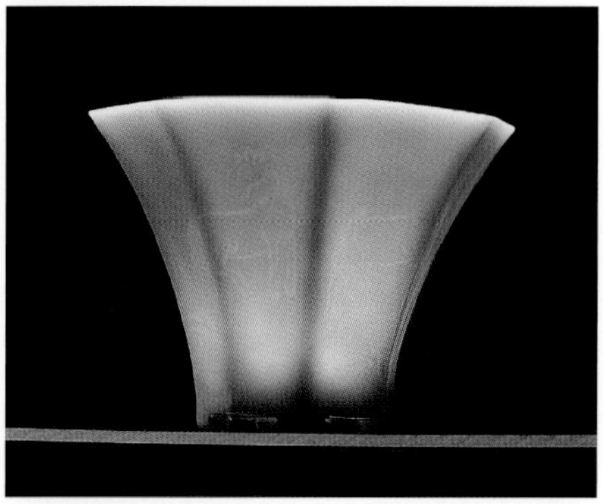

Chinese Blanc de Chine octagonal ornamental cup, molded, with incised *an hua* theme of the *Eight Horses of Mu Wang*, 17th century, back lit, H: 2.36". © *Asian Civilisations Museum, Singapore, acc. no. 2000.3382.* Gift of Frank and Pamela Hickley.

Similar, yet even smaller are a pair of Chinese Blanc de Chine cups with molded dragon designs, also in this Singapore museum. The secret decoration of two four-clawed dragons chasing a flaming pearl, molded in low relief, is revealed when the cups are back lit. With a height of only 1.96 inches even the facial features of the dragons can then be seen. These cups date to the 18th century, thereby pre-dating the invention of lithophanes in Europe in 1827.

Chinese Blanc de Chine pair of cups with molded dragons, 18th century, H: 1.96". © *Asian Civilisations Museum, Singapore, acc. no. 2000.3398.1-2.* Gift of Frank and Pamela Hickley.

One of a pair of Chinese Blanc de Chine cups with molded dragons, 18th century, back lit, H: 1.96". © *Asian Civilisations Museum, Singapore, acc. no. 2000.3398.1-2.* Gift of Frank and Pamela Hickley.

A fine example of an English manufacturer being influenced by translucent Chinese wares, can be seen in a small bowl manufactured by Worcester Porcelain, c. 1760-1770. With a diameter of only 3.86 inches, similar in size to Chinese Blanc de Chine wares, this finely modeled, soft-paste porcelain bowl has a molded floral pattern. When held up to the light, the effect is quite beautiful.

English Worcester porcelain bowl, soft-paste porcelain, with molded floral pattern, c. 1760-1770, Diam: 3.86". *Courtesy Hampshire County Council Museums and Archives Service.* Photo by Neil Hyman.

English Worcester porcelain bowl, soft-paste porcelain, with molded floral pattern, c. 1760-1770, Diam: 3.86", back lit. *Courtesy Hampshire County Council Museums and Archives Service.* Photo by Neil Hyman.

A few rare Qing dynasty porcelain bowls, produced in China before the invention of lithophanes in Europe, are worthy of examination. One example, located in the Seattle Art Museum, is a small finely potted Jingdezhen ware bowl with a reign mark of the Emperor Qianlong (1736-1795) decorated with designs of dragon motifs. The reticulated motifs are filled with nothing more than transparent glaze. Another exquisite example is a Qianlong period bowl located in the Flint Institute of Art, which when back lit, reveals a detailed dragon motif through its paper-thin bodiless form.

There are several other Chinese inventions that merit discussion in relationship to the origins of or inspiration for lithophanes. A later Qing dynasty invention, the so-called "rice pattern" porcelain, is frequently compared to lithophanes due to the light transmitted through the "grains of rice" pattern. Many of these were created in the region of Jingdezhen and are still being made today in China and Taiwan. The crudely formed dried porcelain piece (bowl, dish, teapot, etc.) has the clay carefully scraped away with a special knife to form the curvature of the vessel. The kernel-shaped holes are cut in by a skilled workman. Contrary to popular belief, the rice pattern was not made by pressing kernels of rice into the damp clay. Up to thirty applications of clear glaze were applied, until all the holes were filled. There is clearly no viable connection to lithophanes.

Table screen, Chinese, 18th century, Feicui jade, enamel and gilt, 13.125" (in stand) x 6.5". Handsomely carved translucent jade exhibits four Immortals and an attendant. © *Christie's Images Limited [2007].*

Chinese bowl, Qing dynasty, reign mark of Emperor Qianlong, 1736-1795, Jingdezhen ware, porcelain with reticulated decoration filled in with transparent glaze, H: 2" Diam: 5.25". *Courtesy Seattle Art Museum, Eugene Fuller Memorial Collection, acc. no.* 35.252.2. Photo by Paul Macapia.

Chinese bowl, porcelain, Qing dynasty, Qianlong period (1736-1795), with dragon in the clouds motif, H: 1.375" Diam: 6.5". *Courtesy of the Flint Institute of Arts, Flint, Michigan.* Gift of Mrs. Thelma C. Foy, acc. no. B1956.17.

Due to the plaque format, comparisons have occasionally been made between lithophanes and the porcelain, slate, and jade table screens collected by Chinese scholars in the 17th century and used on their desks. Additionally, the mounting of the screens is in simple or elaborate carved wooden stands similar to those used to mount many lithophane plaques. In the Song dynasty, the Chinese scholar's desk contained the "four precious things," – ink, ink stone, brush and paper. By the 17th century, this list was expanded to include jars and rests for brushes, a variety of water pots and dishes, incense burners, seals, vases – and desk screens. Table or desk screens were made of a variety of materials including porcelain, jade, glass, ink stone, slate and other materials. There are several jade table or desk screens which exhibit a translucency akin to lithophanes and this translucency reveals finely carved images visible from only one side. A pair of Qianlong nephrite jade screens illustrated in *The Splendor of Jade*, are so unusually carved that when illuminated from behind, the carving from the opposite side is not visible. An exquisite 18th century Feicui jade Chinese table screen exhibiting immortals and an attendant, owned by Christie's in New York in 1984, exemplifies the close visual connection between jade screens and lithophanes, with the jade itself reminding one of the similar magical translucency of lithophanes.

Even some of the non-translucent porcelain table screens decorated with fine applied relief designs, show visual connections that are impossible to deny even though the Chinese piece might be carved in relief or has applied relief designs and the other mold-made. One Qing dynasty white glazed porcelain table screen, formerly in the Eumorfopolous Collection and now at the Victoria & Albert Museum, bears a remarkable resemblance to a lithophane, minus the requisite translucency. Another similar table screen, dating from the 1st half of the 18th century, with a clear yellow enamel glaze over an applied relief design of a rooster in a naturalistic scene, is located in the Percival David Foundation in London (PDF 539).

Carved ivory is another popular material that is sometimes compared to lithophanes. In addition to carved ivory, which generally lacks the translucency of porcelain, Chinese lanterns appear to bear some relationship to the invention of lithophane lanterns in Europe and Chinese precedents. Lanterns were so important in China that an annual festival was held in their honor. The Lantern Festival is still celebrated today from the 13th to 17th of the first moon. There were the finest lanterns made of glass or jade and there are also beautiful porcelain lanterns which bear some resemblance to lithophane hanging lanterns.

Finally, when exploring the Asian influences and inspirations for lithophanes, there remain the mystery pieces. These reveal the most magical attributes of porcelain, but little is known about these rare individual pieces. These would include a small teacup with handle in the collection of the Blair Museum. The cup is eggshell thin, obviously mold-made, with a Chinoisserie flair. It is not a lithophane, but it has all the qualities – translucency, molded three-dimensional designs revealed when backlit, and the shiny white precious appearance of porcelain. The origins of this unmarked cup, are presently unknown.

Another possible lithophane precursor can be seen in the form of a stem cup of Chinese origin, possibly dating to the Ming dynasty, with a satiny, rich, unctuous white glaze which appears to be only a handsome white stem cup when seen in reflected light. However, when back lit, an *an hua* or secret decoration is revealed of a five-clawed Imperial dragon seen in underglaze (and innerbody) cobalt and flames in underglaze (and innerbody) copper and the characters "*nei fu*" meaning "Imperial household." Porcelains with this mark fall within the scope of "official porcelain" but the majority of these were sold commercially unlike "Imperial wares."

China clearly provided all the technical and aesthetic inspiration for lithophanes. The most direct connection between Chinese ceramics and lithophanes are the Blanc de Chine wares of China that were copied in France, Germany and England by some of the same porcelain manufacturers who soon after "invented" lithophanes. Those who study "things Chinese," like to joke that there are Chinese origins for everything – porcelain, the fast-moving potters wheel, fireworks, the invention of paper, and old adages ("Confucius says ... "). Now, all that is needed is to find that missing lithophane link – an actual Chinese lithophane plaque made in China prior to the 1820s.

Table screen, Chinese, Qing dynasty, Kangxi period (1662-1722), porcelain, glazed, with relief ornamentation of ducks, lotus, and water on one side, roosters and bamboo on the other, Eumorfopoulos Collection acc. no. c.946.1935, 15.5" x 10" x 6.25". *Courtesy the Victoria & Albert Museum, London.*

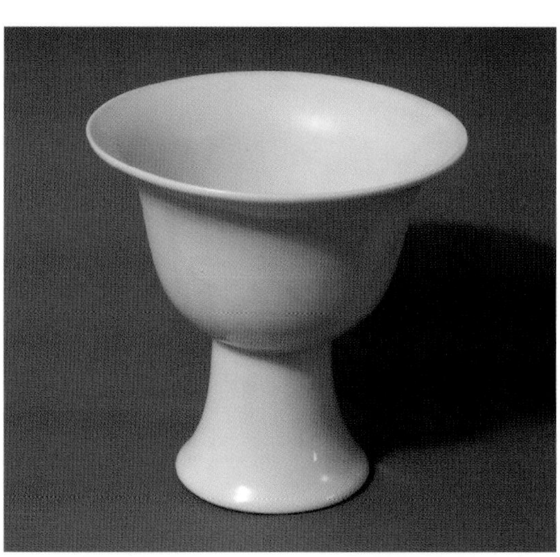

Chinese stem cup, porcelain, with underglaze (and innerbody) cobalt and copper designs of a five-clawed Imperial dragon, flames, and *neifu* characters, possibly Ming dynasty (1368-1644), H: 4" Diam (rim): 4.25" Diam (foot): 2.25". *Courtesy of Margaret Carney and William J. Walker, Jr.*

Chinese stem cup, porcelain, with underglaze (and innerbody) cobalt and copper designs of a five-clawed Imperial dragon, flames, and *neifu* characters, possibly Ming dynasty (1368-1644), H: 4" Diam (rim): 4.25" Diam (foot): 2.25", backlit. *Courtesy of Margaret Carney and William J. Walker, Jr.*

Chinese stem cup, porcelain, with underglaze (and innerbody) cobalt and copper designs of a five-clawed Imperial dragon, flames, and *neifu* characters, possibly Ming dynasty (1368-1644), H: 4" Diam (rim): 4.25" Diam (foot): 2.25", backlit. *Courtesy of Margaret Carney and William J. Walker, Jr.*

Chapter Five
Inspiration for Lithophane Images

While the inspiration for the creation of three-dimensional backlit pictures made of porcelain no doubt came from China, the inspiration for the subject matter of the more than 2,000 different three-dimensional porcelain pictures was derived from engravings, masterpiece and genre paintings, stories from the Bible, scenes from Europe and America, and portraits of characters in history, popular literature, poetry and drama.

Additionally there was another precursor to, or inspiration for, porcelain lithophanes, and that is the "romantic transparencies" of the eighteenth century.[1] These earlier transparencies were not manufactured in porcelain, but were rather paintings created on glass or translucent paper that were meant to be viewed when illuminated by candle flame or oil lamp from behind the image. These transparencies were created by masters such as Gainsborough, Turner, and Friedrich. Subject matter included the eruption of Mount Vesuvius, romantic landscapes, and historical events. These transparencies were so popular that the technique was used not just by artists, but also were produced as prints available, then, to a wider audience.[2] There was even a "how-to" book published in 1799, titled *Instructions for Painting Transparencies*, by Rudolph Ackerman, a famous bookseller and publisher.

There exists a fascinating treatise by Edward Orme, written in 1807, which describes transparencies – prints given translucent highlights by applying a varnish of mastic, canada balsam and spirits of turpentine. These could be glazed and hung against a window or night-light. His work, titled *An Essay on Transparent Prints and on Transparencies in General*, "printed for and sold by the Author" in London, is a work of art itself, including five engraved plates (one double-page), four engravings in the text, thirteen hand-colored aquatints (seven using varnish to make the paper transparent) on ten plates, and one leaf with six specimens of colored varnished paper. The text and plates are watermarked 1804. A copy was offered in 2006 through an antique book seller for $12,500. Orme hired engravers "such as Charles Turner [1773-1857] to engrave mezzotints that were then colored, oiled, and varnished for use as transparent screens, shades, fans, and *faux* stained-glass window ornaments."[3]

A related art from the 19th century is "linophanies" – translucent pictures that were formed by pouring paper pulp into a metal mold, the bottom of which was engraved with the desired design or picture.[4] Subsequent steps include the addition of blotting material and the subjection of the whole to the pressure from an ordinary press. The partially dried pulp still in the mold is then dried either in the open air or artificially by stove or kiln. The resulting linophanies were used in lamp or gas shades, for transparent pictures in windows, etc. The mold was usually engraved, but the picture could also be formed by pressure from a hardened relief-plate.[5]

Every now and then someone would send Mr. Blair a paper "lithophane" specimen for Mr. Blair to examine and, hopefully, purchase. In 1966, a gentleman from Cleveland sent Mr. Blair a photo of a piece backlit, some correspondence and finally a paper lithophane specimen. The subject of the lithophane was *Madonna of the Chair*, 18 inches square, created from a sheet of Italian Fabrino all-rag paper by the Hammermill Paper Company in Erie, Pennsylvania. Apparently it was one of a dozen made in approximately 1921. Its whereabouts are presently unknown. Another Blair Museum member wrote to Mr. Blair in 1983 about these paper lithophanes made in Italy by Fabriani, a company that produced artists' paper. She also referred to them as "filigrammi." Mr. Blair considered these similar to watermarks.

As recently as August 2007, a rare French paper lithophane, c. 1880, was offered for sale on the Internet. The image of two oxen with a worker in a field, in color, measured 5.5" x 4.125" and was offered by a French antiques dealer in Versailles.

In several of the Blair Museum Bulletins, Mr. Blair also made mention of hold-to-light postcards from the late 1800s and early 1900s. Some contained cut-outs on the top layer of the postcard that revealed another colored layer underneath that would be illuminated under light. Another variety of the transparency postcard had a separate image or plain colored tissue between the front and back layers that was revealed when illuminated.

There was clearly great interest in transparent and translucent pictures in the 18th and 19th centuries. This has resulted in a great interest on the part of museums and libraries desiring restoration of these specialty papers – tracing and pigment-coated papers, which unfortunately are vulnerable to various forms of degradation which one does not find with porcelain lithophanes.

Translucent, not transparent, porcelains have a different story. Porcelain does not degrade. Breakage is the only preservation issue. Lithophanes were modeled in wax by skilled craftsmen. They took days or even weeks to complete their task and they were well-paid. They did not sign their work as it was not an original creation of the wax carver, but rather a copy or reproduction of the work of another painter, engraver, or illustrator. Information about some of the 19th century wax carvers has been obtained from factory records, but, in general, these are not names familiar to the public. In contrast, the general public was quite familiar with the subjects of masterpiece paintings and the artists who painted them; characters from popular literature, drama and poetry; stories from the Bible; famous figures in history; royalty and rulers from home and abroad; and the engravings that appeared in popular journals of the mid-19th century. Additionally consumers were attracted to genre scenes of idealized family life, hunting scenes, battle scenes, and places to which they had traveled or wished to someday visit.

Some lithophanes were created through the use of patterns. Several grisaille on paper patterns for lithophanes have been discovered in the archives at KPM, and these are discussed in Chapter Three.

Regardless of their origin, every lithophane tells a story. It is not always left to the collector's own devices to determine which popular artists inspired some of the lithophanes from the 19th century. The *Preis-Courants* from the major German manufacturers (KPM, Meissen, and PPM) occasionally list after the title of the lithophane, "nach Göthe," "nach Rembrandt," "nach Battoni," "nach Peter Hess," meaning "after the painting by Battoni," etc.

Old Master Paintings

Examples of well known painters whose works were converted from oil on canvas to molded porcelain, with probably an engraving or two in between, include Peter Paul Rubens, Leonardo da Vinci, Correggio, Raphael, Pompeo Battoni, François Boucher, and Charles de Steuben. Rubens' (1577-1640) work that translated well from oil to porcelain includes *Descent from the Cross*. Leonardo da Vinci's *The Last Supper* later became KPM 321 N. Correggio (1489-1534) painted *Holy Night*, also referred to as *The Nativity*, which is now at the Gemäldegalerie in Dresden, and which was later copied in Berlin to became the lithophane KPM 256 N (Blair Museum acc. no. 479, 13" x 7"), Meissen 101, and the French version AdT 425 (Blair Museum acc. no. 2611, 9.5" x 7.25" in an elaborate Egyptian-style frame). The French AdT version of *The Nativity*, after Correggio, is illustrated in Chapter Six.

Lithophane, *Das Abendmahl, nach Leonardo da Vinci*, (*The Last Supper, after Leonardo da Vinci*), with stained glass frame, German, 19th century, KPM 321 N, Blair Museum acc. no. 478, lithophane 5.75" x 11.125"; stained glass 8.25" x 13.625". *Courtesy of the Blair Museum of Lithophanes.*

Raphael's (1483-1520) painting of the Madonna was later reproduced in Germany as PPM 271 (Blair Museum acc. no. 446, *La Sainte Vierge*, 8.625" x 6.625," illustrated in Chapter Two). Also translated from painting to porcelain were Raphael's *Sistine Madonna* (illustrated in Chapter Six) and *Madonna della Sedia/ Madonna of the Chair* (also illustrated in Chapter Six). Pompeo Battoni (1708-1787) is known for his *Maria Magdalena*, reproduced as Meissen 96/59 and KPM 17. It can be compared to an engraving by W. French. The Meissen version, after a painting by Correggio was reproduced as Meissen 247, in the 1830s. François Boucher (1703-1770) is well known for his painting *Diana at the Bath*, later converted to lithophane format. The paintings of Charles de Steuben (1788-1856) inspired the lithophanes depicting *Esmeralda*, KPM 255 and PPM 240.

Lithophane, *Maria Magdalena, after Correggio*, German, 19th century, Meissen 247 with 35, 6.5" x 9.5". *Courtesy of Andy Cook.*

Engraving, by W. French after a painting of Maria Magdalena by Battoni. *Courtesy of the Archives of the Blair Museum of Lithophanes.*

Below:
Lithophane, *Maria Magdalena, nach Battoni*, German, 19th century, KPM 17 M, Blair Museum acc. no. 1134, lithophane 7.25" x 10"; stained glass 9.75" x 13". *Courtesy of the Blair Museum of Lithophanes.*

Genre Paintings

Genre painters, popular in their day, but less known today to the general public, whose work was copied into lithophane plaque format include Jacob Becker, Karl Begas, Pierre Auguste Cot, Eduard Daege, Gerard Dou, Ferdinand Hildebrandt, Rudolph Jordan, Wilhelm von Kaulbach, Georg Friedrich Kersting, Franz van Meiris, Friedrich Eduard Meyerheim, Sir John Everett Millais, Esteban Murillo, Johann Heinrich Ramberg, Rourt, Gottfried Schalken, Heinrich Wilhelm Schlesinger, Abraham Solomon, David Teniers, and Sir David Wilkie.

While a detailed listing of genre painters, paintings, and related lithophanes would be appreciated by the most ardent of lithophane collectors, it should be noted that lithophane themes and their derivation have been thoroughly investigated on an item-by-item basis, many of which are cited in the attached bibliography. The 18th century popular novel featuring Paul and Virginia has been the focus of scholarly papers concerning Meissen lithophanes. The KPM lithophane featuring the (little known) Pastor F.D.E. Schleiermacher was featured in an article in a journal in 1987. Georg Friedrich Kersting, 19th century artist and head decorator at Meissen, whose paintings became engravings that became lithophanes by manufacturers in Germany and Wales, was documented in an 85-page article by a German researcher, Bärbel Kovalevski. A few examples derived from genre paintings will be described here and several illustrated.

Engraving, *Auld Robin Grey*, after painting by Sir David Wilkie. *Courtesy of the Blair Museum of Lithophanes.*

Lithophane, *Der Antrag nach einem englische Kupferstich*, (*Auld Robin Grey*), after painting by Sir David Wilkie, German, 19th century, KPM 102 St, Blair Museum acc. no. 982, 12.875" x 10.25". *Courtesy of the Blair Museum of Lithophanes.*

Genre painter Jacob Becker painted *The Shepherd Struck by Lightning*, now in the permanent collection of the Städel Museum in Frankfurt am Main. It was later reproduced as the German lithophane PPM 511 *Der vom Blitz erschlagene Schäfer*.

Friedrich Eduard Meyerheim (1808-1879) was a prolific and popular German genre painter whose many paintings were chosen to be reproduced as lithophanes. A short listing of lithophanes would include KPM 399 and 400 *Milchmädchen (nach Meierheim)*, KPM 391 *Das Landmädchen (nach Meierheim)*, KPM 494 *Speilende Kinder (nach Meierheim)*, and KPM 388 Z *Familienglück (nach Meierheim)*, the latter illustrated in both lithophane and engraving formats in Chapter Seven.

Lithophane *Der vom Blitz erschlagene Schäfer (The Shepherd Struck by Lightning)*, after Jacob Becker, in stained glass frame, German, 19th century, PPM 511, Blair Museum acc. no. 56, lithophane 6.5" x 7.875", stained glass 9.375" x 11". *Courtesy of the Blair Museum of Lithophanes.*

Pierre Auguste Cot (French 1837-1883) was another popular 19th century artist whose painting *The Storm*, belonging to the Metropolitan Museum of Art, is reproduced over and over in lithophane format by various manufacturers, primarily those marked with the P.R. (sickle). He also painted *Le Printemps – Spring*, which can be seen as the lithophane marked P.R. 1309 (Blair Museum acc. no. 1151), depicting and man and a woman on a swing.

Opposite page:
Lithophanous globe lamp, with six lithophane scenes including *The Storm*, colored, after a painting by Pierre Auguste Cot, 19th century, no mark, Blair Museum acc. no. 1914, height 8.5". *Courtesy of the Blair Museum of Lithophanes.*

Gottfried Schalken (1643-1706) was a Dutch genre painter and portrait artist, noted for his mastery in reproducing the effect of candlelight. His painting *Das Mädchen, ein Ei gegen das Licht halden* (*The Girl Holding an Egg Against the Light* or *The Egg Test*) now in Dresden at the Gemäldegalerie, was reproduced as the engraving *Die Eierprobe* (*Proving Eggs*) by W. French, which was then reproduced as the German lithophane PPM 504.

Lithophane, *Die Eierprobe* (*Testing the Eggs*), after a painting by Gottfried Schalken, German, 19th century, PPM 504, Blair Museum acc. no. 419, 7.75" x 5.625". *Courtesy of the Blair Museum of Lithophanes.*

Engraving, *Die Eierprobe* (*Proving Eggs*), by W. French, after a painting by Gottfried Schalken. *Courtesy of the Archives of the Blair Museum of Lithophanes.*

One popular genre painting by Heinrich Wilhelm Schlesinger (1814-1893), later was reproduced as *Vergiß mein nicht!* marked KPM 403 and 405, different size lithophanes with the same *Forget me not!* theme. The stained glass frame is strikingly colorful.

Lithophane, *Vergiß mein nicht!* (*Forget Me Not!*), after a painting by Heinrich Wilhelm Schlesinger, with elaborate stained glass frame, German, 19th century, KPM 405 N, Blair Museum acc. no. 99, lithophane 5.75" x 4.5", stained glass diameter 11.375". *Courtesy of the Blair Museum of Lithophanes.*

Lithophane, *Gruppe fliehender Christen, nach Kaulbach*, German, 19th century, KPM 454 Z, Blair Museum acc. no. 763, lithophane 13.75" x 11.375"; stained glass 17.375" x 14.875". *Courtesy of the Blair Museum of Lithophanes.*

Many lithophane collectors are familiar with Wilhelm von Kaulbach (1805-1874) because a portion of his painting *Die Zerstorung Jerusalems durch Titus* (1846) (*The Destruction of Jerusalem by Titus*) was later reproduced as a lithophane marked KPM 454 Z *Gruppe Fliehender Christen, nach Kaulbach*. The Blair Museum owns two of these, both mounted in blue stained glass. An equal number of collectors will recognize two of his engravings that illustrated Goethe's rendition of the classic *Reineke Fuchs* (*Reynard the Fox*) in the 1800s. These are featured in a lantern panel and beer stein bottom illustrated in Chapter Six.

Some painters may have been popular in their day, but there is little information about them available today. One example is a lithophane created in Berlin, marked KPM 192 Z, based on a painting by Johann Heinrich Ramberg (1763-1840), which was copied as an engraving by J. Jury, based on a text and illustrations by Goethe, *Wer kauft Liebesgötter*.[6] It is illustrated as part of a candle shield in Chapter Six.

One painter who was well-known in his day also served as the head of Decorating at the Division Königlich Sächsischen Porzellanmanufaktur in Dresden at Meissen beginning in 1818. The painter Georg Friedrich Kersting (1785-1847) continued his work in Dresden and was responsible for the development of the designs for lithophanes there beginning in 1828. He was responsible for the selection of motifs for the lithophanes, and in 1828, he brought various forms and examples of lithophanes from the Leipzig Fair to Meissen. Among lithophane collectors he is best known for his adaptation of his painting now at the Düsseldorf Museum of Art, which became an engraving by W.E. Tucker titled *Sour Grapes*, which was published in *Godey's Lady's Book* in 1851, and which was produced as lithophanes by KPM (140 G), Meissen (139) titled *Kinder am Weingeleite*, and finally South Wales Pottery at Llanelly.

Engraving, *Sour Grapes*, by W.E. Tucker for *Godey's Lady's Book* in 1851, after a painting by Georg Friedrich Kersting. *Courtesy of the Archives of the Blair Museum of Lithophanes.*

Two lithophanes based on a painting by Georg Friedrich Kersting, left to right, untitled, Welsh, 19th century, marked South Wales Pottery, Blair Museum acc. no. 548, 5.625" x 4.375"; *Kinder am Weingeleite*, German, 19th century, Meissen 139, Blair Museum acc. no. 8, 7.625" x 6.125". *Courtesy of the Blair Museum of Lithophanes.*

Occasionally one image appears to represent two different stories. Meissen 234, *Girl in Room with Bird Cage,* which depicts a young woman in a green dress (the lithophane is colored) wearing a scarf, seen sewing at a table, with a bird cage in the background, has been identified from two seemingly identical engravings, one titled *Rigolet* and the other *Elsie Gray*. The same theme was produced in porcelain in Berlin as KPM 373 G and in Plaue, as PPM 317, titled *Lachtaube, klein*. The engravings were created by John Sartain based on a painting by Rourt.

Another John Sartain engraving is that titled *Morning Bath,* inspired by the painting by Karl Begas, which was later reproduced as the lithophane PPM 401 (*Die Mohrenwäsche*). The Sartain engraving of the Begas painting notes as part of the engraving, "The Original Picture in the Possession of Elizabeth Queen of Prussia."

Lithophane, *Girl in Room with Bird Cage,* colored, German, 19th century, Meissen 234 (handwritten incised), Blair Museum acc. no. 52, 8.75" x 6.125". *Courtesy of the Blair Museum of Lithophanes.*

Engraving *Elsie Gray,* by A.B. Walter for *Peterson's Magazine.* *Courtesy of the Blair Museum of Lithophanes.*

Engravings and Sartain's Union Magazine

Among the best known and documented of the many journals that reproduced paintings in the form of engravings during the mid-19th century was *Sartain's Union Magazine of Literature and Art*. John Sartain (1808-1897) was born in London, and was apprenticed to an engraver. When he finished his term, he married the engraver's daughter and they moved to the United States where Sartain became Philadelphia's preeminent portrait engraver. Sartain's specialty was mezzotint engravings -- considered the method for most faithfully rendering oil paintings as prints. It is believed that he engraved over 1,500 prints during his career, many of which appeared as illustrations in the leading journals of the day, including *Godey's Lady's Book* and *Graham's Magazine*. He bought the Union Magazine in 1848, in partnership with William Sloanaker. While the magazine was not a financial success, poets such as Longfellow and Poe published with *Sartain's Union Magazine*. Publication ceased in 1852. It has been documented that "whereas only about one hundred magazines had existed in 1825, Americans could choose from at least six hundred in 1850."[7] Apparently four to five thousand magazines were introduced between 1825 and 1850, most surviving for less than two years. It was this "golden age of periodicals"[8] that no doubt assisted in increasing the popularity of lithophanes in the United States. At this time in Europe, the first public museums were inaugurated, allowing increasing numbers of people the opportunity to view masterpiece paintings in person. Many of the engravings now part of the archives of the Blair Museum of Lithophanes, were originally published in *Sartain's Union Magazine of Literature and Art*.

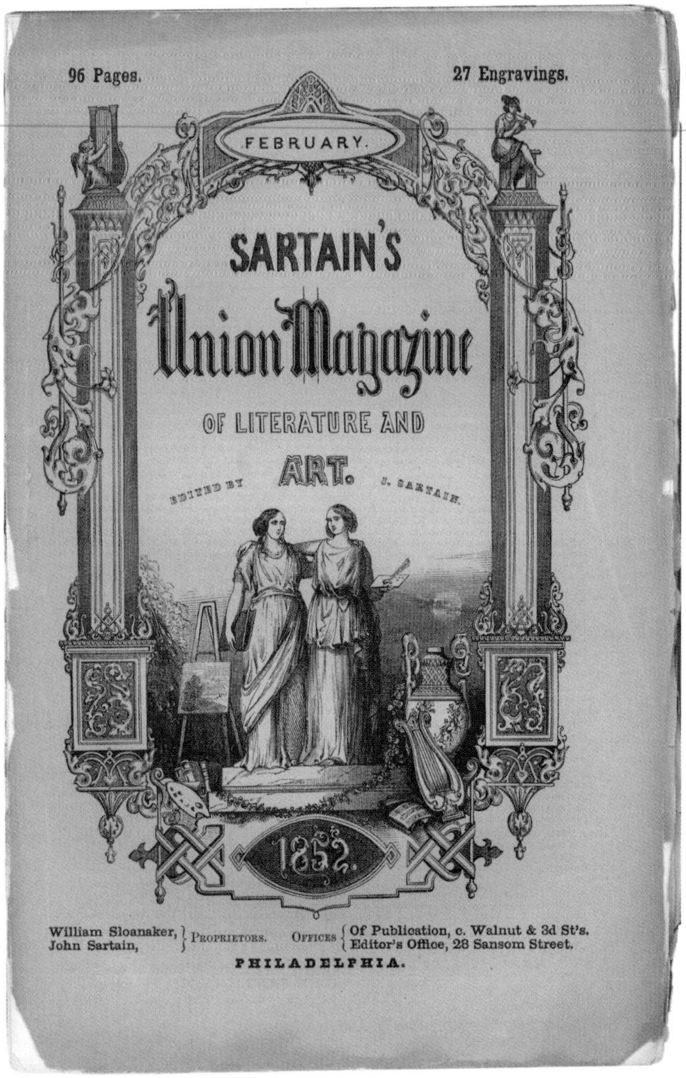

Cover of *Sartain's Union Magazine of Literature and Art*, February, 1852. *Courtesy of Margaret Carney.*

Portraits

There is one aspect of 19th century portraiture that is never mentioned in any art historical treatise on the general topic, yet was wildly popular throughout Europe and the United States during its heyday – lithophanes – with images of Kings and Queens, along with fictional characters from novels and plays. Portraiture was an extremely successful aspect of this nearly forgotten art form. Lithophane portraits exist of Henry Clay, Abraham Lincoln, Garibaldi, Winfield Scott (marked 35, Blair Museum acc. no. 67), and Zachary Taylor. Pope Pius IX appears as a lithophane from Plaue (PPM 235). Russian royalty, Czar Nicholas I and his wife, the Czarina Alexandra Feodorovna, and sometimes their second son, were the subjects of a variety of lithophane portraits, as was Maria Stuart (Mary Queen of Scotts), German Kaiser Wilhelm III (see Chapter Six), Friedrich II (PPM 626), the Prussian Prince and Princess (*Prinz und Prinzessin von Preussen Royale*, PPM 595), and England's Queen Victoria and Prince Albert (Meissen 184). Artists and writers depicted include Goethe, the sculptor Bertel Thorvaldsen, the actor Carl Moor, the singer Jenny Lind, and the Prussian explorer/naturalist Alexander von Humboldt (1769-1856).

A portrait of a king might appear in a lamp shade next to a moralizing lithophane of a sweet child telling her first lie. A tiny erotic lithophane might be in the pocket of a gentleman viewing the lithophanous version of Leonardo da Vinci's *The Last Supper* mounted in a brilliant stained glass frame. While true porcelain had been discovered in China during the Tang dynasty (618-907), it was not created in Europe until 1710 when Johann Friedrich Böttger at Meissen had his first success. Remember that the creator of the first true porcelain in Europe, was an alchemist at the Meissen factory in Dresden, who was hired by the King. Porcelain was as precious as gold then, and therefore it is even more ironic that during the Gilded Age, it was still this rare and exotic material used in the creation of magical portraits for all strata of society to own and enjoy.

While there have been museum exhibitions, coffee table books, doctoral dissertations and such all dealing with 19th century portraiture, the topic of lithophanes is never mentioned. It could be speculated that this is because ceramics, even precious porcelain, is only rarely mentioned in standard art historical treatises. And perhaps if one knows of the existence of lithophanes, they might have been ignored since they generally copied or reproduced masterpiece paintings or engravings. However, in terms of portraiture, this was a rare accessible art form that embraced the needs of the general populace. The portrait sitters were not generally common people, but common people could purchase these portraits that had been incorporated into useful illuminated objects for the home. One fine illustration of this phenomenon is that of Samuel Colt, the inventor of the Colt Revolver. In 1855, while in Berlin, Colt commissioned his own photographic portrait to be made into lithophanes. The resulting 111 lithophanes made by the illustrious Königliche

Porzellan-Manufaktur in Berlin, bearing the backstamp KPM, the number "460" and the scepter mark, were to be sent to his friends and associates as gifts (illustrated in Chapter Seven). Commissioned lithophane portraits were a rare and probably expensive novelty, but were popular in the following decades until electricity also became common and lithophanes in their varying illuminated uses fell out of fashion and were discarded or stowed away in the attic.

Exhibition of lithophane portraits at the Blair Museum of Lithophanes.
Courtesy of the Blair Museum of Lithophanes.

Lithophane portraits were produced of Friedrich Wilhelm III, King of Prussia; Queen Victoria and Prince Albert; Henry Clay; Zachary Taylor; Francoise I, King of France; Goethe; Beatrice; Cardinal Richelieu; Abélard and Heloise; Lincoln; Napoleon; Winfield Scott; the Italian general Garibaldi; Jenny Lind; Martin Luther; Petrarch; and Mary Queen of Scots. The common person could purchase these for a small amount of money and the portrait would be incorporated as part of an illuminated lamp shade, a night light, a tea warmer, or a candle shield. These porcelain conversation pieces, especially the portraits, allowed everyday access to the rich, famous and infamous.

Lithophane, *Queen Victoria and Prince Albert of England*, German, 19th century, Meissen 184 with 15, Blair Museum acc. no. 1460, with metal frame and hanging chain, 8.25" x 7". *Courtesy of the Blair Museum of Lithophanes.*

Lithophane portrait, *Abraham Lincoln*, German, 19th century, PPM 837, Blair Museum acc. no. 4, 5.25" x 4.5". *Courtesy of the Blair Museum of Lithophanes.*

A rare portrait in the Blair collection is that of Abraham Lincoln. In 1965, Laurel Blair was given two original wax models during a visit to the von Schierholz Porcelain Manufacturing plant in Plaue, Germany. One of them was a portrait of Abraham Lincoln. The Lincoln wax was made to commemorate his assassination and the story was told that the wax was never used by the company because they realized when it was completed that they had used an outdated picture of Lincoln. This wax carving depicted him as a younger Lincoln and not as he was at the time of his death. In 1968, Mr. Blair sent a photograph of the wax carving to The Lincoln National Life Foundation in Fort Wayne, Indiana to enquire if they had ever seen a lithophane of Lincoln made from the wax. They had not. However, late in 1976, a collector in California, a Dr. Creighton Reid, contacted Mr. Blair, notifying him that he had a Lincoln lithophane that matched the wax model, also manufactured in Plaue and with the backstamp PPM 837, 5.25" x 4.5". They made a trade in early 1977, and thus the Blair Museum acquired this rare Lincoln lithophane – through the generosity of a new collector who thought it would be more valuable to the Blair Museum than in his own small collection. Dr. Reid wanted to trade for a KPM or PPM colored lithophane. The fragile Lincoln wax model was unfortunately broken when the Museum was moved after Mr. Blair's death. The image of Lincoln was probably based on a photograph of Lincoln taken in Chicago by Alexander Hesler on February 28, 1857.[9] At that time Lincoln was 48 years old and did not yet have a beard. It is believed that the wax modeler added the beard to make Lincoln look more like he did at the time of the assassination. The original Hesler photograph is located in Fort Wayne, Indiana at the Lincoln Museum.

In a Zachary Taylor portrait panel, mounted as a candle shield, he is shown as a general in the Mexican War (1846-1848) before he became president in 1849. Originally it was a sketch by Captain Eaton, *aide de campe* to the General, made at Camargo, Mexico, on August 15, 1846 for George Graham (copyright 1847) who used it as an embellishment in *Graham's Magazine* with the print sold separately. The lithophane was issued either in November 1847 or early in 1848, according to the late Harry Koopman.[10] Zachary Taylor is shown in uniform with spyglass in hand, along with an eagle and a pair of crossed, 15-starred American flags. In this example, located in the Blair Museum, the German-made pedestal and frame are cast iron.

A lithophane portrait of Henry Clay was based on an engraving by T. Doney which was done for *American Review* in 1844. The engraving, in turn, is after a daguerreotype by Anthony, Edwards & Company that was originally exhibited in that enterprise's National Miniature Gallery.[11]

Lithophane, *Henry Clay*, German, 19th century, marked with small "50," Blair Museum acc. no. 132, 8" x 6.375". *Courtesy of the Blair Museum of Lithophanes.*

Lithophane portrait mounted as a candle shield, *Zachary Taylor*, German, 19th century, marked "KK" stamped on front center with tiny "35" on back, "Z. Taylor" signature on front in relief, Blair Museum acc. no. 32, 8.125" x 6.375" with overall height of cast iron stand 23.25". *Courtesy of the Blair Museum of Lithophanes.*

Historic Figures

Historic figures were frequently featured in familiar settings and as the subject of portraits. These included rulers, royalty, religious leaders, and government dignitaries. Napoleon was shown on his horse in a battle scene or talking to a guard (PPM 616 and AdT, Blair Museum acc. no. 898). Christopher Columbus was depicted during his famous voyage. Martin Luther is portrayed after a painting by Hans Holbein (1497-1543) reproduced as a lithophane by Meissen. He is also shown in a Christmas scene with his family (PPM 340 *Luther mit Familie am Weihnachtsabend*).

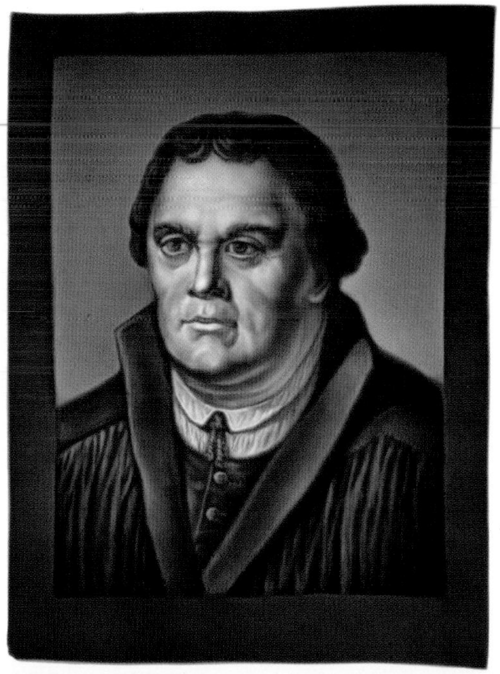

Lithophane, *Martin Luther*, German, 19th century, Meissen 52, Blair Museum acc. no. 1218, 6.25" x 4.75". *Courtesy of the Blair Museum of Lithophanes.*

Lithophane, *Columbus*, German, 19th century, PPM 441, Blair Museum acc. no. 1789, 6" x 7.875". *Courtesy of the Blair Museum of Lithophanes.*

A very dramatic lithophane depiction is that of the princes in the Tower of London, which was produced by KPM as 161 and Meissen as 152. The original painting has been attributed to James Northcote, and the lithophane is a copy of an engraved interpretation of Northcote's painting by Theodor Hildebrand. The painting, engraving and lithophanes are based on the story of the alleged 1483 murder of the two princes, Edward V and his brother Richard, Duke of York. In order to strengthen his claim to the throne, the story goes, Richard II had his two slumbering nephews killed by his servant John Dighton and jailer Miles Forest, after imprisoning the boys in the tower.

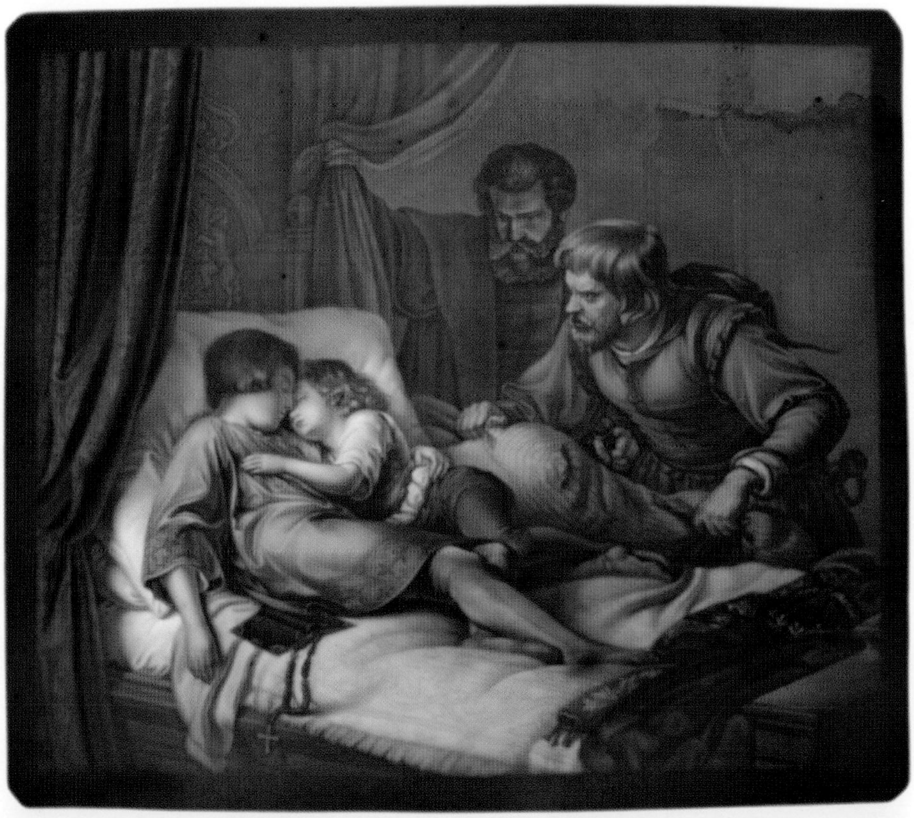

Lithophane depicting the Princes in the Tower, *Die Söhne Eduard's*, German, 19th century, KPM 161 B, Blair Museum acc. no. 1087, 6.125" x 7". *Courtesy of the Blair Museum of Lithophanes.*

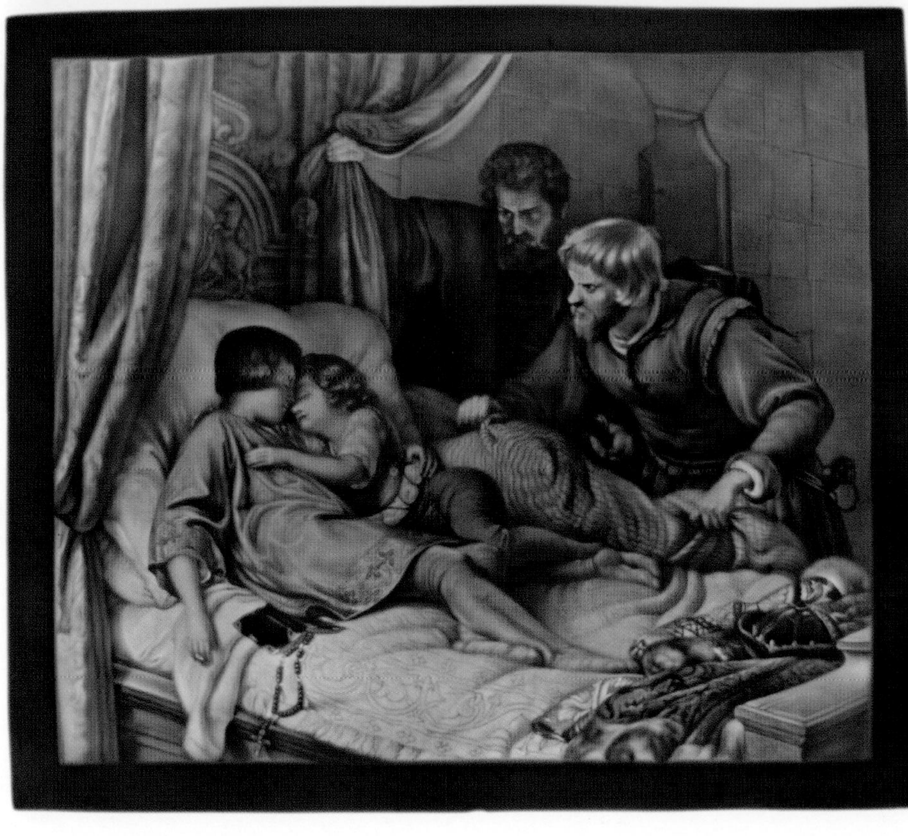

Lithophane depicting the Princes in the Tower, *Die Söhne Eduard's*, German, 19th century, Meissen 152, Blair Museum acc. no. 998, 6.875" x 8". *Courtesy of the Blair Museum of Lithophanes.*

Among the few lithophanes that exhibit controversy or censorship is the pair of portraits of the famous lovers Abélard and Heloise. The Blair Museum collection owns a lithophane of Abélard (1079-1142) in a candle shield (Blair acc. no. 1842, KPM 240 Z). There are two other marvelous versions of this subject, also in the Blair collection, mounted in green velvet Victorian frames. One shows the same image of Abélard and the other in a matching frame, his great love Heloise (1101-1164). If one remembers, Pierre Abélard was the teacher of Heloise. She was brilliant and beautiful and they together possessed a love story unrivaled in history. In the twelfth century, Heloise, the niece of Notre Dame's Canon Fulbert, studied in Paris with Abélard, a professor at Notre Dame twenty years her senior. Their passion resulted in her pregnancy, and her uncle purported to protect Heloise and the baby, thus arranging the wedding of Abélard and Heloise. But she was whisked away to the convent at Argenteuil and forced to give up her child, while Abélard was brutally attacked in Paris and castrated. As a result both were destined to take Holy Orders as Monk and Nun. Abélard and Heloise corresponded for twenty years and they met years later, their love had endured, even though they could not be together. The subjects of these lithophanes both originally had crosses visible on their chests. This pair, mounted in matching green velvet frames, have had the crosses physically ground off their chests, as if to say that their deeds have brought disgrace to the church. There is the implication that the crosses, if present, would indicate some sort of sanction by the church. It is not known when this censorship occurred, but certainly before Mr. Blair acquired them.

Lithophane, *Heloise*, framed in green velvet, with cross removed, German, 19th century, KPM 239 Z, Blair Museum acc. no. 2587, 7" x 5.75". *Courtesy of the Blair Museum of Lithophanes.*

Lithophane, *Abeilard*, framed in green velvet, with cross removed, German, 19th century, KPM 240 Z, Blair Museum, acc. no. 1571, 7" x 5.75". *Courtesy of the Blair Museum of Lithophanes.*

Popular Literature

Popular literature was another source of inspiration for the skilled wax carver. There is an abundance of lithophanes featuring memorable characters including romantic couples such as Faust and Gretchen (or Marguerite) from Goethe, Romeo and Juliet (PPM 587), Abélard and Heloise, and Paul and Virginia.

A novel published in 1788 by Bernardin De Saint-Pierre, *Paul et Virginie*, touted the theme that happiness consists of living according to the dictates of nature and virtue. The novel takes place on the exotic island paradise of Mauritius and is a classic French romantic novel that praises the quest to return to nature. It was a best-seller for half a century. Lithophanes that portray Paul and Virginia include those manufactured by both Meissen and Plaue. Two articles written about lithophanes have focused primarily on this particular popular literature from the late 18th-early 19th centuries.[12] One Meissen example is illustrated in Chapter Ten.

Other memorable characters from literature include the storyteller Scheherazade from *The Arabian Nights*, Esméralda from *The Hunchback of Notre Dame*, Sir Walter Scott's Scottish archer, *Quentin Durward*, from his 1823 historical novel of the same title (KPM 298 N in the Wichita Center for the Arts collection), Shakespeare's Ophelia (PPM 585), William Tell (PPM 653), Don Quixote (*Don Quizotte* PPM 371) and scenes from Goethe's *Reineke Fuchs*, as illustrated by Kaulbach.

Lithophane, *Julie (Juliet)* German, 19th century, PPM 214, Blair Museum acc. no. 427, 7.625" x 6". *Courtesy of the Blair Museum of Lithophanes.*

Lithophane, *Romeo*, German, 19th century, KPM 337 O, Blair Museum acc. no. 414, 9.375" x 7.5". *Courtesy of the Blair Museum of Lithophanes.*

Lithophane, *Scheherazade*, colored, German, 19th century, Meissen 187, 8.75" x 9.5". *Courtesy of Andy Cook.*

Fairy tales are seldom depicted, but a memorable one is that depicting Snow White produced by Plaue titled *Schneewitchen*. Another PPM-marked lithophane celebrates the story of Hansel and Gretel (*Hans und Gretchen* PPM 201).

Lithophane, *Schneewitchen* (*Snow White*), German, 19th century, PPM 582, 7.75" x 6.25". *Courtesy of Andy Cook.*

Esméralda, as mentioned previously, is depicted from the 1831 novel by Victor Hugo, shown as a gypsy girl about 16 years of age, she is always shown with her clever goat Djali, her tamborine, and her seductive dances. The lithophanes include PPM 240 (Blair acc. no. 978) *Esméralda tanzend*, (*Esméralda dancing*) with stained glass frame and the KPM 255 St. plaque *Esméralda* (Blair acc. no. 980, 12.125" x 9.625"), as well as an example mounted as a candle shield (PPM 251, Blair Museum acc. no. 1874, 5.75" x 4.5"). It is a complicated and sad story, where Esméralda dies. The lithophanes reflect the more carefree exploits of Esméralda.

Lithophane, *Esméralda*, mounted in stained glass, German, 19th century, PPM 240, Blair Museum acc. no. 978, lithophane 6.5" x 5.5", stained glass 9.75" x 8.75". *Courtesy of the Blair Museum of Lithophanes.*

Vedute or Scenes of Place

Many lithophanes captured *vedute* or scenes of well-known places in Europe and America, including Heidleburg, Rheinstein, and Lichtenstein (KPM 261 Z, Blair Museum acc. no. 2516, 7.5" x 5.75") castles; Cologne and Strasbourg cathedrals; St. Stephen's Cathedral in Vienna; cathedral interiors such as (possibly) the First Church of Our Lady in Copenhagen; the cities of Coblenz and Ems, Germany; Vevey and Lucerne Switzerland; the fountains of Versailles (see Chapter Two); and the Walter Scott Memorial in Edinburgh. American scenes include Niagara Falls, as seen from the excursion boat *Maid of the Mist*; the President's House in Washington; the Port of Philadelphia; Bastion Falls; a view of a factory near Passaic Falls, Paterson, New Jersey; Genesee Falls, Rochester, New York; West Point; Bay of New York; Mount Vernon; Catskill Falls in Catskill, New York; and Brock's Monument on the Niagara River.

Right:
Lithophane, *Coblenz*, mounted in stained glass at the Glen Iris Inn, 19th century, mark not visible, German, probably PPM 276, lithophane 5.75" x 7.375", stained glass 9.625" x 11". *Courtesy of the Glen Iris Inn, Letchworth State Park.*

Below:
Lithophane, *Innere Ansicht einer Kathdrale, (Interior of a Cathedral)*, Meissen 46 (handwritten incised), Blair Museum acc. no. 935, 5" x 6.75". *Courtesy of the Blair Museum of Lithophanes.*

Of all the areas of lithophane research, investigations into the relationship between original engravings and lithophanes has probably been the best documented. The complete bibliography at the conclusion of this manuscript will permit the enthusiast to explore this topic in further detail. An article by Hans Leichter titled *Berliner Lithophanien: eine fast vergessene grafische Technik des Biedermeier*, is enlightening in terms of presenting a concise listing of 16 engravings depicting monuments and buildings in Berlin and Potsdam, with the artist's name, the engraver's name, the title of the piece and related lithophanes.[13] The published engravings provide proof that they were the model for the porcelain pictures manufactured at KPM. All of these engravings were published by Samuel Heinrich Spiker in his 1833 book *Berlin und seine Umgebung im 19. Jahrhundert.*[14]

Lithophane depicting Moses in the bullrushes, *Die Findung Moses*, colored, German, 19th century, PPM 492, Blair Museum acc. no. 152, 6.75" x 8.375". *Courtesy of the Blair Museum of Lithophanes.*

Religious Themes and Stories from the Bible

Scenes from the Bible and religious themes include Moses in the bullrushes, *Die Findung Moses*. One Plaue version has delicate colors applied on the exterior that are visible even when the piece is not backlit. Other stories pictured include *Jacob bei Laban* (PPM 556) and *Jacob und Rebecca* (KPM 313 N), and one depicting Daniel in the lion's den, *Daniel in der Löwengrube* (KPM 312).

Lithophane exhibit at the Blair Museum featuring *vedute* or scenes of places. *Courtesy of the Blair Museum of Lithophanes.*

Lithophane mounted in a hand screen, *Jacob and Rebecca,* German, 19th century, KPM 313 N, lithophane 5.75" x 4.5" with mahogany wood frame and handle, overall length 13". *Courtesy of Connie Scott.* Photo by John Scott.

There is a beautiful hand screen in a private collection in the United States with a design that was introduced at KPM in Berlin between 1842 and 1846. Marked KPM 313 N, it depicts Jacob and Rebecca, with a depiction of a Biblical scene relating to the story of the stolen blessing. Rebecca is offering Jacob a drink in this depiction. Inspiration for this lithophane can be seen in an engraving located in the Blair Museum archives. This untitled image is inscribed below the image, "And she answered drink my lord and quickly she let down the pitcher upon her arm and gave him drink," and "Genesis XXIV ver. 18."

The Louvre in Paris owns a painting by Émile Signol (1804-1892) titled *Le Christ et la femme adultère* (*Christ and the Adulteress*). Painted in 1840, it became a lithophane in the mid-19th century in Germany and was copied again at Phoenix Pottery in the United States during late 19th century (see Chapter Three). There is a Meissen example in the Blair Museum and the Powerhouse Museum in Sydney, Australia owns KPM 260 titled *Christus mit der Ehebrecherin, nach Signol* (*Christ and the Adulteress, after Signol*) on the KPM *Preis-Courant*.

Engraving, depicting Jacob and Rebecca, 19th century. *Courtesy of the Archives of the Blair Museum of Lithophanes.*

Lithophane, *Christ and the Adulteress*, German, 19th century, Meissen 178 (handwritten), Blair Museum acc. no. 470, 10.125" x 8". *Courtesy of the Blair Museum of Lithophanes.*

A beautiful lithophane depicting *The Priest and the Acolyte* was created in Berlin at KPM and also later copied at the Belleek factory in Ireland. It was based on engravings that were based on a painting by Eduard Daege (1805-1883), a painter living in Berlin. The reflection in the water of the legs of the two figures is transferred somehow miraculously from paper to porcelain. The engraving and lithophane are illustrated in Chapter Seven.

Exhibition of religious themed lithophanes at the Blair Museum. *Courtesy of the Blair Museum of Lithophanes.*

Not surprisingly, there are many lithophanes with a religious or pious intention that do not directly refer to the Bible. Examples would include the Meissen woman church-goer in a Medieval setting (*Kirchgängerin*), a mother praying with her child (KPM 412 *Lieber Gott, mach mir fromm*), *Das Weihwasser* depicting a woman touching holy water (KPM 264 B), and *Der Wohlthätige Pilger, nach Daege*, (KPM 271) after a painting by Eduard Daege.

Above:
Lithophane, *Der Wohlthätige Pilger, nach Daege*, German, 19th century, KPM 271, Blair Museum acc. no. 457, 12.5" x 9.875". *Courtesy of the Blair Museum of Lithophanes.*

Above Left:
Lithophane, *Kirchgängerin*, a woman church-goer with a Medieval church in the background, German, 19th century, Meissen 131 (hand incised) with 27 (impressed), Blair Museum acc. no. 445, 10" x 7.25". *Courtesy of the Blair Museum of Lithophanes.*

Left:
Lithophane, *Lieber Gott, mach mir fromm*, German, 19th century, KPM 412, Blair Museum acc. no. 1664, lithophane 9.5" x 7.5", stained glass frame 12" x 10". *Courtesy of the Blair Museum of Lithophanes.*

Lithophane, *Das Weihwasser* (*The Holy Water*), German, 19th century, KPM 264 B, Blair Museum acc. no. 218, 13" x 10". *Courtesy of the Blair Museum of Lithophanes.*

Genre Themes

It is important not to forget the sometimes excessively sweet depictions of children, puppies and kittens that were popular genre scenes for the young and old alike. Very often these scenes had nothing to do with the reality of living in the 19th century as a child. These were intended to raise sympathetic responses from the viewer. These might include those of sweet little children looking at their image in the mirror, and sentimental subjects such as puppies, kittens, bunnies, and babies.

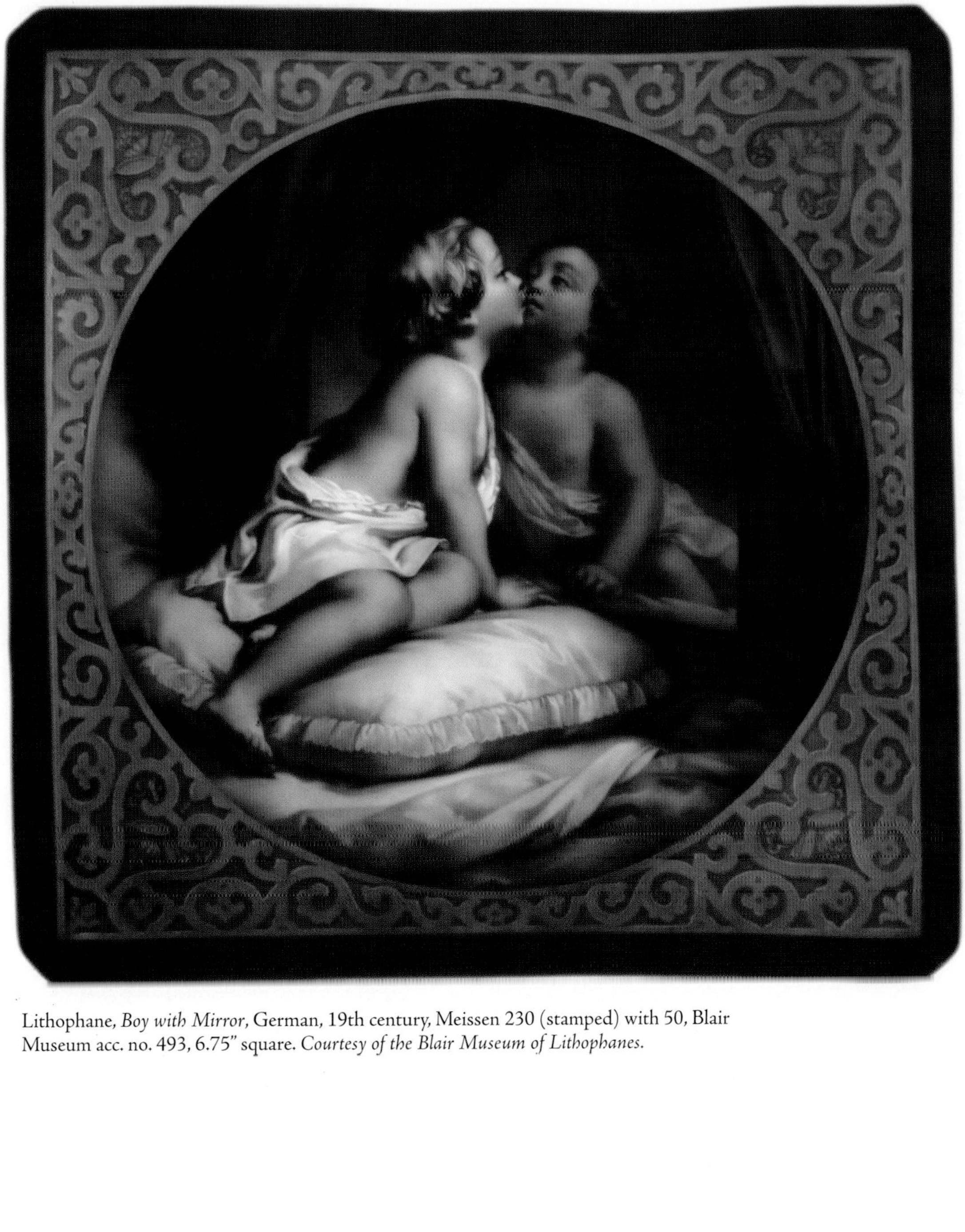

Lithophane, *Boy with Mirror*, German, 19th century, Meissen 230 (stamped) with 50, Blair Museum acc. no. 493, 6.75" square. *Courtesy of the Blair Museum of Lithophanes.*

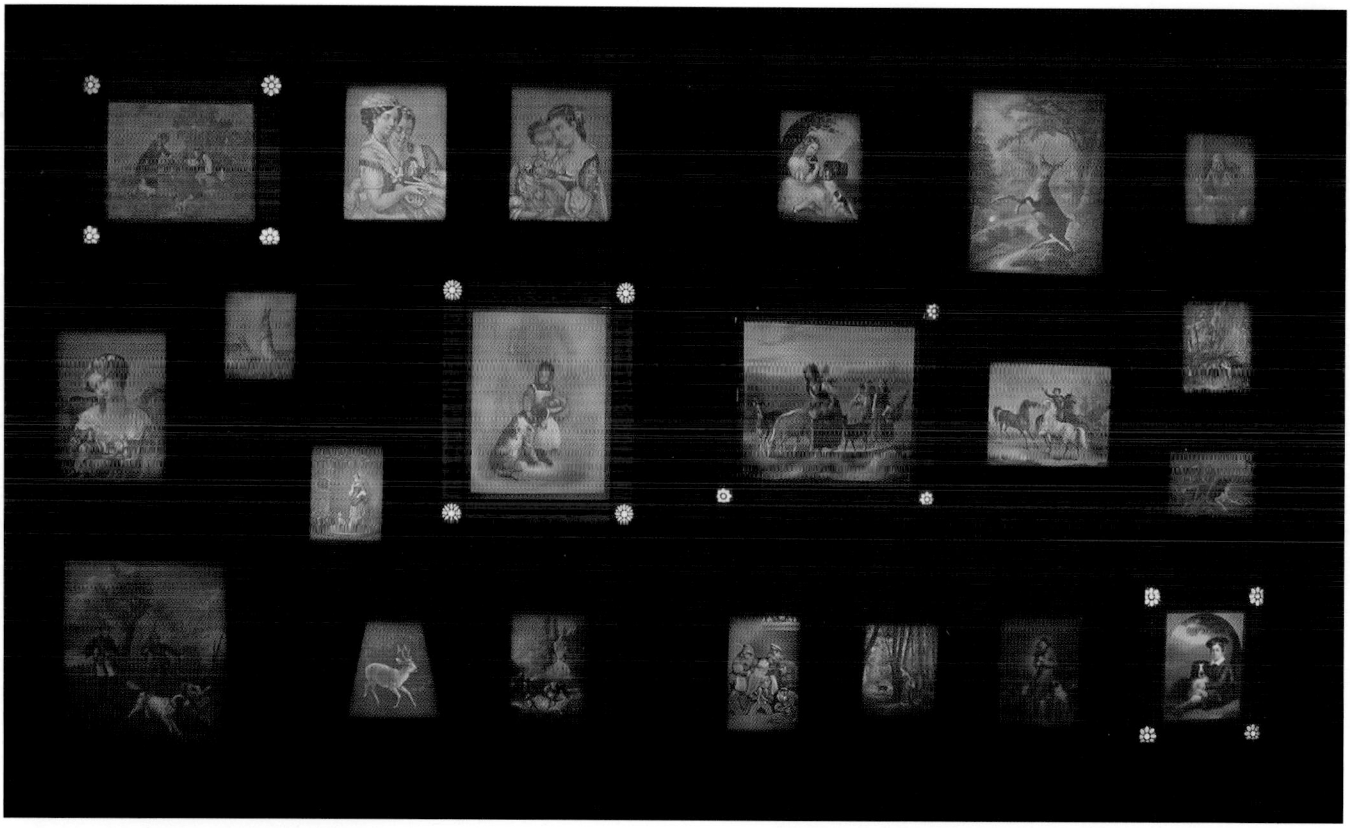

Exhibition of genre-themed lithophanes in the Blair Museum. *Courtesy of the Blair Museum of Lithophanes.*

Lithophane, *Die Neuen Hausgenossen* (*The New Houseguests*), German, 19th century, PPM 513, 5.75" x 4.75". *Courtesy of Andy Cook.*

Lithophane mounted in a candle shield, *Ein Schäfer mit Herde im Sturm* (*A Shepherd with his Herd in a Storm*), German, 19th century, Meissen 12 (incised) and 43 (stamped), 7.75" x 6.125". *Courtesy of Darren King.*

The themes of some of these more saccharine lithophanes, all derived from engravings, are moralizing vignettes, centered around childhood themes of learning a lesson, telling the truth, behaving admirably, and overall goodness and virtue as desirable traits. For instance, some of the engravings that inspired these 19th century porcelain pictures were titled *Deceiving Granny*, *The Happy Family*, *Grandfather's Darling*, *The First Sermon*, and *Master Mischief*.

Some scenes of daily life and activities depicted in lithophane format are of a darker nature. These portray the hardships of life including illness, weathering storms, and hard labor. A German lithophane mounted in a candle shield, presents the image of a shepherd caught in a storm with his herd of sheep. His faithful sheepdog stands nearby, on duty.

Hunting and Battle Themes

In contrast to the sweetness of the aforementioned, would be the lithophanes that depicted hunting scenes that might be favored by men and exhibited in their rooms. These depicted men with guns shooting at birds, deer and bear and trophy kill images. Others were views of a buck being startled out of the woods in the foreground, with the gunfire captured in the brush in the background. Some men also favored battle scenes, on land and sea. A comparison of a Plaue lithophane depicting a sea battle with a French AdT marked piece, shows quite a different effect.

Lithophane, *Seeschlacht*, German, 19th century, KPM 355 N, Blair Museum acc. no. 153, 7.5" x 9.5". *Courtesy of the Blair Museum of Lithophanes.*

Lithophane, soldiers surrendering in an unidentified battle scene, French, 19th century, AdT, Blair Museum acc. no. 901, 6" x 4". *Courtesy of the Blair Museum of Lithophanes.*

Lithophane, *Die Wildschützen* (*The Poachers*), German, 19th century, Meissen 98 with 71, Blair Museum acc. no. 1967, 11" x 9". *Courtesy of the Blair Museum of Lithophanes.*

Lithophane, depicting a shot being fired at a jumping buck, German, 19th century, KPM 342 N, 9" x 7" in metal frame. *Courtesy of the Blair Museum of Lithophanes.*

An occasional lithophane combined sentimentality with the glory and tragedy of war. This combination can be seen in the German lithophane PPM 664, *Hohenschwangau*, which depicts a soldier and grandfather with a missing limb, holding his grandson who is playing with his toy soldiers. One imagines he is sharing memories of battles fought and enemies defeated.

A different presentation combining a sentimental story with a warrior, can be seen in the KPM 128 N lithophane of a soldier with his child. With his sword and armor nearby, a tired and happy warrior hugs his daughter tight.

Humor was a familiar theme adapted from engravings to lithophanes and some of these are described in Chapter Eight devoted to this topic. Eroticism is another theme chosen for pocket-sized lithophanes and this topic is discussed in Chapter Six. Both the humorous and amorous lithophanes involve Victorian mores, costumes, and daily life, not unlike all the others.

It has been noted that those who collected engravings in the mid-19th century, largely the middle class, were not collecting to record visual records of their times, but rather were choosing to decorate their middle-class homes.[15] These porcelain plaques embellished their lamps, night lights, windows, and candle shields. This is the topic to be dealt with in Chapter Six.

The question has been raised that "if a lithophane can be a picture of a painting, why couldn't a painting be a picture of a lithophane?"[16] There are only two known examples of 19th century images with lithophanes. One portrait photograph included a candle shield with a lithophane as part of the decor and was reproduced in an article by Hans Simmler.[17] The other is recorded in a photograph of unknown origin discovered in the Blair Museum archives. This photograph is an image of a painting or a work on paper, depicting a bed-ridden patient and her doctor and perhaps her family. In the foreground, is a lithophane mounted in a candle shield, which can be recognized as PPM 756, *Seemanns Leben*, Blair Museum acc. no. 515, 8.25" x 6.5". Both are illustrated in Chapter Six.

Lithophane, *Hohenschwangau*, German, 19th century, PPM 664, Blair Museum acc. no. 1001, 6.5" x 5.375". *Courtesy of the Blair Museum of Lithophanes.*

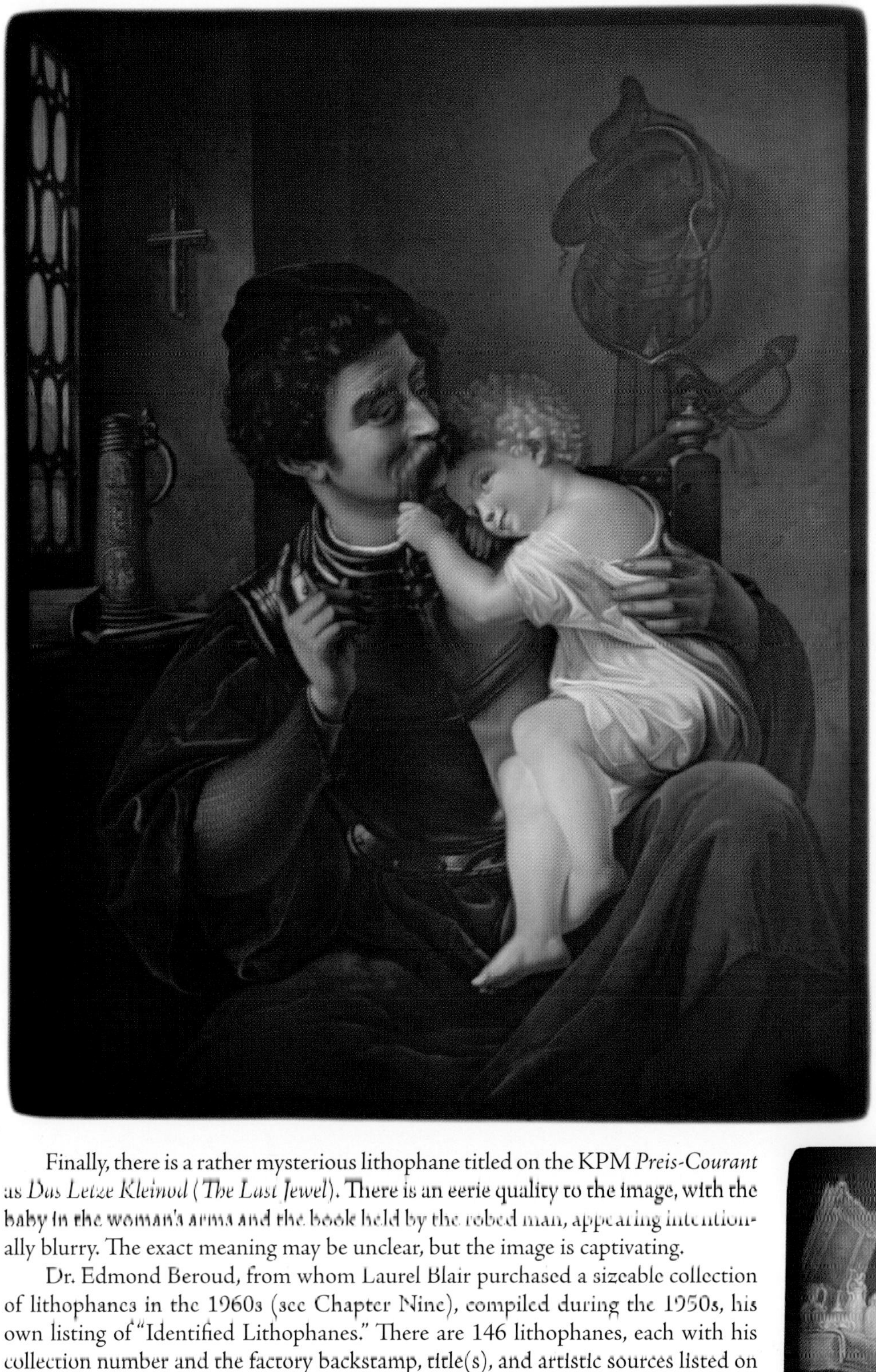

Lithophane, *Der Krieger und sein Kind* (*The Warrior and his Child*), German, 19th century, KPM 128 N, Blair Museum acc. no. 665, 12.75" x 10". *Courtesy of the Blair Museum of Lithophanes.*

Finally, there is a rather mysterious lithophane titled on the KPM *Preis-Courant* as *Das Letze Kleinod* (*The Last Jewel*). There is an eerie quality to the image, with the baby in the woman's arms and the book held by the robed man, appearing intentionally blurry. The exact meaning may be unclear, but the image is captivating.

Dr. Edmond Beroud, from whom Laurel Blair purchased a sizeable collection of lithophanes in the 1960s (see Chapter Nine), compiled during the 1950s, his own listing of "Identified Lithophanes." There are 146 lithophanes, each with his collection number and the factory backstamp, title(s), and artistic sources listed on this carbon-copy listing. A check mark (√) near a listing appears to indicate that he had in his possession that lithophane and original engraving.

Lithophane, *Das Letze Kleinod* (*The Last Jewel*), German, 19th century, KPM 404 B, 12.375" x 10". *Courtesy of Darren King.*

Chapter Six
Lithophane Forms and Functions

Lithophane, *Goldschmidts Töchterlein,*
German, 19th century, PPM 101, Blair Museum acc. no. 7, 6.125" x 7.875". *Courtesy of the Blair Museum of Lithophanes.*

In order to understand why the invention of lithophanes was exactly the right technology at the right time, one must remember that lithophanes are nothing without light. In the 19th century, one literally could not see and appreciate the hidden picture without the porcelain being illuminated by candle light, fireplace flames, the sun, or lighting devices fueled by whale-oil, lard-oil, alcohol, turpentine, or kerosene. Between 1830 and 1860, the heyday of lithophanes, approximately 500 lighting devices were patented.[1] Whales became more scarce, whale oil doubled in price, and new fuels containing combinations of alcohol and turpentine were dangerous due to explosive attributes which had resulted in fatalities. Gas lighting had been introduced before 1830, but was not widely adopted until after the American Civil War (1861-1865). Kerosene was patented by Abraham Gesner of Williamsburg, New York in 1854. The Pennsylvania oil fields were opened up in 1859, and this apparently was the turning point in making cheap and abundant fuel available to the public. In 1847 the Franklin Institute of Philadelphia warned of the "unpleasant, to many eyes, painful, effects of the naked flame of a candle, lamp or gas burner."[2] This is the age of lithophanes.

Plaques

The plaque is the most basic lithophane shape, be it rectangular, square, oval, circular, or trapezoid. Some small plaques are convex. Nineteenth century price lists verify the relative inexpensive nature of the smaller plaques. Whether through breakage or availability, larger plaques (9" x 7") are relatively scarce in public and private collections. Lithophane plaques or panels, large and small, were framed and hung in windows like light-catchers or imbedded more or less permanently in pre-existing window panes for decoration. The detail revealed in the illuminated plaque is often remarkable. Some plaques were made with two holes at the top – utilizing hangers, chains or ribbons to suspend them where ever desired. If one collects lithophanes one soon learns that while there are many recurring lithophane shapes and sizes, they are not all standardized and interchangeable. One might think that all plaques would fit in all candle shields, when, in fact, that is definitely not the case. The flat plaque shape was used in many other functional forms besides sun-catchers – forms that were enhanced by the addition of these illuminated porcelains.

Lithophanes, plaques or more complicated curved cast forms, were utilized to beautify many necessities of 19th century life. They were incorporated into useful illuminated objects for the home. Examples include plaques of all types, candle shields, table screens, lamps and shades, nightlights, tea warmers, combinations of nightlights and tea warmers (called veilleuses théières), fireplace screens, doll house miniatures, complexion fans, beer stein bottoms, interiors of souvenir or commemorative memorabilia, erotica, lanterns, match boxes, devotional home worship pieces, mug and cup interiors, and fairy lamps.

View of the middle section of one exhibition case with German plaques at the Blair Museum. Beginning top left: PPM 705, PPM 1150, KPM 107 G, PPM 511, Meissen 199, KPM 355 N, BPM 512, PPM 101, PPM 756, PPM 1171 (colored), PPM 618, PPM 492 (colored), Meissen 46, and Meissen 234 (colored). *Courtesy of the Archives of the Blair Museum of Lithophanes.*

The appealing, affordable, small flat plaque could be and was easily passed between various companies, just as were the engravings upon which many lithophanes were based. One company would copy another company's idea and issue their own version of the same subject. Some companies apparently went as far as to make a mold of an existing flat panel lithophane, and this resulted in a smaller, less detailed version of the original that was copied. Comparing the same theme between different makers can be very revealing. It is often clear that the wax modelers from each factory were looking at the same engraving for inspiration, but the results are slightly varied, as is the case when comparing lithophanes of the same theme (a maid smoking a pipe) produced at PPM, HPM and probably P.R. (sickle).

Above:
Lithophane, Maid Smoking a Pipe, German, 19th century, HPM 412 R, Blair Museum acc. no. 1123, 5.25" x 4.375". *Courtesy of the Blair Museum of Lithophanes.*

Above Right:
Lithophane, Maid Smoking a Pipe, German, 19th century, PPM 790, Blair Museum acc. no. 1121, 6" x 4.5". *Courtesy of the Blair Museum of Lithophanes.*

Right:
Lithophane, Maid Smoking a Pipe, German, 19th century, marked 1767, Blair Museum acc. no. 1111, 5.125" x 4.25". *Courtesy of the Blair Museum of Lithophanes.*

Perhaps the most appealing plaques for hanging in windows are those with colored or stained glass surrounding the lithophane. Often there is only one color of glass around the porcelain plaque, but whether a single color or multiple colors of glass, the illuminated result is always breathtaking. The colors of glass utilized are red, green, blue, amber, orange, yellow, purple, rose, and lavender. There are many varieties, some with cut glass effects, and others with a stencil pattern on the glass. The windows in the doorway at the Glen Iris Inn in Upstate New York, quite beautifully illustrate the use of stained glass to enhance the drama of the lithophane panels (illustrated in Chapter Seven).

The Blair Museum collection includes several plaques that are mounted as part of existing doors and windows with elaborate stained, etched, and leaded glass mountings. Some windows have as many as nine lithophanes inserted in a frame.

Lithophane, *Allein im Walde* (*Alone in the Woods*), German, design first introduced 1850-59, KPM 395 O, with glass frame, Blair Museum acc. no. 12, 11.25" x 6.5", stained glass 17.75" x 13.5". *Courtesy of the Blair Museum of Lithophanes.*

Window with nine lithophanes, 19th century, German, beginning upper left, KPM incised 26 (Blair 498), KPM 19 (Blair 497), KPM incised 29 (Blair 496), KPM incised 68 (Blair 499), KPM incised 101 above scepter (Blair 500), KPM 84 G (Blair 501), KPM (unclear) 27 (Blair 504), KPM 15 (Blair 503), KPM incised 56 (Blair 502). Overall 19.375" x 16.75". *Courtesy of the Blair Museum of Lithophanes.*

Candle Shields, Table Screens, and Fireplace Screens

After the sun went down, home interiors in the early 19th century were illuminated in several ways. Candles provided light, while fireplaces provided both heat and light. It is sometimes said that electricity caused the decline in popularity of lithophanes as these attractive illuminated porcelain objects were largely created to enhance the flickering movement of flames from wood, wax, oil or gas.

Candle shields were intended to protect ones eyes from the harsh flame of the candle, whether it was in a single stand on the table or mantel, attached to a wall sconce, or suspended from a chandelier. Translucent porcelain provided an excellent candle shield as it not only protected the eyes, but it also presented an illuminated picture for the viewer at the same time. The flickering flame of the candle would have provided additional magical motion to the three-dimensional vision that it backlit.

Dr. Edmond Beroud shown with a lithophane candle shield featuring *Madonna della Sedia (Madonna of the Chair)*, c. 1950s. *Courtesy of the Archives of the Blair Museum of Lithophanes.*

Lithophane mounted as a candle shield, *Madonna della Sedia (Madonna of the Chair)*, German, design first introduced 1828-1836, KPM 104 N, Blair Museum acc. no. 34, diam. 10.125" candle shield height 20.5" with rosewood base and finial. *Courtesy of the Blair Museum of Lithophanes.*

The candle shields that held lithophanous porcelain panels were themselves constructed, often quite elaborately, out of cast iron, wood, gilt wood, antlers, silver, bronze, brass, tin, or other materials. The Blair Museum of Lithophanes owns more than fifty candle shields. The lithophane images in candle shields run the gamut from the German KPM manufactured *Madonna of the Chair*, after a painting by Raphael, a circular lithophane, mounted in a rosewood frame; a scene in the Alps with two deer by a stream with subtle colors on the porcelain surface and a wild antler mounting; to a whimsical mounting of a small oval lithophane surrounded by filigree work and faux gemstones which would have been fastened to a wall sconce. The familiar scene is that of a policeman confronting two children who apparently have been fishing where it is not allowed. While the candle shield stand is placed on a flat surface, wall sconces, are mounted on the wall. The small decorative shade was sometimes in the form of a lithophane, revealing a beautiful detailed picture when backlit. The majority of the wall sconces in the Blair Museum collection were manufactured at Wedgwood.

Above:
Engraving, titled *Madonna and Child*, engraved by Joseph Brown after a painting by Raphael, 19th century. *Courtesy of the Archives of the Blair Museum of Lithophanes.*

Above Right:
Lithophane mounted as a candle shield depicting two deer by a stream, colored, German, 19th century, PPM 1112, Blair Museum acc. no. 2608, H: 9.75" x 8.25", overall 25.5" x 13.25". *Courtesy of the Blair Museum of Lithophanes.*

Right:
One of a pair of oval lithophanes mounted as insect-shaped candle shields that would have been fastened to a wall sconce, 19th century, with filigree work and gemstones, marked PR (sickle) 1681, Blair Museum acc. no. 1741, 3.75" x 2.5", overall 7.75" x 5". *Courtesy of the Blair Museum of Lithophanes.*

Lithophane mounted as a candle shield, *Der Amoretten-Verkauf*, German, originally designed 1837-40, KPM 192 Z, Blair Museum acc. no. 1853, 6" x 4.75", overall candle shield height 18". *Courtesy of the Blair Museum of Lithophanes.*

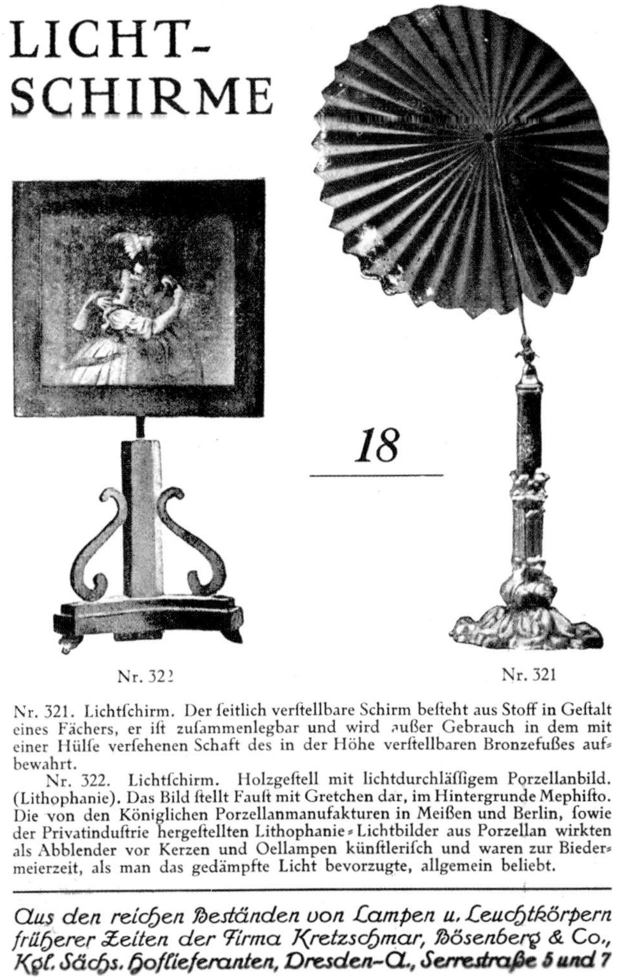

LICHT-
SCHIRME

18

Nr. 322 Nr. 321

Nr. 321. Lichtſchirm. Der ſeitlich verſtellbare Schirm beſteht aus Stoff in Geſtalt eines Fächers, er iſt zuſammenlegbar und wird außer Gebrauch in dem mit einer Hülſe verſehenen Schaft des in der Höhe verſtellbaren Bronzefußes aufbewahrt.

Nr. 322. Lichtſchirm. Holzgeſtell mit lichtdurchläſſigem Porzellanbild. (Lithophanie). Das Bild ſtellt Fauſt mit Gretchen dar, im Hintergrunde Mephiſto. Die von den Königlichen Porzellanmanufakturen in Meißen und Berlin, ſowie der Privatinduſtrie hergeſtellten Lithophanie-Lichtbilder aus Porzellan wirkten als Abblender vor Kerzen und Oellampen künſtleriſch und waren zur Biedermeierzeit, als man das gedämpfte Licht bevorzugte, allgemein beliebt.

Aus den reichen Beständen von Lampen u. Leuchtkörpern früherer Zeiten der Firma Kretzschmar, Bösenberg & Co., Kgl. Sächs. Hoflieferanten, Dresden-A., Serrestraße 5 und 7

German advertisement for *Licht-Schirme* (candle screens), 19th century. *Courtesy of the Archives of the Blair Museum of Lithophanes.*

Other fine examples of lithophanes mounted as candle shields include the KPM 192 Z lithophane titled *Der Amoretten-Verkauf* based on Goethe's text *Wer kauft Liebesgötter?*, another featuring Abélard (Blair acc. no. 1842), a portrait of Zachary Taylor in an extremely elaborate frame with wooden crosses at the top (illustrated in Chapter Five), and one depicting the story of Scheherazade (illustrated in Chapter Five), a similar version of which can be seen at Arolser Schloß. The Blair Museum's *Scheherazade* has a brass stand with a two-part marble base.

An interesting feature of some candle shields is the fact that many of the stands were devised so that the frame holding the lithophane could be raised and lowered with the height of the candle. Others needed to have a candleholder placed behind the shield, while most had the candleholder built right into the frame, which was convenient and efficient.

One collector and authority on lithophanes, Hans Leichter, has written extensively about the powerful relationship between the manufacturers of cast iron candle shield stands and the creators of porcelain lithophanes in Berlin before 1850, during what is now referred to as the Biedermeier Period. He relates in great detail, the original founding of the two companies by the royal family and their success in creating these 19th century treasures.[3] While some collectors are most appreciative of the lithophanes, and somewhat freely exchange one plaque for another in a candle shield stand, other collections focus on the cast iron. The Birmingham Museum of Art in Birmingham, Alabama, is highly regarded for its cast iron collection, and the lithophanes are regarded as secondary to these metal objects. Hans Leichter's discoveries give one a reason to prize both as a harmonious unit.

One of the major 19th century manufacturers of cast iron candle shield stands was E. G. Zimmermann, located in Hanau, Germany. An original 1854 advertisement illustrates that candle shields with "porcelain transparencies" were available. In a 1975 letter to Bernard Rushton, a lithophane researcher, the company noted that they remembered producing cast iron candle shields about 80 years before, but that their factory records were all destroyed in World War II.

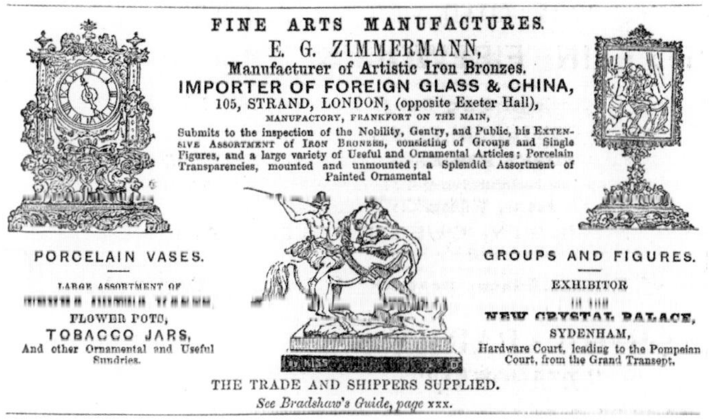

Original advertisement for the E.G. Zimmerman Company, which was published in the London publication *The Art-Journal Advertiser*, November 1854. *Courtesy of the Archives of the Blair Museum of Lithophanes.*

Lithophane triptych mounted as a candle shield, *Mignon*, German, design originally introduced 1850-59, KPM 422 Z, Blair Museum acc. no. 36, 10.5" x 13". *Courtesy of the Blair Museum of Lithophanes.*

Just like the porcelain plaques contained in the candle shield, the candle shields vary tremendously in size. The smallest are miniature, made for doll houses of the 19th century, and measure only 1.75" x 1.25", with the candle shields having an overall height of 4.75". Some examples of larger candle shields include the large KPM 422 Z, 10.5" x 13" triptych titled *Mignon* – an opera in three acts based on Goethe's story *Wilhelm Meister's Lehrjahre*, each panel with a German inscription, or a large Meissen candle shield titled *Juden vor Babylon*, the lithophane measuring 6.625" x 9.75". And then there is every size in between and possibly a few larger. A look at the German *Preis-Courants* indicates that there does not seem to be a standardization of sizes that would facilitate the interchanging of the lithophanes from candle shield to candle shield.

Archival photograph of a grouping of candle shields in the Blair Museum of Lithophanes, including a miniature doll house candle shield. *Courtesy of the Archives of the Blair Museum of Lithophanes.*

Engraving, *The Exiles at Babylon*, engraved by Johnson, the original by Hendemann, published in *Sartains Magazine* in 1851. *Courtesy of the Archives of the Blair Museum of Lithophanes.*

Lithophane, *Juden vor Babylon* (*Jews before Babylon*) mounted as a candle shield, German, 19th century, Meissen 127 (hand incised), Blair Museum acc. no. 1850, lithophane 6.625" x 9.75", frame 18" x 10.75". *Courtesy of the Blair Museum of Lithophanes.*

Oddly enough, as popular as lithophanes were in the 19th century, there are very few representations of them either in paintings or vintage photographs of the era. A black and white image of a painting or drawing containing a lithophane was discovered in the archival materials left behind by either Laurel Blair or Edmond Beroud. It has no notes on it nor is there anything in the records that give a clue to its origin. However it is a mystery more so because of the imagery of a doctor at a woman's bedside, with worried relatives hovering, and a lithophane candle shield in the foreground – depicting the scene referred to as *Seemanns Leben* produced by Plaue (PPM 756, Blair no. 515, 6.5" x 7.875").

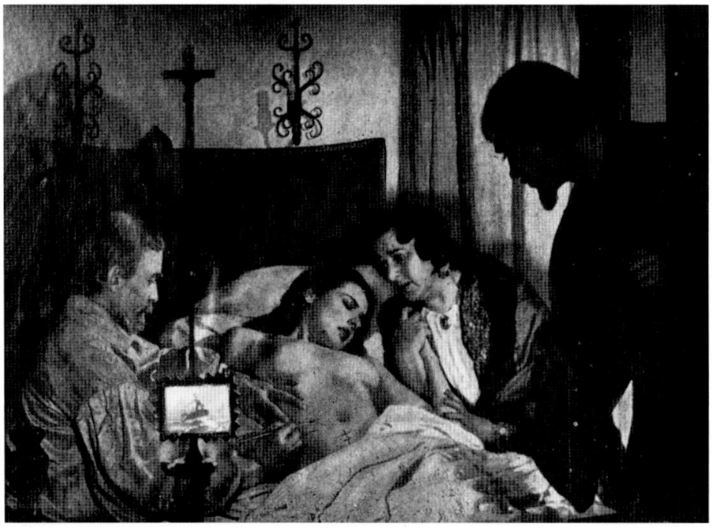

Unknown painting or drawing with lithophane candle shield (*Seemanns Leben*, PPM 756, Blair no. 515, 6.5" x 7.875") featured in foreground. *Courtesy of the Archives of the Blair Museum of Lithophanes.*

Lithophane, *Seemanns Leben*, German, 19th century, PPM 756, Blair Museum acc. no. 515, 6.5" x 7.875". *Courtesy of the Blair Museum of Lithophanes.*

Table Screens and Fire Screens

The table screen or fire screen had a similar function to that of candle shields and hand screens. While some may be confused and think these larger plaques mounted in free-standing framework were fire place screens, it simply is not so. Fireplace screens, which are rare, have cast iron framing and are larger. The cast iron would not melt or burn near the open flames. On the other hand, large plaques, mounted in wooden frames, were not intended to be placed by an open fire, or the framework would have been destroyed. Rather these beautiful objects were used as table screens, much like the Chinese had been using them for centuries – to protect the desk sitter from draughts, or the annoyance of flickering flames. The European version apparently appeared in the middle of the 17th century, and was referred to as a cheval screen, "consisting of a pair of separate trestle legs, each supporting an upright, between which was mounted on sliders a framed panel."[4]

Some of the most spectacular lithophanes in the Blair Museum collection are mounted as table screens. This would include one of the ultimate lithophane plaques, Mount Vesuvius in full eruption over the Bay of Naples at night on August 10, 1832. Only one other lithophane version of this image of Mount Vesuvius is known, which has the incised number "3" corresponding to the KPM *Preis-Courant*. It is mounted in one of the three large oak framed panels salvaged from Woburn Abbey and now in a private collection (illustrated in Chapter Seven). Other smaller versions of Mount Vesuvius are known, including a small Meissen plaque mounted as a candle shield in the Blair Museum collection and a small unmounted plaque produced by the Königliche Porzellan-Manufaktur in the mid-19th century. At first glance the images seem somewhat similar, but the smoke curls upward in the Meissen version and veers to the right in the KPM version.

Lithophane, Mount Vesuvius, mounted as a table screen, German, 19th century, no marks, Blair acc. no. 2101, lithophane 10.625" x 14.75", framed in stained glass and wood, dimensions 17.125" x 18.625". *Courtesy of the Blair Museum of Lithophanes.*

Lithophane, *Vesuv, Landschaft (Mount Vesuvius, landscape)*, mounted as a candle shield, German, 19th century, Meissen 5, Blair acc. no. 1947, 6.375" x 4.75". *Courtesy Blair Museum of Lithophanes.*

Lithophane, *Ausicht des Vesuvs*, German, c. 1828-36, KPM 99 S, Blair Museum acc. no. 150, KPM 99 S, 5.375" x 3.75". *Courtesy of the Blair Museum of Lithophanes.*

There are several other interesting table screens in the Blair Museum collection. One of the most elaborate frames in the entire Blair collection measures 17.75" x 13" overall, and features a 9.5" x 7.25" porcelain version of Correggio's *The Nativity*, mounted in an elaborate Egyptian-style inlaid frame. The lithophane, marked AdT, is from France. The frame is comprised of various colored woods and inlaid mother-of-pearl decorated at the top with what might be interpreted as the symbol of life, and at the bottom, the boat carrying the deceased. It is hard to say which is more distracting, the mesmerizing lithophane or the captivating frame itself. A similar theme, in a table screen format, is a porcelain reproduction of the *Sistine Madonna* by Raphael. The detail in this beautiful porcelain plaque is unbelievable. When backlit, scores of putti are visible in the background, but the viewer's eyes are drawn to the Madonna and Child and then to the two putti at the base of the frame. The frame is exquisite in its attention to detail – as though it was the outside window of a Gothic cathedral with red stained glass medallions.

Lithophane, *The Nativity*, by Correggio, mounted as a table screen, 19th century, French, AdT 425, Blair Museum acc. no. 2611, 9.5" x 7.25", frame 17.75" x 13". *Courtesy of the Blair Museum of Lithophanes.*

Lithophane, *Madonna del Sixto*, (*Sistine Madonna*), by Raphael, mounted as a table screen, German, 19th century, Meissen 83 (hand incised) and 50 (stamped), wooden frame with red stained glass, Blair Museum acc. no. 225, lithophane 11.375" x 9" frame 22" x 13.25". *Courtesy of the Blair Museum of Lithophanes.*

Lithophane, *Faust und Gretchen (Faust and Marguerite)*, 19th century, German, KPM 130, Blair Museum acc. no. 358, lithophane 13" x 11", frame 14" x 12.5". *Courtesy of the Blair Museum of Lithophanes.*

Lithophane portrait of the King of Prussia, Friedrich Wilhelm III in a wooden table screen frame, *Bildnißs Sr. Majestät des Königs Freidrich Wilhelm III*, German, 19th century, KPM 117, Blair Museum acc. no. 1851, 10.75" x 9.625", wooden stand 19" x 13.5". *Courtesy of the Blair Museum of Lithophanes.*

Another large table screen depicts Marguerite and Faust embracing, with Mephistopheles peering through a window in the background. A rather ingenious feature of this particular table screen is the wood screw located at the base that can be used to increase or decrease the width of the holder.

A large 11" x 10" lithophane portrait of the King of Prussia, Friedrich Wilhelm III, was produced by KPM in the 19th century and mounted as a table screen measuring 19" x 13.5". The lithophane image was based on a painting by Ernst Paul Gebauer (1782-1865). This same portrait was reproduced as a lithophane at KPM (no. 100), c. 1838, and an example is currently in a private collection in Germany.

There is only one fireplace screen in the Blair Museum collection (Blair Museum acc. no. 332). It is comprised of a cast iron frame measuring 21.5" x 16.5", with stained and etched glass, and four small unmarked lithophanes (each 2.75" x 2.75") mounted in the corners. There are two identical lithophanes featuring cats and two featuring an old woman.

Complexion Fans or Hand Screens

Complexion fans or hand screens were a clever invention popular in Victorian times, which protected the waxy makeup of both men and women from the threat of meltdown from the heat of the fires, lamps or candles of the time. While no one waved these complexion "fans" through the air, these beautiful and useful devices also protected one's eyes from the light and heat. The porcelain plaque was mounted at the end of a handle, much in the manner that a lithophane is fastened into a candle shield stand. The fashionable person would hold the screen or fan in front of his or her face, literally shielding the face from the heat source. The porcelain was not affected by the heat and neither was the waxy makeup of the bearer. Additionally, with the plaque situated between the person's eyes and the fire, the person with the complexion fan was treated to a splendid view of the image on the porcelain, illuminated by the glow of the embers. It has been noted that the hand screen evolved in the late 18th century "when a face flushed by the fire's heat was not regarded as pretty."[5] While the porcelain lithophane hand screens were often mounted in sturdy metal frames with metal handles, other materials were used to construct hand screens, including wood or papier mâché. The male counterpart to the hand screen has been described as plain and utilitarian, and was "designed to fit into a slot on the back of a chair."[6] To the uninitiated it seems as though complexion fans or hand screens which incorporated lithophanes should be abundant. But if the Blair collection is any gauge, not many of these devices survived the passing of time and the perils of breakage.

There are only three examples of hand screens in the Blair Museum collection. One depicts a young girl testing the water wit h her toes while her friends watch. The lithophane is from the Plaue factory, marked PPM 83. It is comprised of a cast iron frame and a wooden handle. This combination of materials would have resulted in a lighter weight object that would have been less tiring to hold. Another complexion screen in the collection depicts the ascension of Christ and it is framed in brass. The third complexion fan is that of a gentleman recognizable as Francis I, the porcelain plaque probably manufactured by AdT with a wood turned handle and papier-mâché border. These were published in an article in the winter 1990-1991 issue of the *Fan Association of North America Quarterly*, volume IX, no. 3.

Lithophane, *Badende Kinder*, mounted as a complexion fan, 19th century, German, PPM 83, Blair Museum, acc. no. 412, lithophane height 7.625" x 6", with frame and handle 16.5" x 6.25". *Courtesy of the Blair Museum of Lithophanes.*

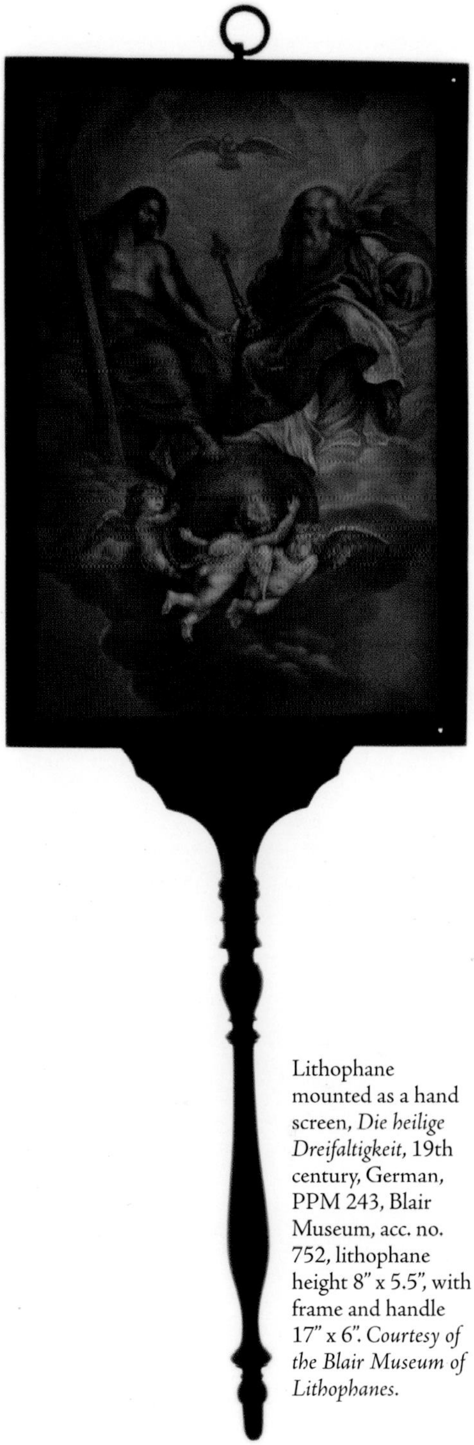

Lithophane mounted as a hand screen, *Die heilige Dreifaltigkeit*, 19th century, German, PPM 243, Blair Museum, acc. no. 752, lithophane height 8" x 5.5", with frame and handle 17" x 6". *Courtesy of the Blair Museum of Lithophanes.*

Lithophane, *Francis I*, mounted as a complexion fan, 19th century, marked 493, Blair Museum, acc. no. 381, lithophane 5.75" x 4", with frame and handle 9.25" x 7.25". *Courtesy of the Blair Museum of Lithophanes.*

A fine pair of complexion fans is in a private collection. Although the fans were bequeathed to this individual, it is not a coincidence that she is a major fan collector, too. Her pieces, mounted in almost Medieval-looking 19th century hand screen frames, are both manufactured by AdT near Paris. The stunning mounts are identical. One lithophane image depicts an interior scene of perhaps a castle or a manor house, a knight in armor is petting the faithful dog at his side, and a veiled, gowned woman stands in a nearby doorway with a young boy behind her clutching her skirt; a female servant is seen peering through the partially opened doorway. A similar lithophane can be seen in the collection of the Blair Museum, acc. no. 851, measuring 3.625" x 2.25" and marked "25." The other complexion fan is also an interior scene and depicts two seated women, with a robed man holding a spindle of yarn, and a child on a stool at their feet. A fence is the backdrop for this genre scene.

Two additional handscreens are illustrated in Chapters Three and Ten, one from a private collection depicting *Jacob and Rebecca* and another from Llanelly, Wales, depicting an angel at night. During the heyday of lithophanes in the mid-19th century there must have been many complexion fans or hand screens in fashionable homes. Today there seem to be less than ten with lithophanes that have survived.

Lithophane mounted as a complexion screen in paper cardboard frame, French, 19th century, AdT, lithophane 3.625" x 2.5", frame 9.625" x 7.5", handle length 8.25". *Courtesy of Sandy Melnikoff.* Photo by Paul Simeone.

Lithophane mounted as a complexion screen in paper cardboard frame, French, 19th century, AdT, lithophane 3.625" x 2.5", frame 9.625" x 7.5", handle length 8.25". *Courtesy of Sandy Melnikoff.* Photo by Paul Simeone.

Erotica

If one examines a survey of worldwide ceramics from early times to contemporary, there are not that many people, places and cultures that have produced what might be viewed as erotica made of ceramic materials. However, the cultures that have produced such objects are not insignificant. The earliest would be the Greeks and Romans, in terms of painted pottery from the Greeks circa 6th century B.C. and the embossed Roman Arretine wares from the 1st century A.D. While the Greeks may have been portraying every day scenes of fertility rituals involving phalluses, and gentle love making among the various or same sexes, the Romans liked sweet love scenes in red gloss ceramic ware. The Peruvian potter also may have been portraying everyday sex life in their extremely explicit terra cotta sculptures of couples that date circa 200-500 A.D. There is an occasional Italian maijolica, tin-glazed earthenware plate with erotic overtones dating from the 16th century as well.

If the Chinese made early ceramic erotica it has not survived. But in the late Qing dynasty, circa the late 1800s, there are many small, pocket-size ceramic sculptures that are playful or even whimsical on the exterior or top, but when opened or viewed from below, anatomically correct images are plainly visible. Once again, whether these ceramic objects from Greece, Rome, Peru, Italy and China were meant to be titillating or merely instructional, is not known.

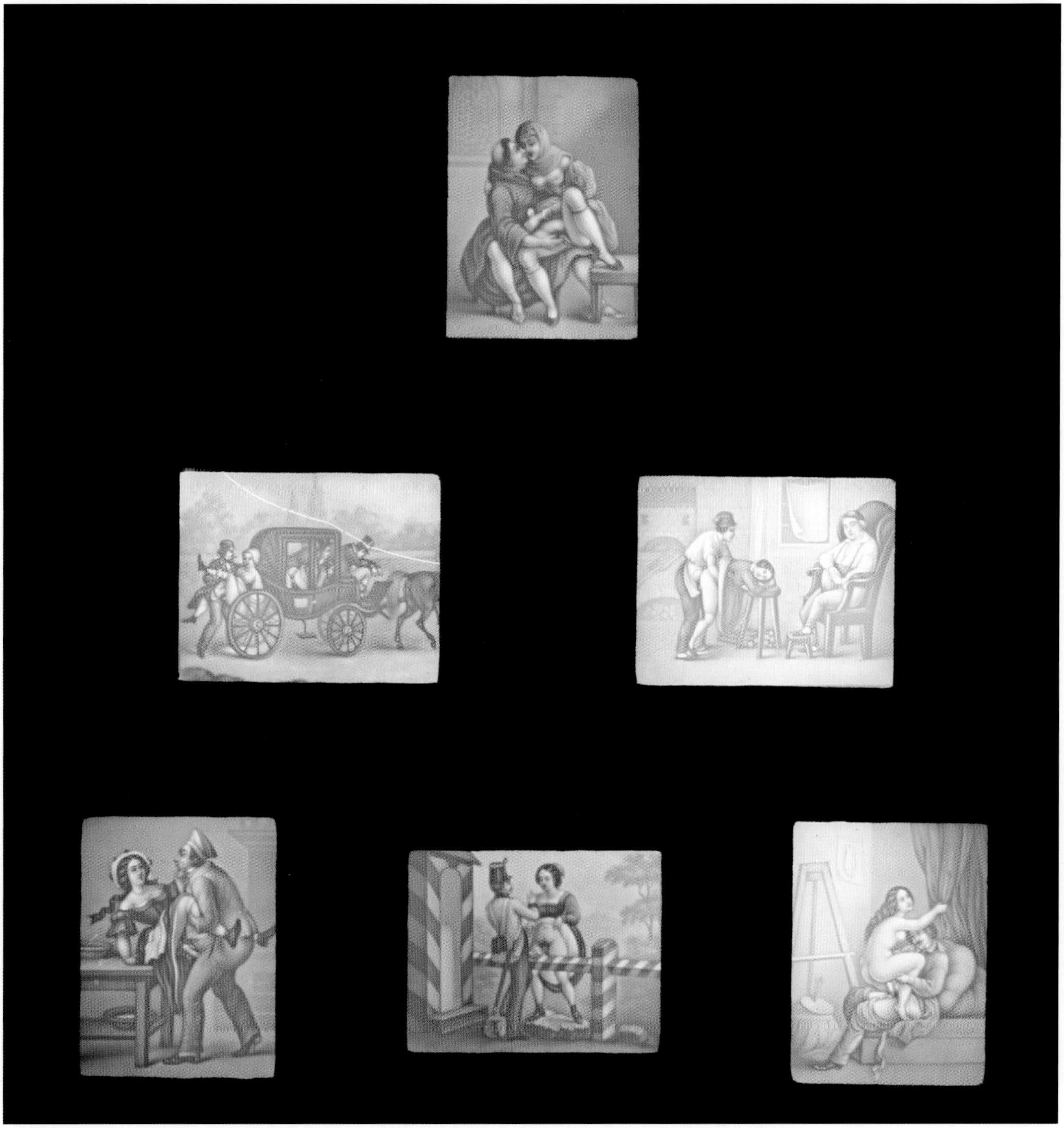

Set of erotic lithophanes mounted behind illuminated false print box, 19th century, German, marks unknown, Blair Museum acc. nos. beginning at top, 2853, 2854, 2855, 2856, 2857, and 2858, lithophanes, each approximately 2.125" x 2.75", overall dimension of box 16" x 14". *Courtesy of the Blair Museum of Lithophanes.*

What is known, is that for all the sense of stereotypical Victorian prudery or conservativeness, there were wonderful small erotic lithophanes produced by unnamed companies in the 19th century. Like many erotic objects, these were small and intimate, able to fit in one's pocket. In fact, in the case of lithophanes, they seem to have been marketed in small boxes or cases for easy transportation, not unlike adult toys arriving in one's mailbox in discreet plain brown wrappers. Another indication that these lithophanous erotic objects were not ready for popular consumption among the masses, was that some were concealed behind false print boxes, only to be viewed when the false print lid was unhinged and lifted to reveal a delightful array of porcelain erotic back lit visions.

Small in all measurable dimensions, most measuring just a few inches at their extreme edge, the erotic lithophanes are large in terms of creativity. Each is a tiny Victorian vignette of man, woman and sometimes, beast, in various Victorian costumes, having graphic sexual encounters. Picture servants, the military, the devout, the artistic, and the occasional donkey and monkey, all involved in not-so-innocent sexual frolicking. Anyone could own these and no doubt many sets were destroyed due to prudish censorship from the time of their inception up to this very day. To destroy these small lithophanes with erotic scenes is such a shame, because they show the costumes and customs of the day, and they simultaneously portray the Victorian sense of humor.

The Blair Museum owns several sets of erotic lithophanes, including the group of six that were mounted, backlit, inside a false framed print box, only to be viewed after unhinging the print frame and lifting the glass. Other examples in the collection were kept in tiny multi-compartmentalized boxes for discreet carrying and viewing. Some of these in the Blair collection are marked with a stamped number such as 10, 14, 18, 30, 33, 34, 35, and some have no mark at all.

The Kinsey Institute for Research in Sex, Gender, and Reproduction in Bloomington, Indiana, has a set of six erotic lithophanes, probably German, measuring 3.75" x 3.125" (Kinsey Institute acc. nos. A402Q A001-A006a-b/ISR 2767-2772a-b). The couples are copulating on a couch, in a dining room, in a carriage, in Elizabethan costumes, and elsewhere. While these date from the 19th century, the Kinsey Institute also owns a set of eight plastic versions with different erotic scenes of couples or *ménage à trois* and even foursomes. The latter were likely created during the 1960s or later. They were acquired in 1985.

Small erotic lithophane featuring a donkey, 19th century, German, Blair Museum uncatalogued, 2.125" x 2.75". *Courtesy of the Blair Museum of Lithophanes.*

In 1951, an antique dealer in Reading, Pennsylvania offered Dr. Beroud seven original "old plaster moulds, to make small lithophanes...they show mens [sic] relations with women, quite interesting...they are for sale at $50.00 for lot... Should be valuable for historical interest."[7] The antiques dealer claimed that the molds had been brought to America by an English potter 75 years earlier. Dr. Beroud sent a check to the dealer and expressed interest, and that might account for the five small plaster molds in the Blair collection. Each one-piece mold is of an odd, irregular form, and has been cracked and repaired.

There are erotic lithophanes in private collections, but in general, the terms private and erotic go together and do not invite announcement. A collection of six in a discreet carrying case were for sale in Versailles via ebay in late January 2007. The starting bid was $1,800 and there were no bids at that price. Other collectors with private collections of erotica, seem to want to keep them just that, private. But there are valid reasons why the collections of lithophane erotica might not be too numerous. This was just the case involving the broken, ceramic fragments excavated near the City Custom House in London and published in 1996. The cache of porcelain pieces turned out to be "imported pornography in the round, seized and smashed by the Customs authorities under legislation introduced in 1857."[8] These include lithophane shards, which, as the author pointed out, "may be the only specific evidence available for just what, in ceramics, was considered too outrageous for Victorian England."[9]

Small plaster one-piece press molds for erotic lithophanes, 19th century, Blair Museum acc. nos. 2859-2863, irregular sizes, approximately 4.25" x 3.25" x 0.75". *Courtesy of the Blair Museum of Lithophanes.*

Miniatures for Dollhouses

Even adults remain fascinated by the miniature lithophane lamps and candle shield plaques created for the Victorian child's dollhouses. Tiny single cast lampshades and candle shields were created along with other miniature items to be treasured by the young 19th century homemaker and her doll friends – and later by generations of collectors. These are some of the most sought after lithophane collectibles. The miniature lampshades are as small as a thimble and the plaques that fit in tiny cast iron candle shields frames are approximately the size of a postage stamp. They are exact replicas of the full-size versions, and just as functional, with places for the candles. The ones in the Blair Museum collection have all been converted to electricity for use in the exhibits.

Miniature lithophanes mounted in dollhouse lamps and candle shields, German, 19th century, beginning left, Blair Museum acc. nos. 164, 165, 166, 162, lithophanes 1.75" x 1.25", overall candle shield height 4.75", overall lamp height 4.25". *Courtesy of the Blair Museum of Lithophanes.*

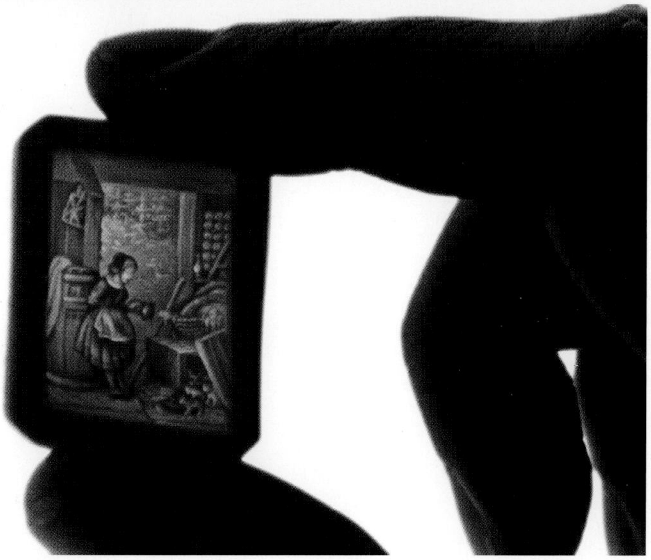

Miniature lithophane plaque in the fingers of Mr. Laurel Blair, founder of the Blair Museum of Lithophanes, c. 1966. *Courtesy of the Archives of the Blair Museum of Lithophanes.*

Some miniatures are unmounted plaques, usually depicting children and their pets. There are also miniature chamber pots that were sold as souvenirs, with tiny lithophanes in the bottoms of the pots. There are even child's versions of tea warmers with four small lithophanes mounted in the base.

Five miniature lithophanes, German, 19th century, Plaue, marked beginning upper left 1005, 1010, PPM 987, 1038, 1008, each 1" x 0.75". *Courtesy of the Blair Museum of Lithophanes.*

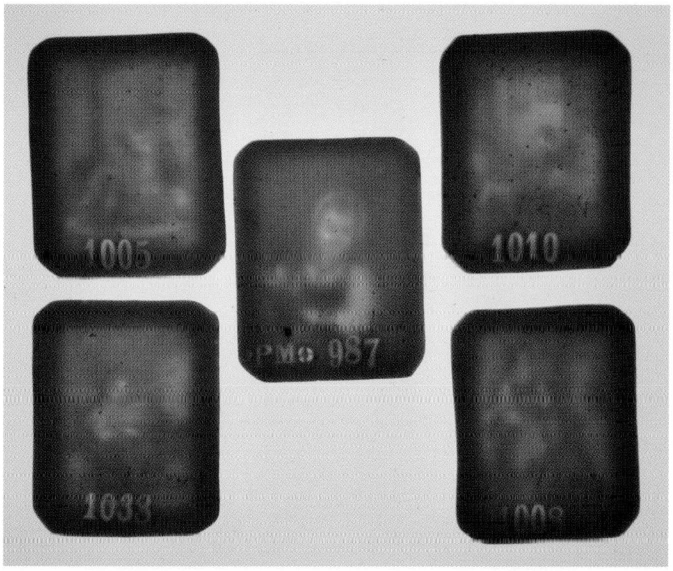

Five miniature lithophanes showing back stamps, German, 19th century, Plaue, marked beginning upper left 1005, 1010, PPM 987, 1038, 1008, each 1" x 0.75". *Courtesy of the Blair Museum of Lithophanes.*

Fairy Lamps

Fairy lamps are candle-burning lamps that are both decorative and functional. The name most closely associated with fairy lamps is that of Samuel Clarke, a British candle maker by trade, and a patent-holder for the devices he invented during the Victorian era to hold his candles. He applied for a series of patents for "improved candles" beginning in 1857, and in 1885 patented his candle cup. His lamps each had a dome and a lamp cup that was usually embossed with his trademark and logo consisting of a fairy holding a wand. This is why the name fairy lamp became attached with these pieces. Other companies imitated Clarke's fairy lamps, even though he granted licenses to other glass and porcelain manufacturers in the United States, the United Kingdom, and Europe. It should be noted that there is an international club devoted to the subject of fairy lamps – both Victorian and contemporary. There is a multitude of information available at www.fairylampclub.com.

The Blair Museum collection has only eight true fairy lamps that incorporate lithophane panels within the design, according to Mr. Blair's notes. There are several that are plentiful and have found their way to many collections of fairy lamp collectors, including the one that the Bob and Pat Ruf *Fairy Lamps* book refers to as *Little Miss Muffet*, depicting a little girl frightened by a frog in her food dish. Others that are less common, include the very obviously Victorian night light in the shape of a Victorian bathing cart, complete with woman's head appearing in the carriage door window.

Two-piece painted porcelain Victorian bathing cart night light with three lithophanes, 19th century, marked P.R. (sickle) and 44, Blair Museum acc. no. 2506, overall height 11.25", top 7" x 3.5" x 4.75". *Courtesy of the Blair Museum of Lithophanes.*

Two-panel lithophanes in the form of a domed lamp, design referred to as *Little Miss Muffet*, 19th century, no mark, Blair Museum acc. no. 278, overall height 4.75", saucer diam. 3.5", dome diam. 4.125". *Courtesy of the Blair Museum of Lithophanes.*

Colored lithophane in the form of a domed lamp, *Fanning the Flames of Love*, with monkey working the bellows, 19th century, no marks, 5.25" x 8". *Courtesy of Graham and Helen Pullen.* Photo by Graham Pullen.

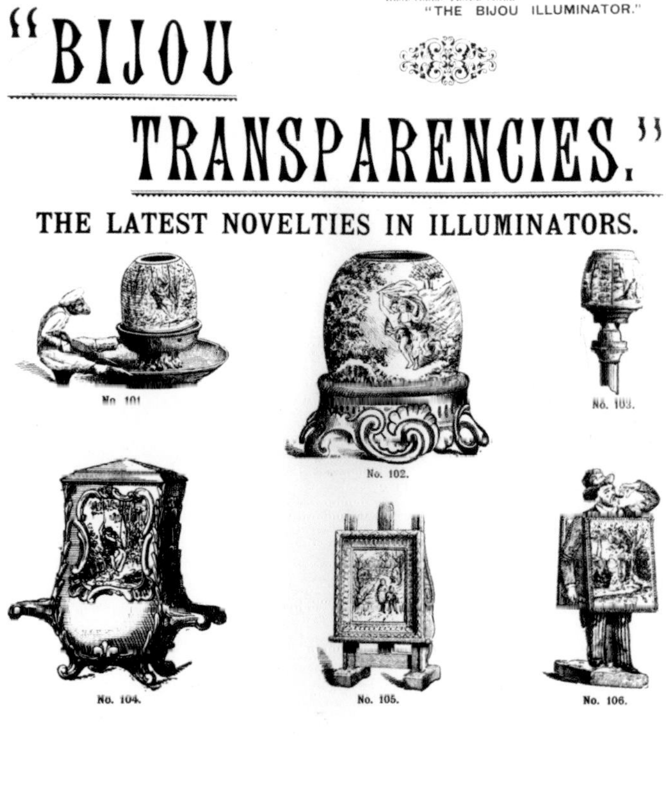

Advertisement for the British importers J. Stembridge & Co., for Bijou Illuminators from 1888. *Courtesy of the Archives of the Blair Museum of Lithophanes.*

An unusual colored domed lithophane lamp mounted on a large saucer with a somewhat eccentric-looking ceramic monkey using a bellows to fan the candle flame of the lamp, is located in a private collection in the United Kingdom. This same unusual piece can be seen in an advertisement for the British importers J. Stembridge & Co. in 1888. Modern day domed lithophane lamps of high quality are being manufactured in France by Bernadaud of Limoges.

Gothic Chapel night light with four lithophane plaques, French, 19th century, marked AdT 216, AdT, AdT 522, and AdT, Blair Museum acc. nos. 686, 687, 688, and 689, overall 11.5" x 10" x 6.5". *Courtesy of the Blair Museum of Lithophanes.*

Night Lights

Night lights in the 19th century would have had multiple uses. While they could have been used for illuminating a small area in order to read, many appear to be more ornamental than practical. One of the most beautiful and unusual night lights in the Blair Museum collection is the Gothic church-shaped night light with four French AdT-marked lithophane panels all with scenes of priests and altars. The stained glass panels along with the religious-themed lithophanes are mesmerizing. This piece was loaned to the J. Paul Getty Museum for the exhibition *Devices of Wonder: From the World in a Box to Images on a Screen,* November 13, 2001 – February 3, 2002.

There are a variety of nightlights that contain lithophanes. A rare type is often referred to as a pastille burner. While it had been a centuries old practice to use aromatic herbs to provide some indoor air freshener, it was in the early 19th century that specially-prepared compounds were compressed into pastilles and burned in ceramic vessels specifically designed for this purpose. These pastille burners were often shaped like little cottages and were manufactured in a number of well-known factories. The pastille would burn slowly and send smoke up the chimney of the container. Grainger, Lee & Co. of Worcester produced these in the early-to-mid-19th century and the lithophane panels frequently depict a sentinel at his post challenging Napoleon and the pastille burner is shaped like a sentry box or in one example, an English castle gatehouse. Another original subject is that of Belisarius. Only a few pieces have survived (see Grainger, Lee & Co. entry in Chapter Three), even fewer are marked with the proper Grainger, Lee & Co. mark, and most have firing cracks or show other kiln firing or construction irregularities.

Two pastille burner night lights, featuring Napoleon and a sentinel at his post and Belisarius, English, 19th century, Grainger, Lee & Co. of Worcester, height 7". *Courtesy Graham and Helen Pullen.* Photo by Graham Pullen.

Veilleuses and Veilleuses Théières

The French term veilleuse (pronounced "vay-euz") has been defined as a ceramic utensil that has several parts, which is used for warming food or beverages, by means of a bowl, cup, or teapot that rests on a hollow pedestal containing a lamp (or godet). Originally the veilleuse was used in the sickroom or for infant care, but after 1800 it became popular for use in the bedroom by a single individual. In German literature the term for these is frequently the French term réchaud. Some of these have lithophane panels as part of the pedestal, and those with this attractive embellishment are eagerly sought by collectors. A veilleuse théière includes a teapot (théière) on the upper portion. These are often described as combination nightlight and tea warmer. Pieces were illustrated in the 19th century as part of a Schierholz (Plaue) *Preis Courant*.

The Blair Museum of Lithophanes has in its possession ten complete veilleuses théières, including the flamboyant gilded version signed by Jacob Petit that is illustrated in Chapter Three. A less exuberant yet beautiful example in the Blair collection is a four-part (base, night light, teapot, lid), unmarked piece with lithophanes on a Gothic cathedral theme.

A page from an undated 19th century Schierholz (Plaue) *Preis-Courant* illustrating various uses for lithophanes, including placement as part of a veilleuse théière. *Courtesy of the Schloßmuseum Arnstadt.*

Lithophanes as part of a four-piece (base, night light, teapot, and lid) veilleuse théière (night light tea warmer with teapot), 19th century, unmarked, overall height 10.25". *Courtesy of the Blair Museum of Lithophanes.*

While some tea warmers are austere in design, others have gilding and bright overglaze enamel decoration. Another unique tea warmer in the Blair Museum collection is of pentagonal form, white porcelain, with five lithophane panels. It is marked "Petit," and thus is French in origin. Its five sides include images of Marguerite and Faust, a scene with soldiers, a seated dancer and a helmeted horseman and is illustrated in Chapter Three.

The Freed collection of porcelain veilleuses théières on exhibition in the Trenton, Tennessee City Hall, claims to be the largest in the world, numbering 525. Within this collection are a very small number of beautiful examples of combination nightlight and tea warmer with teapots on top and illuminated lithophanes beneath. Another substantial collection of veilleuses théières was gathered by the American author Frances Parkinson Keyes (1885-1970). Her collection is now located in her former home in New Orleans, the Beauregard-Keyes House in the Vieux Carré. She was so captivated by veilleuses that she mentioned them in several of her novels. Veilleuse scholar and author Harold Newman, donated his collection to the Wadsworth Atheneum. This collection, the third largest in the world, includes three which have lithophane plaques and are of French origin.

Lithophanes as part of a veilleuse théière with gilding and overglaze red decoration, with three scenes, one depicting a young girl mending a boy's pants, 19th century, incised "25" on base, Blair Museum acc. no. 2503, overall height 12". *Courtesy of the Blair Museum of Lithophanes.*

Lanterns

One of the most beautiful and captivating uses for lithophanes is as panels in hanging lamps or lanterns. These lithophane lanterns, once fueled by oil and other sources, are relatively scarce. The Blair Museum has twelve hanging lanterns, some with four sides, and several with five or six sides.

Hanging lantern with four lithophane panels, each colored, German, 19th century, marked PPM 260, PPM 261, PPM 262, PPM 263, Blair Museum acc. nos. 1909, 1910, 1911, 1912, lithophanes each 6" x 4.75", each side 12" x 7.5", overall lantern height 23". *Courtesy of the Blair Museum of Lithophanes.*

If one tours the Blair Museum there is a hanging lantern in the foyer and another in the lobby (with five others in a hallway). The docent presenting the tour invariably notes that the lantern in the lobby, manufactured in Germany in the 19th century with four colored Plaue lithophane panels, is illustrated in the *Encyclopaedia Britannica*. Mr. Blair was proud of the fact that he was instrumental in persuading them to include an entry under the heading "lithophanes." It was a victory in disseminating knowledge about the subject. In October, 1964, the editorial assistant at *Encyclopaedia Britannica* had written in response to Mr. Blair's inquiry about the absence of a "lithophane" entry, "Thank you for your letter of August 8. We hope you will pardon our unseemly delay in responding. We have checked various articles that would be related to lithophanes, in the present set and manuscripts we have for future editions, and have found no reference to lithophanes. However, you may be sure that when lithophanes are once again a matter of general interest and importance, Britannica will include information on the subject."[10] By at least 1974, there was an entry in the encyclopaedia, and every year since. Legend has it that Mr. Blair wrote the entry, but in fact he corrected the errors in their entry and provided information for their reference. In a letter written in 1976, Mr. Blair contradicts this, saying, "...I allowed the *Encyclopaedia Britannica* to write the article in their new edition and furnished the pictures, but there were errors in the article. I had no part in the writing or editing of the article."[11]

In a September 1952 advertisement in *The Spinning Wheel*, the owner of the hanging lantern, Dr. Beroud, touted the unique features of this piece. He described the cast iron frame decorated with four lion heads and the four lithophanes colored in delicate pastel shadings. But above all he emphasized that each side of the lantern was a complete unit. When removed from the lantern each side becomes a separate panel that can be hung in a window. Each lithophane panel is surrounded by four bull's eyes in blue blown glass.

There are other types of lanterns in the Blair Museum collection, including some that might fall into the category of night lights or fairy lamps because of their form or function. A small four-sided metal lantern with three lithophane panels is notable for its beautiful rendition of Wilhelm Kaulbach's illustration from Goethe's *Reineke Fuchs* text published circa 1847. On the front of one of the lithophane panels, hidden by the frame, is the identification of the scene.

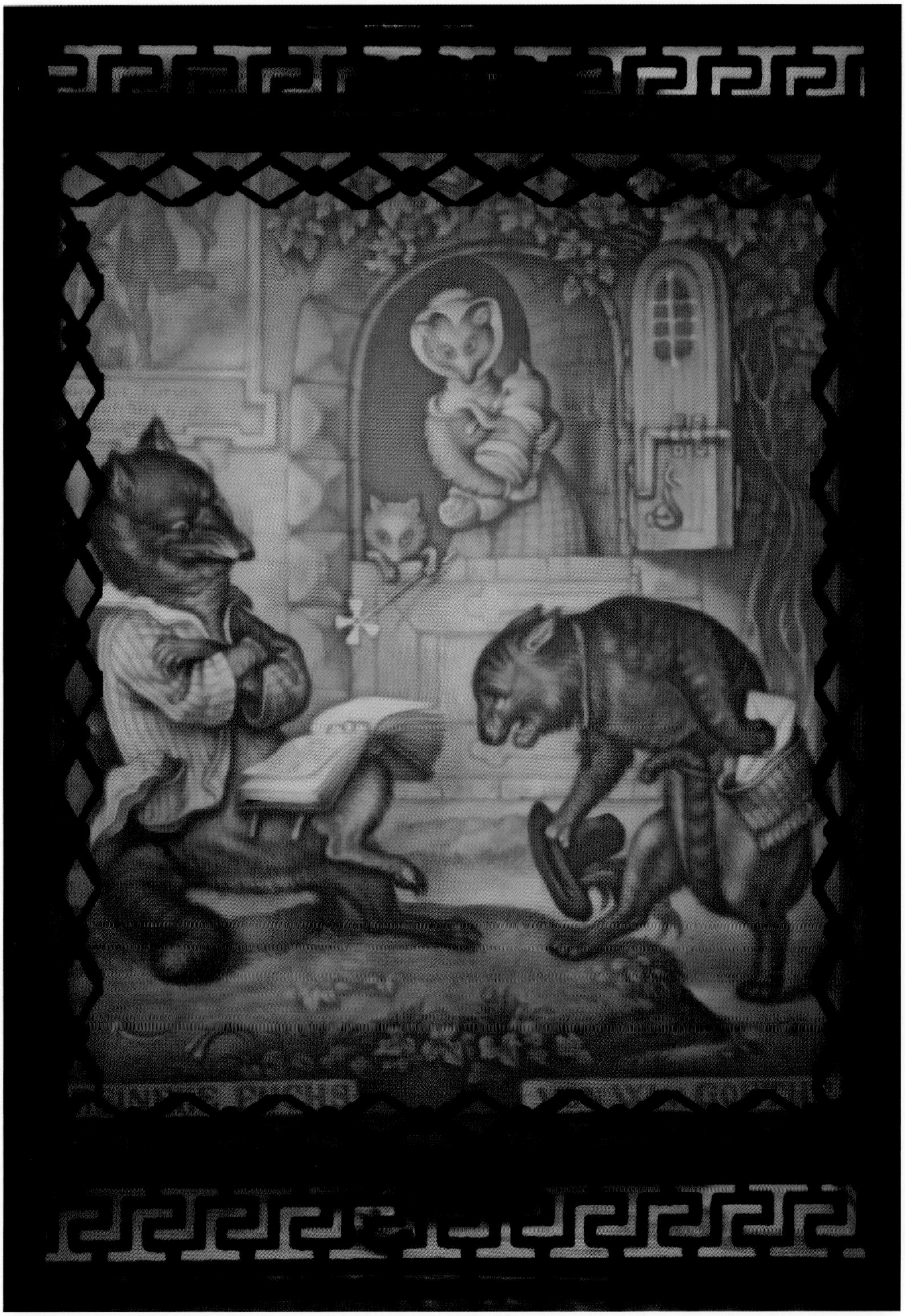

Front view of a four-sided lantern with three lithophane panels, including the Kaulbach illustration for Goethe's *Reineke Fuchs* (*Reinecke der Fuchs B*), German, 19th century, PPM 367, Blair Museum acc. no. 1923, lithophane 5.75" x 4.75", overall lantern 9.25" x 6.375". *Courtesy of the Blair Museum of Lithophanes.*

Engraving, *Reineke Fuchs*, by Rudolf Rahn after the illustration by Wilhelm Kaulbach. *Courtesy of the Archives of the Blair Museum of Lithophanes.*

Page from the 1857 Stuttgart edition of Wolfgang von Goethe's *Reineke Fuchs*, illustrated by Wilhelm von Kaulbach. Published by J.G. Cotta'ßcher.

32 Dritter Gesang. III. 15—22.

Möget ihr Segen von Gott nach meinem Wunsche genießen.
Aber er dachte nicht so in seinem verräthrischen Herzen;
Neue Tücke sann er sich aus, er wollte den Boten
Wieder geschändet nach Hofe senden. Er nannte den Kater
Immer seinen Neffen, und sagte: Neffe, was setzt man
Euch für Speise nur vor? Man schläft gesättiget besser;
Einmal bin ich der Wirth, wir gingen dann morgen am Tage
Beide nach Hofe: so dünkt es mich gut. Von meinen Verwandten

Lamp Shades

One of the earliest uses for the flat or curved plaques, were as panels in lamp shades, be it 4, 5, 6 or even 8-sided. There would be a metal frame or armature where these plaques would slide in and out of brackets. Some of these are the easily recognizable trapezoid shape that instantly identifies their usage. Trapezoid plaques are abundant in collections.

Trapezoid lithophane lampshade plaque, Rolandseck on Rhine River, colored, German, 19th century, marked PPM 1171, Blair Museum acc. no. 137, 5.25" x 4.5" x 8.5". *Courtesy of the Blair Museum of Lithophanes.*

Exhibit of Mr. Blair's collection when the museum was located in his home in Toledo's Old West End, featuring several rows of trapezoid shade panels and lampshades. *Courtesy of the Archives of the Blair Museum of Lithophanes.*

The largest single cast lithophane lampshade in the world was made at the Lithophanie Francaise factory about 1875 and is located in the Blair Museum. It measures 17.75" in diameter and is 10.25" in height. Dr. Beroud apparently offered this for sale for $250 in July 1952 as can be seen in an advertisement. Perhaps it was intended as a ruse to attract interested collectors? An identical shade (without the base) is located in a private collection in Germany.

There are many fanciful lithophane lampshades in the Blair Museum collection, with manufacturers in Germany, England, France and Belgium. Wedgwood examples are illustrated in Chapter Three, as are others. Certain companies are best-known for their lithophane lampshades, primarily those marked "Lithophanie Francaise."

Originally Victorian era lithophane lampshades were in use with oil fluid lamps but were later also incorporated into gaslight fixtures. Some were even used with Gone-with-the-Wind type lamps.

The largest single cast lithophane lamp shade, circa 1875, marked Lithophanie Francaise, Blair Museum acc. no. 1878, diam. 17.75" height 10.25", overall height 24.75". *Courtesy of the Blair Museum of Lithophanes.*

ONLY KNOWN EXAMPLE IN THIS SIZE
of a unique Lithophane Porcelain shade. Height 12". Bottom dia. 17½". 4 beautifully blended Hunting Scenes. Ormolu base, electrified.
Priced at $250 complete.
Stamp please with inquiry.
ART STUDIO — EDMOND BEROUD
Collector-Importer of Lithophanes
7205 Sellers Ave., Upper Darby, Pa.

Advertisement placed by Dr. Beroud in the July 1952 issue of *The Spinning Wheel*. *Courtesy of the Archives of the Blair Museum of Lithophanes.*

On rare occasions, there has been a merging of two functional forms into one successful piece. Such is the case with the veilleuse théière that was converted to a beautiful lamp, complete with a single cast lithophane shade. Veilleuses have been the subject of several books by Harold Newman, who used a few Blair Museum examples to illustrate his text. One of the "personages" type veilleuses théières described in the Newman books is owned by the Blair Museum. The subject is the figure of a nun holding a teacup, the Blair example in white porcelain left undecorated, with the upper portion of the nun's body forming the teapot, and the skirt portion containing space for the warmer and/or light. There is no lithophane incorporated into this basic, popular form. In the case of the Blair piece, it has been converted to a lamp, with a marvelous single cast lithophane shade decorated, appropriately enough, with angels and religious figures. The teapot spout is located on the headdress, her arm is the handle, and the lid has become the opening where the lamp stem is attached. These figures were mold-made and an unknown number of examples were produced.

Single cast lithophane lampshade with four religious scenes, part of veilleuse théière personage of a nun, 19th century, no mark, Blair Museum acc. no. 1793, shade height 8" diam. 12", overall lamp height 20.25". *Courtesy of the Blair Museum of Lithophanes.*

Steins, Cups and Mugs

What is the one undeniable fact about what happens when one magically discovers a lithophane at the bottom of a tea cup, saki cup, coffee cup, or beer stein? After the surprise and delight phases have concluded, one is destined to pick up every cup and stein seen in an antique shop, just to check and see if it contains a precious lithophane in the bottom.

Just imagine ones surprise upon draining a beer stein at a festival and discovering a depiction of an angry *hausfrau*, awaiting the return of her drunken spouse, portrayed in the bottom of the drinking vessel. 19th and early 20th century German beer steins with lithophane bottoms are called Mettlachs, named so after the Villery and Boch Co. of Mettlach, Germany. Some had images in the bottom of scenes of Munich or other famous cities and others had scenes from the opera *Faust*. Some commemorated military service and they are frequently referred to as regimentals or reservists. Their lithophanes reflect a patriotic and humorous tone. Austria and Bohemia also produced such military-related steins with lithophanes. It is likely that the nude figures discovered as lithophanes in the bottoms of some steins indicate that the stein is of later than 19th century origin, perhaps even after World War II.

The beer steins that were destined for lithophane bottoms would have begun as basic cylinders with the circular lithophane added in the green unfired stage and then the two would fuse together in the kiln firing.

Stein in the form of a nun, exterior view, with lithophane bottom depicting a Wilhelm Kaulbach illustration from Goethe's *Reineke Fuchs*, German, 19th century, no mark, Blair Museum acc. no. 323, 6.625" x 3.75" x 5.25". *Courtesy of the Blair Museum of Lithophanes.*

Many lithophane stein images are related to the theme of the stein exterior, such as the biking image in the bottom of the "L.A.W. Bicycle" stein ("L.A.W." stands for the Legion of American Wheels). Another example is the World's Greatest Fair mug from St. Louis, with a lithophane of the Palace of Liberal Arts (Blair Museum acc. no. 194).

Stein in the form of a nun, interior view of lithophane bottom depicting a Wilhelm Kaulbach illustration from Goethe's *Reineke Fuchs*, German, 19th century, no mark, Blair Museum acc. no. 323, 6.625" x 3.75" x 5.25". *Courtesy of the Blair Museum of Lithophanes.*

Page from the 1857 Stuttgart edition of Wolfgang von Goethe's *Reineke Fuchs*, illustrated by Wilhelm von Kaulbach. Published by J.G. Cotta'ßcher.

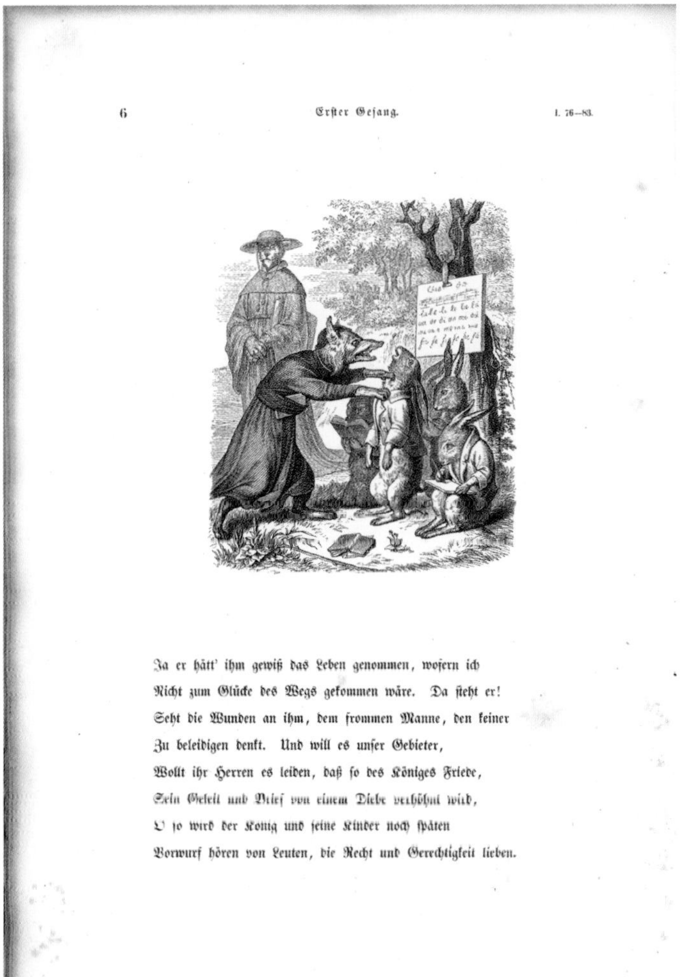

6 Erster Gesang. I. 76–83.

Ja er hätt' ihm gewiß das Leben genommen, wofern ich
Nicht zum Glücke des Wegs gekommen wäre. Da steht er!
Seht die Wunden an ihm, dem frommen Manne, den keiner
Zu beleidigen denkt. Und will es unser Gebieter,
Wollt ihr Herren es leiden, daß so des Königes Friede,
Sein Geleit und Brief von einem Diebe verhöhnt wird,
O so wird der König und seine Kinder noch späten
Vorwurf hören von Leuten, die Recht und Gerechtigkeit lieben.

Stein in the shape of a 19th century bicycle, exterior view, with a lithophane depicting a bicycle excursion on the interior bottom, German, 19th century, no mark, Blair Museum acc. no. 719, 4.5" x 3.25" x 3.25". *Courtesy of the Blair Museum of Lithophanes.*

Lithophane featured in the bottom of a stein in the shape of a 19th century bicycle, the lithophane depicting a bicycle excursion, German, 19th century, no mark, Blair Museum acc. no. 719, 4.5" x 3.25" x 3.25". *Courtesy of the Blair Museum of Lithophanes.*

Not surprisingly, steins with lithophane bottoms, frequently depict on the interior a drinking-related scene — a vat room in a monastery (Blair Museum acc. no. 1920), a king drinking a mug of beer (Blair Museum acc. no. 2595), or a couple in a tavern (Blair Museum acc. no. 2594). There are even dribble steins or puzzle mugs with lithophane interiors – nudes, of course. Colored lithophanes at the bottoms of steins are considered rare.

Information about beer steins and their lithophanes is abundant, with prolific illustrations in the several encyclopedic books by Eugene Manusov concerning character steins, which were mainly produced between 1850 and 1930. The crosshatch (#) mark that appears as a factory backstamp on some steins and nightlights is an underglaze cobalt mark that the German manufacturer Plaue used.

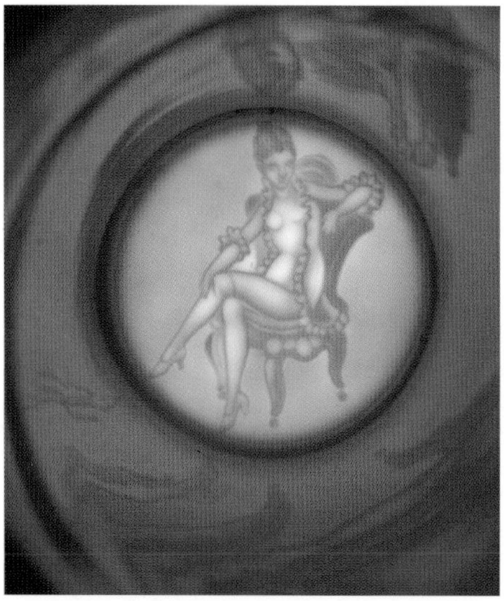

Lithophane depicting a nude woman, in the bottom of a dribble beer stein, German, no mark, Blair Museum acc. no. 810, height 7.5" diam. 4.5". *Courtesy of the Blair Museum of Lithophanes.*

The multitude of tea cups with geisha images is covered in Chapter Three, under the heading "Japan." These may be the best known of all forms of lithophanes, prolific in sales on the Internet, even though they do not date from Victorian times.

Teacup with a geisha lithophane in the bottom, Japan, 20th century, Blair Museum acc. no. 1757, height 2" diam. 3.75". *Courtesy of the Blair Museum of Lithophanes.*

In a related usage, lithophanes occasionally were found in the bottoms of shaving mugs or cups and commemorative cups not intended for practical use, but rather to be kept as souvenirs of a visit to a special location. The Blair collection includes cups and plates commemorating the coronation of King Edward in 1902, paired with Alexandra, of course. The collection additionally includes cups that were souvenirs from places such as Milwaukee (Blair Museum acc. no. 171), Manchester (Blair Museum acc. no. 246), and the King's house in Dresden (Blair Museum acc. no. 251).

A few drinkers will be delighted to find a rare lithophane of a Kewpie image visible as they drain their cups. These were manufactured in Germany by Royal Bayreuth c. 1915. Although it was an international craze, for the most part, porcelain Kewpie dolls and related items were made in Germany early in the 20th century.

Plate paired with matching mugs with interior lithophanes depicting the coronation of King Edward in 1902 and Queen Alexandra, early 20th century, no mark, Blair Museum acc. nos. 243 A,B and 249 A,B, cup height 2.625". *Courtesy of the Blair Museum of Lithophanes.*

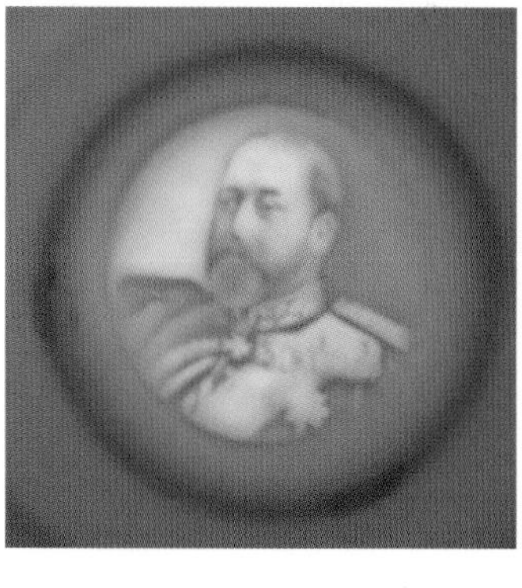

Interior lithophane from commemorative cup and plate set, honoring the coronation of King Edward in 1902, early 20th century, no mark, Blair Museum acc. no. 243, cup height 2.625". *Courtesy of the Blair Museum of Lithophanes.*

Interior lithophane from commemorative cup and plate set, honoring the coronation of King Edward in 1902, depiction of his wife Alexandra, early 20th century, no mark, Blair Museum acc. no. 249, cup height 2.625". *Courtesy of the Blair Museum of Lithophanes.*

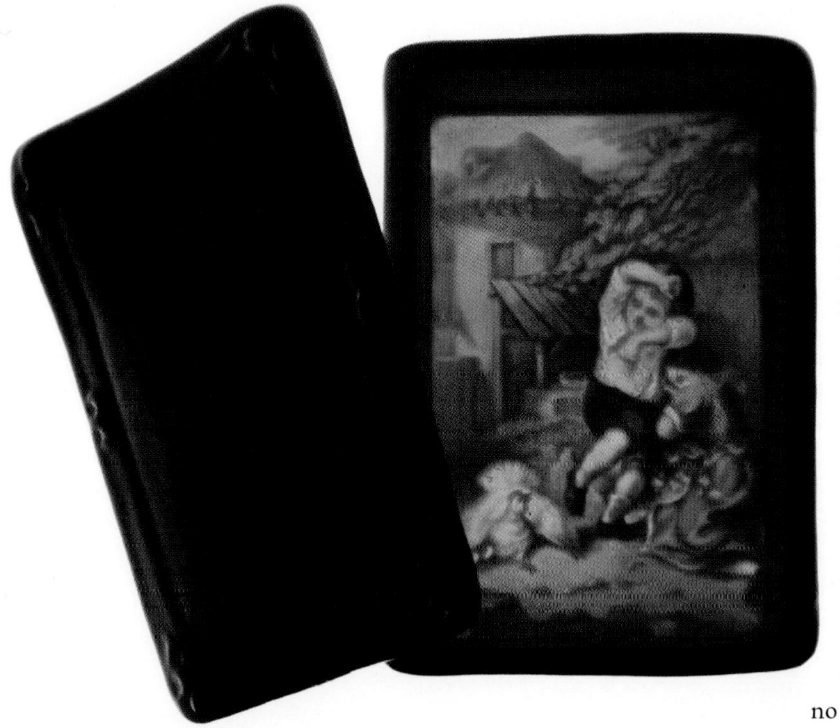

Match box, two-piece, with interior lithophane, probably German, 19th century, no mark, Blair Museum acc. no. 190, 3" x 2". *Courtesy of the Blair Museum of Lithophanes.*

Match Boxes

If having a tea party in Victorian times, using one's very own single-serving teapot, reading a book by the gentle light from the night light/tea warmer component of a veilleuse théière, was a magical experience, then how does the experience of using a match box with a lithophane in the bottom compare? One might think that the boxes were impractical, because the match box would have to be empty to appreciate the lithophane and one would have to hold a match or other illuminating device below the small panel to appreciate its beauty. They were definitely meant to hold matches, as some are labeled "matches" on the cover in gilded script. They are lovely to behold (empty and backlit), and they do a fine job of holding matches, but they do not serve both functions simultaneously. The lids are separate from the boxes, some with painted designs on the covers.

There are nine match boxes in the Blair collection, with lithophane scenes such as that of an angel playing a harp, a mother sewing while seated on a couch with her daughter watching, a young man playing a violin with a dog nearby, and other various scenes with children and dogs.

Novelty Items

There are a number of lithophane-related items that defy categorization and therefore fall under the label of "novelty items." These include a pair of binoculars with a pair of nudes viewable through the eye pieces (Blair Museum acc. no. 205), a loving cup (three handles) with a portrait of Robert Burns in the interior (Blair Museum acc. no. 250), and a nut cup with a lithophane of Admiral Dewey (Blair Museum acc. no. 373) and another with a portrait of Admiral Schley (Blair Museum acc. no. 374).

Plates

The circular plates, all about dessert plate size, were clearly not meant to be used to serve cake or pie, but were rather commemorative in nature. All appear to be recent, with images of John F. Kennedy, Albert Schweitzer, Albert Einstein, Bela Bartok, and Michelangelo, and most were made by Herend Porcelain in Hungary. Others, with no marks of the manufacturer, depict special places such as George Washington's birthplace, a music hall in Berlin, Cologne Cathedral, or the Brandenburg Gate. Some have holes drilled in the base to facilitate hanging in a window.

Vases

Kirsten Pliquet (Rather) noted in her 1982 Master's Thesis, *Lithophanien der KPM-Manufaktur Berlin (1828-1865)* that vases with lithophanes were rare.[12] The examples she cites were produced at Meissen and were of the classical krater form. There are no examples of vases with lithophanes in the Blair Museum collection.

Plate with scalloped rim and lithophane interior featuring the Cologne Cathedral, *Dom zu Koeln*, in relief on plate front, probably German, unknown date, no mark, Blair Museum acc. no. 737, diam. 6.75". Courtesy of the Blair Museum of Lithophanes.

Chapter Seven
Lithophanes *in situ*

Most lithophanes that one encounters in the 21st century are plaques that have been incorporated into lamp shades, candle shields, veilleuses, or other objects created in the 19th century. Collectors, dealers, and the occasional museum will display them as such, or even as individual "light catchers" hanging in windows.

What one seldom witnesses is the lithophane in its originally intended environment – part of a home. Usually the lithophane formed the central feature of a window or door, surrounded by colorful stained glass. In the United States there are many homes dating from the 19th century, yet seeing a lithophane *in situ* is a rare occurrence. There could be several reasons for this, including the fragile nature of these porcelain plaques and a constantly changing aesthetic from the 19th century to the present.

Perhaps it is the rarity of the occurrence that makes it even more exciting to locate a lithophane or many lithophanes where they were originally installed during the 19th century. Nearly equally exciting is finding the uncommon 19th century black and white photograph of a lithophane in use. Several interesting examples of both instances can be cited.

Despite the popularity of lithophanes in Europe and in the United States, it was not common to have lithophanes mounted as more-or-less permanent architectural fixtures in doors and windows. These special instances would have involved the lithophanes being selected as a feature prior to the design or renovation of a home, rather than as an added afterthought. It may also indicate that the American homeowner had traveled to Europe prior to the home construction and fell in love with lithophanes and decided to incorporate them into their new home as an aesthetic statement. All of the known homes that had or still have original lithophanes installed are rather magnificent in their size, style and flavor. There are several documented cases in the United States that one can use to illustrate this point.

Because, for the most part, the United States was settled from East to West, the older homes are located in the Eastern or Northeastern region of the U.S. And it stands to reason that the more older homes that there are, the greater the odds that special features such as lithophanes would be included. Examples can be cited in New York, Connecticut, New Hampshire, and Washington, D.C.

President's House, Gallaudet University

House One is the name given to the President's house at Gallaudet University in Washington, D.C. This fine, c. 1867-68 Victorian Gothic home was constructed as the residence of Gallaudet University's founding president, Edward Miner Gallaudet. It is interesting to note that the plans for the grounds and future buildings surrounding the President's home were created by landscape architects Olmstead, Vaux, and Company, the same designers who created the plans for both Central Park in New York City and the Capitol grounds in Washington, D.C. The 20 room President's home itself, was designed by Frederick Withers, an associate of Olmstead and Vaux.

What would be more appropriate adornment for this Victorian home than the popular Victorian art form known as lithophanes? President Gallaudet had traveled to Europe several times prior to 1867, when he is known to have stayed there for several months. It is probable that during one of these trips he purchased two large, stunning lithophanes for installation in the President's new home.

The President's house at Gallaudet University, shown c. 1930. *Courtesy of the Archives at Gallaudet University.*

Original, linen blueprints show the location of the two 11.5" x 9.5" lithophanes, situated in the windows on either side of the doorway, between the Hallway and Plant Room (Sun Room). The lithophanes would have been visible to those entering the Plant Room via the Hallway or to guests walking by the Plant Room enroute to the Dining Room. A vintage photograph shows the lithophanes as they were originally installed, with plants visible through the open door, inside the room, and stunning stained glass measuring 4' x 2' surrounding each lithophane. Tall vases with floral motifs are nearby.

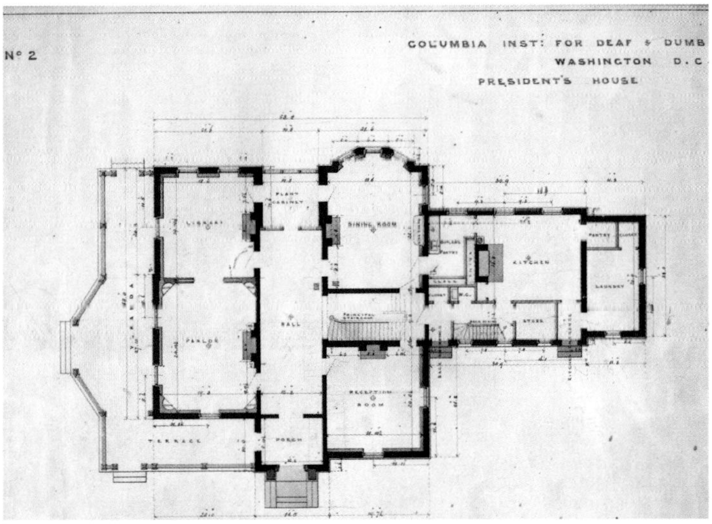

Original blueprints for President's home, Gallaudet University, showing the location of the lithophanes in the sunroom doorway. *Courtesy of the Archives at Gallaudet University.*

Original installation of two lithophanes in President's home at Gallaudet University, shown c. 1870. *Courtesy of the Archives at Gallaudet University.*

Both lithophanes are marked with backstamps that identify the manufacturer as the Königliche Porzellan Manufaktur or Royal Porcelain Manufactory of Berlin, the original designs date from the 1840s. The lithophane to the left of the Plant Room entranceway is marked KPM 258 Z. According to the KPM *Preis-Courant* list, the piece is titled *Das Wunder der Rose* or *The Miracle of the Rose.*

The woman in the lithophane wears a crown and robe and an angel in the form of a cross hovers above her head. A bearded man holds one edge of her apron, which reveals abundant roses within. It depicts Saint Elizabeth and the Count of Thuringia. Elizabeth (1207-31) was a princess in Hungary. At the age of fourteen she married Count Ludwig who died a mere six years later. Afterwards Elizabeth entered the Franciscan Order and devoted the rest of her life to caring for the sick and needy in the city of Marburg until she died. She had rather a devout following in Germany, and is frequently depicted in the art there. Her crown symbolizes her royal birth, while the roses are her most common attribute.

The Blair Museum of Lithophanes owns at least five versions of *Das Wunder der Rose*, none of which is the KPM 258 Z version. Two of the plaques are unmarked, Blair Museum acc. no. 655 measuring 9.875" x 8", and Blair Museum acc. no. 1301, measuring 5" x 4.25". Two others bear the German mark PPM 272 (Blair Museum acc. no. 657) and PPM 185 (Blair Museum acc. no. 1665) and measure 8.5" x 6.75" and 5" x 4.125" respectively. A fifth example is part of a fairy lamp, and it bears the KPM 292 backstamp (Blair Museum acc. no. 1582), and measures 6" x 4.75".

Lithophane, *Das Wunder der Rose*, German, design first introduced 1840-41, KPM 258 Z, 12" x 9.5". *Courtesy of the Archives at Gallaudet University.*

Lithophane, *Familienglück (nach Meierheim)*, design first introduced 1848-50, German, KPM 388 Z, 12" x 9.5". *Courtesy of the Archives at Gallaudet University.*

The other lithophane installed in the entranceway to the Plant Room in the President's home at Gallaudet University bears the backstamp KPM 388 Z and is listed on the *Preis-Courant* with the title *Familienglück (nach Meierheim)* or *The Happy Family*. This charming lithophane features children playing with a cat and kittens while adults look on. This was also published as an engraving, based on the painting by Friedrich Eduard Meyerheim from 1847, but was titled *The Happy Family* or *Häusliches Glück*. One can see from both the Gallaudet University and Blair Museum examples, that the lithophane includes only the central portion of this print.

The two lithophanes were removed during a major renovation of House One in 1983 or 1984. They were carefully transferred to the Archives at Gallaudet University for safekeeping.

Engraving, *The Happy Family* or *Hausliches Glück,* engraved by A.H. Payne, based on an original painting in 1847 by Friedrich Eduard Meyerheim (1808-1879), published by A.H. Payne, Dresden and Leipzig. Note the KPM 388 Z lithophane only includes the central portion of the print. *Courtesy of the Archives, Blair Museum of Lithophanes.*

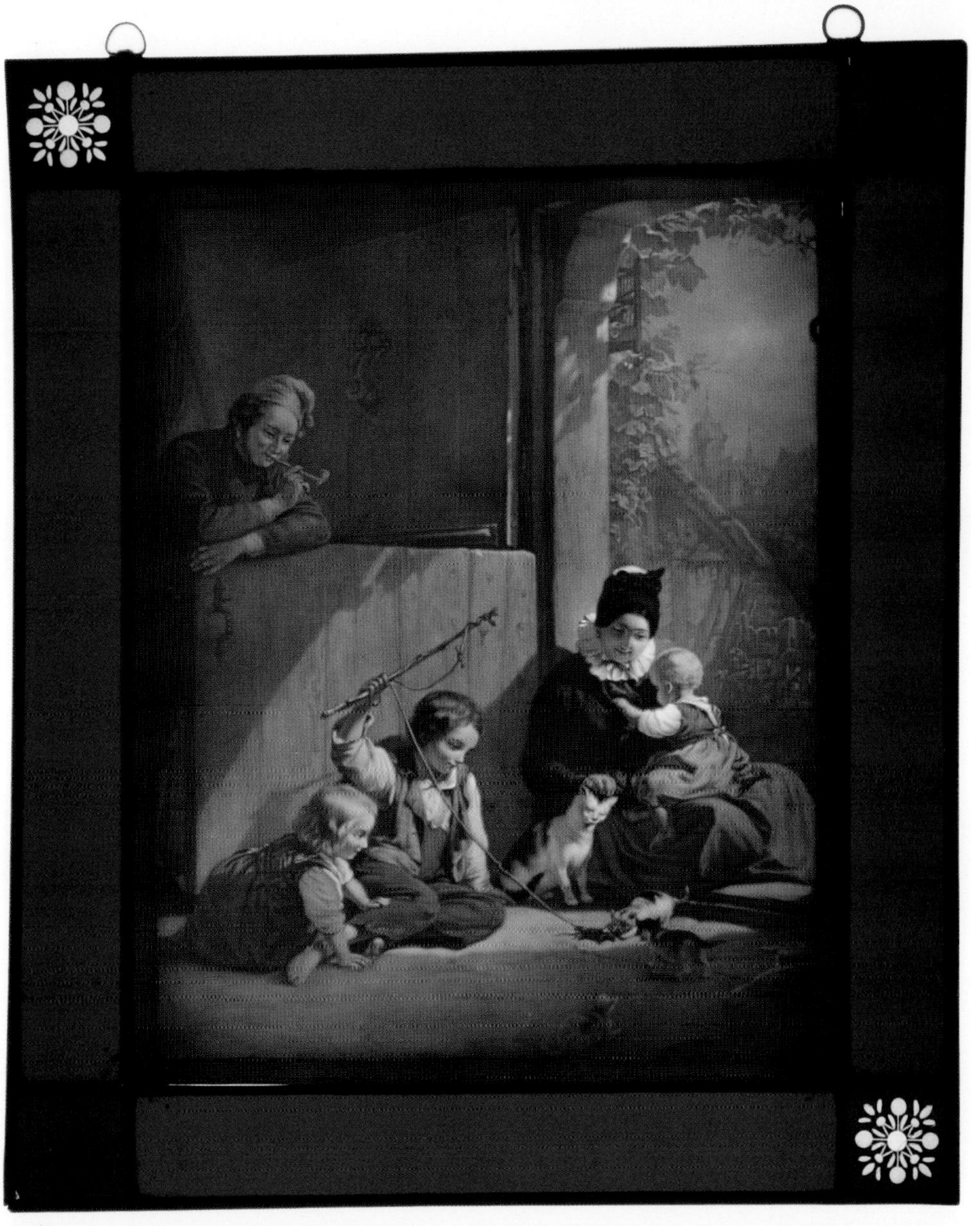

Lithophane, *Familienglück (nach Meierheim),* German, KPM 388, design first introduced 1848-50, Blair Museum acc. no. 224, 12.125" x 9.75". *Courtesy of the Blair Museum of Lithophanes.*

The Glen Iris Inn, Letchworth State Park

Nearly a decade before Edward Miner Gallaudet traveled to Europe and purchased his two Berlin lithophanes, another person with a vision traveled to Europe and purchased at least twelve lithophanes that were subsequently installed in his home in Upstate New York. William Pryor Letchworth has been described as "a Buffalo industrialist, a Quaker, an intellectual, a humanitarian and above all, a visionary. He was also an historian, conservationist, social reformer, philanthropist and environmentalist."[1]

In 1858, while looking for a country retreat, he took the train to the region of New York near the Genesee River Gorge that had once been a lumbering area, and fell in love with the region's valley, river and waterfalls. At that time he saw an old homestead that had been constructed in two phases in 1830 and 1850. He acquired the property in 1859. The original homestead was on 190 acres, which grew to more than 1,000 before it was donated to the State of New York.[2] He named the estate Glen Iris, connecting the beauty of the landscape with Iris, the goddess with "the cloak of many colors, trailing across the sky in a rainbow curve."[3] It is interesting to note that the Genesee Falls in Rochester, New York, are depicted in lithophanes produced in Europe about this same time.

In 1880, alterations were made to the Glen Iris estate by Buffalo architect Alexander F. Oakey. At that time the interior was "completely rearranged, detailed and finished with the most up-to-date aesthetic detailing and appointments."[4] There were rare albumen photographs, oil paintings by regional artists, and lithophanes. It is published that twelve of these are "remaining throughout the Inn,"[5] indicating that there originally may have been more. It is known that he purchased the lithophanes during an 1857 European tour. This trip was prior to his first encounter with what would become his country estate and therefore the lithophanes were purchased with the idea that they would be installed in his home, but the site had not yet been identified.

The Glen Iris Inn, Letchworth State Park, Castile, New York, with *in situ* lithophanes from the 19th century.
Courtesy of Letchworth State Park.

A comparison of the present locations of the twelve remaining lithophanes, with several undated postcards, indicates that at least four were moved among various upstairs windows, and two were moved downstairs to a parlor area. The most breathtaking installation is original with the 1880 renovation – eight lithophanes, mounted with four on either side of the main entranceway to the Glen Iris. All are surrounded by stunning red, green, blue, yellow, white, and purple stained glass. Most are German and marked with BPM backstamps, several are broken, and most have had white paint applied to the flat back portion of the lithophane. Two are colored with delicate pigments that have been made permanent by a second firing in the kiln.

View from interior downstairs hallway facing the entrance, the Glen Iris Inn, showing eight 19th century lithophanes, *in situ*. *Courtesy of Letchworth State Park.*

THE LITHOPHANES

Upper right side of the doorway:
BPM 564 two girls with a pigeon
two children outdoors (backstamp painted and not visible)
PPM 118 *Dom zu Köln*
PPM 481 *Geigenspieler* (*Violinist*)

Upper left:
BPM 540 *Priest and Acolyte*
BPM 592 *Die Loreley*
Coblenz (backstamp covered by lead framing)
BPM 574 two women in kitchen
boy in front of large fireplace (color)

In the downstairs parlor:
BPM 515 lady in elegant costume
KPM 467 B *Bacharach am Rhein*

Upstairs:
cupid sharpening his arrow
child with puppies and dog
(both installed in upstairs window so backstamps are not accessible)

An interesting comparison can be made between the BPM 540 version of *The Priest and the Acolyte* in the entranceway at the Glen Iris Inn, the original colored engraving, and the KPM 263 G example in the Blair Museum collection.

Engraving, colored, *The Priest and the Acolyte. Courtesy of Archives Blair Museum of Lithophanes.*

Lithophane, *The Priest and the Acolyte*, German, 19th century, BPM 540, with stained glass framing, Glen Iris Inn entranceway, 5.75" x 3.75". *Courtesy of Letchworth State Park.*

Lithophane, *Der Meßsner und der Chorknabe, nach Daege*, German, KPM 263 G, design first introduced 1842-46, Blair Museum acc. no. 483, 13" x 10", stained glass 16" x 13.25". *Courtesy of the Blair Museum of Lithophanes.*

Every lithophane has a story, though the origins or inspirations of some lithophanes have yet to be discovered. In the lithophane window panels surrounding the doorway of the Glen Iris Inn, is a lithophane depicting a violinist shown in an arched window. This scene is also found in museum and private collections. At first glance, one wonders whether it is a portrait of a particular person or just a lyrical rendering of a romantic violinist. A book written by A. Görling, B. Meyer, and A. Woltmann, titled *Art Treasures of Germany, A Collection of the Most Important Pictures of the Galleries of Dresden, Cassel, Brunswick, Berlin, Munich and Vienna, with Portraits of the Most Celebrated Masters and Explanatory and Biographical Notices*, published in Boston, circa 1880, solves the mystery of the origins of this and several other popular lithophanes. The lithophane was inspired by an engraving by W. French, titled *G. Dow*, after a painting by Gerard Dow. The volume recounts the story of Gerard Dow, as written by the subject himself in an essay "The Minuet." It is a fascinating story that takes place in Leiden, in Dow's atelier. Dow (also spelled Dou or Douw) was a painter (Dutch 1613-1675) of some lofty reputation who has been compared with Rembrandt and Teniers. In fact he worked in the studio of Rembrandt from 1628 to 1631. His paintings may be found in the permanent collections of the Rijksmuseum, The Hague, the Louvre and the Metropolitan Museum of Art. In addition to his skills as an engraver and painter, he was also a gifted violinist. To make a long story shorter, one of his two painting pupils, Franz van Mieris, was hoping to convince Dow's wife Brigitta to run away with him on the very day of Brigitta and Gerard's wedding anniversary. That evening, just as Mieris was in the act of tempting Brigitta to escape with him, Dow strode to the open window, violin in hand, and proceeded to play a melancholy tune, followed by the minuet to which he and his wife had happily danced on their wedding day. It will come as no surprise that Brigitta decided at that very instant that she loved only her husband Gerard and they lived happily ever after. She later confessed to him how the violin melody that he played in the arched window that evening had recaptured her heart and afterwards he prized the violin even more because it had "regained for him his choicest treasure."[6]

The lithophanes remaining in the windows at the Glen Iris allow a visitor in the 21st century to appreciate how the installation of lithophanes would have embellished the grand homes of the late 19th century Victorian period. It is a rare reminder of a different aesthetic in an era not that long ago.

Today the Glen Iris is known as the Glen Iris Inn, a favorite dining and overnight destination nestled among the beauty of Letchworth State Park, which now includes more than 15,000 acres, including the 1,000 donated by William Pryor Letchworth in 1907.

Lithophane, *Geigenspieler*, German, 19th century, PPM 481, with stained glass framing, Glen Iris Inn, 6.25" x 5.25". *Courtesy of Letchworth State Park.*

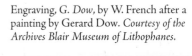

Engraving, *G. Dow*, by W. French after a painting by Gerard Dow. *Courtesy of the Archives Blair Museum of Lithophanes.*

Lithophane, colored, *G. Dow*, German, 19th century, BPM 578, Blair Museum acc. no. 9, 5.25" x 3.875". *Courtesy of the Blair Museum of Lithophanes.*

Surry House, Surry, New Hampshire

New Hampshire has many charming villages nestled in rolling hills, each with a fascinating history. The village of Surry is no exception. Surry is home to nearly 680 people and was named in honor of Sir Charles Howard, Earl of Surrey, Duke of Norfolk and hereditary Earl Marshall of England. The population hasn't changed dramatically since the first census of 448 residents was recorded in 1790. The county of Surrey in England became known for its manufacture of surreys, or horse drawn pleasure carriages, that were first introduced into the United States in 1872. The village in New Hampshire was settled in 1764 and incorporated in 1769 from parts of Gilsum and Westmoreland. Surry Mountain lies east of the village and there precious amounts of mica, copper, lead, silver and gold were mined. Otherwise the region has always been a prime agricultural resource.

This village is where Surry House was built in 1865 and where one finds a most magical lithophane depicting Mount Vesuvius mounted above the fireplace mantel. The present owners believe that this is an original feature of the house. Now lit by a light bulb, legend has it that the previous owner of the house (it is now a bed & breakfast) lived in the house for twenty years and never could figure out how to access changing the light bulb – and apparently they never had to. One has to wonder if this house was among the first to be lit by electricity around the time of the Civil War, or whether the fireplace fire itself lit this marvelous lithophane. This rare lithophane appears to be one of a pair, each complementing the other, the other being located in a private collection, originally from Woburn Abbey. The Woburn Abbey lithophanes will be discussed in more detail later.

Opposite page:
Surry House interior view with Mount Vesuvius lithophane installed above fireplace mantel. *Courtesy Mary Anne Bonafair and Eileen Duffy, Surry House Bed and Breakfast.* Photo by Mark Corliss.

Lithophane, *Mount Vesuvius,* mounted as part of one of three framed panels originally from Woburn Abbey, design first introduced 1828-1836, German, KPM 34, approximately 16.5" x 16". *Courtesy of Andy Cook.*

Lithophane, *Mount Vesuvius,* 19th century, mark not accessible, 19" x 18". *Courtesy of Mary Anne Bonafair and Eileen Duffy, Surry House Bed and Breakfast.* Photo by Mark Corliss.

Armsmear, Hartford, Connecticut

An early 20th century renovation of the Samuel Colt home, Armsmear, in Hartford, Connecticut, effectively removed the opportunity for one to view *in situ* the more than 100 lithophanes originally inset into the windows. However, photographs taken between 1857 and the 1861 remodeling, show lithophane usage at its most extravagant level. It has been written that Samuel Colt, best known for his invention of his revolver, probably first saw lithophanes at the 1851 Great Exhibition at the Crystal Palace in London, where his revolvers were also displayed.[7] While in Berlin in 1855 he purchased at least one hundred lithophanes that were subsequently mounted in the windows of his home in Hartford.[8] He chose particular themes for each area of the home, including religious themes and fables for the nursery, humor for the billiard room, inspirational for his own upstairs bedroom, and portraits and scenic views for other spaces such as his wife's private rooms.[9]

What is most interesting about the story of Samuel Colt (1814-1862) and lithophanes is that while he was in Berlin in 1855, he also ordered his own lithophane portrait to be created after a photograph by P. Graff of Berlin.[10] This oval porcelain plaque, with the KPM (Königliche Porzellan Manufaktur) backstamp, scepter and number "460" is 7" x 5.75".[11] One hundred and eleven of Colt's closest friends and associates appear to have been destined to receive his lithophane portrait as a gift.[12] While his cousin's lithophane portrait was apparently produced in a more limited edition for family members, this phenomenon raises the question of how many lithophane portraits were honoring the sitter and how many were vanity pieces made in the fashion of the day to be sent to admirers.

Many of the lithophanes that were subsequently removed from the doors and windows of Armsmear are now in the collection of the Wadsworth Atheneum, due to the bequest of Colt's widow.

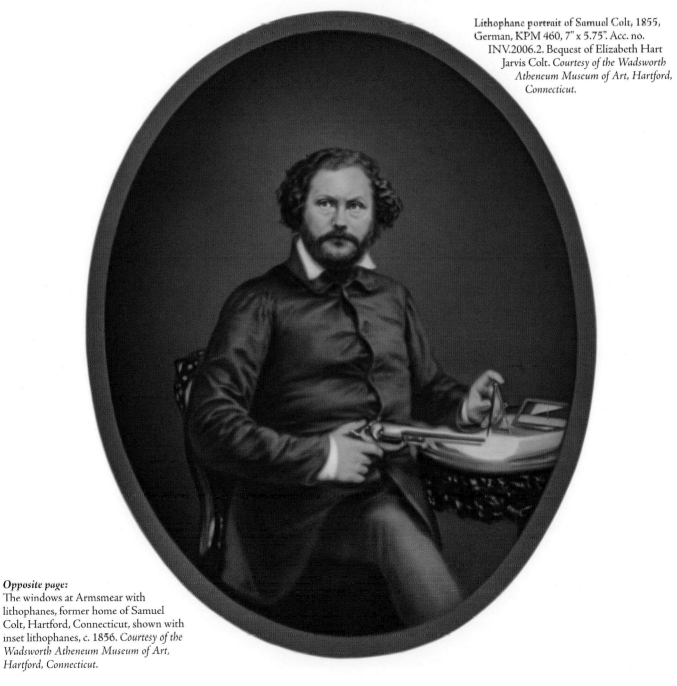

Lithophane portrait of Samuel Colt, 1855, German, KPM 460, 7" x 5.75". Acc. no. INV.2006.2. Bequest of Elizabeth Hart Jarvis Colt. *Courtesy of the Wadsworth Atheneum Museum of Art, Hartford, Connecticut.*

Opposite page:
The windows at Armsmear with lithophanes, former home of Samuel Colt, Hartford, Connecticut, shown with inset lithophanes, c. 1856. *Courtesy of the Wadsworth Atheneum Museum of Art, Hartford, Connecticut.*

Campbell House, St. Louis Missouri. *Courtesy of Campbell House Museum, St. Louis, Missouri.*

Historic photograph, c. 1885, showing lithophane globe lamp, *in situ*. *Courtesy of Campbell House Museum, St. Louis, Missouri.*

Campbell House Museum, St. Louis, Missouri

Another method for documenting historic lithophanes that remain in original 19th century homes is via vintage black and white photographs. There is a very rare and beautiful lithophane globe shade, still on its original lamp base, which is located in Campbell House in St. Louis, Missouri. This differs from the previously cited examples of lithophanes *in situ* due to the fact that it was not an original inset architectural feature, but rather can be documented by mid-19th century photographs which show the lamp in the Master Bedroom.

This lamp has been located on the same table in this magnificent historic home since at least 1885 when the photographs were taken. According to Museum records, the "Campbell ledgers," there was a shopping trip to Philadelphia in June 1855, where a number of purchases were made from a lighting manufacturer, Cornelius and Baker. The Museum therefore attributes this lamp to this source even though they were not likely the manufacturer of this particular lamp. Speculation could also be made that the lamp was purchased during an 11-month tour of Europe in 1867, though it bears strong resemblance to at least one other globular lamp, now in the collection of the Blair Museum of Lithophanes, that bears a similar number and letter backstamp and is additionally marked "G.A.S. Philad." (see illustration under G.A.S. entry, Chapter Three). This would imply that both were manufactured in Philadelphia, but it is more likely that both were manufactured by Meissen in Germany, with one marked with an American retailer's insignia.

Detail of lithophane globe lamp, 19th century. German, Meissen, 2626, Z 72, 75, height 7.875", diam. 6.75". *Courtesy of Campbell House Museum, St. Louis, Missouri.*

The lampshade measures a height of 7.875" and the diameter is 6.75" and has two backstamps on the decorative panels featuring a snake approaching a bird and its nest with eggs among scrolling acanthus. Each repetitive decorative panel is located between the three genre scenes, two of mothers with children and the third depicting children picking flowers. On the rim of the shade base is "2626," and "Z 72" and "75" are at the tops of two of the decorative panels. The numbers on the globe refer to Meissen manufacture. The base for the shade is comprised of bronze, marble and white metal and originally would have been a gas-burning lamp (now converted to electricity). On this base one finds a standing figure of a warrior with a sword, helmet and mailed armor, and a brass column supporting the lithophane lampshade.

The house was built in 1851 and it was the long-time home of Robert Campbell, a fur trader and entrepreneur.[13] The Campbell family lived in the house from 1854 to 1938. The house is now a museum, founded in 1943, and since 1999 it has been completely restored to its former Victorian splendor of the 1880s. Ninety per cent of the home's original furnishings were saved, and this has made the home a rare opportunity to see the Victorian era *in situ*. The meticulous renovation of the home was based on the same rare 1880s photographs that verified the lithophane lampshade placement in its original setting.

Detail of lithophane globe lamp, 19th century, German, Meissen, 2626, Z 72, 75, height 7.875", diam. 6.75". *Courtesy of Campbell House Museum, St. Louis, Missouri.*

Detail of lithophane globe lamp, 19th century, German, Meissen, 2626, Z 72, 75, height 7.875", diam. 6.75". *Courtesy of Campbell House Museum, St. Louis, Missouri.*

Woburn Abbey, United Kingdom

While lithophanes are considered a European art form of the Victorian era, they were clearly popular in the United States and incorporated into the lives of many. The extant examples of 19th century lithophanes remaining *in situ* are rare, but they appear no less rare in Europe. Some attribute this to the wars that occurred on European soil and the damage to commercial buildings, churches, and homes. Once again, similar to that in America, a change in aesthetic disposition may have caused the lithophanes that were architecturally set in windows and doors to be systematically removed during subsequent renovations and remodeling. There remain some interesting examples worth citing.

There exists an example of lithophanes that have been removed from their original location, yet due to the retention of their monumental framed mountings, they retain the freshness and power that they must have had during their glory days in Victorian England. Three oak frames measuring 84" tall by 42.5" wide originally contained 175 lithophane panels organized within brass grids. These oak panels were sold to a private collector during a 2004 Christie's auction. They had likely been removed from their original location in Woburn Abbey during the demolition of the decaying East Wing circa 1949-50. These framed panels were salvaged and remained in storage for another fifty years.

The history of the Woburn Abbey site is of interest as it dates to 1145 when Hugh de Bolebec founded a Cisterian Abbey at Woburn, which exists today in the region known as Bedfordshire. While the Abbey suffered first from poverty, then treasonous monks, rumored ghosts of at least one Abbot haunting, later neglect, and at least one visit from Queen Elizabeth, it remains today one of the great stately treasure houses of England. In 1547, King Edward VI had granted the monastery to Sir John Russell, the first Earl of Bedford. Woburn Abbey thus became home to the Duke and Duchess of Bedford and their family. It is here that important events took place and significant art collections were amassed. At least one of the later Dukes by inheritance was apparently opposed to modernization which may have led to the general decay and dry rot found in the East Wing where the lithophane panels were originally located. It is a pity that apparently no photographic records exist of that Wing of Woburn Abbey, now demolished.

Four hundred years after the monastery was presented by the King to Sir John Russell, tragedy and the accompanying estate taxes forced the 1955-era Duke and Duchess of Bedford to open up part of Woburn Abbey as a tourist attraction. Today guests can visit a nearby Safari Park and visit the beautiful objects that were collected and remain as part of this treasure house. While today's visitors can hold their weddings, receptions, dinners, seminars and corporate events at Woburn Abbey and can see paintings by Van Dyke; English, Japanese, German and French porcelain; sculpture and more; the three framed lithophane panels are preserved elsewhere.

Framed panel with lithophanes, 84" x 42.5", originally inset in Woburn Abbey, 19th century, German, various marks and sizes. *Courtesy of Andy Cook.*

The three framed wooden panels with their translucent porcelain pictures, have miraculously survived more-or-less intact for more than 170 years. It is believed that they were purchased in Germany by Major-General Lord Sir George William Russell (1790-1846) while he was in the British diplomatic service.[14] His duties included British Envoy to Stuttgart (Württemberg) from 1834 to 1835 and then to Berlin (Prussia) from 1835 to 1841.[15] Both of these locations would have provided the perfect opportunity to see the lithophanes made by the outstanding manufacturers of the 19th century. Not coincidentally, all of the lithophanes in the Woburn panels are German, and appear to date no later than the 1830s. The German manufacturers include Meissen in Dresden and the Königliche Porzellan Manufaktur in Berlin, with some lithophanes unclearly marked "GM-" which are believed to have been produced at the Henneberg factory in Gotha.[16]

Section from Woburn Abbey panel, featuring large lithophane of Mount Vesuvius, 19th century, German, (KPM) 3, 15" x 10.5". *Courtesy of Andy Cook.*

There are many shapes and sizes included in the lithophanes installed in the Woburn panels and they are equally diverse in subject matter, chronicling many significant historical events in Europe, as well as displaying portraiture, copies of religious paintings, scenes of cities and churches, illustrations from popular literature, and genre scenes. One example of a religious subject is Correggio's *Holy Night*, a Meissen lithophane measuring 9.5" x 7.25". Peter Hess was the original artist of the painting titled *Cossack Raid* on which the 8" square Meissen lithophane from Woburn Abbey was based.

Section from Woburn Abbey panel, featuring *Cossack Raid*, 19th century, Meissen, 8" square. *Courtesy of Andy Cook.*

Section from Woburn Abbey panel, featuring Correggio's *Holy Night*, 19th century, Meissen 101, 9.5" x 7.25". *Courtesy of Andy Cook.*

Arolser Schloß, Arolsen, Germany

There are European sites with 19th century lithophanes still in their original placement in windows. The best of these might be Arolser Schloß (or Chateau), located in Arolser, Germany. While the major Baroque portion of Arolser Schloß was constructed in the 1700s (it had begun as a monastery circa 1526-30), a significant feature was added to the residence during the second half of the 19th century. At that time, four magnificent windows were installed with lithophane groupings, each set featuring up to fourteen lithophanes mounted in spectacular stained glass. It is significant that the stained glass surrounding the lithophanes dates earlier, from the early 19th century.[17]

Postcard image of Arolser Schloß, c. 1918. *Courtesy of William J. Walker, Jr.*

Originally there were forty-eight German lithophanes installed in the windows, of which forty-two still remain. Twenty-seven of these were manufactured at the porcelain factory at Plaue-on-Havel located in Thuringia, including three marked PMP that were added during a subsequent restoration. Fifteen were produced at the Meissen factory in Dresden, Germany. One Meissen lithophane illustrates the story of *Scheherazade*, in translucent porcelain. Other Arolser Schloß lithophanes are based on famous paintings, religious topics, historical events, portraits, genre scenes, and inspiration from literature. Shakespeare's classical characters of Romeo and Juliet each have their own lithophane, produced at Plaue (PPM 213 and PPM 214, respectively). Representing more contemporary literature are two lithophane examples featuring Paul and Virginia, from the popular novel, *Paul et Virginia*, of the 18th century by Bernardin De Saint-Pierre. Published in 1788, this romantic fictional story with an exotic flavor, embraces the concept that happiness consists of living within the dictates of nature and virtue. It was a bestseller for half a century.

A painting by the artist Georg Friedrich Kersting (1785-1847), now at the Düsseldorf Museum of Art was reproduced as a lithophane at Arolser Schloß. Titled *Kinder am Weingeleite*, it features two children in a window by a grape vine. It was produced at Meissen, but this same lithophane was also produced at Königliche Porzellan Manufaktur in Berlin (KPM 140 G) and later at Llanelly (South Wales Pottery). The engraving by W.E. Tucker of the same subject, titled *Sour Grapes* was published in 1851 in *Godey's Lady's Book* (see illustrations Chapter Five).

There are numerous genre scenes depicted in these stunning windows, children with bunnies and puppies, and some representing humor. A favorite is *Der Geniestreich*, featuring a pupil drawing a caricature of his teacher, not realizing that the teacher is right behind him (see illustration Chapter Eight). This lithophane title is a play on words – and can be dually interpreted as a "stroke of genius" or a "genial prank." The only historical theme featured at Arolser Schloß is one commemorating the Battle of Lutzen in 1632. While the owners of the Arolser Schloß are recorded, it is not known who decorated the various rooms or who chose to add the lithophanes in the second half of the 19th century. No matter who elected to add this feature to the residence, they truly reflect the aesthetics of the times.

Lithophanes in windows at Arolser Schloß, mid-19th century. *Courtesy of the Building Management of the State of Hesse.*

Lithophane window, designed by Károly Csapvári Csapek (1904-1976), Church of St. Eustace, located Herend, Hungary, Herend Porcelain, 1934, 92" x 49", and consists of 54 pieces. *Courtesy of the Church of St. Eustace.*

Church of St. Eustace, Herend, Hungary

There is still another lithophane masterpiece *in situ* that is worth the price of an airfare or train ticket to Hungary. The company that created this *tour de force* is Herend Porcelain, which is explored in detail in Chapter Three. While Herend had created a few rare lithophanes in the 19th century, no company in either the 19th or 20th century has duplicated the magnificence of this church window which can still be viewed by appointment at the Roman Catholic Church of St. Eustace (Szent Euszták in Hungarian). It is located in the village of Herend, in northwest Hungary. The Church itself has its origins in the 18th century, but the porcelain window was designed by Károly Csapvári Csapek (1904-1976) in 1934. The subject of the window is St. Elizabeth of Hungary, the daughter of King Andrew II. She was known as the protector of the poor. The lithophane window measures 98.5 inches high and 59 inches wide, and consists of 54 pieces. The individual pieces are framed in lead and covered outside by glass and wire. There are inscriptions in the corners in two triangles. One is inscribed, "Herend Porcelain Company Year 1934 K. Csapvar design," and the second, "Herend Porcelain Company Year 1839 Through Work to Honor," accompanied by the company logo of the crown.

The original window installed in the church was damaged during World War II, so in 1947 they used an identical window, made at the same time, to replace the badly damaged parts. The original window was placed in the south wall of the sanctuary, but during the church renovation in 1975, the window was placed in the south side of the nave for better visibility.[18]

Entally Estate, Tasmania

There are several other opportunities to see lithophanes *in situ*. If one travels to the town of Hadspen, Tasmania, there are three large German KPM lithophanes located in this remote location within the library of a colonial house called the Entally Estate.

The Swiss Cottage, Osborne House, Isle of Wight

On another island far removed from Tasmania, is Osborne House on the Isle of Wight in the United Kingdom. It originally had two lithophanes, now in storage, that were placed in the windows of the Swiss Cottage on the estate. Osborne House was built by Queen Victoria and Prince Albert in 1848. The nearby Swiss Cottage, built in 1854, was constructed as a royal playhouse for their children, the princes and princesses, with all the furnishings in the two-story, 2,500 square feet cottage provided on a slightly smaller scale. Both lithophanes are 17.75" x 15" in size (including the very elaborate frames for hanging in a window) and are decorated with Alpine scenes.

Postcard image of the Swiss Cottage, Osborne House, Isle of Wight, United Kingdom. *Courtesy of William J. Walker, Jr.*

Louisa's Place, Berlin, Germany

Still another journey could be made to Louisa's Place, a turn-of-the-century mansion house hotel dating circa 1904, located in Berlin and named after the Prussian Queen Luise (1776-1810). One of the fine features of this German hotel is the lithophanes that adorn the stairway. The most prevalent theme of their 19th century lithophanes is that of significant Berlin architectural monuments such as the Brandenburg Gate, the Castle of Berlin, and the Concert Hall. Other lithophanes portray King Friedrich II.

The first time a person gazes at a 19th century lithophane, that individual is often mesmerized by the translucent three-dimensional picture. The phenomenon is a new experience and the viewer is captivated and charmed. Yet a moment later someone's cell phone rings or an airplane flies overhead and the viewer is jolted back to the 21st century and their present environment – a friend's home, a department store, an antique shop, a museum, or a clever gift shop. Just imagine what it would be like to view the lithophane as a 19th century family member might – with a flickering flame behind the porcelain candle shield, or the flame of an oil lamp lighting a breath-taking lithophane lampshade, fireplace flames dancing behind a large fireplace screen, or daylight streaming through the image hanging in a sunny window. After viewing just one or two lithophanes in their vintage 19th century environments, the urge for the visitor might be to take up permanent residence in Campbell House in St. Louis, the Glen Iris Inn in Castile, New York, or Surry House in New Hampshire. Or one might need to find his or her own 19th century lithophane to take home and cherish.

Lithophane depicting Brandenburg Gate, German, 19th century, inset in window at Louisa's Place, Berlin. *Courtesy of Louisa's Place, Berlin.*

Pair of lithophanes, *Der Lustige Schornsteinfeger* (*The Merry Chimney Sweep*), German, 19th century, inset in window at Louisa's Place, Berlin. *Courtesy of Louisa's Place, Berlin.*

Chapter Eight
Lithophanic Humor

When one thinks of the 19th century, stereotypical images may present themselves. Images of Victorian England complete with prudish, conservative beings in the costumes of bygone eras might immediately come to mind. The lithophanes of the 19th century generally do reflect what one might view as conservative morals and behavior, just as did the paintings and engravings upon which the lithophanes were based.

Despite this narrow Victorian stereotype, there is generous humor to be discovered among the lithophane motifs. This is one of the most appealing aspects of this nearly forgotten Victorian art form. The Blair Museum of Lithophanes collection includes more than its share of porcelain lithophanous pictures that make one smile. Several favorites must be mentioned and illustrated. For instance, one French example with the AdT (Alexis du Tremblay) backstamp (on the front) depicts a group of monkeys with goat legs providing a whisker trimming for a dapper cat. While the print source has yet to be identified, there is more humor here than just the artist poking fun at the ideas of Charles Darwin and evolution.

Similar in some ways, is the Meissen lithophane *Eine Affenfamilie* (*A Monkey Family*) which bears the backstamps 156 and 61. It depicts three monkeys, two in 19th century costume, with one wielding a kitchen implement forcing another out the window as he yanks on his tail.

Lithophane, Cat and Monkeys, 19th century, French, AdT 309, Blair Museum acc. no. 870, 6" x 4.125". *Courtesy of the Blair Museum of Lithophanes.*

Another lithophane appears to depict a young artist sketching a caricature of his teacher – who the student does not realize is standing right behind him as he obliviously sketches away. There is a beauty and spirit to this lithophane, with trouble waiting in the wings. The manufacturer of this lithophane is Meissen in Dresden, and its German title as listed in the *Preis-Courant* from 1846, is *Der Geniestreich* which can be rather humorously translated as "A Stroke of Genius."

Lithophane, *Der Geniestreich* (*A Stroke of Genius*), 19th century, German, Meissen no. 157 with 70, Blair Museum acc. no. 1125, 7.875" x 6.25". *Courtesy of the Blair Museum of Lithophanes.*

A little knowledge of German or access to a German dictionary provides even greater understanding of the humor in the lithophane marked PPM and produced by the Plaue Porzellanmanufaktur located in Plaue-on-Havel, Thuringia, part of Germany. Perhaps the quintessential example of 19th century humor as depicted in porcelain, is the classic that illustrates in illuminated glory, a humble couple "enjoying" a museum gallery full of sculpture of nudes and suits of armor. The homely lady in the picture appears eager to leave the uncomfortable museum setting, while her spouse feigns scholarly appreciation for the female nude sculpture form before him. Even the suit of armor and the portrait painting on the wall appear to be leering at the nude. The humor in this simple scene is compounded when the sign hanging in the gallery is translated from its German into English basically telling the gallery visitors "we kindly ask you not to touch the objects" (in German "Man bittet die Gegenstände nicht zu berühren"). It is a classic. The Blair Museum has several versions of this German masterpiece – both small and large, some with the addition of colored glazes, in rustic candle shield frames.

Detail of lithophane, Victorian Art Lovers, 19th century, German, PPM 1133, Blair Museum acc. no. 611. *Courtesy of the Blair Museum of Lithophanes.*

Lithophane, Victorian Art Lovers, 19th century, German, PPM 1133, Blair Museum acc. no. 611, 7.125" x 5.625". *Courtesy of the Blair Museum of Lithophanes.*

There is, however a humorous prequel or sequel to this lithophane made at Plaue in the 19th century. The same couple is depicted slightly earlier or later that same day during their museum visit. Marked with the factory backstamp PPM 1124, the couple is focused now on a sculpture of a dragon with claws. While the man appears to be using his large hat as a shield protecting his eyes from seeing the donation box at the base of the sculpture, his wife peers on, and a pickpocket hovers behind the couple, engaged in pilfering the man's wallet. Little did they know that they did not need to be pretending not to see the donation box, as all of their cash is being cleverly removed without their consent by another museum visitor.

Lithophane, *Der bestrafte Neuierige* (*The Peeping Tom Being Punished*), 19th century, German, KPM 267 B, Blair Museum acc. no. 1024, 8.25" x 6.875". *Courtesy of the Blair Museum of Lithophanes.*

Lithophane, Museum Pickpocket, 19th century, German, PPM 1124, Blair Museum acc. no. 610, 7.125" x 5.625". *Courtesy of the Blair Museum of Lithophanes.*

More humor can be seen in another lithophane of German origin that is sometimes referred to as *The Peeping Tom*. This plaque was created in Berlin by the Königliche Porzellan-Manufactur and carries the backstamp 267 B and the title from an early KPM *Preis-Courant* is *Der bestrafte Neugierige* (*The Peeping Tom Being Punished*). It depicts two young women foiling a peeping tom – preparing to dump a bucket of water on his head as he sneaks a peek through a door that is ajar. While the origin of some of these lithophanes is unknown, an engraving of the Peeping Tom, titled *Le Curieux Puni*, and measuring 13.75" x 10.5" is located in the Blair Museum archives. The engraving was created by Jules Ciere from a painting by Vallou de Villeneuve.

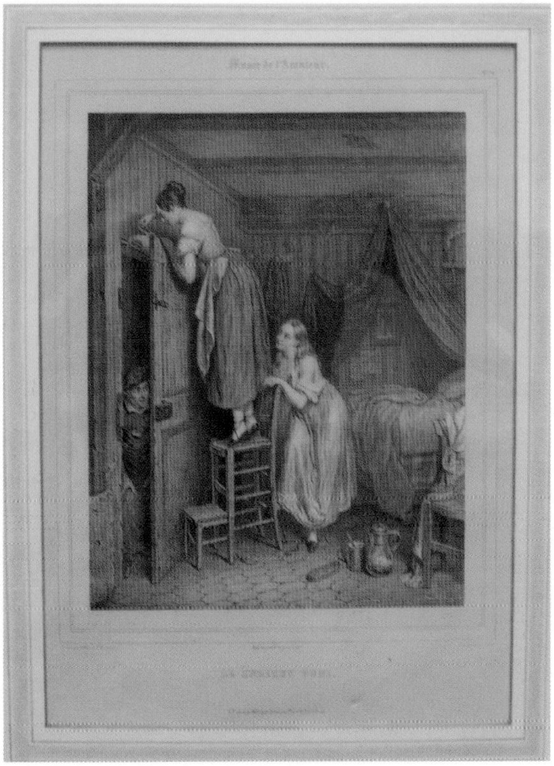

Engraving, *Le Curieux Puni*, by Jules Ciere after a painting by Vallou de Villeneuve, 13.75" x 10.5". *Courtesy of the Archives of the Blair Museum of Lithophanes.*

A lithophane depicting a smiling, soot-covered chimney sweep and the efforts others are making to keep him from contaminating them as he teeters along, tangled in his ladder, was manufactured in Germany in the 19th century. Marked PPM 705, the alleged girlfriend of the chimney sweep, the butcher, and all of those surrounding the local butcher shop, are humorously portrayed as they sidestep the advancing and staggering soot-covered worker. The official title of this lithophane, as listed on the PPM *Preis-Courant* from the 19th century, is *Der lustige Schornsteinfeger*, which could be translated *The Merry Chimneysweep*. While one doesn't see too many chimney sweeps these days, or even butcher shops, every viewer can relate to this humorous predicament.

Lithophane, *Der Lustige Schornsteinfeger* (*The Merry Chimney Sweep*), 19th century, German, PPM 705, Blair Museum acc. no. 96, 7.75" x 6.125". *Courtesy of the Blair Museum of Lithophanes.*

Lithophanes and other related art forms, are considered pre-cinematic, and are delightful when they illustrate humorous sequential events such as those seen in two panels on a six-sided lamp shade in the Blair Museum's collection. In one panel a happy rendezvous is about to take place as a friend lends his back to assist his friend in reaching his sweetheart at her window. In the next scene we see that the happy rendezvous has been thwarted by a large dog that caused the two men to tumble, taking down the flower box on the window ledge as woman looks on in surprise.

Lithophane (left), one panel on a six-sided lampshade, *Der glückliche Rendezvous* (*The Happy Rendezvous*), 19th century, German, PPM 678, Blair Museum acc. no. 1806, 6.25" x 4.625". Lithophane (right), one panel on a six-sided lampshade, *Das verunglückte Rendezvous* (*The Rendezvous That Met With an Accident*), 19th century, German, PPM 677, Blair Museum acc. no. 1805, 6.25" x 4.625". *Courtesy of the Blair Museum of Lithophanes.*

Some of the motifs that one might find amusing involve Victorian people with some nudity included. An example would be the 19th century German lithophane marked PPM 762 which when backlit reveals a woman checking the inside of her gown, supposedly for fleas. Titled *Die Flohjagd* on the 19th century PPM *Preis-Courant*, one translation could be *The Flea Hunt*.

Lithophane, *Die Flohjagd* (*The Flea Hunt*), 19th century, German, PPM 762, Blair Museum acc. no. 1028, 6.25" x 5.5". *Courtesy of the Blair Museum of Lithophanes.*

Other lithophanes involving either a little or a lot of nudity are the often amusing small erotic lithophanes. For instance there is one depicting a human frolicking with a donkey and another where a man and a woman are shown embracing. In the case of the latter, the man has his pants around his ankles and a cat is using his exposed posterior as a scratching post. These are thoroughly examined and illustrated in Chapter Six.

Lithophane, erotic, depicting a cat and a partially clothed couple, 19th century, German or French, stamped 14, Blair Museum acc. no. 2519, 2.25" x 2.875". *Courtesy of the Blair Museum of Lithophanes.*

In the 21st century, Victorian humor may be evident in a 19th century lithophane, but the exact meaning is lost. Such is the case with the German (Meissen) caricature of a politician, with possible traces of color remaining, which pictures the man seated at a table with a candle clearly burning a hole in his hat. Not wanting to leave anything to chance, the lithophane is labeled, on the front, "Ein Politiker." This design was discontinued in 1851, so perhaps the coloring was added later and therefore was not as permanent as pigments applied by the original manufacturer.

Victorian humor as seen in lithophanes seems to have transcended the borders of countries, factories, and even time. The Germans and French produced them at factories in Berlin, Dresden, Plaue, and Paris in the 19th century. The humor allows an insight into Victorian times, but more importantly illustrates the timelessness of human behavior.

Lithophane, *Ein Politiker* (*A Politician*), 19th century, German, Meissen 75 (handwritten) and 19 (stamped), with faint traces of color pigment on the exterior. Blair Museum acc. no. 1547, 5.75" x 3.75". *Courtesy of the Blair Museum of Lithophanes.*

Chapter Nine
History of the Blair Museum of Lithophanes

If one has witnessed the magic of lithophanes first hand, it is not too difficult to see how one might become so captivated with these translucent porcelain plaques that little else would matter. This was exactly the case with Laurel Blair (born Toledo, Ohio, September 6, 1909; died September 23, 1993) and his passion for collecting lithophanes. Apparently Mr. Blair believed that collectors are made, not born. He has been quoted as saying, "As a child, I collected a few stamps, but I became bored with them. Neither of my parents or brother or sister was a collector, except that my mother had a set of Wedgwood dishes I always liked."[1] Others might observe his behavior and say he was a born collector from the beginning, collecting musical boxes, orchids, bourdalou (women's urinals used in carriages), scissor cuttings, and wax sculpture with enthusiasm. He considered these other collecting forays as "phases" and his earlier collecting of books, cufflinks, tiepins and statues and even music boxes as the prelude to his serious collecting of lithophanes. What is different about his lithophane collection is that he ended up with the largest collection in the world. However, it was his enthusiasm for collecting other objects that lead directly to his introduction to lithophanes. As it has been eloquently stated, "When you're looking for one thing and accidentally discover something of greater interest, it's called serendipity."[2] And this is the story that will be presented now.

Mr. Blair's collecting of musical boxes lead him to join the International Musical Box Society that was comprised of enthusiasts from the United States, England and Switzerland (considered the home of musical boxes). In October 1961, a meeting of musical box collectors was held at the home of Dr. and Mrs. Byron O. Merrick, a veterinarian living in Berlin Heights, Ohio. There his guests were treated to not only his extensive collection of music boxes, but also his Staffordshire ware figures, miniature lamps, fairy lights, and art glass.

Mr. Blair described his first encounter with lithophanes in an unpublished and undated typescript:

> But there was a small item hanging in the window behind a music box. It was a white plaque of porcelain and because it was daylight and (because of) the light coming through the window the picture was gorgeously defined and instead of being the usual two dimensions of most pictures, where the artist has to accomplish his ends through perspective with a brush or pen, here was three dimensions in this small white piece that made me stop and contemplate its beauty. I had never seen anything like it before and there was another close by which was equally as beautiful in all of its details.

Apparently Dr. and Mrs. Merrick owned four of these porcelain plaques and it was not long before Mr. Blair was inquiring of the Merricks as to what they were. As he later wrote, he "fell in love."[3] He stated that he "couldn't spell my new loved one's name," so he "went back to the doctor and he spelled it" for him.[4] The reply, of course, was "lithophanes," and Mr. Blair was at the beginning of his investigation of this Victorian art form. When he returned to Toledo, he could only find mention of lithophanes in an older dictionary, not in either the current abridged or unabridged dictionaries or encyclopedias at the local library. His searching led him from Toledo libraries to those at the University of Michigan, with little success – just a few meager articles in old magazines. While this lack of current information frustrated him, it only made him more determined to learn about these magical porcelain pieces.

Several months later, on December 26th, Mr. Blair was in New York City with his family, as was their tradition. His brother George volunteered to go shopping with him the next day – to antique stores in the City, and there they found fifteen or twenty lithophanes and his collection was begun. The first was purchased on December 27, 1961, at a shop on Third Avenue. During this shopping excursion he acquired six curved pieces that he later found out were intended to be Inserts in metal tea warmers. His brother George found one 4" x 5" lithophane depicting Christ. After they found another 6 small lithophanes the next day, George Blair drolly remarked "Let's get the corner on the market," yet he never purchased any others since that trip to New York.[5]

His search for lithophanes resulted in Mr. Blair attending antique shows and visiting dealers throughout the Northeast United States. It wasn't long before his enthusiasm caused him to place advertisements in antique journals and newspapers such as *Hobbies, Antiques, Antique Journal* and the *Antique Trader*. Over the years he traveled the world, visiting art fairs, collectors, antique dealers, libraries, and all the major porcelain manufacturers in Europe, including von Schierholz in Plaue, Meissen, and more. It probably wasn't long before Laurel Blair came across the names of well-known lithophane collectors, Dr. and Mrs. Edmond Beroud.

Mr. Blair relaxing during travels, c. 1960s. *Courtesy of the Archives, Blair Museum of Lithophanes.*

The Berouds had begun collecting in 1947. An original list by Dr. Beroud noted the purchase of a PPM lithophane, *The Hermit*, on February 10, 1947. Both Dr. and Mrs. Beroud were French. Edmond was born in Tallahassee and was educated from age twelve in France. There he married Jeanne, and they moved in 1922 to Philadelphia, where he became a successful dentist. Their collection began with the discovery of a couple of broken lithophanes in an antique shop in Philadelphia.[6] Over an expanse of fifteen or twenty years they had acquired approximately 1,600 lithophanes of every size, shape and function. The collection was amassed by advertising in trade magazines, antique hunting on the East Coast and via "scouts" collecting for them on the Continent and in England.

Dr. and Mrs. Edmond Beroud with a favorite lithophane globe lamp, c. 1950s. *Courtesy of the Archives of the Blair Museum of Lithophanes.*

By 1963, Laurel Blair had acquired nearly 506 lithophanes, including about thirty-two that he had purchased directly from the Berouds prior to meeting them.[7] He had corresponded with them previously, sharing enthusiasm for lithophanes. In November 1962, he had written to the Berouds, "From all the conversations and letters in which your name has appeared, I could almost feel that I know you, and someday I certainly hope that I can meet you and see your collection of lithophanes."[8] At that time Mr. Blair owned 325 different lithophanes.[9] The correspondence continued, and he finally met them in January 1963, in Miami, Florida where they had retired in 1957.

In correspondence from the Berouds to Laurel Blair dated May 2, 1963, Dr. Beroud wrote, "With the 506 lithophanes you already have in your possession..." that Laurel was the second best collector, but if he bought his (Dr Beroud's) "entire collection, along with all the datas, letters, stories of lithophanes we have gathered over the years...will make you without a doubt FIRST MAN ON THE TOTEM POLE."[10]

During this first trip to visit the Berouds in January, 1963, Laurel Blair purchased "a few choice items... as they had so many items that they couldn't show them off or enjoy them."[11] At one point in his correspondence Dr. Beroud described the lithophanes as "his babies," and he tallied up Laurel's wish list of lithophanes from the Beroud collection, just 116 items, with the prices he (Dr. Beroud) paid for them (not including expenses attached to acquiring them) totaling $3,676.60.[12] At the same time he invited Laurel Blair to come for a visit, assuring him that he was certain that they "can come to an agreement."[13]

They corresponded frequently during the next year and Mr. Blair visited them again about a year later. This time they discussed the possibility of keeping the collection in tact, with Mr. Blair acquiring the entire collection and setting up a museum of lithophanes. In

Dr. Beroud with backlit lithophane display, c. 1950s. *Courtesy of the Archives of the Blair Museum of Lithophanes.*

the first collectors' bulletin, Mr. Blair recalled the following story. "With that they mentioned a price for which I could purchase the entire collection. It was so reasonable that I, a Scotchman, didn't even haggle one cent, and also I happened to have enough in the bank so that I could write a check right then and there! How fortunate could anyone be?"[14] Although the exact price paid for the Beroud collection is not known, the prices noted in correspondence ranged from $10,000 for the entire collection to $10 per lithophane (roughly $16,280).

Beroud collection displayed in their home, c. 1950s. *Courtesy of the Archives of the Blair Museum of Lithophanes.*

Through the years, his brother George would remain an ardent supporter of all "things lithophane" that Laurel Blair encountered. In a letter dated February 11, 1964, it appeared quite clear that Laurel had purchased the entire Beroud collection when George addressed his brother Laurel as "Dear Lithophane Tycoon," and said, "Congratulations! I am glad that you did it. The collection couldn't be in better hands. I am anxious to learn of your plans for it. It probably will never make you rich, but it will be a significant contribution in the field of Art. It assures you of everlasting fame."[15]

Blair family Christmas in Red Hook, New York, 1966, left to right, Georgia Blair (Laurel's mother), Dorothy Blair (George's wife), Laurel, George, Gee Gee (George's daughter). *Courtesy of Gee Gee Blair.*

The Blair Museum of Lithophanes' opening on March 2, 1965 was announced in the *Toledo Blade* the following morning. Journalist Louise Bruner wrote, "Guests at last night's opening of the unique Blair Museum of Lithophanes, 220 Columbia St., weren't sure whether a lithophane was a tropical plant, seafood, a foreign car, or a citizen of a newly created African state."[16] The article announced that his "hobby" had created a collection of more than 2,300 – the largest collection in the world. It recounted his first encounter with lithophanes just four years before and detailed a bit of the history. At that time his Museum was comprised of four rooms with mirror-back display cases and individual lighting for the 800 examples on display. Located in a historic neighborhood in Toledo, the building housing the collection was a Victorian era brick Italianate stable or carriage house that was, at the time, 80 years old. Mr. Blair lived in a portion of the structure and the lithophanes and carved waxes occupied the adjoining spaces. The newspaper announcement also noted that it took ten months for the installation of the collection. At the time of the opening, Mr. Blair had plans to travel to Europe in May to research lithophanes more thoroughly and then write a book. This 19th century historic structure, once the home of a prosperous seed merchant who imported craftsmen from Italy to construct its three ornate marble fireplaces, burned down in 1980, years after the collections had moved to a larger home.

Carriage House, 220 Columbia Street, Toledo, original location of the Blair Museum of Lithophanes, 1965. *Courtesy of the Archives of the Blair Museum of Lithophanes.*

It was only a few years later, in October 1972, that Mr. Blair found the collections had grown extensively, so he relocated to a very fine Victorian mansion in Toledo's Old West End historic district, and moved the collections and exhibits there to 2032 Robinwood.[17] He lived on the second floor, with the collections displayed in five large galleries located on the first floor. The collection remained there until the house and collection were donated by Mr. Blair to the City of Toledo at the time of his death at the age of 84 on September 23, 1993. Laurel Blair was a Toledo native, a graduate of the University of Michigan, at one time the president of the Blair Realty Co.; yet he is best remembered as a "character" who grew orchids, collected lithophanes and wax carvings, and then very carefully bestowed this unique gift to the City of Toledo.

There is only one puzzling aspect to the collection with which one would like to query Mr. Blair. Why and when did he make the decision that he wasn't going to attempt to collect each and every unique and distinctive lithophane? Even in 1967, when he was still relatively new to the research and development of his lithophane collection, he was offered a lithophane, via a letter and accompanying photograph, a portrait, circa 1835, of a woman. This came from a reputable source. His response to the offer was as follows, "The Blair Museum has approximately 2,300 lithophanes, and although this one of yours is an excellent example of the art, we have stopped purchasing any more plaques or panels, as although we do not have this particular one in the collection, we know that we can not purchase and should not purchase every one as it is already impossible to display the entire collection at one time."[18] He states further on in this same letter that he is still seeking pieces other than panels, yet in his membership newsletters, he was known to offer for sale rare pieces which the Museum did not even own, including lamps and candle shields.

Blair Museum of Lithophanes, 2032 Robinwood, Toledo, c. 1979. *Courtesy of the Archives of the Blair Museum of Lithophanes.*

Every few years, Mr. Blair held collector club member meetings in Toledo, the final one being held in October 1990. These occasions were usually sparsely attended but some people traveled from the United Kingdom and elsewhere to see his marvelous collection. In addition to providing copious time with the Museum's massive lithophane collection, Mr. Blair always included field trips to antique fairs, museums, and invited contemporary lithophane artists from Michigan, New York, and Arizona, to provide live demonstrations.

Participants in the Blair Museum of Lithophanes' Collectors meeting, October 1990. Back row, second from left, Eve Coleman, United Kingdom, fifth from left, David Failing, contemporary lithophane artist, and far right, Laurel Blair. *Courtesy of John and Eve Coleman.* Photo by John Coleman.

Laurel Blair with a small portion of his lithophane collection, c. 1965. *Courtesy of the Archives, the Blair Museum of Lithophanes.* Photo by Steve Warren.

Mr. Blair struggled for years to find a home for his collection of lithophanes. He had investigated donating the collection to the Toledo Museum of Art, the Old West End Association, and the University of Michigan Museum of Art. The Toledo Museum of Art was not a likely home for the Blair Museum's lithophane collection for a number of reasons, not the least of which concerned the fact (although Mr. Blair had probably forgotten) that they had sold their 17 lithophanes to Dr. Beroud in 1954 for $125.[19] Apparently Mr. Blair had offers for the collection to be relocated to Europe. Therefore, he was pleased but perhaps a bit skeptical when the City of Toledo agreed in May 1993, to take the collection and continue to provide a museum for the public to enjoy. From his nursing home in Winter Haven, Florida, Mr. Blair noted, "Toledo is the favorite city. I'm happy now that the city of Toledo is going to be taking over the entire museum," and he continued, "It occupies all my heart ... and I don't want to see it go down the tubes."[20] At that time there was still debate over whether or not the museum would reopen at the same Old West End location that it had previously occupied, or perhaps be relocated to the Toledo Botanical Garden.

The Museum was established within the City of Toledo governance, by Ordinance no. 321-93, passed May 11, 1993 and April 18, 1994. A Trust fund was established to support the Museum in perpetuity at the time of Mr. Blair's gift to the City. At the time of Mr. Blair's death, an auction was held in Detroit at DuMouchelles, in April 1994, to sell other contents of Mr. Blair's estate, including Wedgwood, majolica, bronze sculpture and silhouettes.

It took almost ten years of remarkable tenacity for the Advisory Board of the Blair Museum of Lithophanes to interact with the City of Toledo in seeing the collection boxed up and stored while a small home located at the Toledo Botanical Gardens was renovated to suit the exhibition of the collection. The Blair Advisory Board consisted of Robert Huebner, Peggy Grant, Greg Knott, and Sandra Wiseley. While all of the Blair Advisory Board was instrumental in the transition from private museum to public, special mention must be made of Bob Huebner who dealt with the City on a daily basis during the renovation of current Museum space. It is an extreme understatement to say that this was no easy task. In July 2002, the public and dignitaries were invited to the opening of the Blair Museum of Lithophanes. The important collection of carved wax sculpture had been sold to support the cost of building renovation.

Since the grand opening in 2002, the Museum has been open year round by appointment for groups of ten or more. This may seem odd to some, but this is only continuing Mr. Blair's tradition. A small fee is charged per guest. Of course, Mr. Blair always opened for members when they contacted him in advance and he was not traveling in Europe or Asia. The Museum initially opened on Saturdays 1-4 p.m. from May through September, but has increased free public access to include the weekends 1-4 p.m.

Original Blair Museum Advisory Board at the grand opening of the Blair Museum of Lithophanes, July 2002, left to right, Kattie Bond, Sandra Wiseley, Robert Huebner, Peggy Grant, Gregory Knott, and Robert Zollweg, *Courtesy of Sandra Wiseley.*

An exterior view of the Blair Museum of Lithophanes, 2007. *Courtesy of the Archives of the Blair Museum of Lithophanes.*

Robert Huebner passed away on May 4, 2004, but a few months before he died, he hired the first curator for the Museum since its founder, Laurel Blair. Margaret Carney, a ceramics historian with a Ph.D. in Asian art history and thirty years of professional museum experience had moved to the area in 2003, and she was flabbergasted when she and her husband had visited the May plant sale at the Toledo Botanical Garden and noticed that there was a museum devoted to lithophanes in Toledo. She actually could not believe that there was a museum devoted to this topic anywhere, let alone Toledo, Ohio. A few years earlier she had been trying to investigate the topic of lithophanes and knew there was no book on the subject, so she visited the Museum and wrote Mr. Huebner about the possibility of writing a book and serving as curator. She was hired and began work January 2004.

Blair Museum Curator, Dr. Margaret Carney, newly appointed, May 2004. *Courtesy of the Archives of the Blair Museum of Lithophanes.*

The curatorial position has been funded through the generosity of Mr. George Blair, Laurel Blair's brother, who is famously known as Banana George. Always wearing his trademark banana yellow suit, or wet suit, eyeglasses, etc., Banana George, born January 22, 1915, holds the world's record for the oldest barefoot water skier. His achievements are the stuff of legends.

Museum benefactor Banana George Blair (in yellow) shown with Bill Walker and Margaret Carney onboard Seine River champagne luncheon cruise in Paris, June 2005. *Courtesy of the Archives, the Blair Museum of Lithophanes.*

The Museum's Advisory Board has made some changes in the past few years and now includes Associate Board members, too. The Board consists of chair Heide Klein, Posy Huebner (Mr. Blair's cousin and widow of Robert Huebner), Peggy Grant, Bill Mies, and Dennis Seffernick. Associate Board members include Greg Knott, Jim Larrow, Georgia (Gee Gee) Blair, Brad Huebner, and Sandra Wiseley. Since 1993, there have been more than a half a dozen directors of the department of Parks, Recreation and Forestry that have interacted with the Blair Board on behalf of the City of Toledo.

Blair Museum Advisory Board, 2005, left to right, Greg Knott, Sandra Wiseley, Heide Klein, Larry Anderson (City of Toledo), Peggy Grant, Posy Huebner, Kattie Bond (City of Toledo), Dennis Seffernick, Jim Larrow, Margaret Carney, and Brad Huebner. *Courtesy of the Archives of the Blair Museum of Lithophanes.*

A docent program was established to keep the Museum open to the public on weekends and to provide quality tours to the many first-time visitors to the Museum who are not familiar with the Victorian art of lithophanes. A core group of volunteers has been active since the opening in 2002, and they include Louise Bankey, Nancy Durnford, Betsy Ford, Peggy Grant, Posy Huebner, Mary Karazim, Heide Klein, Greg Knott, Jim and Sharon Larrow, Doris McEwen, and Sandra Wiseley. In addition, more recently joining the docent program are Sally Bergsmark, Barbara Britsch, Barbara Brown, Carol Ann DuBrul, Mary Louise Glen, Christine Goslin, Robert Gosling, Marie Harr, Brad Huebner, Carole Kiroff, Judith Lerner, Jocelyn Marinescu, Donna Martin-Isard, Bill Mies, Deanna Johnson, Pat Scharf, Dennis Seffernick, Lillian Spaulding, Joan Wiley, and Gene and Chuck Williams. While the docent enrichment program is one of the curator's responsibilities, Posy Huebner has undertaken coordinating the volunteer schedule for weekends and special tours.

Exhibition installation expertise as well as computer knowledge for the Museum has been provided by Kurt Hanushek, while membership and computer database talents are a gift of Marilyn Kehl who worked with Mr. Blair beginning in January 1985.

A key aspect of Mr. Blair's collecting and museum activities was his bi-monthly *Lithophane Collectors' Club Bulletins* for the Blair Museum of Lithophanes and Carved Waxes. He began issuing these bulletins on March 15, 1976, and a total of ninety-seven bulletins (approximate number since some issues were missing and others had supplements) were issued prior to his death in 1993. The bulletins had multiple features, including charming travelogues from his worldwide travels to collect lithophanes and carved waxes; the advertisement of "extra" lithophanes, frequently illustrated, that he would offer to members to purchase for their private collections, thereby funding his subsequent expeditions; disseminating information about lithophane history and manufacture; and more.

The bulletins can best be viewed as ongoing research by Mr. Blair, as they included statements that unintentionally contained mistakes that were subsequently corrected by club members via written correspondence, with the corrections published in the following bulletin. This all predated email and the Internet, but the frequency of his publication (usually six times a year) allowed for the speedy transmission of information. The bulletins offered a great vehicle for Mr. Blair to share his knowledge and test it among other avid collectors.

The bulletins are famous for reporting Mr. Blair's extensive travels inside and outside of the United States. In a bulletin published in 1990, while reporting on his fascinating 26-day trip to South Africa, he mentioned that his visit to Tanzania marked his 62nd country that he had visited in his lifetime. While in South Africa he was the guest of a lithophane collector, saw baboons in the wild, and visited a nude beach. This man really knew how to live.

The bulletins additionally offered some statistics for the collector. Not only did he discuss the forbidden-by-public-museums topic of the value of the lithophanes, he kept track of his membership and announced those figures, too. Mr. Blair frequently wrote in the bulletin about how many members there were and where they lived. His first issue in 1976, notes there were 15 U.S. states represented in the Club. By the publication of Bulletin No. 2 he had members from nineteen states and England. Several months later he could announce there were eighty-three members from twenty-three states and England and Canada. And by the end of the first year, he noted there were 100 members from 25 states, Canada, England and Germany. By April 1977, he could boast of 125 members from 26 states, England, Germany, Canada, and France. He advertised in 20 different magazines looking for lithophanes. He held the first meeting of the lithophane collector's club in Toledo on June 29, 1979, where they could view 1,100 lithophanes on exhibition in his Museum. In 1980, there were 150 Museum members from 36 states and 6 countries in Europe.

The bulletins were generally well received by the member collectors and generated copious correspondence.

Blair Museum docents, October 2004, left to right: Barbara Britsch, Posy Huebner, Kurt Hanushek, Marilyn Kehl, Betsy Ford, Margaret Carney, Sandra Wiseley, Heide Klein, Shirley Fischer, Doris McEwen, Mary Karazim, Louise Bankey, Greg Knott, and Nancy Durnford. *Courtesy of the Archives of the Blair Museum of Lithophanes.*

Brief mention should be made of the other focus of Mr. Blair's collecting in addition to lithophanes, carved waxes. These waxes were not the carved waxes that served as the models for the lithophanes from the 19th century. Rather, these are stand alone carved wax sculpture, a technique known in ancient Egypt and revived intermittently ever since. The Blair collection, now dispersed, numbered over 500. At least one of the wax carvings was so precious that it occupied its own seat on a 747 flight from England in the early 1970s. They range in dates from ancient Egypt to the 1980s. At the time it was probably the most comprehensive collection of art waxes in the United States.

It was actually during Mr. Blair's visit to the von Schierholz Porcelain factory in Plaue in 1965, that he became intrigued with the subject of wax carvings. The factory administrators had presented him with two original carved waxes of the type that were used in the production of lithophanes in the 19th century. As he later noted, "... I had never really seen or held a wax in my hand,"[21] before this experience. He "didn't have any idea at that time that it would turn out to be the start of a collection."[22] He began investigating the larger topic of wax carvings, which had a long and fascinating history. Without elaborating on the history of wax carvings, suffice it to say that Mr. Blair became extremely knowledgeable about the topic and acquired many rare and unusual pieces for his collection over the years.

He was proud that the oldest piece in his wax carving collection, a wax head sculpture, dated circa 300 B.C. and was reportedly from the tomb of Osiris, the god of the underworld. According to the dealer from whom he purchased the wax, "it had been wrapped around the Pharaoh's favorite falcon to preserve it."[23] While the majority of his collection was from the 18th and 19th century, and a few from the 20th century, he knew the whole history of wax portraiture during the Renaissance, wax effigies of kings and queens made for funeral corteges, anatomical wax body parts made for teaching when cadavers were not allowed in the 16th century, and waxes encrusted with jewels and enamel overlays.

His collection included wax flowers that might have been favored in a Victorian home setting, a Spanish Pieta, and a wax carving depicting the Punic War of about 200 B.C. – complete with Hannibal and his men, elephants, and horses all fighting the Romans. It was his beautiful miniature sculpture of Queen Charlotte, wife of King George III that was so precious that he bought her a seat on a 747 flight from England. She sits on a sofa with patterned upholstery, wearing a stunning gown and wig. A Spanish baptismal scene is another of the treasures, which incorporated lace and satins with the wax figures. Some one-inch relief portraits created from wax were made in England during the 19th century and were important to his collection. His wax collection included pieces from Egypt, Denmark, Russia, England, Spain, the United States and more. At the time of Mr. Blair's death, most of the wax collection was sold in order to raise funds to support the Blair Museum of Lithophanes in its new home.

Some might be critical that this book has too many references to Mr. Blair's own relentless search for information about lithophanes from libraries, museums, collectors, researchers, art dealers, and factories. Two letters from an admirer in late 1967, seem to summarize the Blair book-writing situation at the time. Adelaide Dember wrote, "I do think you should write your book. I do think that you have it mostly completed except for drafting the material and putting down the facts. Get busy and good luck on your book and publish same in 1968. This should be your New Year Resolution."[24] Mr. Blair had sent her Harold Newman's book on Veilleuses, which included several with lithophanes. Mrs. Dember continued, "I regret that your book shall not be the first article on lithophane. Do you know this man and how come that you let him get ahead of you."[25] He must have responded because she sent another letter a few weeks later. She continued in the same vein as her last correspondence, "You must write your book and give expression to your museum. This book will enlighten and bring to life your entire effort. Somehow, there seems to be a gap of unfinished summary and climax to this subject. Since you have done so much research and physical display of these beautiful items, you should conclude your work with this final persute [sic] to this entire subject."[26]

SMALLEST MUSEUM: Toledo's smallest accredited museum is the Blair Museum of lithophanes and wax carvings, presided over by Laurel Blair (above) at 2032 Robinwood Ave.

Mr. Blair shown in a newspaper photograph with his carved wax of Queen Charlotte, wife of King George III, who once occupied an airline seat next to him on a 747 flight from Europe in the 1970s. Photo courtesy of the *Toledo Blade*.

Chapter Ten
Museum Collections

While the Blair Museum of Lithophanes located in Toledo, Ohio, possesses the largest collection of lithophanes in the world, totaling more than 2,340 as of 2007, there are lithophanes in well-known museums such as the Metropolitan Museum of Art in New York, the Victoria & Albert Museum in London, the Smithsonian Institution's National Museum of American History in Washington, D.C., the Österreichisches Museum für Angewandte Kunst (MAK) in Vienna, the Musée National de la Porcelaine Adrien-Dubouché in Limoges, and many others worldwide. Unfortunately, the millions of people who visit these museums annually seldom have the opportunity to see a lithophane at these institutions unless they make a prior research appointment and visit these objects kept perpetually in storage. The good news is that one can visit the Blair Museum of Lithophanes in Toledo, Ohio, and see on display all of the lithophanes owned by the Met, the V&A, the MAK, and the NMAH, in addition to hundreds of others. Not meant to be comprehensive, a sampling of other institutional collections with lithophanes is provided here. Well-known institutions with just a smattering of lithophanes are listed, as well as more specialized or obscure public collections that may become destination attractions for lithophanophiles.

Laurel Blair began communicating with Jessie McNab, one of the curators at the Metropolitan Museum of Art in 1962. The Metropolitan Museum of Art never displays their six lithophanes to the public, so one might wonder why this collection is known at all. When illustrating articles, many writers turn to large well-known institutions for the loan of illustrations to publish. The Metropolitan Museum of Art loaned lithophane images for several key articles in the 1950s, including four of their six lithophanes illustrating an article by Amelia E. Rawding titled "Lithophanes: Art of the Victorian Era," which was published in *Hobbies* magazine in July 1958.

The Metropolitan Museum of Art collection is comprised of six German lithophanes, four Meissen and two KPM. The two with KPM backstamps are actually a pair. One of the pair depicts an old man with a smile and a staff. Titled *Der verliebte Alte*, (*The Old Man In Love*), it measures 5.875" x 4.875", and is marked with a scepter and KPM 183 and St. The companion to the old man *and* companion piece in the lithophane set, depicts a young woman in peasant costume, *Ein Mädchen, spottend, Pendant zu No. 183* (KPM 184 St.) H: 5.875" W: 4.875". The title links this lithophane with the former, and the title also notes she is mocking the old man.

Other lithophanes in the Metropolitan Museum of art include *Maria Magdalena, nach Battoni*, Mary Magdalene after a painting by Pompeo Battoni (1708-1787), a Meissen lithophane marked with the numbers "96" and "16" measuring 6.75" x 9.875"; a Meissen lithophane *Dresden von der Brühl. Terrasse*, with an incised mark "118"; a Meissen lithophane of a coastal scene, *Seeprospect mit Sonnenaufgang* (*Seascape with Sunrise*), with figures in the left foreground and one on horseback, and the incised marks "36" and "43," measuring 6.5" x 8.25"; and *Kirchgängerin, groß* (*Woman Church-goer, large*), depicting a woman in late Gothic style costume, with the ruins of a Gothic building in the background. This piece, according to the Meissen *Preis-Courant*, was introduced in 1836. It is marked "131" and "59" and it measures 9.5" x 7.25". All of these pieces were donated to the Metropolitan Museum of Art by W.L. Hildburgh in 1936 and bear the accession numbers 36.116.1-6. These are all excellent examples of German lithophane production from the 19th century and worth an appointment with the curator.

Lithophanes in the Blair Museum of Lithophanes that match the pair in the collection of the Metropolitan Museum of Art. *Der verliebte Alte* (*The Old Man in Love*), German, design first introduced 1836-37, KPM 183 B, Blair Museum acc. no. 1571a, 5.75" x 4.75" and *Ein Mädchen, spottend, Pendant zu No. 183* (*A Mocking Girl, paired with no. 183*), German, KPM 184 B, Blair Museum acc. no. 1570, 5.75" x 4.75". *Courtesy of the Blair Museum of Lithophanes.*

Lithophane in the Blair Museum of Lithophanes that is similar to the PPM 630 *Erste Class* lithophane in the Victoria & Albert Museum collection as well as one from the collection of the Hampshire County Council Museums and Archives Service marked PPM 730. *Erste Class (First Class)*, after the original 1855 painting by Abraham Solomon, *First Class – The Meeting*, PPM 618, 19th century, German, Blair Museum acc. no. 999, 8.25" x 7.75". *Courtesy of the Blair Museum of Lithophanes.*

The Victoria & Albert Museum is another world-class museum with a small but fine collection of lithophanes. These are stored off-site and can only be viewed by prior appointment with the curator. The collection includes nine lithophanes from Germany, and one from France. Seven were produced in the 19th century by the Plaue Porzellan Manufaktur located in Thuringia. These include Cologne Cathedral from the south (inscribed "Dom zu Koln"), 6" x 8" including the lead frame, marked PPM 118 (V & A acc. no. C.175-1933); a lithophane depicting the *Madonna*, marked PPM 208 (V & A acc. no. circ. 73-1971); a scene in a railway carriage, after *Erste Class* (*First Class*), a painting by Abraham Solomon (1824-62), marked PPM 630, measuring 7" x 5" (V & A acc. no. C.97-1935); a lady in a day dress standing near foxgloves, *Süsses Verlangen* (*Longing for Sweetness*), measuring 6" x 4", marked PPM 592; *Hasenjagd* (*Rabbit Hunt*), framed in metal alloy, measuring 6" x 5", marked with the Plaue backstamp PPM 447 (V & A acc. no. C.16a-1971); and a woman spinning yarn, marked PPM 679, *Die Hausfrau aus der Glocke*, measuring 6" x 4" (V & A acc. no. C.16b-1971). There are other German pieces from two different factories also included in this collection. One piece is marked HPM 163, which is probably from the Hennebergsche Porzellan Manufaktur in Gotha, measuring 7" x 5" and depicts a woman in 19th century dress leaning on her chair in a bedroom (V & A acc. no. C.96-1935). The other two German pieces are Königliche Porzellan Manufaktur lithophanes. One is marked KPM 384 B *Das Landmädchen, nach Meierheim* (*The Farm Girl, after Meierheim*), a peasant woman standing in a field with gleaner's rake on right shoulder, with a cloth bundle of corn on her head and a goat to her left. This piece was produced in Berlin in the mid-19th century. It measures 9" x 7" (V & A acc. no. C.16c-1971). The other piece, with a KPM 305 B backstamp, *Eine schlafende mutter mit ihrem Kinde*, depicts a child embracing a woman lying in bed and measures 7" x 6" (V & A acc. no. C.75-1964). The one French lithophane is in the form of a candle shield mounted in a wooden frame, with the backstamp AdT and "85". It pictures an oriental scene of a boat in a lake in front of a building with a dome, amid palm trees in a hilly landscape (V & A acc. no. C.15-b-1969).

The Wyck is a National Historic Landmark house and garden located in Germantown in Philadelphia, Pennsylvania. The house, constructed in 1690, with alterations in 1824, was home to nine generations of the same Quaker family. It houses significant 18th and 19th century furniture, ceramics and needlework collections, including some remarkable lithophanes.

The lithophane collection includes two five-sided lampshades with trapezoidal lithophane panels (one with German lithophanes, including canal scenes, Wyck acc. no. 78.143), a student lamp, and three candle shields. One candle shield has a Biblical scene of Jesus and the disciples (Wyck acc. no. 78.28), another displays a fishing scene (Wyck acc. no. 78.29), and the final one is the most significant. The Wyck candle shield with a lithophane depicting *William Penn's Treaty with the Indians*, bearing a rare G.A.S. backstamp, is a rarity and is described in detail and illustrated in Chapter Three.

Another public institution with lithophanes is Baggs Memorial Library at the Ohio State University in Columbus, Ohio. Their collection includes around 10 objects which meet the definition of lithophane, some with more or less translucency, that were all created by Walter Ford in the late 1930s or early 1940s. His extensive research concerning photo processes on ceramics is elaborated on in several chapters, including Chapters Two, Three, and Five. The collection at OSU includes small portraits of Ross Purdy, a leader with the American Ceramic Society, and others affiliated with Ohio ceramics, such as Edward Orton.

Lithophane portrait of Ross C. Purdy, an administrator with the American Ceramic Society, by Walter Ford, c. late 1930s, Baggs Memorial Library acc. no. 1997.373, 3.75" x 2.3125". *Courtesy Baggs Memorial Library, Department of Art, The Ohio State University.*

Other U.S. museums have lithophanes that, although unmarked, were probably created by Walter Ford. In addition to the portrait of Ross Purdy, Baggs Library also has a 4.375" x 3.5" portrait of Franklin Delano Roosevelt (Baggs acc. no. 1997.364). FDR subject lithophanes can also be seen in the collection of the Blair Museum and the Lightner Museum in St. Augustine Florida. All of these 20th century lithophane images of FDR created by Walter Ford are lacking the clarity seen in 19th century lithophanes.

Lithophane, jar shaped lamp, featuring photographic type image of Franklin Delano Roosevelt on one side and probably Alf Landon on the other, created by Walter Ford, c. 1939-40, no marks, Blair Museum acc. no. 1602, 8" x 5" x 3.5". *Courtesy of the Blair Museum of Lithophanes.*

The Birmingham Museum of Art in Birmingham, Alabama has a small collection of lithophanes. What is most interesting about their collection is that their focus has been on early 19th century cast iron, not the porcelain plaques themselves. They have one of the largest collections of cast iron objects in the world, including candle shield stands, watch holders, candlesticks, inkwells, tobacco boxes, pin cushions, and more, all created during the heyday of cast iron, between 1800 and 1850, in Germany, Austria, and Bohemia. It is a fascinating history that is intertwined with the popularity of lithophanes.

The Birmingham Museum of Art's lithophane collection includes a piece depicting the courtship of a couple, produced at the Plaue Factory marked PPM 229, titled *Brautwerbung* (*Courting the Bride*), (BMA acc. no. 1986.289.2); a family scene, marked with the number 1782; and three Meissen lithophanes – *Martin Luther* with incised 52 and impressed 50, (BMA acc. no. 1986.289b); *Eine Kirche* (*A Church*) incised with 108, (BMA acc. no. 1986.298.3); and *Der Krieger und sein Sohn* (*The Warrior and his Son*), incised with numbers 143 and 59 and an X (BMA acc. no. 1986.289.4a).

The Henry Ford Museum in Dearborn, Michigan has approximately 1 million visitors annually. It would be an ideal setting and location to view lithophanes within their reconstructed domestic environments. However, only a visit to storage or their website would provide one the opportunity to view their German five-sided lampshade with lithophane panels manufactured at the Plaue Factory in the 19th century (acc. no. 29.1329.29) and several other pieces of unknown origin.

The House of the Seven Gables in Salem, Massachusetts has a paneled lampshade displayed on a converted oil lamp base. Another specialized East coast museum with published lithophanes is the Mariner's Museum in Newport News, Virginia. Sometimes publications do not get the facts correct and those errors are perpetuated. That was the case with it being reported that the two lithophanes in the Mariner's Museum were manufactured in the United States at Phoenix Pottery.[1] A 1966 article repeated the "facts" from an earlier 1954 article in *Antiques Magazine*.[2] Rather than being American lithophanes, they are both from Germany. While the stein has no marks, it was identified in 1954 as German by Robert A. Elder, Jr., from the Smithsonian Institution's Division of Ethnology. The stein bears an American Naval Insignia which first came into use in 1870, and the lid, with a pewter mount, is in the form of an officer's cap.[3] The lithophane visible in the bottom of the empty stein depicts a sailor and his sweetheart. The other lithophane in their collection, a plaque, has the backstamp PPM 220, which depicts *Seeschlacht* (*Sea Battle*) showing a battle between French and English fleets, listed on the *Preis-Courant* for Plaue Porzellan Manufaktur.

The Kinsey Institute's collection of erotic lithophanes is unique and is detailed in Chapter Seven. No other museums have admitted to having this variety of lithophane in their collection.

The J. Paul Getty Museum in Malibu, California is famous for its acquisitions, yet owns only five lithophanes, including two Belleek, one of a cathedral and the other of a seated woman. These are part of the Getty Research Institute collection. Their KPM version of *Christ and the Adulteress* includes the Latin inscription at the bottom of the lithophane *Qui sine peccato est vestrum primus in illiam lapidem mittat* (*Let he who is without sin cast the first stone*).

It is mounted as a candle shield. They additionally have two other lithophanes in their Werner Nekes collection of optical devices – a French plaque depicting Napoleon and a lampshade.

One museum in the U.S. with a fine and important collection of KPM lithophanes is the Wadsworth Atheneum in Hartford, Connecticut, with more than seventy-five lithophanes in their permanent collection. Many of these are from the Samuel Colt collection and from his historic home Armsmear, and some pieces are awaiting cataloguing. The Smithsonian Institution's National Museum of American History has a fine collection of eight lithophanes, all German marked PPM (nos. 28, 32, 39, 102, 114), KPM (no. 299) or HPM (248 R), and a very rare lithophane made at Phoenix Pottery in the United States, depicting *Christ and the Adulteress* (illustrated in Chapter Three).

Lithophane, untitled, 19th century, French, AdT ('m" on back), 3.93" x 3.315". *Courtesy of the Hampshire County Council Museums and Archives Service, acc. no. 1980.22.17.*

One of the best-kept secrets among lithophane collectors is a public collection located in Wichita, Kansas, at the Wichita Center for the Arts – the largest public collection of lithophanes outside of the Blair Museum. The fine collection originally donated to the Wichita Art Association was from the estate of Pat Zoller McEwen, a former member of the Blair Museum. She and her husband Owen corresponded with Dr. Beroud about their collection in the 1950s. In 1969 they loaned work for an exhibition at the Wichita Art Association. Years later, after the bequest, an exhibition of a portion of this gift was held January 22 through February 26, 1984. The collection includes approximately 200 objects, including candle shields, lampshades, tea warmers, and plaques, with more than 320 individual lithophanes. The collection is largely German with KPM, PPM and Meissen represented, as well as a few marked AdT or P.R. (sickle). The collection does not meet the organization's current mission relating to regional artists, so it is seldom displayed.

The Philadelphia Museum of Art has been collecting lithophanes since as early as 1896-97, when it acquired two rare lithophanes produced by Phoenix Pottery in Phoenixville, Pennsylvania. Both were donated via a trustee who acquired them from Edwin Atlee Barber, who purchased them directly from the factory. The Museum also owns a set of eight unmarked lithophane globes, each 4.875" in height with a diameter of 6.875". In their European decorative arts collection is a Meissen plaque (no. 199 impressed) that depicts the romantic story of *Paul and Virginie*, and three PPM plaques that are part of a lampshade (PPM 94, PPM 121, and PPM 122).

Without providing details, each of the following museums also owns at least one lithophane: the Houston Museum of Decorative Arts, Chattanooga, Tennessee; Museum of the City of New York; the Strong Museum, Rochester, New York; the State Museum of Pennsylvania, Harrisburg; and the Carnegie Museum of Natural History in Pittsburgh. Sometimes in the United States lithophane collections are owned by organizations dedicated to preservation. Such is the case with Historic New England, located in Haverhill, Massachusetts, which claims to be the oldest, largest, and most comprehensive regional preservation organization in the country. Their 19th century lithophane collection includes lamps, lampshades and plaques, all with PPM or KPM backstamps.

There are many museums outside the United States that feature lithophanes in their permanent collections. Once again, few examples are on public view and most must be seen by prior appointment. The Hampshire County Council Museums and Archives Service, in England, has a collection of 44 lithophanes and several plastic versions, too. Only one lithophane is currently on display in their Allen Gallery, Alton, Hampshire – an AdT-marked nightlight with mountain scenes. The others are in storage. The collection ranges from Plaue pieces, such as PPM 781 *Das erste Gebet* (*The First Prayer*), and *Frankfurt* (PPM 577), and other German KPM and HPM plaques, as well as French examples. An unusual lithophane with the AdT mark on the front and an "m" on the back, is described in their records as "two men on the seashore ministering to, or murdering, a third." Their collection includes plaques, nightlights, steins, mugs and more. They additionally own a Japanese 20th century tea service with circular geisha lithophanes in the cup interiors. Theirs is the largest public collection of lithophanes in the United Kingdom.

Other museums in the United Kingdom with lithophane collections include the Worcester Porcelain Museum in Worcester (Grainger, Lee & Co.), the Cheltenham Museum and Gallery in Cheltenham, the Potteries Museum in Stoke-on-Trent, the Parc Howard Museum and Art Gallery in Llanelli, the Carmarthenshire County Museum, Wales, and the National Museum and Galleries of Wales (South Wales Pottery). There are also several private collections in the United Kingdom with breathtaking lithophanes.

While some collections in Europe were no doubt impacted from damage received during World War II, there remain substantial collections throughout England, France, Norway, Hungary, Germany, Austria, and elsewhere.

The MAK or Österreichische Museum für Angewandte Kunst in Vienna, not only owns the three 19th century Viennese (Wiener Porzellanmanufaktur) lithophanes that were donated to the MAK in the 19th century and are described in Chapter Three, but they also own three manufactured in Plaue and marked with PPM backstamps.

Germany's museums with lithophane collections include the Museum für Kunst und Gewerbe in Hamburg, Staatliche Kunstsammlungen in Dresden, the Kesner Museum in Hanover, the Bayerisches Nationalmuseum in Munich, the Museum für Angewandte Kunst in Cologne, Museum Hanau in Hanau, the Museum für Angewandte Kunst in Frankfurt am Main, and the Kunstgewerbemuseum in Berlin.

The Deutsches Speilzeugmuseum Sonneberg in Thuringia is a museum devoted to toys. It has at least thirteen lithophanes in its collection including those marked KPM, PPM, BPM, and HPM. These include a depiction of *The Last Supper*, Martin Luther at Christmas with his family, and children with their pets.

The Nordiska Museet in Stockholm has a rather extensive collection of lithophanes, totaling about 30, candle shields, plaques, lampshades, with German marks (KPM, PPM, Meissen) and French marked P.R. (sickle). Motifs include the two princes sleeping in the tower, two girls looking at grapes, landscapes, and children with puppies and baby goats.

Other museums containing at least one lithophane include the Hermitage Museum in St. Petersburg, Russia; the Sevres Musee de Porcelaine, Sevres; the Rijksmuseum, Amsterdam; the Bernische Historisches Museum, Berne, Switzerland; the Hamina City Museum in Finland, the Klasterec Museum, Klasterec, Czech Republic; Monk's House Museum, Manchester, United Kingdom; Museu del Cinema, Girona, Spain; the Royal Copenhagen Porcelain Factory Museum in Copenhagen, Denmark; the Royal Museum of Scotland in Edinburgh; the Swiss National Museum in Zurich; and the Town Museum in Porsgrunn, Norway.

There is also a lithophane collection located in the Château de Charles VII, Mehun-sur-Yèvre, France. Charles VII was born in 1403 and died in 1461, centuries before lithophanes were invented. The connection between Charles VII and the lithophane collection is a mystery.

In Australia, the Powerhouse Museum in Sydney has three lithophanes in its permanent collection. One is that of the KPM 260 O version of *Christus mit der Ehebrecherin, nach Signol* (*Christ and the Adulteress*); another PPM 318, *Die Unschuld* (*The Innocent*).

Chapter Seven has been dedicated to the topic of where one can visit 19th century lithophanes as they were originally installed, in their original surroundings, *in situ*. These include museums such as the Campbell House Museum in St. Louis and the Arolser Schloß in Arolsen, Germany. Several of the other locations included *in situ*, are not museums per se, but might welcome visitors, including St. Eustace Church in Herend, Hungary and the Glen Iris Inn at Letchworth State Park, in Castile, New York.

One can tell by this sampling of just a portion of museums, that there are lithophanes just waiting to be rediscovered. Just remember to make an appointment with the curator or collections manager in advance of arrival, if viewing lithophanes in person is a priority.

Lithophane in the Blair Museum of Lithophanes that matches one in the permanent collection of the Philadelphia Museum of Art. *Paul and Virginia*, 19th century, Meissen 199/74, Blair Museum acc. no. 1017, 10.25" x 7.5". *Courtesy of the Blair Museum of Lithophanes.*

Chapter Eleven
Glass, Plastic, Edible and other Lithophanes or Lithophanous Pictures

If translucency is a key requirement for creating lithophanes, then many translucent materials have been explored over the years as components of lithophanes (defined as a hidden image revealed when an object is backlit). Some of these variations have already been described in previous chapters concerning Chinese inspiration (jade table screens and Chinese lanterns) and the 18th century precursor to lithophanes – the romantic transparencies created by painting on glass or paper. Additionally, as mentioned previously there were clever related inventions such as "linophanies," described by Jacobi in his *The Printer's Handbook* of 1891, still another type of translucent picture made with paper pulp. Clearly, transparency and translucency have long intrigued creative individuals.

Even after lithophanes were the rage in Europe and widely available, there were those who wanted to create a similar phenomenon using materials available to the average creative person who did not know how to carve beeswax, make a plaster mold, prepare porcelain, and fire a kiln. This exact topic was the focus of an 1875 article in the *Crockery & Glass Journal*, titled "Lithophanous Pictures." While the author praises the virtues of porcelain lithophanes, she recommends creating a similar effect by using layers of parchment cemented together, with the end result "which are in all respects similar to porcelain."[1]

With some frequency, three-dimensional watermarks on paper have been compared to porcelain lithophanes. In the case of watermarks, the thickness in the paper is varied to alter the amount of light transmitted. Sometimes these links have lead to important discoveries. Apparently the company Delcam, located in the United Kingdom, began making lithophanes in 1991, while they were researching computer-generated watermarks.[2] Delcam is a software company that had its beginnings through collaborations with Cambridge University.

There have been succinct explorations of glass as it relates to the 19th century and lithophanes. Both Gustav Pazaurek in *Glaser der Empire und Biedermeierzeit*, published in 1923 in Leipzig, and an article by Stanislav Urban published in 1971 in the *Glass Review*, discuss the work of the Bohemian Karl Pfohl (1826-1894). His "lithophanies" have been referred to as "masterpieces of the art of glass carving," and were created circa 1864 by carving and engraving glass of different colors and then laminating the panels to create the illusion of three-dimensionality. Like porcelain lithophanes, they had to be illuminated or placed against the light to be appreciated. The origin of these glass lithophanes dates from the 1830s in what was then Bohemia. Specimens by Karl Pfohl are rare. Mr. Blair referred to these examples as cased glass, art glass or cameo glass, but acknowledged they were called lithophanes and he wished to acquire an example for the Blair Museum.

Additionally, there has been a small amount of literature generated concerning what has been referred to as "glass lithophanes." In her book *Lore of our Land Pictured in Glass*, author Bessie M. Lindsey illustrates a Lincoln lithophane as the book's frontispiece, and later in the book describes it as "a rectangular plaque of milk-white glass, a transparency, also bears a well executed portrait of Lincoln."[3] She believed the portrait, 11" in length and 8" in width, was based on a Brady photographic profile taken February 9, 1864. Apparently a method of making lithophanes from press-molded opal glass was patented by Hobbs, Brockunier & Leighton of Wheeling, West Virginia, in 1871. The products that resulted were lampshades with decorations that resembled the porcelain type. Members of the Blair Museum occasionally sent Mr. Blair photos and information about oddities such as a lithophane lampshade with what was believed to be "albumen photos on white glass."[4]

What is known about the evolution of translucent porcelain lithophanes into plastic is that the man who sold the vast majority

Lithoplastic, *William Penn's Treaty with the Indians*, 20th century, molded plastic, 6.25" x 7.875". *Courtesy of the Blair Museum of Lithophanes.*

of his collection to Mr. Blair in the 1960s, Dr. Edmond Beroud, was successful in creating "lithoplastics" of his favorite porcelain lithophanes beginning in the 1950s. In fact, a worn typescript dated May 1, 1950, records this accomplishment, "TO WHOM IT MAY CONCERN: This is to prove that I conceived the idea of reduplicating the lost art of Lithophane in plastic. By varying the thickness of plastic so the heavy parts represent the shaded parts of the picture and the thin parts the highlights. The processing is done by carving a picture in Wax, then transferring it to plaster or metal molds. The plastic can be then pressed or injected in the mold and heated a 120 degrees F. for half an hour. (1/2) It then became a finish Lithoplastic." Edmond Beroud's name is typed below and three signatures witnessed. This dentist had molds made out of bronze from existing lithophanes, and the resulting plastic versions, when viewed with transmitted light, were nearly as detailed as the original porcelain. And, of course, they did not break and they could be used as temporary replacements for missing panels in a lampshade. He even made colored lithoplastics.

In 1977, Dr. Beroud offered to members of the Blair Museum, 35 examples of lithoplastics in sizes ranging from 3" x 3.5" to 11" x 9". Themes he had selected included *Esmeralda, Maria Stuart, William Penn's Treaty with the Indians*, and more. He made these of a special plastic one at a time, by hand. In 1977, the Blair Museum sent Christmas lithophanes as gifts to all the members. These were created in a factory for this special occasion. In the early 1990s, long after Dr. Beroud had sold his lithophane collection to Mr. Blair, he enjoyed his former hobby via all the lithoplastics decorating his home – as substitutes for his favorites in porcelain. He noted that small boys throwing stones at his lithoplastic lamp in his yard, caused no damage.

Backstamp marking on a "Lithoplastic" made by Dr. Edmond Beroud, 20th century. *Courtesy of the Blair Museum of Lithophanes.*

An acquaintance of Dr. Beroud was Adrian Nagelvoort, a chemical engineer living in Utah, who at one time worked at the United States Resin Corporation. He developed a method of making lithophanes from photographs, and in the 1950s there was massive correspondence between the two referring to "plastifanes" and "mold-made" photography. As a dentist, Dr. Beroud would have known a great deal about making molds and apparently Mr. Nagelvoort had talents along the same lines. Nagelvoort made the plaster molds and Beroud the lithoplastics. These two were definitely ahead of the times when thinking about a market for plastic lithophanes with personalized photo portraits. Beroud wrote to Nagelvoort, "It occurred to me that if you could sell plastifanes to the Mormons of their shrines over there, I probably could sell Independence Hall to the tourists over here, so I am enclosing a negative of it."[5] In a letter dated May 1, 1957, Nagelvoort wrote to Beroud, "I have had an offer of financing a shop to make them by a Texas man. He was very much intrigued with them. He thought there would be many who would want their own portraits made in plastifane and would pay as much as $100 for such." They were also making and marketing earrings, an "artistic and novel T.V. lamp with plastifane plaques," and photo water marks for fine paper companies. They thought they could sell the lamp and picture combinations by the thousands as "T.V. just now – is the big fad."[6] These explorations of plastic lithophanes began so early, that it was in 1952 that Dr. Beroud wrote to Mr. Nagelvoort that he liked his idea of changing the name of the product from lithoplastic to plastifane. The new plastifane body was made of "Castelite," manufactured by the Castelite Company of Woodstock, Illinois.

Over the following years, a number of individuals and companies dabbled in plastic lithophanes. However, the next one hears of plastic lithophanes on a large commercial scale is decades later. In July 1997, while on a business trip to a molding company in Somerset, United Kingdom, Francis Dufort stopped to buy a sandwich. He noticed an antiques market on the other side of the road and "being a keen collector of curios" he went to have a look. He recalls, "I saw a white rectangular plaque lying on a table. Noticing the curious texture on the surface I asked the dealer what it was. He showed me how when held to the light an image was clearly visible. I was completely enchanted by the plaque and bought this and a second lithophane."[7] As he worked in plastics, it occurred to him at the time that this item could be manufactured in plastic.

It was a year later that he decided to see if he could manufacture plastic lithophanes. He cast a mold in aluminum resin from one of the two lithophanes he had purchased. This proved that the principle would work. After much research he found a piece of engraving software capable of converting grayscale images into engraving tool paths. Dufort noted that it was extraordinary that the software company had never made an injection molding die using their software. He also became acquainted with a company in Birmingham involved in engraving stamps for striking coins. Their engraving machinery was a perfect match for cutting precision molds in aluminum. He supplied a suitable picture, and the first mold was made. Dufort applied for a patent for the complete process of converting a grayscale image into a die for injection molding. He recalls, "I showed the first samples to a contact I had at Kellogg's and had immediate interest in the idea of producing an in-pack promotion Insert based on a plastic Lithophane." He discovered a great deal of interest from all his contacts in the promotion industry and he felt confident that this was a "great new process which was both magical in the way the image appeared from a simple piece of plastic as well as being cost effective to produce."[8]

As a result, Dufort set up a company to exploit the technology and he employed a designer to help him devise applications. His good friend Rob Stevenson came up with the name Epix at the same time eMail, eCommerce, and eShopping were popular buzz names. This same friend also came up with the first big promotion for Quaker. The Quaker promotion featured a set of collector cards depicting soccer players.

There were technical advances along the way. His company commissioned special translucent pigments which would create the best visual effect and they worked with a local molding company to perfect the process. The patent issues took time to resolve as there were objections to their patent application from various parties who had a vested interest in selling software and making molds. Epix prevailed, and they were granted the first of 14 European patents in 2000.

Epix, located in Cornwall, United Kingdom, has worked with a number of promotional companies worldwide to produce over 1 billion plastic promotional items, ranging from collectible jigsaw pieces to ice cream sticks. The successful promotions have involved end user clients such as Quaker, Nestle, Weetabix, McDonalds, Unilever, Bimbo Kraft, Frito-Lay, and many others. They now have a dedicated facility for prototyping and sampling, while the manufacture takes place in either China or the country of use. In Turkey alone, 300 million ice cream sticks have been produced. Dufort proudly notes, "The patents have many years to run and the process now known as Epix Technology has many years of potential sales ahead of it."[9]

Examples of plastic Epix lithophanes, various sizes and themes, 21st century, United Kingdom. *Courtesy of the Blair Museum of Lithophanes. Gift of Francis Dufort.*

A related product which has been deemed "tastier" rather than more tasteful than the porcelain or plastic versions, was also developed in 2003 by Dufort Associates and the process has been licensed to Chocpix Ltd. Chocpix, located in Durham, UK, has been described as "a design and production company that makes clever use of existing technology to produce novelty chocolate confectionery molds and rapid prototype packaging. The novelty feature is a hidden detailed picture – revealed by simply holding the translucent chocolate up to any bright light."[10] A report from 2006 states that they have three employees with a planned expansion to fifteen.

Chocpix novelty chocolates are produced using the latest proven CAD/CAM technology and injection molding equipment. The company creates cost effective design molds and packaging for the final product and outsources the chocolate production to local companies, thus allowing Chocpix to operate without warehouses and storage facilities. Basically, the company can scan any picture into the computer and etch the design in a block of plastic. The details are then able to be transferred to the product poured into the mold, in this case chocolate. The company can detail chocolate down to one tenth of a millimeter, and the promotional possibilities are endless. They also offer personalized chocolate, allowing the customer to supply photographs or personal messages. They use thin slabs of opaque white chocolate, and the result is a 3-dimensional effect when held up to the light, with all the details clearly revealed. Just as lithophanes won awards for their European companies in the 19th century, at its first public launch in 2004, Chocpix won an award for best British innovation among 1,500 trade stands at the world's leading chocolate exhibition in Cologne.

Chocpix (image of sheep in a field) in its original promotional packaging, molded white chocolate, 21st century, United Kingdom, 4.25" x 5.75". *Courtesy of the Blair Museum of Lithophanes.* Gift of John and Eve Coleman.

From chocolate photographic images to photographic images in polymers, lithophanes appear to be in the revival mode. Light Affection is a company founded in 2002 by Lisa Mann. Located in California, Light Affection specializes in creating one-of-a-kind personalized pieces. Most of their sales are accomplished online, and their business has been growing by word-of-mouth. The founder is a mechanical engineer who worked in the CAD/CAM industry for 10 years. It is the combination of her entrepreneurial spirit, education, and the love of design that have made Light Affection successful. Mann's science background accounts for her ease in explaining the relationship between the development of math and the application. All of these skills helped translate a picture into a three-dimensional object using CAD/CAM technology. While some have attempted to create lithophanes from translucent acrylic materials, Light Affection wanted to create their product from a material that would mirror the qualities of porcelain. The result was a translucent body that is a blend of natural materials and a polymer.

One fascinating observation by Light Affection founder Lisa Mann, is the connection between technology and art. She believes the majority of their clients have never heard of lithophanes and would never have known of their existence if it were not for technology – their use of digital cameras and the computer. This is the same technology which has allowed Light Affection to create one-of-a-kind pieces without using a master or a mold, or an extremely experienced artisan, for that matter.[11]

Light Affection issues a unique serial number and authenticity card with each piece. As their advertisements note, "Light Affection turns any personal photograph into a glowing work of 3-D art." They offer a variety of sizes and a truly unique gift that makes the customer want to investigate further this art form that refuses to be permanently "lost." An Internet search will display numerous other companies who make lithophanes using CAD/CAM or related processes, some even offering online tutorials.

Light Affection composite nightlight image from a photograph of a 2002 wedding, c. 2005, framed 4.25" x 3.25".

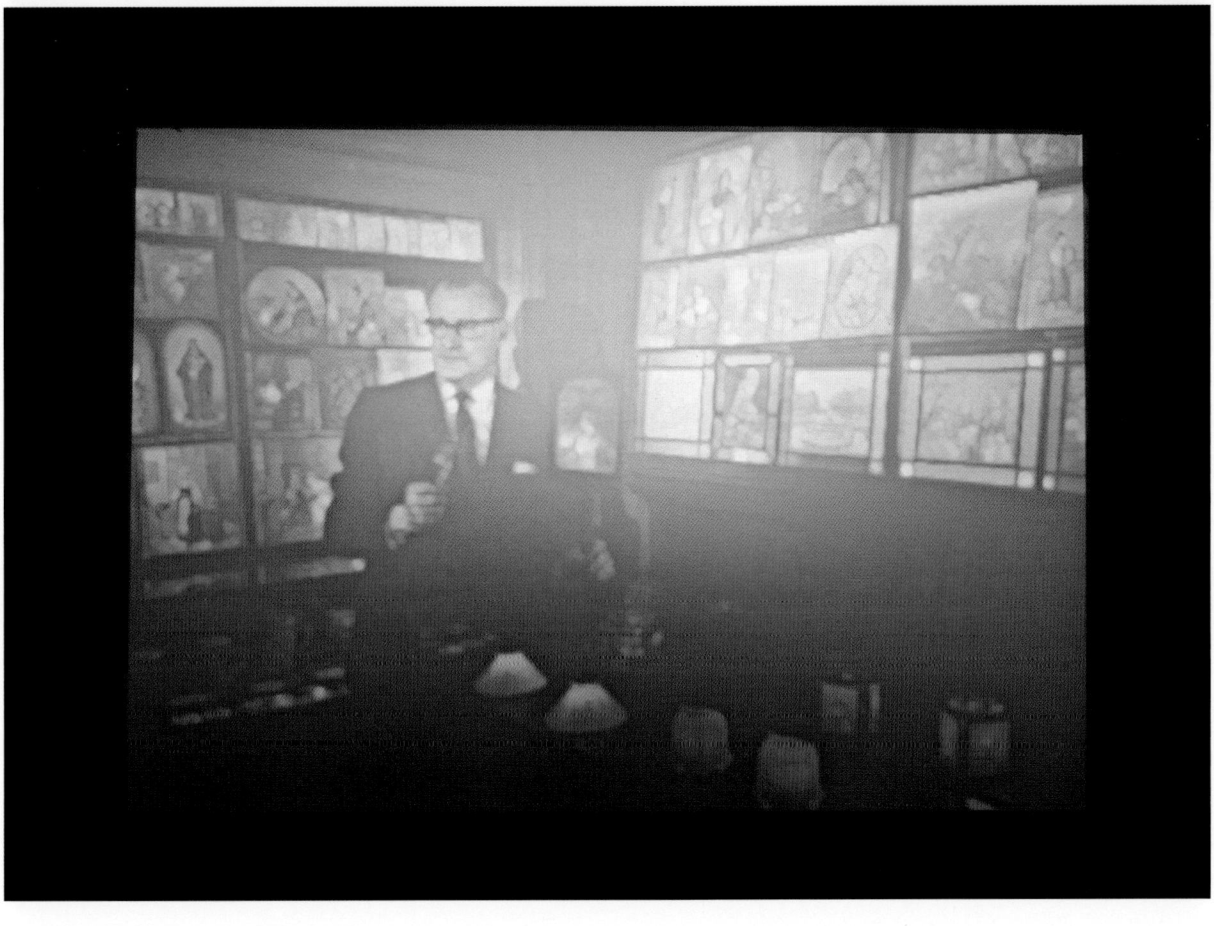

Light Affection composite light image of Laurel Blair shown with a small selection of his lithophane collection, from a 1960s black and white photograph, c. 2006, framed 5" x 7". *Courtesy of the Blair Museum of Lithophanes.*

Chapter Twelve
Twentieth Century and Contemporary Lithophane Artists

In addition to the companies that have a long history of manufacturing lithophanes and are continuing to make them today, described in Chapter Three, including Bernardaud and Haviland in France; Herend in Hungary; Rörstrand in Sweden; Vista Alegre in Portugal; and Von Schierholz in Germany, there are contemporary artists and specialized manufacturers who are enhancing our home and office environments with their lithophanes. Some of these pieces are created by means of traditional wax carving processes and many others are made through photo-mechanical or CADCAM processes. Those using materials other than porcelain, for example, a composite or polymer, are described in Chapter Eleven. Some artists are working with translucency as a primary issue, and whether or not the term "lithophane" is used in describing the work, has not restricted the listing of that artist.

Alpha Gene Blue

Alpha Gene Blue was a Native American artist who lived near Phoenix in the Southwest United States. She signed her lithophanes on the front with the "backstamp" of her surname "Blue." There are twelve lithophanes in the permanent collection of the Blair Museum created by Mrs. Blue. The subject matter is diverse and varied, including reclining nudes (Blair Museum acc. nos. 329 and 1393), Jesus walking on water (Blair Museum acc. no. 327), Santa Claus (Blair Museum acc. no. 1249), a portrait of a Native American chieftain (Blair Museum acc. no. 330), a witch riding a broom (Blair Museum acc. no. 1248), and genre scenes. Her connection to lithophanes makes an interesting story. Mrs. Blue was an employee of a gentleman who was head of a dental supply store who himself owned a collection of lithophanes. When she saw her boss's collection she was fascinated, and even though she had no formal art training, she developed her own instinctive techniques for creating original lithophanes. Mr. Blair claimed in his *Bulletin* no. 25, dated April 15, 1980, that she, "never traveled and has never been in a museum in her life!" She began making lithophanes in the 1950s or 1960s, and entered some of her creations in several art shows. In 1965 she entered two into the Arizona State Fair, Fine Art Division, and received Honorable Mention and a ribbon. She began her acquaintance with Dr. Beroud after a lithophane collector in the Phoenix area saw her work and alerted Dr. Beroud.

In Blair *Bulletin* no. 25, dated April 15, 1980, Mrs. Blue presented detailed directions and supplies for making lithophanes. These step-by-step directions are thorough, even including details about making colored lithophanes.

Mr. Blair visited Mrs. Blue in her studio in May 1980 and reported about the visit in Blair *Bulletin* no. 26, dated June 23, 1980. During that visit she showed him her wax carving talents.

Mrs. Blue visited Toledo and the Blair Museum several times, including in the fall of 1983, when she provided a wax carving demonstration for the other participants in the lithophane collector's meeting that Laurel Blair organized on a regular basis. She corresponded frequently with Mr. Blair about matters regarding lithophanes, kilns, problems with raw materials, and health issues.

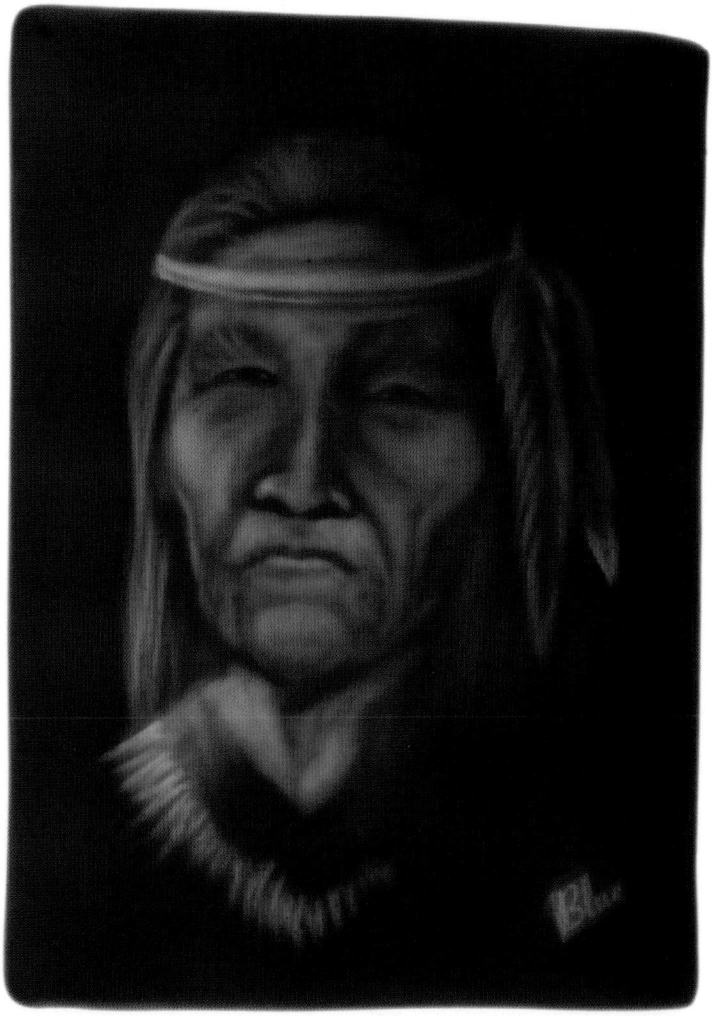

Lithophane, *Chieftain*, 20th century, by Alpha Gene Blue, Native American, signed "Blue," Blair Museum acc. no. 330, 3.625" x 2.5". *Courtesy of the Blair Museum of Lithophanes.*

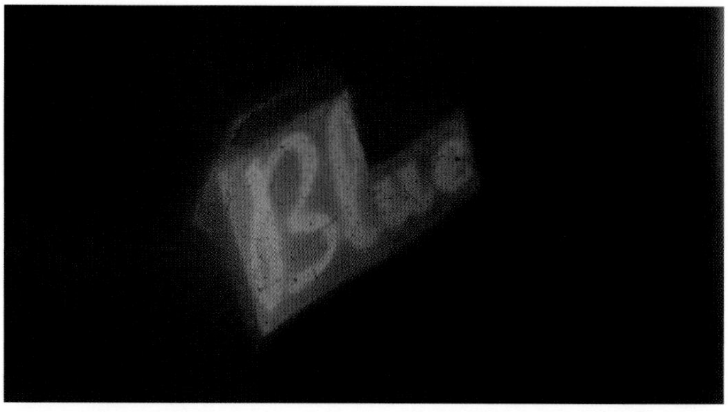

Detail of artist's signature, "Blue," on *Chieftain* lithophane by Alpha Gene Blue, 20th century, Blair Museum acc. no. 330. *Courtesy of the Blair Museum of Lithophanes.*

David Failing carving wax model for lithophane. *Courtesy of David Failing.*

David Failing and Schmidt-Failing
Utica, New York

In 1983 when David Failing (b. 1951) attended an International China Painters Convention, he had no way of knowing that it would lead to a lifelong career, the art of creating lithophanes. While at Fredonia College, where he earned a fine arts degree, he had never heard of a lithophane. When he first saw reproductions of antique lithophanes at the convention he was so intrigued by their beauty that he became determined to create his own art in the medium.

Failing's search for information on the creation of lithophanes led to a dead end. The only thing he found was that the 19th century originals were made from the plaster molds taken from carved waxes. It took years of experimentation to develop just the right wax, which turned out to be not sticky beeswax, but jeweler's wax. He learned to transfer his drawings to the wax by using a special carbon paper. As Failing said, "I couldn't just go to an art store and request lithophane carving tools."[1] He made some of his own tools and also uses dental and plaster tools to carve the wax, creating just the right depth. He removes the wax one thin layer at a time, with one shaving being perhaps two-thousandths of an inch.[2] Making the molds and then finding just the right porcelain was the next hurdle to conquer. The process of creating an original design and following through to the finished product can take months. In the beginning there was also the additional problem of how to display these new creations so that they could be lighted to show the exquisite designs. Five years later he was ready to show his creations at local art and craft shows. The response was exciting.

When researching the lithophane, Failing found that there was a Lithophane Museum located in Toledo, Ohio, and contacted the curator, Laurel Blair. Blair felt that Failing had a unique talent and was pleased to see someone turning out original work. He invited Failing to visit the museum in 1984 and show some of his work, opening a new customer base and inspiring even more original designs and new lamp styles.

By 1991, Failing had introduced his first colored lithophane and soon found that the modern day collector preferred these. He also designed an enclosure for the light source, creating an accent lamp that could be enjoyed without the glare of an exposed light bulb. This was quickly followed by a complete lampshade of porcelain lithophane panels, leaded together in the Tiffany style.

Most of the lithophanes Failing creates are limited editions and each is signed. He remains committed to Victorian themes. Over the years his lamps have been sold in the United States, Canada, and Great Britain. His company, Schmidt-Failing, Ltd., remains a small family owned business and Failing takes pride in making the highest quality lithophanes possible. Still the greatest joy for the artist comes from watching the expression of someone who is unfamiliar with this lost art when they see a lithophane light up. It's still magic.[3]

Walter Ford

The concept of photo process on ceramics, originating in the 19th century, was explored in depth in the 1930s and 1940s by a ceramic engineer at the Ohio State University in Columbus, Walter Ford. A paper on this topic, titled "Application of Photography in Ceramics," was published by the American Ceramic Society in January, 1941. This article referenced the use of photo-mechanical processes in the production of ceramic products dating back to the early 1800s. Walter Ford is examined, in detail, in Chapter Two.

Walter Ford shown working at Ford Ceramic Arts, Columbus, Ohio in 1938. *Courtesy of Sandy Schroth.* Photo by Ivor-Gordon.

Octagonal lithophane with metal banding on edge, Sailing Ship, 1988, by David Failing, American, signed "David Failing 1988" on front and "48/1000 © SF LtD" on back, Blair Museum acc. no. 1940, 6.5" x 7.75". *Courtesy of the Blair Museum of Lithophanes.*

David Jefferson
Ann Arbor, Michigan

He isn't that old, but David Jefferson was really a pioneer in the contemporary lithophane art field. Jefferson remembers that his first serious introduction to lithophanes occurred around 1974, when a local collector brought several antique lithophane panels to his studio in Ann Arbor. This collection had been purchased from Laurel Blair. These lithophanes differed from the ones Jefferson had seen in the bottoms of Japanese teacups and German beer steins that his parents had collected. He thought that the quality and fine detail of these almost photographic German KPM lithophanes was remarkable and they were so thin, they lit up with a minimal amount of light. At that point he decided to try and make his own lithophanes.

As a ceramicist, he had been experimenting for several years with translucent high fire porcelains, but discovered there were several difficulties he had to overcome to produce lithophanes. These issues involved discovering how the original 19th century lithophanes were created and finding a source of fine quality parian porcelain. He molded an original antique lithophane in plaster and then made wax copies of the original from the plaster mold. All of this was done very carefully, as the antique lithophane was on loan! The waxes were then cut up to examine the various gradations that made the image. During his early experimentation he and his studio partner (his wife, Kathleen) visited Mr. Blair to learn more about lithophanes – their history and manufacture, and to start their own collection. Their studio's first original lithophanes were made by pressing found objects, such as antique buttons, jewel boxes, buckles, frames and anything with an interesting design or texture, into plasticine. At that point they discovered that they could carve into the plaster mold itself. The porcelain used to make china dolls was the best material they could find for making lithophanes at the time, but the results did not compare with the 19th century German lithophanes. They sold their first lithophane window hangings and light boxes at the 1977 Ann Arbor Art Fair. Jefferson remembers them as rather dark panels with stained glass borders. Over the years he and his wife continued to experiment with various materials such as industrial rubbers, silicones and dental waxes that would increase the clarity of the lithophanes.

After consultation with the few remaining domestic china manufacturers in the early 1980s they began a long association and friendship with Dr. John Jones, head ceramic engineer at Lenox China Co. At that time Lenox China was not interested in making lithophanes, but Dr. Jones independently made and sold them the fine white porcelain they had long desired. They were then able to increase their production and make a unique variety of lithophanes such as miniature lamps for doll houses, thimbles, cups, candle screens, window-hangings, light boxes, Christmas ornaments, lampshades, and night-lights. An illuminated lithophane sculpture for the 1986 National Governors Convention was one of their many custom commissions.

By 1989, the Jeffersons began to investigate computer generated (CAD-CAM) engraving as a possibility for making any lithophane image they wanted. At that time, most CAD-CAM imaging was one dimensional, so they needed to customize an engraving program to include a gray scale format. They also had to learn to use a computer for creating the artwork they wanted to engrave. After much trial and error they got it on line and working. The CAD-CAM system provided the capability to produce many new images including custom work for hotels and wedding portraits.

Their business grew and they did trade shows every six months. The buyers at the gift shows expected to see a new collection every time and Jefferson recalls that it was exhausting to produce all the molds necessary to meet the sales demands. At their peak they were producing 2,500 lithophanes a month. At the same time they started producing colored lithophanes, which were so popular that people still inquire about them. Their staff included casters, mold makers, sanders, painters, kiln loaders (and unloaders). A mold would only last about 25 castings before retirement and they had to have at least 10 working molds for each design as they lost an average of thirty percent to breakage from handling and kiln cracking. The kilns cycled every 12 hours and they had 5 kilns running night and day. Finally, everything had to be boxed and shipped to their customers. During their fifteen years of lithophane production, more than 1,100 different subjects were created.

Their success in the lithophane art business lead to their retirement from that particular art form after about fifteen years. Jefferson and his wife have since reinvented themselves as artists and found a variety of different creative outlets. The octagon-shaped studio outside Ann Arbor is still jammed full of old and new lithophanes and retains the flavor of the studio of a Renaissance man, with tools and books and raw materials and antiques around every corner.

Single cast conical lithophane lampshade with fishing scene and Dutch wind mill, David Jefferson, 20th century, American, stamped in italics "Jefferson Art", Blair Museum acc. no. 2100B, Height 4", Base Diam. 5". *Courtesy of the Blair Museum of Lithophanes.*

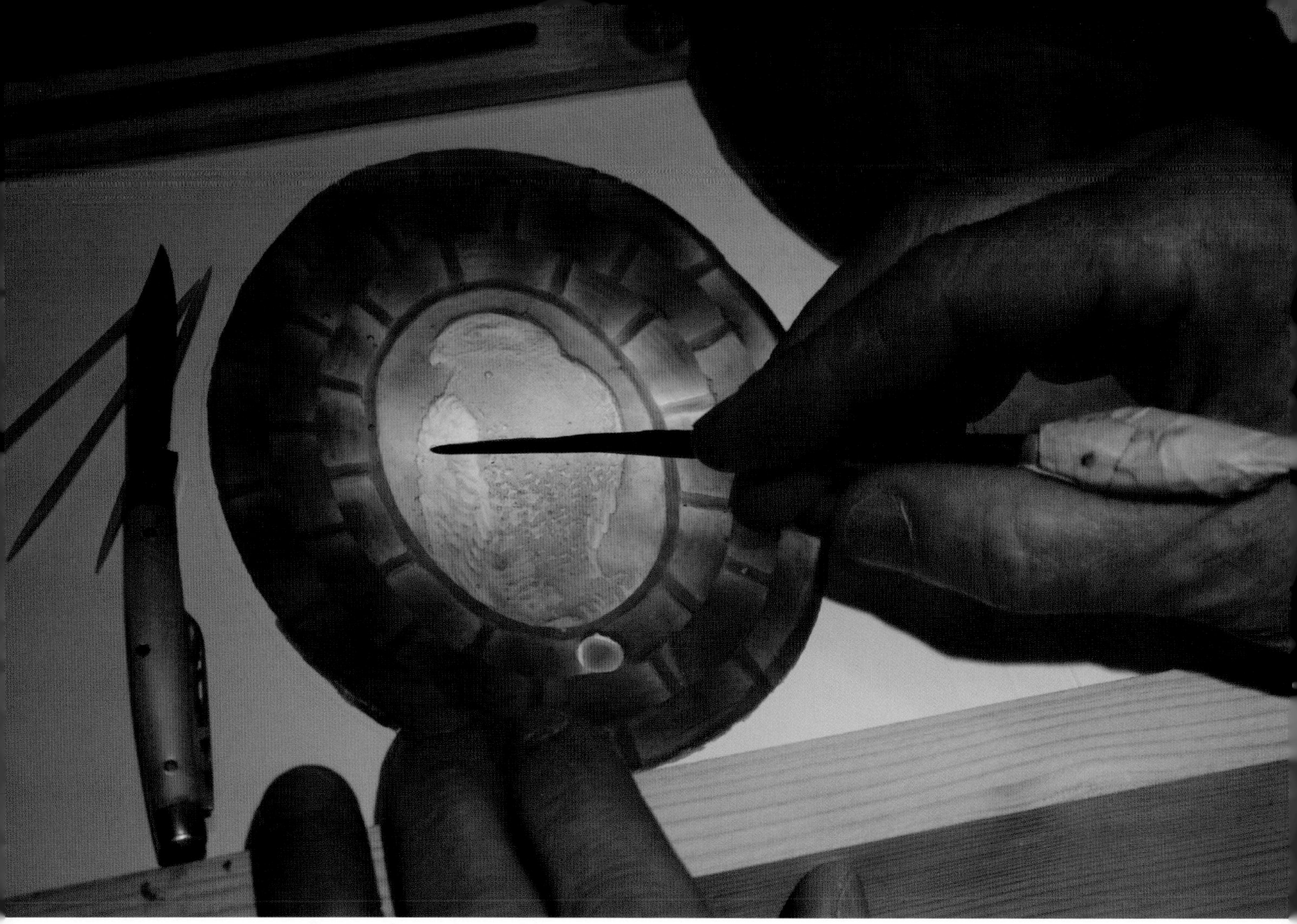

Curt Benzle touching up photomechanical wax model, c. 1995, 5" x 4". *Courtesy of the Artist.*

Curt Benzle
Huntsville, Alabama

A number of individual artists in the United States have been making lithophanes since the 1970s, one even establishing his own company for larger scale production. These individual artists would include Curt Benzle, a contemporary maker now located in Huntsville, Alabama, who has both carved his own wax models and utilized a photo process in the creation of his own original lithophanes. Benzle has been working with translucent ceramic materials since the 1970s when he was an undergraduate student at the Ohio State University. At that time, Margaret Fetzer, a ceramics professor at OSU, learned of Benzle's interest in porcelain and shared some lithophane treasures from the OSU collection.

He attended graduate school at Northern Illinois University beginning in 1974 and studied with Gib Strawn, thus developing a body of work that focused on the stamping and carving of porcelain, ceramic stains, and the transmission of light. In 1979, he moved back to Ohio, where he met Laurel Blair in Toledo. Mr. Blair was delighted to find an artist who shared his passion for translucent porcelain and was eager for Curt Benzle to reproduce lithophanes from the Blair Museum collection as a commercial product. Instead Benzle continued his creation of an original line of lithophanes that incorporated traditional carved wax techniques with his ongoing interest in stained porcelain.

Benzle met with Walter Ford in 1982, and became intrigued by the concept of photo-mechanical processes in the production of ceramic products. After extensive research of his own, Benzle developed a technique for creating lithophanes using photographic images. This is described in his own words as follows:

> The technique for making a photographic plate with sufficiently deep relief to generate a plaster mold is surprisingly similar to the relatively well known technique used in gelatin plate printmaking. The primary modification is the addition of a dichromate that will make the gelatin solution photosensitive. Either potassium or ammonium dichromate can be used with the primary difference being that ammonium dichromate is slightly stronger. A good starting point for experimentation would be: 100 gm Knox gelatin (unflavored), 2.5 gm ammonium dichromate, 300 cc water. Slowly heat the mixture until melted (heat slowly and avoid over-heating the mixture). Once melted, pour the fluid onto a sheet of ¼" plate glass surrounded by a ¼" reservoir of plastiline. Dry the plate in total darkness (I used my dehydrator). Once dry, place a negative on top of the gelatin mixture and expose under photo lamps (exposure times vary but start with 30 minutes). Wash the exposed plate under water to reveal the relief image. A plaster mold may then be pulled from the gelatin plate.[4]

Mr. Benzle cautions that both ammonium dichromate and potassium dichromate can cause skin irritation and proper safety precautions should be taken, including at least rubber gloves and a respirator during the plate making process. While Benzle's fascination with photo process on ceramics was short-lived once the mystery was solved, he has not lost interest in carving the original waxes used in producing his own lithophanes and translucent porcelain objects.

Curt Benzle currently has around ten lithophane designs in production.

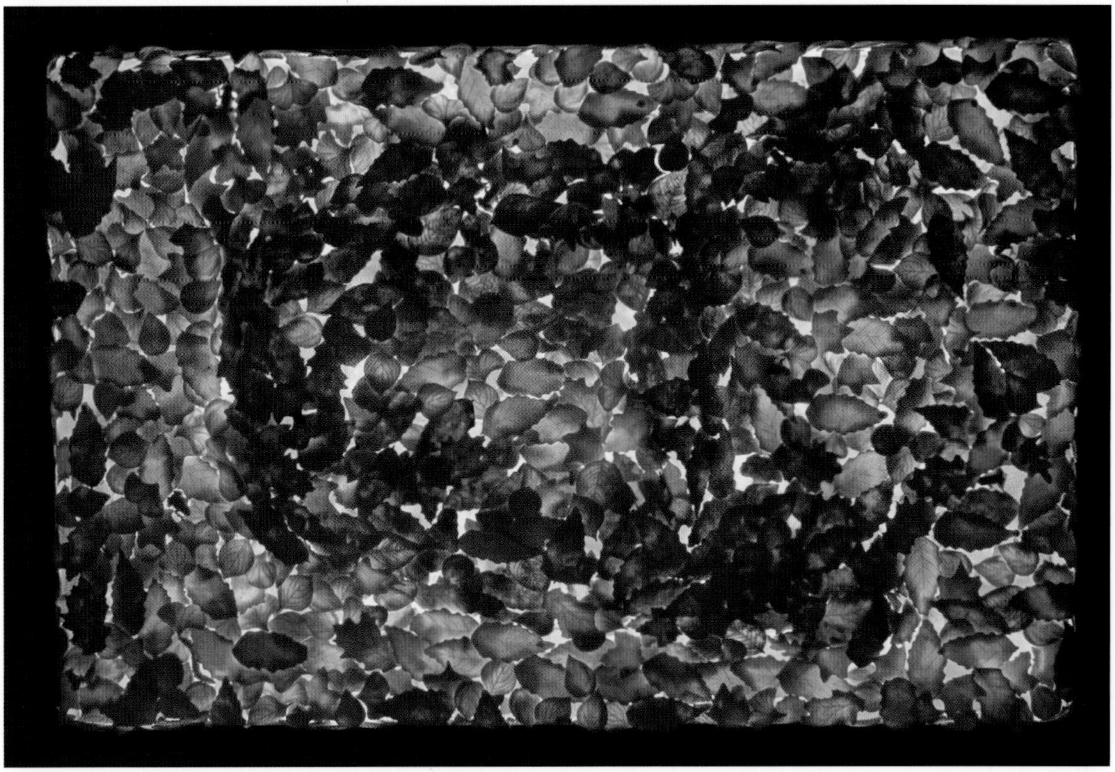

More Than Meets the Eye, c. 2006, Curt Benzle, 4' x 3'. *Courtesy of the Artist.*

Detail of frogs and leaves from *More Than Meets the Eye*, c. 2006, Curt Benzle. *Courtesy of the Artist.*

Nicolai Klimaszewski
Groton, New York

Sometimes an artist's view of the art work of a different era is surprisingly different than that of the pure consumer who has never touched clay in its unfired state. Contemporary artist Nicolai Klimaszewski's observations are perceptive, yet capture the feelings of many who view lithophanes for the first time, "A well-crafted lithophane can exhibit an astonishing range of subtle and precisely nuanced tones. This viewing experience becomes even more magical with the understanding that one is looking through a clay surface."[5]

Klimaszewski has written that "the best lithophanes produced in the nineteenth century were hand-carved, even those that have a photographic appearance to them. Skilled artists worked from photographic references while carving a translucent wax slab that mimicked the behavior of translucent porcelain."[6] It is interesting that his first attraction to lithophanes and the related intaglio process of *émaux ombrants*, was the photographic quality of both carved surfaces, which he only later discovered were produced from models carved by hand. He knew that Walter Woodbury had used a chemical process to produce photographic relief surfaces as early as 1865, so it was surprising to him that lithophanes were not produced through photomechanical means.

In the early 1990s Klimaszewski began experimenting with computer carved photographic surfaces and by 1994 he had his first operational prototype. His homemade machines run on his own homemade software that translates the grey scale contained in a photograph into a carved surface. From this he is able to create lithophanes, *émaux ombrants* tiles, Woodbury-process prints, and other experimental forms.

Mr. Klimaszewski has recorded three ways to make lithophane originals. The first, reproduced here, is related to the 19th century practice of carving beeswax models. The other two, Walter Ford's chemical process for producing lithophanes from photographs, is explained in Chapter Two, while the application of digital technology to produce lithophanes from photographs is easily available at many Internet sites. He does however, suggest that the novice may wish to have a sample carved by an Internet vendor and then experiment with this plastic model before investing in costly equipment. One may also consult his website at www.klimco.com

Hand-carving original art for the production of lithophanes, in the words of the artist:

> The best lithophanes produced in the nineteenth century were hand-carved, even those that have a photographic appearance to them. Skilled artists worked from photographic references while carving a translucent wax slab that mimicked the behavior of translucent porcelain. Most likely the carving tables were near a window and had an angled mirror beneath them to provide constant illumination.
>
> I highly recommend a wax from the Kindt-Collins Company (800-321-3170) called KC-1767-x. It is a dry white wax with excellent carving properties, it casts easily, and does a reasonable job of mimicking the behavior of light going through porcelain. A five-pound chunk should be enough wax to make more than a dozen lithophane panels 5 x 7 inches.
>
> To make a 5 x 7 inch slab of wax ¼ inch thick:
>
> 2 pieces of 8 x 10 inch glass, one clean, one with silicone applied.
>
> 3 pieces of ¼ inch thick wood strips (balsa from a hobby store is o.k.).
>
> 6 metal spring clamps.

Andres Serrano & Sister Agnes, Nicolai Klimaszewski, porcelain lithophane construction with vintage image on right, 11" x 14". *Courtesy of the Artist.*

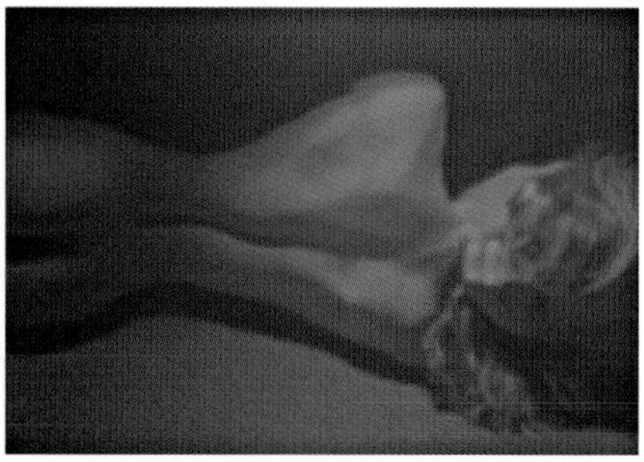

Lithophane made from cherry-avocado soap, *Becky's Back,* Nicolai Klimaszewski, 4" x 5.5". *Courtesy of the Artist.*

Arrange 3 wood strips on clean glass in a 5-7-5 U-shape. Place the other glass on top and secure with spring clamps. Put it in an oven at 200 degrees F to warm it.

Melt some wax in a double boiler. Use a thermometer in the wax and do not exceed 200 degrees F. When liquid, stir well to distribute the solids contained in the wax and cast into the warm glass mold on the open 7-inch side, letting the wax run in against the plain glass. Let the wax cool slowly, then remove the silicone treated glass and the wood strips. The remaining glass will be useful to support the wax while working and will also aid in forming of the plaster mold.

Carry out the carving over a light source and try to ignore the somewhat unattractive surface that emerges; concentrate instead on the light-dark image being transmitted through the wax. Mistakes can be repaired by using hot tools and adding wax. If more opacity and whiteness are desired, a small amount of white colorant sold for use in candle making can be added to the double boiler. When the carving is finished, cast a plaster mold, press or cast the clay into it, dry, and fire. It is useful to make a few quick studies to establish the entire workflow. The studies will also show that the finished porcelain image contains a little more contrast than what the wax indicates.[7]

Marty Kubicki and The Porcelain Garden

The Porcelain Garden was established in 1982, through the combined talents of Marty Kubicki and Liesa Smith. Their lithophane story, told from the viewpoint of Marty Kubicki, is an interesting one.

Educated as an electronics engineer, Mr. Kubicki moved to California in 1977. He became friends with the owners of a ceramics studio located just across the street from where he lived. Just at the time he was becoming disillusioned with the direction of his career, he was offered a position working in the ceramics studio, painting decorative ceramics. It was there that he learned about casting, glazing, and firing ceramics. After a few years, he and his partner began designing a line of home decorative accessories, first in earthenware, and later in porcelain. He says, "We were drawn to the beauty, the translucency, and the enigmatic character of working with this difficult material."[8] Then in 1981, he was approached by an artist at an art festival. He recalls, "She held in her hand a flat piece of etched porcelain, but it was difficult to discern the design in the etching. She then held the panel up to a light, and a remarkably detailed image revealed itself." Needless to say, he was enthralled by what he saw. He learned from this woman that she had a collection of lithophanes, and had tried to reproduce them with little success. While she was giving up her quest, he and his partner embraced the idea and purchased her collection, including porcelain plaques, plaster molds and several acrylic reproductions. He spent the following nine months learning how to make molds and at the same time worked on his casting techniques. "Our initial idea was to simply attach a porcelain panel to a night light, and to test market them that way. So there we were, at an art festival with our existing line of decorative porcelain, and in the back of the booth we had one little electrical strip with some night lights plugged in. People were drawn to them like moths to a flame! The initial reaction was so overwhelming, that it did not take us long to completely abandon our previous work and devote all our energy to creating these amazing night lights. Initially we were just making reproductions of the old patterns that we have in our collection. I also began to actively collect lithophanes. Over the next ten years I amassed a collection of about 240 antique lithophanes." Most of these are unmounted KPM and PPM panels, along with trapezoids, several lampshades, tea warmers, steins, and teacups, and even some colored pieces.

Marty Kubicki touching up a plaster lithophane mold for the Porcelain Garden. *Courtesy of the Artist.*

The story does not end there. He recalls, "Over time, while working on correcting flaws in the molds, we eventually learned how to carve our own original designs. This opened up a whole new world to us, as we were no longer limited by designs produced 130 years ago. We were very excited, because for the first time in modern history, we could take this antique art form and start interpreting contemporary designs into it, and progress the art into the 21st century. This also allowed us to design larger pieces that could be incorporated into table lamps that had not been made before." Current production involves a combination of carving and CAD. All of their porcelain pieces are designed, cast, finished and fired in their studios in California. They use only kiln-fired porcelain, not any resin or epoxy or porcelain blends. They produce over 50,000 lithophanes annually – roughly 160 designs. He concludes, "After 25 years, I still get excited to see a new design come out of the kiln and be held up to the light for the first time. Lithophanes are my life, my passion, my love, and I will continue to work with them until my body no longer allows it."

Filling lithophane plaster molds with porcelain slip at the Porcelain Garden. *Courtesy of the Porcelain Garden.*

Greenware porcelain lithophanes just out of the plaster molds at the Porcelain Garden. *Courtesy of the Porcelain Garden.*

Chris Wight

Around 1996-98, a Scottish ceramic artist and designer, Chris Wight, researched lithophanes and began experimenting with the translucency of bone china and the tonal changes of carved images. While pursuing his BA and then later his MA in ceramics at Staffordshire University he had studied surface pattern and design. A work placement at Wedgwood had provided his first encounter with a lithophane mold and that triggered further investigation. His creations in the mid to late 1990s dealt with large-scale translucent surfaces and carvings that were less detailed than that found in a lithophane. His panels, screens and vessels are luminescent and frequently incorporate other materials along with the bone china, such as toughened glass, aluminum, Perspex and stainless steel. Although at present he claims he is not actively researching lithophanes, his current work in bone china still utilizes amazing creativity and technical expertise to explore and exploit the translucency of the material along with demonstrating a masterly understanding and display of good design. More information about Chris Wight can be discovered at www.cone8.co.uk website.

Other contemporary lithophane artists and companies that use plastic, composites or polymers are discussed in Chapter 11. These makers include Light Affection, Epix, and more.

Whether one accesses lithophanes through vintage 19th century lithophanes at the Blair Museum in Toledo, plug in nightlights with Maxfield Parish print images purchased on Ebay, photomechanically produced wedding photo night lights of dearly beloveds, contemporary artwork in translucent porcelain discovered at a local holiday craft fair, or plastic promotional versions in with lunch box snacks, each invites the viewer to step into a magical world. Despite recent advances in digital imaging, computers, and communication, the innovations of the 19th century remain magical in terms of lithophanes.

Fish Screen, 1997, by Chris Wight, bone china, lead came and wenge, each panel Height: 196 cm. x 80 cm. *Courtesy of the Artist.*

Appendix A
English Translation of Original 1827 French Baron Bourgoing Patent for Lithophanes, no. 5117

COPY OF PATENT NO. 5117 – PATENT OF A FIFTEEN YEAR INVENTION, DATE JANUARY 12, 1827, TO THE SIEUR DE BOURGOING IN PARIS, FOR THE PROCESS OF LITHOPHANY

Like lithography, lithophany reproduces and multiplies the original work of the designer, but the new process is, for most subjects, infinitely more rapid than any of those known up to now. It offers the advantage, too, of allowing the use of a great number of different materials, from transparent colors and glazes to glass, porcelain; hard and precious stones, their imitations, and every other substance capable of taking the most beautiful polish, and to keep without any change.

TRANSLUCID LITHOPHANY
First Process

Although lithophanic products give, at will, the effect of ordinary as well as transparent pictures, the painter prefers to do his first work on a glazed surface which is colorless, covered by a light coat of transparent color; then it is only by mechanical methods that the subjects thus produced are molded and multiplied so as to result in either opaque pictures, to serve as ornaments for all kinds of objects, or panes, screens or other transparent things.

The reliefs which are to produce these results are modeled by means of a principle entirely different from that used in engraving, either in intaglio or in relief. It is not the shapes of the objects, their projections or hollows, which determine the prominences and recesses of the lithophanic surface; the inequalities are only determined by shadow and highlights. The effect of these reliefs cannot be imagined; looked at in any other way than letting light rays through them, show only a shapeless piece of work; but, held to a light or to daylight through a window, suddenly become pictures as remarkable for their softness and harmony as for the absence of any trace of an engraving tool, and above all, for the fidelity of reproduction of the original work; but this new art would be incomplete if its results could only be applied to transparent objects. Two processes can be followed to transform into opaque pictures the subjects first treated as translucid lithophany.

Second Process

Any subject having been cast from the original in transparent colored material then receives, on the side of the relief, a coat or background of a white or opaque substance (china clay for example); thus it becomes a real picture, showing all the gradations from the deepest shadow to the sharpest highlights. It would have been enough, to obtain this effect, to give the colored material a great degree of translucence than to that intended for transparent pictures; the light actually passes through the latter, while the others only show up by the reflection of the white substance which makes up the background.

Third Process
Lithophany with Soft Shadows

This third process consists of touching up in black the impression of the relief, which, the "clear-fading" variety, is superposed by a white substance. The relief cast for this kind of picture is nothing more than a transparent colored material, but white and diaphanous, in appearance somewhat like porcelain enamel or the crystal called opal glass. In the clear-fading pictures, it is the white background which, seen through the different thicknesses of a color material, produces the desired effect. In the soft shadow method, on the contrary, it is the shadows in a background of black, brown, violet, or some other dark color, which come to the surface of the picture, tempered and modified by the more or less thick coats of a white material through which they have come.

In these two kinds, the surface of the picture is a perfectly smooth plane; the back may also be; the carvings of the lithophanic surface are in the middle of the thickness of the picture.

These two processes are employed in turn according to the subjects; the first gives more vigor to the shadows and contours; the second produces soft, vaporous tones which lend themselves to marine views and landscapes. This kind, carried out to the perfection of which it is capable, can give finished pictures, and nuances with as much softness as an agate, doubled naturally with a darker material. The process with softened shadows offers the additional advantage of giving at will different shades to the dark background, so as to obtain pictures, not with a gray or bister ground, but in natural colors.

By means of the three processes here described, India ink, sepia and water colors can be united in polished, unchanging material; the softness obtained without any trouble by the thickness equals what the most able brush cannot produce without much time and effort.

The inventor proposes to request a patent on transparent lithophanic pictures of every material and applicable to every usage for which they may be adapted; for the second and third processes, objects of every size which may be foreseen, such as:

Framed pictures, folding screens in arabesques, white wooden chair backs, or painted in white sunbursts, then varnished in colors;

Boxes and fancy objects: objects replacing glazed cloth, shading or softened shadows, by mean of reliefs in bright varnished metal in colors, or in black metal varnished in white; for natural or artificial stones to be used in jewelry, either transparent or set in gold or silver.

For all kinds of vases, tables, center tables or china sets, shaded; by means of white earthenware covered with a coat of glazing or colored enamel or in softened shadow; black earthenware coated with white or diaphanous enamel; for all objects, in a word, capable of being cast and reproduced by the three methods detailed above.

It will be noted that, in these three kinds, the original picture may give an endless number of impressions, producing casts more numerous and perfect, from a lithophanic picture, than from other reproductive arts, which work from a single model, and each cast dulls and sharpness.

To make this art available to painters who would experience difficulty in painting on transparent material, a method has been developed which allows the artist to continue with his style.

This fourth procedure consists of painting on white marble without checks, with colors or lacquers which are transparent but with some thickness. The artist produces in this way, directly and with the aid of his brush alone, pieces as capable of being cast and reproduced as those from a picture painted originally on a transparent surface.

LITHOPHANY
Explanation of Lithophanic Processes in all their Details

This new art produces, as has just been said, by means of different thicknesses of materials white and colored, every shade of light and shadow of a picture.

These pictures may be, as desired, transparent or opaque; although the former are only the least important branch of the new invention, we may start with the detailed explanation of the process employed in this part of the lithophanic art; processes since discovered, and which transform into ordinary pictures subjects first treated as transparent.

TRANSLUCID LITHOPHANY PART ONE

To produce the original of the diaphanous pictures, like those shown in the gallery, a colorless glass was taken, surrounded by a border of putty about one centimeter thick; this glass having been placed horizontally on a tripod. Melted colored wax is poured, in sufficient quantity to cover the whole surface of the glass, this first coat to form the sky of the subject, and must be very light, and arranged so as to just cover the background.

The proportion to keep between the thicknesses and the transparency of the materials being the basis of every lithophanic operation, the waxes with the strongest colors, pour subjects which are wanted in higher relief, are only light applied for pictures where greater thickness is desired. It will be explained how the various subjects require alternately higher or lower reliefs.

The wax flowed on the picture being still liquid, the glass slab is slightly inclined toward one of the upper corners, so as to make darker the upper parts of the sky of the landscape. At the same time, care is taken to lightly shake the inclined slab, so as to produce in the wax, just as it hardens, some more or less pronounced waves, to give the effect of clouds. Often, at the first try, this can be done in this way; lucky accidents which need only a few lines with the chisel or graving tool to give the character of clouds. Other times one must melt the wax again and let it cool with the same precautions, and to blow on the places which are to be the lightest in tone.

This operation is repeated until satisfactory result are obtained by this almost accidental cooling of the colored wax; skies formed like this are always quite light and soft.

When it comes to placing distant mountains against the sky thus put on, other, very thin coats of wax are poured on the lower part, which, flowing in the directions given, produce, often by themselves, movements which a little working with the chisel are enough to transform it into distant peaks covered with snow, their sides ringed with trees to the summit; hills full of buildings, belfreys and other objects standing out in light colors against the dark background; in a word, to correct the defects in outline in the imagined subjects, or to make them more nearly resemble what it is desired to imitate, in reproducing scenes from nature.

These first procedures, which are very long to describe, are quite rapid to execute; it takes on a few minutes to arrange the sky and distant objects of the landscape up to two feet in height.

The background being thus arrived at, you proceed by various operations to bringing about the foreground.

Melting the wax and flowing it by means of a watering can with a flattened spout is almost always preferred as the quickest method. However, sheets of wax, varying in thickness, are employed, cut and applied in place; this is used mostly for walls of buildings in the foreground, for landscapes and interiors, this type of subject requiring large surfaces all of one shade, which wax sheets provide more easily than melted wax. An expedient must be noted which, especially for interiors, is a great help to shorten the work. This consists of tracing according to the ordinary laws of perspective, all the lines marking the joints of the stones of a wall, so as to push up on one side of the line the wax routed out, and then smoothing it with the finger; in this way it shows the highlight of the upper side of each stone and the shadow of the lower side. The figures of people, where they are the principal interest of the picture, are carved with the chisel; in landscapes and pictures where they are subdued and small they are produced by quicker methods. For this effect, sheet copper can be cut out, a half a line thickness, of figures in all attitudes and all sizes, from one line to eight; horses, cattle, dogs, etc., in the same proportions, are made the same way. These figures, whose outlines are the same as those in ordinary reliefs, differ from them essentially in the engraving of their two sides; this engraving, in fact, does not give the highs and lows of figures in ordinary relief, but just their lights and shadows, from which are calculated their thicknesses.

The cuts will give an idea of this difference between the reliefs used in sculpture or engraving, and the lithophanic reliefs.

The sphere, taken for example, only shows in cuts A and B a lenticular projection or hollow, like a globe either in ordinary low relief or in intaglio, like in a figure of Atlas or Uranus. The same subject, treated in lithophany, shows us in the cut a sphere of an entirely different aspect: circular in its outline like the globe A, it differs in its inside working, where a luminous point is seen in the hollows and reliefs, in the form of a crescent, which is to be the ball's shadow when light shines through it. What has just been said of the sphere applies to any other figure. A transparent stone, engraved in intaglio or in relief in the ordinary manner, and held to the light, shows, besides the outlines, the carved shapes of the figures; but these shapes will never look like anything but a bas relief, without shadows thrown, without background, without light and dark; here, on the contrary, you produce, with just the help of casting, thicknesses, and figures lighted like in paintings. Lithophany can then be defined as an art which, by means of cast reliefs, bring real pictures of all possible kinds.

By using a hundred figures cut out of copper, as has just been said, one can put any desirable variety in groups of lithophanic landscapes; the same person in profile can at will be placed walking from left to right or from right to left; it is only necessary to turn the cut out figures; the same horse can at will be a white horse against a dark background, or a black horse placed on a light background, according to whether the figure has been pressed into the wax, or left inlaid, producing a relief in copper. If you wish to show a piebald horse, or some other object made up of black and white parts, the outline of the figure is modeled, by turns, hollow and in relief.

These figures thus obtained, and made, at while, dark or light, and walking from one side or the other, can be infinitely varied still more by means of accessories used with them; hats, cloaks, plumes, etc., being added with the chisel.

These metal figures left in the wax, where they have the effect of reliefs, can only be used for transparencies to be cast and reproduced. In original pictures painted as samples, one cannot use figures made up in advance, these originals being perforce complete pictures, transparent in all their parts, and capable of giving an idea of what a copy would be, cast in solid material. These original pictures, being finished, you proceed by means of casting to produce as many copies as desired.

PART TWO

Plaster is first flowed on the original wax. A matrix in the same material (plaster) was taken on the first plaster.

On this second coat of plaster is flowed the mold in copper, tin or again in plaster, to reproduce copies of the original work.

Several reasons have made necessary these four successive castings: in the first place, the impossibility of flowing any other material but plaster on the original wax.

Secondly, the advantage, in all engraving work, of cutting out in a mold what is to be in relief on a cast.

Lastly, however, to prevent any miscasting between the matrix and the cast, which often contain, both of them, as many objects, projecting as hollowed out, great precautions have to be taken. First, here are the names for the casts and matrices used.

The first piece of work in wax is called Aperçu (A).

The first flow of plaster, or second result, is called Base (B).

The second flow of plaster, or third result, receives the denomination Contre-epreuve (C).

The fourth piece of work, out of copper or mother material, is called Definitif (D).

Finally, from this Definitif cast come the copies, Exemplaires (E).

These names were chosen so that their initials would indicate their order in the lithographic process.

The first and second plaster coats being easily confounded by the workers, it was thought best to always flow the bases in white plaster (BB), and the second flow in colored plaster (CC). On these bases are made all the relief parts, which, on account of their thinness, it would be long and hard to model first on the original wax; thus, the branches and twigs of trees without leaves in winter scenes, the balustrades of a bridge, spears, swords, people's staffs, etc. are preferably carve out on plaster bases.

It is possible even to work by carving the matrix, correcting the work done on the bases, adding highlights to the reliefs made in them; placing, in winter landscapes, snow clinging to branches, etc.

On the metal positives made up one may retouch the parts which require greater sharpness: faces, hands, embroidery, people's clothes, regular railings, the upper parts of gothic windows, etc.; all these objects are corrected and finished with the chisel on the metal molds.

However, it is not always necessary to go to the expense of metal molds; plaster positives suffice when it comes to make copes in china.

The details given above explain fully how all kinds of diaphanous pictures are produced, such as panes, transparent framed screens, etc., in any material; to produce them in glass, in enamel, in wax or gum, you have only to mold the positives in such and such a substance, capable of taking impressions.

These different casting operations, going back to known processes, do not need to be described here.

Now we must explain how translucid lithophane pictures are transformed into ordinary pictures.

PART THREE

To obtain the first kind of opaque pictures, we have taken the base in white plaster of some subject; we have flowed a second coat of wax, or preferably colored and transparent resin, which we then pressed with a glass plate to make it thinner and with a smooth surface. We were careful to press the glass on the resin while still soft, hard enough so that the most prominent objects of the white relief would be veiled by as fine a coat of resin as possible; it is clear that these very tops of the relief, seen through paper thin resin, appear almost white, while the colored resin was deeper present masses of more or less pronounced shadow. In this way the thicknesses of the transparent colored material give, in translucid lithophany, all the tones of light and shade desired. You need only give the resin more transparence than the wax of the lithophane screens. The latter is really pierced by the light itself, whereas the resin of the (clair-ternis) is pierced only by the reflection given the white reliefs which it covers. What has just been said of wax and resin is true by analogy of harder materials: such as white porcelain, or translucid lithophany, while for the transparent coatings of opaque pictures, it would be better to use glass, enamel and other colored but limpid substances.

It is superfluous to remark that it is immaterial, to obtain (clair-terni) pictures, to flow the transparent substance on to the white reliefs cast in advance, or else to pour the white and opaque substance on the casts made first in diaphanous material. The sample herewith was obtained in this way; on a first coating of wax lightly colored, and with a low relief, was flowed a double coating of plaster. This sample may appear a bit dark, perhaps, as the was here replaces only imperfectly the resin or colored glass.

These (clairs-ternis) will be put to good use in replacing painting on china. The bottoms of plates and other objects will be cast on lithophane positives, and then covered with a light coat of colored transparent enamel; they will present pictures perfectly polished on the surfaces, and reproducing the original work with extreme fidelity. We will not go into more ample details on the application of the different combinations possible of white and opaque materials, or metallic and highly polished, doubled with transparent substances; from white woods or painted white, then engraved and polished, to tin plate or cast tin, and china and other white earths capable of being enameled; all substances can be at will used in the (clairs-ternis). The processes employed will be the same as those in use up to now by the different industries which work in these materials.

PART FOUR
LITHOPHANY IN SOFTENED SHADOW

The second type of opaque lithophane pictures is only the counterpart of the first; it consists, in effect, of casting in black the matrices of the lithophane reliefs, and covering them with a very light coat of white, diaphanous enamel like the crystal known as opal glass. In this kind of production, it is the shadow of the background coming to each point of the polished surface of the picture, after being softened or more or less effaced by traversing different degrees of thickness of a white material; the two kinds have the same result by opposite means, as, in the two cases we arrive by the thicknesses of white to black, passing through all the intermediate shades. All subjects can then be treated at will as (clair-terni) or as softened shadow; but the latter, more difficult to obtain by reason of the uncertain effects of fire on the milky white glass, will have, in the copies which come out well, a softness still greater than that obtained by the (clairs-ternis). The effects of fog, the smoke of battle, marines and other similar subjects, portraits of women, the imitation of velvet and light cloth, will be the result more particularly of this type.

Carried to the perfection which it should attain, it will give pictures which, by their fine polish and softness of their shading, will present the aspect of agates whose transparent coats were naturally assembled by chance, so as to produce a landscape or portrait.

With the two types which we have just been descrived, it will be possible to take subjects before covering them with enamel, and in this way may have pictures in colors.

PART FIVE
TRANSPARENCY OF SUBSTANCES USED

The exact estimate of the transparency of the materials used being, in the first three branches of lithophany, the first of all conditions for the success of the picture, we must figure out a means of measuring it satisfactorily. Two instruments have been thought out for this purpose.

Before describing these instruments, it is useful to establish a distinction between the two kinds of pictures whose transparency they will measure. That of colored, limpid glass can only really be evalued by the same scale as that of materials with a cloudy, milky transparence. In the colored glass, it is the depth of the color which grows by reason of the thickness of the plaque; in the opal glass, it is the opacity which grows by means of this same thickness. Pure, perfectly white crystal is the point of departure or zero of these two scales. The other extremity of their subdivisions is for colored glass, blue for example, the degree of the coloration, where the blue tint is so dark that it can be taken for black. As for the colored glass called opal crystal, it is by passing through all the transitions of whitish transparence that this glass soon has only the half transparency of china, and arrives finally at the absolute opacity of chalk or plaster. The two instruments have then, for their particular aim, one to measure to what degree the glass has been colored; the other, to what point it will have been rendered cloudy.

For the first of these instruments, we take two thick glass plaques, 20 centimeters long by three centimeters wide; these two bands are joined together by a copper mounting, which keeps them one of top of the other, inclining them five degrees. One of these plaques is movable around an axis on the hinge placed at the point of the angle formed by the intersection of the inside surfaces of the glass bands. Under one of these bands is a movable needle, following the whole length of the instrument. The same band is divided in equal parts, by a simple geometric operation. This graduation is made so that each subdivision is placed where the material between the two sides of the angle would be 1, 2, 3, etc. centimeters thick, always measuring this thickness, not from the perpendicular brought down from a point of one of the sides of the angle on the other side; but from the line which, drawn from this point on the opposite side, is equally inclined to the two sides of the angle, and forming with them the base of an isosceles triangle. This line, whose length shows the thickness of the material held between each point of the two sides of the angle, is merely the chord of this angle placed on circles of different radiuses. Thus, the chord of an angle of 5 degrees, applied to a circle with a 50 cm radius, is one cm long, which should be more than enough to measure the transparency of a very slightly colored glass, so at 50 cm distance from the top of the angle is placed the last subdivision, and which shows the maximum of the evaluation of the transparent thicknesses. One could really make the sides longer, but the instrument would then be unwieldy with no useful purpose, as lithophane reliefs can only be made with raised surfaces (**) cm high, and colored glass, which is not totally dark unless this thickness, being too light to produce any effect in (clair-terni), and even less in translucid lithophany.

To make this instrument to measure the transparency of the wax, resin or colored water representing glass of the same tint, you merely pour the substance into the inside of the angle; the point where the moveable needle ceases to be visible, placing the instrument on a white surface, gives the degree of transparency on the material so placed.

However, as it would be impracticable to measure in the same was melted glass, we must use iron tongs which close and leave between their jaws the different portions of the space contained between the plaques.

Experience and use of this instrument alone can determine the lengths to give these measurements;

The whole of their length; that is to say, the first tongs, the triangle of the apex, and the four others, the trapeziums which follow at 10 centimeters. By means of these tongs we can take the hot glass and put it against the scale of transparency, after letting it harden. We must simply take the precaution of choosing, appropriately, the tongs which seem to fit, according to the proportion of colored material placed in the crucible.

This instrument has never been very exact, as total obscurity does not take place at a certain point, but imperceptibly; but it does for a somewhat exact estimate for the composition of glass, as lithophane reliefs do not demand a precise degree of transparency; this transparency can vary in the same picture, without causing any trouble, by 10, 20 or even 30 degrees.

The second instrument is constructed on the same principle; only, as milkiness runs on a scale much shorter than limpid, colored transparency, we give smaller dimensions to the second instrument.

Some substances, such as tinted wax and opal, turquoise blue or rose crystal, being at once cloudy and colored, must be put to the measurement of the two instruments.

Such are the different methods that are employed in the three branches of lithophany. It must be added that, to bring this art within range of artists who experience difficulty in painting transparent, either vertically, or placing the colored glass on a slanted easel under a horizontal mirror, we may imagine we are painting on a ground of close grained marble, and just with the aid of the brush, by means of very transparent colors having some thickness, we make on this white background, and directly, (clairs-ternis) capable of being cat and reproduced in the same way as those made from pictures first painted transparent. This method furnishes by consequence the means of transporting onto cloth and as if on paper, cast pictures which owe their effects solely to the transparence and thickness of the colors of which they are composed. It may be seen that, after all these operations here described, this one will present little difficulty; but the art of lithophany promises such vast assemblage of different and useful results, that we have had to confine ourselves, in the beginning, to making a choice; as for the exploitation of these processes, it is proposed to start with objects in china, glass and enamel.

Since lithophane pictures are all produced by means of rather pronounced reliefs, it will be possible to reproduce or make larger, by means of a portrait enlarger, the works of artists which we may wish to reproduce in different dimensions.

Appendix B
English Robert Griffith Jones Patent

A.D. 1828 . . . . N° 5626.

Ornamenting China.

JONES' SPECIFICATION.

TO ALL TO WHOM THESE PRESENTS SHALL COME, ROBERT GRIFFITH JONES, of Brewer Street, in the County of Middlesex, Gentleman, send greeting.

WHEREAS His present most Excellent Majesty King George the Fourth did, by His Letters Patent under the Great Seal of Great Britain, bearing date at Westminster, the Thirteenth day of March, One thousand eight hundred and twenty-eight, in the ninth year of reign, give and grant unto me, the said Robert Griffith Jones, His especial licence, that I, the said Robert Griffith Jones, my executors, administrators, and assigns, and such others as I, the said Robert Griffith Jones, my exors, admors, and assigns, should at any time agree with, and no others, from time and at all times during the term of years therein mentioned, should and lawfully might make, exercise, and vend, within England, Wales, and the Town of Berwick-upon-Tweed, my Invention of "A METHOD OF ORNAMENTING CHINA AND CERTAIN OTHER COMPOSITIONS WHICH I DENOMINATE 'LITHOPHANIC TRANSLUCD OR OPAQUE CHINA,'" communicated to me by a certain Foreigner resident abroad; in which said Letters Patent there is contained a proviso that I, the said Robert Griffiths Jones, shall cause a particular description of the nature of the said Invention, and in what manner the same is to be performed, to be inrolled in His Majesty's High Court of Chancery within two calendar months next and immediately after the date of the said in part recited Letters Patent, as in and by the same, reference being thereunto had, will more fully and at large appear.

2 A.D. 1828.—N° 5626.

Jones' Method of Ornamenting China.

NOW KNOW YE, that in compliance with the said proviso, I, the said Robert Griffith Jones, do hereby describe the manner in which the said Invention is to be performed by the following description thereof (that is to say):—

The said Invention of a Method of Ornamenting China and certain other Compositions which I denominate Lithophanic Translucid or Opaque China, consists in producing the effect of a design or shadowed drawing in china or other semi-transparent or semi-opaque compositions, such as coloured glass, by adapting the thickness of the various parts of the substance of such semi-transparent composition according to the outlines and to the lights and shadows of the design or shadowed drawing which is to be represented upon the same, in order that the said china or composition being viewed against the light may, by the difference of thickness of its various parts, transmit more or less light through the same, so as to exhibit the lights and shadows of the forms intended to be represented as a design or picture; (that is to say,) the parts intended to exhibit the deeply shadowed parts of the picture or design (when the china or composition is viewed against the light) must be of a competent thickness (according to the degree of transparency or of opacity of the china or composition) to resist the passage or transmission of the light in a great degree, whilst in those parts of the picture or design which are intended to exhibit the bright lights the china or composition is reduced to a very thin substance in order that the light may readily penetrate through the same, and also of all the intermediate lights and shadows between the darkest and the brightest, the thickness of the substance of the china or composition is to be adapted to let through as much or as little of the light as will give the required effect of light and shadow to every part of the intended design or picture. And as to the means of executing such ornamental designs or shadowed drawings upon china and other compositions, a suitable model must first be made in plastic wax, which is spread out in a layer upon the surface of a plate of glass, the substance of the wax being previously prepared or tinted in a suitable manner to give it such degree of opacity or transparency as will in some degree correspond with that of the china or other composition which is to be ornamented, and also the thickness of the layer of wax which is poured out in a melted state upon the surface of the glass must be regulated according to the degree of light that it is capable of transmitting through its substance. Upon the surface of the wax so prepared the artist must proceed according to the means usually practised for modelling wax, to cut away and reduce the thickness of the layer of wax at all those parts which are required to exhibit the light parts of the picture or design, leaving the other parts which are to exhibit the shadows of the full thickness of the wax, and even adding wax in particular places to give an extra thickness where necessary to attain the effect of the deepest shadows; and occasionally for particular objects which are to be exhibited with very defined shadows, they may be cut out as profiles and forms in paper or in pasteboard, or in wood, metal, or other suitable substance, and stuck upon the surface of the wax, the surfaces of such objects being carved in relief to give them different thicknesses in different parts. Or when defined objects as aforesaid are to be represented by lights instead of shadows, suitable profiles or forms cut out as aforesaid in pasteboard, wood, metal, or other suitable substance may be pressed upon and imprinted into the surface of the wax and then withdrawn, so as to leave hollow cavities in the wax in order to reduce the thickness thereof, as the nature of the design requires. In thus modelling for lithophanic china the artist must use discretion and ingenuity for the attainment of the required effect of the particular subject or design he undertakes, and no precise rules or directions can be given; he must employ the various means above stated with judgment, and as he may find them best adapted to obtain the representation of the different effects of light and shade required in the various parts of the piece. As an example, suppose the design to be represented in lithophanic china is a landscape, the artist must first pour over the whole surface of a glass plate surrounded with a suitable border of putty and warmed, a thin layer or coat of wax of suitable thickness and tint as aforesaid to form the ground for the model of the picture, and then by inclining the glass gently one way or another, while the wax is still fluid, he may cause a somewhat greater thickness to flow to particular parts, and he may by dexterous management of agitation, and by blowing with the breath while the wax is cooling, cause it to settle in waves with gradual differences of thickness, which by the help of slight alterations and amendments may afterwards be modelled into the proper thicknesses to exhibit the effects of clouds, and the variations in the thickness of the wax which are necessary to exhibit the effect of distant mountains may be produced by applying additional layers of fluid wax upon the original ground of wax, which was first spread upon the glass, such additional wax when in a fluid state being spread out in directions suitable to the forms of those mountains by blowing the fluid wax gently with the breath, and also by moulding it with a scraper or modelling tool so as to lay it thinner on those parts intended to be light, for instance, the tops of the mountains or those most in the distance, and thicker at the parts intended to be shaded. The first set of the fluid wax will not always produce the desired effect, and then it must be scraped off wholly or in part, and the wax may be

remelted at particular parts by partial application of heat, and the surface must be afterwards remodelled. The surface of the wax being thus prepared of suitable thickness for modelling the back ground, greater thicknesses must be given for the deepest shadows and the subjects in the foreground. Figures of men and animals, and strong and decided forms, such as buildings or trees, may be produced by cutting out those forms in lamina of hard wax and fixing them in their proper places, or else fresh layers of fluid wax may be added, and the surface carved and modelled to the forms required. When such figures form the principal subject of the design, they should be moulded with the scraper or knife to reduce the thickness at all those parts of each figure which are intended to exhibit lighter shades, whilst the darker shadows must be raised into a considerable thickness of wax. The projections and excavations upon the various parts of the surface of lithophanic china are not (as in the case of common embossing and modelling in relief) carved according to the real forms of the subject, but are intended to adapt the degree of thickness of the china at every part according to the intensity of light and of shadow which is requisite to represent the subject, and hence a lithophanic model or lithophanic china, when viewed upon an opaque ground, presents an irregular, indistinct, and unfinished surface, with very little of the effect of the design, for, like transparent paintings, the lithophanic china must be viewed against the light to exhibit the light and shadow of a picture. Hence during the process of modelling the design in wax as aforesaid, the model must be frequently held up to the light to examine the progress and effect of the work and to govern the modelling accordingly. The model in wax or original design being prepared by a judicious application of the various means above described, and of all other suitable means usually practised in modelling in wax, a cast or mould must be taken from the model in plaister, which mould will consequently be in reverse to the model; then from such mould the required number of casts or copies may be obtained in china, in the manner commonly practised for taking casts of ornamental figures in china. If it is desired to produce a very finished and delicate design with a strong effect of light and shade, the first plaister cast or mould which is taken from the wax model, and in reverse thereto, may be retouched by carving and cutting away at all those parts which are required to exhibit very deep and defined shadows and dark outlines, such as would have been difficult to execute with sufficient relief and sharpness on the surface of the wax model. For instance, the naked branches of trees, railings, the outlines of buildings, figures, and similar objects, which must be represented by dark lines, should be carved out in the hollow parts of the first mould. From that first mould when so prepared

a cast should be taken either in plaster or in china, which will be a counterpart of the original model, but more perfect and in higher relief at all the shadowed parts and dark outlines. That cast should be again retouched, in order to cut away and reduce the thin parts where requisite, to improve the parts which are to exhibit the lights, by carving or graving the surface to reduce the thickness of those parts. Lastly, a metal mould of pewter, tin, or type metal, or brass, or other suitable metal, should be taken from the said cast, and the finishing touches for the sharp outlines and deep shadows may be engraved in the hollows of that metal mould. For instance, to attain the effect for the more delicate strokes of the design, such as the lineaments of the face, the hands, the embroidery of garments, suitable finishing touches must be put in with the graver. These operations of retouching upon the hollow moulds and the metal require even more skill and attention than the first operation of modelling in wax, because the artist can only judge of his work by his previous knowledge of the effect it will produce. In order to guide him as to the depth of cut he is to make with his graver, the impressions or casts for highly finished lithophanic china are taken from the last metal mould when prepared as above described, and such impressions and casts are to be burned and treated in every respect in the same manner as ornamental figures in china or biscuit are usually treated, and the surface of the lithophanic china may be further ornamented in colours, and glazed if thought desirable.

In witness whereof, I, the said Robert Griffith Jones, have hereunto set my hand and seal, this Thirteenth day of May, in the year of our Lord One thousand eight hundred and twenty-eight.

ROB^T G. (L.S.) JONES.

AND BE IT REMEMBERED, that on the Thirteenth day of May, in the year of our Lord 1828, the aforesaid Robert Griffith Jones came before our said Lord the King in His Chancery, and acknowledged the Specification aforesaid, and all and every thing therein contained and specified, in form above written. And also the Specification aforesaid was stamped according to the tenor of the Statute made for that purpose.

Cox.

Inrolled the Thirteenth day of May, in the year of our Lord One thousand eight hundred and twenty-eight.

LONDON:
Printed by GEORGE EDWARD EYRE and WILLIAM SPOTTISWOODE,
Printers to the Queen's most Excellent Majesty. 1857.

Appendix C
KPM Preis-Courant

PREIS-COURANT

der

Königlichen Porzellan-Manufactur in Berlin

über

porzellanene transparente Lichtschirmplatten.

Zahlbar in Preufsischem Courant, den Thaler zu 30 Silbergroschen.

Nummer der Platte.	Benennung der Gegenstände.	Viereckig hoch (Zoll.)	Viereckig breit (Zoll.)	Rund-Durchmesser (Zoll.)	Verkaufspreis (Thlr.)	Verkaufspreis (Sgr.)
1.	Amor-Kopf	—	—	6	—	10
2.	Der Besuch, nach einem englischen Kupferstiche	12½	9¼	—	4	—
3.	Ansicht des Vesuvs	10½	14½	—	5	—
4.	Eine alte Frau in einem Buche lesend	5¼	3½	—	—	10
5.	Landschaft mit einer grossen Eiche	5¼	3½	—	—	10
6.	Winterlandschaft	3½	5	—	—	10
7.	Landschaft, ein Bauernhaus im Vordergrunde	3½	5	—	—	10
8.	dergl. im Vordergrunde eine Frau am Ziehbrunnen	5¼	3½	—	—	10
9.	Ein russischer Courier, in einer Kibitke mit 3 Pferden	3½	5	—	—	10
10.	Landschaft, im Vordergrunde Reiter, im Hintergrunde Gebirge	3½	5	—	—	10
11.	Seeküste mit segelnden Schiffen, ein Fischerhaus im Vordergrunde	3½	5	—	—	10
12.	Die Wilddiebe	12½	10¼	—	4	—
13.	Bildnifs Göthe's	9	6½	—	1	5
14.	Die Elisabethkirche in Breslau	4½	6¼	—	—	15
15.	Das Schlofs Fischbach in Schlesien	3½	5	—	—	10
16.	Landschaft, mit aufgehender Sonne	6¾	8½	—	—	25
17.	*Maria Magdalena*, nach Battoni	6¼	9½	—	1	5
18.	Leuchtthurm mit scheiternden Schiffen	9¼	8½	—	1	5
19.	Die Ansicht von Dresden	3½	5	—	—	10
20.	Eine Ansicht des Vesuvs	19½	18	—	30	—
21.	Der Geiser auf Island	5¼	3½	—	—	10
22.	Johannes-Kopf	—	—	5¼	—	10
23.	Familienscene, nach Teniers	3¼	2¼	—	—	6
24.	Eine in der Kirche vor einem Marienbilde knieende weibliche Figur	3¼	2¼	—	—	6
25.	Scene aus Marie von Avenel, von Walter Scott	3¼	2¼	—	—	6
26.	Das Innere eines Rittersaals, ein Knappe knieend vor einer weiblichen Figur	3¼	2¼	—	—	6
27.	Zankende Frauen	3¼	2¼	—	—	6
28.	Kreuzgewölbe eines Klosters	3¼	2¼	—	—	6
29.	Ein Mannskopf, nach Rembrand	3¼	2¼	—	—	6
30.	Die St. Stephanskirche in Wien	7¼	5	—	—	25
31.	Der Dom in Meifsen	8¾	6½	—	—	25
32.	Eine Burg mit drei Thürmen am Meeresstrande	3½	5	—	—	10
33.	Spielende Katzen	3¼	2¼	—	—	6
34.	Eine Ansicht des Vesuvs	19½	18	—	30	—
36.	Landschaft, im Vodergrunde eine grofse Windmühle	5¼	3½	—	—	10
37.	Landschaft mit englischen Wettreitern	3½	5¼	—	—	10
38.	dergl. mit Rindvieh im Vordergrunde	3½	5¼	—	—	10
39.	Das Innere einer Kapelle mit einer betenden Figur	5¼	3½	—	—	10
40.	Landschaft mit einem Hühnerhunde	3½	5¼	—	—	10
41.	Das Innere einer Kapelle mit einer betenden Figur	3¼	2¼	—	—	6
42.	Landschaft, im Vordergrunde eine grofse Windmühle	3¼	2¼	—	—	6
43.	Der Geiser auf Island	3¼	2¼	—	—	6
44.	Landschaft, eine grofse Eiche im Vordergrunde	3¼	2¼	—	—	6
45.	dergl. mit Rindvieh im Vordergrunde	3¼	2¼	—	—	6
46.	dergl. mit Meeresküste und Schiffen	3¼	2¼	—	—	6
47.	Eine alte Frau in einem Buche lesend	3¼	2¼	—	—	6
48.	Landschaft	3¼	2¼	—	—	6
49.	dergl. im Vordergrunde eine Frau am Ziehbrunnen	3¼	2¼	—	—	6
50	Landhaus des Prinzen Wilhelm, Onkel Sr. Maj. des Königs von Preufsen, in Cöln	4¼	5¼	—	—	10
51.	Drei Kinder am Meeresstrande (des Schiffmanns Kinder)	8¾	6½	—	1	5
52.	Ein Mädchen am Ziehbrunnen	9¼	6¼	—	—	25
55.	Eine Frau mit einem Kinde im Gewittersturme	9	7	—	1	5
56.	Eine alte Frau aus dem Fenster schauend	3¼	2¼	—	—	6
66.	Engels-Kopf, nach Raphael	—	—	5¼	—	10
67.	Ein Engels-Kopf	—	—	5¼	—	10
68.	Eine Frau mit einem schlummernden Kinde in einem Zimmer, am Fenster	5¼	3½	—	—	10
70.	Ein Trinker, nach einem niederländischen Bilde	5¼	3½	—	—	10
71.	Ein Mädchen mit zerbrochenem Milchkrug	3¼	2¼	—	—	6
72.	Landschaft mit Uhlanen zu Pferde	5¼	3½	—	—	10
73.	Amor-Kopf, nach Mengs, in ausgefülltem vertieften Viereck	9½	9½	—	2	10
74.	Belisar mit dem Knaben am Meeresufer	8¼	6½	—	1	5
75.	Ein alter Schäfer mit seiner Heerde im Regenwetter	8¼	6½	—	1	5
80.	Amor-Kopf, nach Mengs	—	—	5¼	—	10
81.	Bildnifs Sr. Majestät des Königs Friedrich Wilhelm III.	7¼	5¼	—	—	25
82.	Ein Mädchen am Ziehbrunnen	5¼	3½	—	—	10
83.	Meeresküste, vom aufgehenden Monde beleuchtet	3½	5¼	—	—	10
84.	Winterlandschaft	3½	5¼	—	—	10
85.	Zimmer aus der Alhambra	5¼	3½	—	—	10
88.	Christus am Kreuz	8¼	7	—	1	5
91.	Christus mit dem Abendmahlskelch, Brustbild	8¼	6½	—	1	5
92.	Zephyr-Kopf	—	—	6	—	10
93.	Ein Mädchen an der Thür eines Bauernhauses	8¼	7	—	1	5
94.	Morgenländische Landschaft	5¼	3½	—	—	10
95.	Winterlandschaft, zwei Reiter auf einem Pferde	5	3½	—	—	10
96.	Sixtinische Madonna, nach Raphael	10½	9	—	1	20
97.	Das Brockenhaus	4¼	6	—	—	10

Nummer der Platte.	Benennung der Gegenstände.	Viereckig hoch (Zoll.)	Viereckig breit (Zoll.)	Rund-Durchmesser (Zoll.)	Verkaufspreis (Thlr.)	Verkaufspreis (Sgr.)
98.	Ein Mädchen über einen Steg gehend, vor ihr eine Ziege	8¾	6½	—	1	5
99.	Ansicht des Vesuvs	5¼	3½	—	—	10
100.	Bildnifs Sr. Majestät des Königs Friedrich Wilhelm III.	6¼	4½	—	—	10
101.	Ein junger Mann, ein Mädchen durch den Bach tragend	8¼	7	—	1	5
102.	Der Antrag, nach einem englischen Kupferstich	12½	9¼	—	4	—
103.	Hagar in der Wüste	8¼	7	—	1	5
104.	Madonna della Sedia	—	—	9½	1	20
105.	Prinz von Preufsen	9	6½	—	1	5
106.	Ein Mädchen auf einem Sopha sitzend und den Schuh bindend	11¼	9¼	—	1	20
107.	Warnung vor der Wassernixe (zwei Figuren in einem Kahn)	8¾	7	—	1	5
108.	Das Innere einer gothischen Kirche	6¼	4½	—	—	15
109.	Die St. Stephanskirche in Wien	4½	6¼	—	—	15
110.	Kapelle in Oswitz bei Breslau	6¼	4½	—	—	15
111.	Prinzefs Karl, Gemalin des Bruders Sr. Maj. des Königs von Preufsen	9	6½	—	1	5
112.	Das Innere der Cathedrale zu Worcester	19½	18	—	30	—
113.	Bildnifs des Professors Dr. Schleiermacher	—	—	6½	—	10
114.	Eine Dame vor einem Spiegel stehend und sich schnürend	11½	9¼	—	1	20
115.	Das Brandenburger Thor in Berlin	4½	6	—	—	10
116.	Das Opernhaus in Berlin	4½	6	—	—	10
117.	Bildnifs Sr. Majestät des Königs Friedrich Wilhelm III.	10½	9½	—	1	20
118.	Bildnifs des Geheimen Raths Heim	—	—	6½	—	10
119.	Himmelfahrt Christi, Altargemälde zu Dresden	12½	6½	—	1	20
120.	Die neue Wache in Berlin	4½	6	—	—	10
121.	Das Innere einer Kirche, Säulengang	4½	6	—	—	10
122.	Das Zeughaus in Berlin	4½	6	—	—	10
124.	Das Schauspielhaus in Berlin	4½	6	—	—	10
125.	Das Museum in Berlin	4½	6	—	—	10
126.	Der Weinprober, nach Pistorius	12½	10½	—	4	—
127.	Peristil aus dem Vatican	19½	18	—	30	—
128.	Der Krieger und sein Kind	12½	10	—	1	20
129.	Der Klosterhof, nach Lessing	10½	13	—	2	20
130.	Faust und Gretchen	10½	12½	—	2	20
131.	Die Heimkehr	13½	11	—	4	—
132.	Ein englisches Rennpferd (Plenipotentiari)	10½	11¼	—	1	20
133.	Der erste Kummer, ein Knabe weinend, dessen Vogel gestorben	5¼	7½	—	—	10
134.	Ein Knabe auf der Trommel schlafend, neben ihm ein Hund	5¼	7½	—	—	10
135.	Die Italienerin in einer Laube	8¼	6½	—	1	5
136.	Die Griechin sitzend	5¼	4½	—	—	10
137.	Ein englisches Rennpferd (Riddlesworth)	10½	11¼	—	1	20
138.	Das Universitätsgebäude in Berlin	4½	6	—	—	10
139.	Der Heirathsantrag auf Helgoland	7¼	9	—	1	20
140.	Maria mit dem Kinde auf der Flucht	7¼	6½	—	1	5
141.	Drei spielende Kinder	5	6	—	—	10
142.	Der zweite Hof im Königl. Schlosse zu Berlin	4½	6	—	—	10
143.	Der Weinprober, nach Pistorius	7½	6½	—	1	5
144.	Die Nätherin	7¼	5¾	—	—	25
145.	Die Weindiebin	7¼	5¾	—	—	25
146.	*Mort de Medore*	6½	8	—	1	5
147.	Die Werdersche Kirche in Berlin	4½	6	—	—	10
148.	Das Königl. Schlofs in Berlin, von der langen Brücke aus gesehen	4½	6	—	—	10
149	Der Krieger und sein Kind	6¾	5½	—	1	5
150.	Die Heimkehr	7½	6½	—	1	5
151.	Faust und Gretchen	6	7	—	—	25
152.	Der erste Hof im Königl. Schlosse zu Berlin	4½	6	—	—	10
153.	Nicolaus, Kaiser von Rufsland	6¾	6	—	—	15
154.	Kaiserin von Rufsland	6¾	6	—	—	15
155.	Der Edelknabe	7½	6½	—	1	5
156.	Russischer General Paskewitsch	6¾	6	—	—	15
157.	Das Edelfräulein	7½	6½	—	1	5
158.	Die Kirchengängerin	7½	6½	—	1	5
159.	Schlofs auf der Pfaueninsel	4¼	6	—	—	10
160.	Der König von England, Wilhelm IV., ganze Figur	9½	6½	—	1	5
161.	Die Söhne Eduard's	6	7	—	—	25
162.	Faust und Gretchen im Garten	6	7	—	—	25
163.	Tankred und Armide	11¼	10½	—	1	20
164.	Musicirende Genien	3½	3½	—	—	6
165.	dergl.	3½	3½	—	—	6
166.	dergl.	3½	3½	—	—	6
167.	dergl.	3½	3½	—	—	6
168.	Landschaft mit einem spanichen Hühnerhunde	3½	5¼	—	—	10
169.	Die Schneekoppe und Wiesenbaude	4¼	6	—	—	10
170.	Der Raub des Hylas	8¼	8¼	—	1	5
171.	Wasserhund und eine herabstürzende Ente	3½	5¼	—	—	10
172.	Hühnerhund und fortfliegende Waldschnepfe	3½	5¼	—	—	10
173.	Eine Albaneserin	5¼	4½	—	—	10
174.	Zwei im Walde schlafende Kinder	4¼	5¼	—	—	10
175.	Zwei im Walde spielende Kinder	4¼	5¼	—	—	10
176.	Die kleine Näscherin	—	—	5½	—	10
177.	Die kleine Leserin	—	—	6½	—	10
178.	Jagdstück, zwei Jäger auf der Hühnerjagd	9¼	8½	—	1	5
179.	Mutter, die ein Kind füttert	—	—	6½	—	10
180.	Psyche betrachtet den schlafenden Amor	5¼	4½	—	—	10
181.	Entführung der Psyche durch Amor	5¼	4½	—	—	10
183.	Der verliebte Alte	5¼	4½	—	—	10
184.	Ein Mädchen, spottend, Pendant zu No. 183.	5¼	4½	—	—	10
185.	Spielende Amoretten	3½	3½	—	—	6
186.	dergl.	3½	3½	—	—	6
187.	dergl.	3½	3½	—	—	6
188.	dergl.	3½	3½	—	—	6
189.	Die Haarflechterin	7¼	6½	—	1	5
190.	Victoria, Königin von England	11	8½	—	1	20
191.	Christus am Kreuz	5¼	3½	—	—	10
192.	Der Amoretten-Verkauf	5¼	4½	—	—	10
193.	Bäuerin mit Amor auf der Schulter, hinter ihr ein Lamm	5¼	4½	—	—	10
194.	Eine Dame auf einem Balkon, Brustbild	8	6½	—	1	5
199.	Die Ohrenbeichte	11½	9½	—	1	20
205.	Zwei Kinder, Brustbild	—	—	7½	—	15
206.	Christuskopf mit der Dornenkrone	—	—	5¼	—	10
207.	Glienicke, mit der Ansicht von Potsdam	5¼	6¼	—	—	15
208.	Die Ansicht Glienicke vom Babertsberge	5¼	6¼	—	—	15
216.	Die Russische Kirche bei Potsdam	5¼	6¼	—	—	15
225.	Ansicht des Babertsberges, von der Wasserseite, bei Potsdam	5¼	6¼	—	—	15
226.	Das neue Palais bei Potsdam	5¼	6¼	—	—	15
231.	Der Babertsberg bei Potsdam	5¼	6¼	—	—	15
235.	Laura	7¼	5¾	—	—	15
236.	Petrarca	7¼	5¾	—	—	15
237.	Das wiedergefundene Kind	5¼	7¼	—	—	10
238.	Das gerettete Kind	5¼	7¼	—	—	10
239.	Heloise	7¼	5¾	—	—	15
240.	Abeilard	7¼	5¾	—	—	15
241.	Das neue Packhofgebäude in Berlin	5¼	6¼	—	—	15
242.	Statue Guttenberg	6	4½	—	—	10
243.	Bildnifs Schiller's	6¼	5¾	—	—	10
244.	Bildnifs Goethe's	6¼	5¾	—	—	10
249.	König Friedrich Wilhelm IV. und Elisabeth, Königin von Preufsen	7½	6½	—	1	5

Nummer der Pl.	Benennung der Gegenstände.	Viereckig hoch (Zoll)	Viereckig breit (Zoll)	Rund-Durchmesser (Zoll)	Verkaufspreis Rthlr.	Verkaufspreis Sgr.
250.	Eine Mutter mit einem Kinde am Weihkessel	11½	9½	—	1	20
251.	Das Rendezvous	11½	9½	—	1	20
252.	Undine	11½	9½	—	1	20
253.	Bildnifs Sr. Majestät des Königs Friedrich Wilhelm IV.	11	9½	—	1	20
254.	Madonna del Lago	8½	8½	—	1	5
255.	Esmeralda	11½	9½	—	1	20
256.	Die Geburt Christi, nach Correggio	12½	6½	—	1	20
258.	Das Wunder der Rose	11½	9½	—	1	20
259.	Die Abnahme Christi vom Kreuz, nach Rubens	12½	6½	—	1	20
260.	Christus mit der Ehebrecherin, nach Signol	11½	9½	—	1	20
261.	Das Schlofs Lichtenstein	7½	5½	—	—	15
263.	Der Mefsner und der Chorknabe, nach Daege	12	9½	—	1	20
264.	Das Weihwasser	12½	9½	—	1	20
265.	Der Liebesengel, nach Begas	9½	9½	—	1	5
266.	Baiersche Bauermädchen, einen Brautkranz auswählend	11½	9½	—	1	20
267.	Der bestrafte Neugierige	8	6	—	1	5
268.	*L'Algerienne*	10½	13½	—	1	20
269.	dergl.	6½	8	—	1	5
270.	Schiller's Standbild in Stuttgart, mit Prospect	7½	5½	—	—	15
271.	Der wohlthätige Pilger, nach Daege	11½	9½	—	1	20
272.	Das schmollende Ehepaar, nach Hasenclever	8½	11½	—	1	20
273.	Schiller's Standbild in Stuttgart	6½	5½	—	—	10
274.	Zwei Mädchen in der Sylvesternacht, nach Kleine	9	7½	—	1	5
275.	Zwei angelnde Kinder	6½	5½	—	—	10
276.	Zwei italienische Frauen mit Kindern, nach Riedel	9	7	—	1	5
277.	Fernanda, mit einem Lichte in der Hand	5½	4½	—	—	10
278.	Louise, in einem Kahn sitzend	5½	4½	—	—	10
279.	Die Wahrsagerin, drei Figuren, nach Kretius	9	7	—	1	5
280.	Ein Herr und eine Dame im Regen	9	7½	—	1	5
281.	Mutterfreuden	5½	4½	—	—	10
282.	Drei badende Kinder, nach Steinbrück	9	7½	—	1	5
283.	Thisbe, nach Steinbrück	9	7½	—	1	5
284.	Herzog Ulrich vor Hohen-Neuffen	7½	5½	—	—	15
285.	Die Himmelskönigin, nach Daege	12½	6½	—	1	20
286.	Eine von zwei Engeln getragene Seele	9	7½	—	1	5
287.	Eine betende Italienerin, nach Mues	8½	7	—	1	5
288.	Eine Mutter sitzend, mit ihrem Kinde	9	7½	—	1	5
289.	Zwei Figuren, ländliche Musik	9	7	—	1	5
290.	Mönche, mit Botanik beschäftigt	11½	9½	—	1	20
291.	Der Mefsner und der Chorknabe, nach Daege	5½	4½	—	—	10
292.	Das Wunder der Rose	5½	4½	—	—	10
293.	Zwei Kinder mit Blumen spielend	12½	9½	—	1	20
294.	Mein kleiner Liebling	5½	4½	—	—	10
295.	Der kleine Schotte	5½	4½	—	—	10
296.	Walter Scott's Denkmal in Edinburgh	7½	6	—	—	15
297.	Der wohlthätige Pilger, nach Daege	5½	4½	—	—	10
298.	Quentin Durward	8½	7	—	1	5
299.	Das Rendezvous	5½	4½	—	—	10
300.	Christus erster Ausgang	7½	8½	—	1	5
301.	Ein Mädchen mit einer Katze auf dem Arme	7½	5½	—	—	15
302.	Der Fischerknabe, nach Goethe	13½	10½	—	1	20
304.	Schlofs Rothenberg	5½	7½	—	—	15
305.	Eine schlafende Mutter mit ihrem Kinde	7½	5½	—	—	15
306.	Die Brautschmückung	5½	4½	—	—	10
307.	Brustbild eines jungen Mädchen, mit aufgelöstem Haare	7½	5½	—	—	15
308.	Brustbild eines jungen Mädchen, an einer Blume riechend	7½	5½	—	—	15
309.	Der talentvolle Malerlehrling	6½	5	—	—	10
310.	Walter Scott's Denkmal in Edinburgh	13½	10½	—	1	20
311.	Der Tiroler und sein Mädchen	5½	4½	—	—	10

Nummer der Pl.	Benennung der Gegenstände.	Viereckig hoch (Zoll)	Viereckig breit (Zoll)	Rund-Durchmesser (Zoll)	Verkaufspreis Rthlr.	Verkaufspreis Sgr.
312.	Daniel in der Löwengrube	5½	4½	—	—	10
313.	Jacob und Rebecca	5½	4½	—	—	10
314.	Christus und der Zinsgroschen	5½	4	—	—	10
315.	Die Sängerin Jenny Lind, Kniestück	9½	7½	—	1	5
316.	Christus im Tempel lehrend	5½	4	—	—	10
317.	Maria's Flucht nach Egypten	5½	4	—	—	10
318.	Die Auferstehung Christi	5½	4½	—	—	10
319.	Christus am Oelberg	5½	4½	—	—	10
320.	Die Sängerin L. Tuczek, Kniestück	9½	7½	—	1	5
321.	Das Abendmahl, nach Leonardo da Vinci	5½	10½	—	1	5
322.	Die Verspottung Christi	5½	4½	—	—	10
323.	Christus nach der Abnahme vom Kreuze	9	7½	—	1	5
324.	Christus am Oelberge	5½	4½	—	—	10
325.	Zwei Bachantinnen	5½	4½	—	—	10
326.	Die Weinschmecker, nach Hasenclever	8½	11½	—	1	20
327.	Die drei Marien	12½	7½	—	1	20
328.	Madonna, nach Murillo	12½	7½	—	1	20
329.	Der gute Camerad	7½	9½	—	1	5
330.	Der erste Freund	7½	9½	—	1	5
331.	Zwei italienische Frauen mit einem Kinde	9	7½	—	1	5
332.	Der Wolf im Schaafstalle	7½	9½	—	1	5
333.	Die Unterhaltung	7½	9½	—	1	5
334.	Gretchen in der Kirche	9	7	—	1	5
335.	Der Untergang des Vengeur (Seeschlacht)	7½	9	—	1	5
336.	Eine Seeschlacht	7½	9	—	1	5
337.	Romeo	9	7½	—	1	5
338.	Julie	9	7½	—	1	5
339.	Zwei Kinder mit Reisern (Winter)	5½	7½	—	—	10
340.	Anleitung zur Wohlthätigkeit	9½	7½	—	1	5
341.	Das genesene Kind	9½	7½	—	1	5
342.	Ein angeschossener Hirsch	9½	7½	—	1	5
343.	Ein Hirsch, welcher über Jagdzeug springt	9½	7½	—	1	5
344.	Ein Mädchen, einen Hund liebkosend	9½	7½	—	1	5
345.	Eine Kindergruppe mit einem Hunde	9½	7½	—	1	5
346.	Zwei Hasen	5½	7½	—	—	10
347.	Ein Fuchs	5½	7½	—	—	10
348.	Ein Sommer-Fuchs	5½	7½	—	—	10
349.	Der Fischer und seine Kinder (Pendant zu No. 339.)	5½	7½	—	—	10
350.	Madonna (Pendant zu No. 104.)	—	—	9½	1	20
351.	Pabst Pius IX.	6½	5½	—	—	10
352.	Mendelssohn Bartholdi	6½	5½	—	—	10
353.	Jacob und Rahel	7½	9½	—	1	5
354.	Gräfin Landsfeld	5½	4½	—	—	10
355.	Seeschlacht	7½	9	—	1	5
356.	Seeschlacht bei Trafalgar	7½	9	—	1	5
357.	Der Nachmittag	7½	9	—	1	5
358.	Die Ankunft beim Vicar	7½	9½	—	1	5
359.	Der Eifersüchtige	7½	5½	—	—	15
360.	Die Bewerbung	7½	5½	—	—	15
361.	Die Bitte am Kreuz	9	7½	—	1	5
362.	Aschenbrödel	12	9½	—	1	20
363.	Alex. von Humboldt	12	9½	—	1	20
364.	Ave Maria	7½	9	—	1	5
365.	Mädchen mit Kaninchen spielend	7½	9½	—	1	5
366.	Zwei Kinder mit Ziegen	7½	9½	—	1	5
367.	Badende Mädchen	7½	6	—	—	15
368.	Badende Frauen	7½	6	—	—	15
369.	Sara in der Hängematte	11½	9½	—	1	20
370.	Champagner-Scene	9½	7½	—	1	5
372	Die Unschuld	9½	7½	—	1	5
373.	Lachtaube	9½	7½	—	1	5
374.	Portrait, Lucilie Grahn	11½	9½	—	1	20
375.	Allein in der Welt	11½	9½	—	1	20
376.	Ein Kind in der Wiege	—	—	6½	—	10

Nummer der Pl.	Benennung der Gegenstände.	Viereckig hoch (Zoll)	Viereckig breit (Zoll)	Rund-Durchmesser (Zoll)	Verkaufspreis Rthlr.	Verkaufspreis Sgr.
377.	Portrait, Heinrich v. Gagern	6½	5½	—	—	10
378.	Sara in der Hängematte	5½	4½	—	—	10
379.	Folgen einer Perrücke	5½	4½	—	—	10
380.	Portrait Sr. Majestät des Königs Friedrich Wilhelm IV.	7	5½	—	—	15
381.	Portrait des Prinz von Preufsen	7	5½	—	—	15
382.	*A travers champ* (mitten durch's Land)	7½	9½	—	1	5
383.	*Chemin faisant* (bei Gelegenheit)	7½	9½	—	1	5
384.	Das Landmädchen (nach Meierheim)	9	7½	—	1	5
385.	Portrait des General von Wrangel	7	5½	—	—	15
386.	desgl. Graf von Brandenburg	—	5½	—	—	15
387.	desgl. Prinz Friedrich Wilhelm, Sohn des Prinzen von Preufsen	7	5½	—	—	15
388.	Familienglück (nach Meierheim)	11½	9½	—	1	20
389.	Portrait Königin Elise von Preufsen	7	5½	—	—	15
390.	desgl. Prinzefs von Preufsen	7	5½	—	—	15
391.	Das Landmädchen (nach Meierheim)	5½	4½	—	—	10
392.	Allein in der Welt	7	5½	—	—	15
393.	Alexisbad	5½	7	—	—	15
394.	Berührung des Zephir	11	6½	—	1	5
395.	Allein im Walde	11	6½	—	1	5
396.	Portrait vom Minister von Manteufel	7	5½	—	—	15
397.	Die Unschuld	5½	4½	—	—	10
398.	Lachtaube	5½	4½	—	—	10
399.	Milchmädchen (nach Meierheim)	5½	4½	—	—	10
400.	desgl.	9	7½	—	1	5
401.	Die Harzerin	7½	6	—	—	15
402.	*Le Georgonne et Grillandata*	9	7½	—	1	5
403.	Vergifs mein nicht!	9	7½	—	1	5
404.	Das letzte Kleinod	12	9½	—	1	20
405.	Vergifs mein nicht!	5½	4½	—	—	10
406.	*L'education de la nature*	5½	7½	—	—	15
407.	*L'education du monde*	5½	7½	—	—	15
408.	Undine, oben halbrund	15½	11	—	2	20
409.	Undine	7	5½	—	—	15
410.	Portrait des Ministers von der Heydt	7½	6	—	—	15
411.	*Going With the Stream*	8½	12	—	1	20
412.	Lieber Gott mach mich fromm	9	7	—	1	5
413.	Die Erwartung	9	7½	—	1	5
414.	Ein Schnupfer — Wohl bekomm's	5½	4½	—	—	10
415.	desgl. — Nehmen Sie eine Priese	5½	4½	—	—	10
416	Christus am Kreuz, nach Dürer	5½	3½	—	—	10
417.	Morgenandacht	7	5½	—	—	15
418.	Lieber Gott, mach mich fromm	5½	4½	—	—	10
419.	Die Erwartung	5½	4½	—	—	10
420.	Denkmal, Friedrich II.	4½	3½	—	—	10
421.	Margarethe	5½	4½	—	—	10
422.	Mignon	13¾	10	—	2	—
423.	Badendes Mädchen, nach Riedel	9	6½	—	1	5
424.	desgl.	5½	6½	—	—	10
425.	Franz Joseph, Kaiser von Oesterreich	7½	6	—	—	15
426.	Graf Egmont's letzte Augenblicke	7½	9½	—	1	5
427.	Mignon und ihr Vater	9	5½	—	—	20
428.	Mignon denkt an die Heimath	7	3½	—	—	10
429.	Mignon sehnt sich nach dem Himmel	7	3½	—	—	10
430.	Mohrenwäsche, nach Begas	5½	6½	—	—	15
431.	Standbild Friedrich Wilhelms III.	4½	3½	—	—	10

Nummer der Pl.	Benennung der Gegenstände.	Viereckig hoch (Zoll)	Viereckig breit (Zoll)	Rund-Durchmesser (Zoll)	Verkaufspreis Rthlr.	Verkaufspreis Sgr.
432.	Die Pachterstochter	7½	5½	—	—	15
433.	Portrait der Königin von Baiern	9	7½	—	1	5
434.	Komm her, nach Meierheim	9	7½	—	1	5
435.	Der zerbrochene Schlitten	3½	3½	—	—	6
436.	Die beiden Studenten	3½	3½	—	—	6
437.	Prinz von Wales	3½	3½	—	—	6
438.	Knabe mit Pudel	3½	3½	—	—	6
439.	Der lustige Bauersmann	3½	3½	—	—	6
440.	Die Winzerfamilie, nach Begas	7½	5½	—	—	15
441.	Die Pachterstochter	5½	4½	—	—	10
442.	*La petite friponne*	9	7½	—	1	5
443.	Schlafende Brüderchen	9	7½	—	1	5
444.	Rheinfall bei Schaffhausen	4½	6	—	—	10
445.	Madonna mit dem Kinde, nach Murillo	12½	7½	—	1	20
446.	Jobs der Nachtwächter, nach Hasenclever	4½	6	—	—	10
447.	Madonna mit dem Kinde, nach Murillo	7½	6	—	—	15
448.	Amor und die Wassernixe	—	—	6½	—	10
449.	Eine Scene bei der Wiege	4½	6	—	—	10
450.	Der Lautenspieler	6	4½	—	—	10
451.	Ein Mädchen mit Tambourin, Pendant	6	4½	—	—	10
452.	National-Denkmal	4½	3½	—	—	10
453.	Eine Dame rauchend	7½	6	—	—	15
454.	Gruppe fliehender Christen, nach Kaulbach	13½	11	—	3	—
455.	Eine Neapolitanerin mit ihrem kranken Kinde	9	7½	—	1	5
456.	Der Reichthum	9	7½	—	1	5
457.	Die Armuth	9	7½	—	1	5
458.	Unschuldige Liebe, Mädchen mit Katze	7½	6	—	—	15
459.	Dergl. Mädchen mit Hund	7½	6	—	—	15
460.	Portrait des Erfinders der Revolvers (oval)	—	—	—	—	20
461.	Eine Neapolitanerin mit ihrem kranken Kinde	6	4½	—	—	10
462.	Denkmal von Blücher, Gneisenau und Yorck	4½	3½	—	—	10
463.	Stolzenfels am Rhein	5½	7½	—	—	10
464.	Das Krankenbett	9	7	—	1	5
465.	Godesberg am Rhein	5½	7½	—	—	10
466.	Das Mittagsmahl	7½	6	—	—	15
467.	Bacharach am Rhein	5½	7½	—	—	10

In Betreff der von aufserhalb eingehenden Bestellungen ist zu bemerken, dafs alle nur mögliche Aufmerksamkei und Sorgfalt angewendet wird, um die Verpackung der Porzellane richtig und gut zu bewirken. Der resp. Empfänge kann sich also wegen fehlender Stücke oder vorkommenden Bruchs nur an den Fuhrmann oder Schiffer halten, welche die Waare überbringt, und es wird Seitens der Königl. Manufactur auf keinen Fall ein Ersatz geleistet. Uebrigens bleib es jedem Käufer freigestellt, die erstandenen Waaren aufser der Manufactur verpacken zu lassen, oder Jemanden zu beauftragen, der beim Einpacken zugegen ist, wenn dasselbe in der Manufactur geschieht.

Appendix D
Meissen Preis-Courant

PREIS-COURANT
von
LITHOPHANIEN
der
Königl. Sächs. Porzellan-Manufactur zu Meissen
und
deren Niederlagen zu Dresden und Leipzig.

№ der Platte.	Benennung der Gegenstände.	Sächsische Zoll hoch.	breit.	Durchmesser.	Weiss. Rf	Ng	S	Bunt gemalt. Rf	Ng	S
5.	Vesuv. Landschaft	7	5 3/4	—	—	14	—	1	17	—
9.	Lustschloss Pillnitz	5	6 3/4	—	—	12	—	1	10	—
16.	Johannes, rund, gross	—	—	8	—	14	—			
24.	Bivouac	7 1/4	9	—	—	19	—	1	25	—
33.	Zephyrköpfchen, rund	—	—	6 1/2		14	—			
35.	Venus in Wolken	8 3/4	6 1/2	—		14	—	1	22	—
47.	Amor nach Mengs, rund	—	—	8	—	14	—	1	22	—
49.	Christus am Kreuz	8 3/4	6 1/2	—	—	14	—	1	12	—
50.	Seesturm	6	7 3/8	—	—	11	—	1	12	—
51.	Orientalischer Sclavenhandel	4	2 1/2	—		9	5			
52.	Martin Luther	6 3/4	5	—	—	9	5			
53.	Madonna della Sedia nach Raphael, rund	—	—	10 1/2	1	7	—	2	25	—
57.	Melanchthon	6	—	—	—	9	5			
58.	Engel der spanischen Madonna, rund	—	—	5 3/8		7	—		26	—
59.	Eine Katzenfamilie	5 1/8	3 3/4	—	—	7	—		16	—
60.	Meissner Dom, äussere Ansicht	10 3/4	8 1/2	—	—	28	—			
61.	Prospect Dresden	5	7	—	—	9	5	1	3	—
65.	Madonna della Sedia, rund		—	9	—	28	—	2	15	—
73.	Engel nach Raphael, rund	—	—	7 3/4		14		1	3	—
74.	Frau mit Kind im Gewittersturm	8 1/2	6 1/4	—	—	14	—	1	22	—
80.	Christus mit Kelch	7 1/2	6 1/4	—	—	14	—	1	17	—
82.	Landschaft mit Wassermühle	6 1/4	8 1/2	—	—	23	—	1	22	—
83.	Madonna del Sixto	10 1/2	9 1/2	—	1	17	—	3	13	—
86.	Hagar in der Wüste	8 1/4	6 1/4	—	—	14	—	2	—	—
89.	Engelskopf nach Raphael, rund	—	—	7 1/2	—	14	—	1	3	—
91.	Schloss zu Meissen	4	6	—	—	9	5	—	28	—
92.	Kirche mit Sonnenaufgang	9 1/2	7 1/4	—	—	23	—	1	12	—
94.	Madonna del Sixto, klein	10 1/4	8	—	1	3	—	3	—	—
96.	Maria Magdalena nach Battoni	7 1/4	10 1/2	—	1	3	—	2	20	—
98.	Die Wildschützen	11 1/2	9 1/2	—	—	28	—	2	15	—
99.	Ein Engelskopf	—	—	5 3/4	—	14	—	1	3	—
100.	Ein Zephyrkopf	—	—	5 3/4	—	14	—	1	3	—
101.	Die heilige Nacht nach Correggio	10 1/4	7 3/4	—	1	17	—	3	5	—
103.	Ein Mädchen vor der Toilette	10 3/4	6 3/4	—		23	—	2	—	—
111.	Kosaken-Ueberfall nach Peter Hess	8 1/4	8 1/2	—		23	—	2	10	—
112.	Himmelfahrt nach Mengs, Altargemälde in der katholischen Kirche zu Dresden	11 1/2	7 3/4	—	1	26	—	6	17	—
113.	Mädchen und Jüngling im Kahn	8 1/2	6 3/4	—	—	14	—	1	12	—
115.	Der Kuss von Göthes Faust nach Retzsch	7 3/4	9	—	—	19	—	1	17	—
116.	Mädchen am Spiegel	11	8 1/2	—	—	23	—	1	22	—
118.	Dresden von der Brühlschen Terrasse	7 1/4	9	—	—	19	—	1	26	—
119.	Faust und Gretchen im Garten	7 1/4	9	—	—	19	—	2	—	—
122.	Böttcher am Fass sitzend, gross	11 3/8	9	—	—	19	—			
124.	Heirathsantrag auf Helgoland	7 3/8	6 3/8	—	—	14	—	1	22	—
127.	Juden vor Babylon	7	10 1/2	—	—	14	—	2	10	—
128.	Der Raub des Hylas, rund	—	—	7	—	9	5	1	17	—
129.	Der Edelknabe	6 1/4	5 3/4	—	—	9	5	1	7	—
130.	Kirchgängerin, klein	6 7/8	5 3/8	—	—	9	5	—	28	—
131.	Kirchgängerin, gross	10 1/2	7	—	—	19	—	1	17	—
132.	Knabe, schlafend auf Trommel	5	6	—	—	7	—			
134.	Madonna mit schlafendem Christus-Kinde	7 3/8	6 3/4	—	—	14	—	1	12	—
135.	Mädchen in einer Laube sitzend	7 5/8	6 1/4	—	—	14	—	1	17	—
136.	Eine schlafende Venus	6	7 3/8	—	—	14	—	1	12	—
137.	Die Heimkehr, gross	12 3/4	10	—	—	28	—	2	25	—
139.	Kinder am Weingeleite	8 3/4	6 1/2	—	—	14	—	1	22	—
143.	Der Krieger und sein Sohn	7	6	—	—	9	5	1	12	—
144.	Kinder am Weingeleite, gross	10 1/2	7 3/4	—	—	19	—	2	5	—
147.	Jäger am Baum schlafend	6 1/2	7 1/4	—	—	9	5	—	28	—
148.	Jäger auf Baum kletternd	6 1/2	7 1/2	—	—	9	5	—	28	—
149.	Italienisches Mädchen	5 1/2	4 1/4	—	—	7	—	—	26	—
150.	Ein Jagdhund	4	5 1/4	—	—	7	—	—	21	—
151.	Christus-Kind	8 3/4	6 3/4	—	—	14	—	1	17	—
152.	Die Söhne König Eduards von England	7 3/4	9	—	—	19	—	2	5	
153.	Monument König Gustav Adolph's von Schweden bei Lützen	9 3/4	7 3/8	—	—	19	—	1	[illegible]	

№ der Platte.	Benennung der Gegenstände.	Sächsische Zoll hoch.	breit.	Durchmesser	Weiss. Rf	Ng	S	Bunt gemalt. Rf	Ng	S
154.	Odaliske	10 1/4	7 1/2	—	—	16	—	1	1	—
156.	Eine Affenfamilie	8 1/4	6 1/2	—	—	14	—			
157.	Der Geniestreich	8 3/8	6 3/4	—	—	14	—	1	2	—
158.	Die Beichte	10 1/2	7 7/8	—	—	19	—	2		—
160.	Dame auf Altan an Geländer	7 1/2	6 1/2	—	—	9	5	1		—
162.	Niederländer Bauerfrau	5 1/4	4 1/4	—	—	4	5	—	21	—
163.	Niederländer Bauer	5 1/4	4 1/4		—	7	—	—	2	—
164.	Christuskopf, rund	—	—	4 3/4	—	4	5	—	2	—
165.	Die vollbrachte Pilgerreise	7	10 1/2	—	—	14	—	2	1	—
167.	Die bestrafte Neugierde	9 3/4	7 3/4	—	—	19	—	2		—
173.	Münchner Mädchen	10 1/2	8	—	—	23	—	2	1	—
174.	Der Schutzengel	—	—	—	—	23	—	2		—
177.	Mutter mit Kind	8 1/4	6 3/4	—	—	14	—	1	1	—
179.	Esmaralda, gross	11	8 3/4	—	—	23	—	2	1	—
180.	Christus vor der Ehebrecherin, klein	9 1/4	7 1/2	—	—	19	—	1	2	—
181.	Esmaralda, klein	9 1/4	7 1/2	—	—	19	—	1	2	—
182.	Prospect Meissen	7	8 7/8	—	—	19	—	2	-	—
183.	Tyrolerin mit Kind	7 3/8	6 3/8	—	—	14	—	1	1	—
185.	Hochländer Brautpaar	10 1/2	8	—	—	23	—	2	1	—
186.	Mutter mit Kind, „Meine gute liebe Mutter!"	8 1/2	6 3/4	—	—	14	—	1	1	—
187.	Scheherazade	9	10 1/4	—	—	28	—	3	1	—
188.	Romeo und Julie	9 1/8	7	—	—	19	—	2		—
189.	Dame in Domino	8 1/4	6 3/4	—	—	14	—	1		—
190.	Das Geplauder	8 3/8	6 3/4	—	—	19	—	1	1	—
191.	Waldpartie	7	8 1/8	—	—	19	—	1	2	—
192.	Kind mit Katze	9 1/8	7 3/4	—	—	23	—	2	-	—
194.	L'amour filial (kindliche Liebe)	10	7 3/8	—	—	23	—	2	-	—
195.	Amorette ☐ klein	4	3 1/2	—	—	5	5			
196.	do. do.	4	3 1/2	—	—	5	5			
197.	Eremit, Mutter mit Kind labend	11	8 3/4	—	—	23	—	2	1	—
198.	Schiffbrüchige von Eisbären angefallen	9	10	—	—	23	—	2	2	—
199.	Paul und Virginie, von Schopin	10 3/4	8	—	—	23	—	2	—	—
200.	Badende Kinder von F. Steinbrück	10 1/8	8	—	—	23	—	2	10	—
201.	Der Liebestraum	10 1/8	8	—	—	23	—	2	—	—
202.	Der Beduinenraub	11	9	—	—	23	—	2	10	—
203.	Thorwaldsen's Portrait	7 3/4	6 1/2	—	—	14	—			
204.	Mädchen vor dem Balle	9 3/4	8	—	—	23	—	2	—	—
205.	Mutter Kind beten lehrend	6 3/8	8 3/4	—	—	19	—	1	25	—
206.	Dresden von Mitternacht	7	9	—	—	19	—	1	26	—
207.	Pillnitz	7 1/4	9 1/4	—	—	19	—	1	26	—
208.	Angelnde Kinder	6	5 1/4	—	—	9	5	1	3	—
209.	Mit Blumen spielende Kinder	7 1/2	7 1/2	—	—	14	—	1	22	—
210.	Mutterstolz	7 3/8	9	—	—	19	—	1	26	—
211.	Ave Maria	5 1/4	7	—	—	9	5	1	7	—
212.	Papst Pius IX.	8 1/2	6 3/4	—	—	14	—	1	22	—
213.	Testamentspiel der Kinder	8 1/2	6 3/4	—	—	14	—	1	22	—
214.	Hirtenkinder mit Ziegenbock	7 3/8	8 3/4	—	—	19	—	2	5	—
215.	Venus im Bade	6	8	—	—	14	—	1	8	—
216.	Clavierspielerin nach Netscher	8 1/2	7	—	—	14	—	2	—	—
217.	Virginie im Bade	10 1/2	8	—	—	23	—	2	10	—
221.	Jagdpartie	7 1/2	9 1/2	—	—	19	—	1	17	—
222.	Sylvesternacht	8 1/4	6 3/4	—	—	14	—	2	—	—
223.	Paul und Virginie sich führend	10 1/2	8	—	—	23	—	2	10	—
224.	Das Geheimniss	8 1/2	10 1/2	—	—	23	—	1	22	—
225.	Unterricht der Treue	8 1/2	10 1/2	—	—	23	—	2	10	—
226.	Zwei Mädchen in Rococco-Costüm	8 1/2	10 1/2	—	—	23	—	2	10	—
227.	Zwei Mädchen mit Brieftaube	10 3/4	8 1/2	—	—	23	—	2	10	—
228.	Mädchen mit Spiegel	7 1/2	7 1/2	—	—	14	—	1	22	
229.	Zwei Mädchen mit Hahn	10 3/8	8 1/8	—	—	23	—	2	10	—
230.	Knabe mit Spiegel	7 1/2	7 3/8	—	—	14	—	1	22	—
231.	Mann und Frau } Italiener	6 3/8	5 3/8	—	—	7	—	1	—	—
232.	do. do. } Italiener	6 3/8	5 3/8	—	—	7	—	1	—	—
233.	Hamburger Frau mit Ziege	8 1/4	6 3/8	—	—	14	—	1	12	—
234.	Mädchen im Zimmer mit Vogelbauer	8 3/8	6 3/8	—	—	14	—	1	12	—
235.	Dame im Ballkleide	8 3/8	6 3/8	—	—	14	—	1	17	—
236.	Mädchen im Bade	10 3/8	8 1/8	—	—	23	—	2	10	—
237.	Frau mit Kind in der Küche	10 3/8	8 1/8	—	—	23	—	2	10	—
238.	Ansicht von Prag	10 3/8	8 1/8	—	—	23	—	2	10	—
239.	Die Elfen	10 1/4	8 1/8	—	—	23	—	2	20	—
240.	Eine Nymphe	10 3/8	8 1/8	—	—	23	—	2	5	—
241.	Schloss Wesenstein	7	8 7/8	—	—	19	—	1	26	—
242.	Sr. Maj. König Johann von Sachsen	9 5/8	8 3/8	—	—	23	—	3	8	—
243.	Ein betender Engel	7 3/8	6 1/8	—	—	9	5	—	26	—
244.	Hirtenfamilie	8 7/8	10 1/8	—	—	23	—	2	20	—
245.	Winzerfamilie	9 5/8	8 1/4	—	—	19	—	2	15	—
247.	Magdalena nach Correggio	7	10 1/4	—	1	3	—			

Druck von C. E. Klinkicht & Sohn in Meissen.

Appendix E
PPM Preis-Courant

PREIS-COURANT

über

transparente Lichtschirme

von

C. G. SCHIERHOLZ & SOHN

in

Plaue bei Arnstadt.

Agraffen zur Befestigung an die Platten, um solche an die Fenster zu hängen, von Neusilber, Eisen und Mannheimer Gold. – **Decorirte** Lichtschirme der doppelte Preis wie **weiss.** Es kann auch jede beliebige Ansicht oder Genrebild gefertigt werden, wenn die Kosten vergütet werden.

№	Benennung.	Leipziger Zoll		Sgr.
		hoch.	breit.	
2	Warnung vor der Wassernixe	7¾	5¾	10
3	Krieger und Kind	7¼	6¼	10
4	Kirchengängerin	7½	6½	10
5	Faust und Gretchen im Garten	5¾	6¾	8
6	Faust und Gretchen	5½	6¾	8
7	Heirathsantrag	6¾	7½	12
10	Christus beim Abendmahl	8¼	6¾	18
11	Himmelfahrt	9¼	6¼	18
12	Madonna del Lago	7¼	6¾	10
13	Johannes	7¼	6	10
15	Madonna della Sedia	7½	6¾	10
16	Edeldame	7¼	6½	10
17	Edelknabe	7¼	6½	10
18	Zwei Kinder in der Weinlaube	7½	6	10
20	Die Heimkehr	7¼	6¼	10
21	Schlafende Kinder im Walde	4⅜	5	5
22	Spielende Kinder	4⅜	5	5
23	Frau und Kind mit Lamm	5⅛	4½	6
24	Entführung der Psyche	5⅛	4½	6
25	Amor und Psyche	5⅛	4½	6
27	Tankred und Armide	7⅜	6¼	10
28	Albaneserin	5⅜	4½	6
29	Verliebter Bauer	5⅜	4½	6
30	Mädchen spottend	5⅜	4½	6
33	Dame auf dem Balkon	7¾	6¼	10
34	Die Ohrenbeichte	9	6¼	18
39	Kind vom Hund gerettet	5	7	8
40	Kind vom Hund erkannt	5	7	8
41	Schiller Portrait	6½	5½	8
42	Schiller im Park	7¼	6	10
43	Göthe Portrait	6½	5½	8
44	Göthe im Park	7¼	6¼	10
47	Odaliska	6¾	7¼	12
48	Lichtenstein	7½	5½	10

№	Benennung.	Leipziger Zoll		Sgr.
		hoch.	breit.	
49	Petrarca	7	5½	8
50	Laura	7	5½	8
53	Tyrolerin	6¾	5½	8
56	Kreuz-Abnahme	9¼	6¼	18
62	Abeillard	7	5½	8
63	Heloise	7	5½	8
64	Römerin	7¼	6	10
66	Romeo und Julie	7¼	6	10
67	Meine gute Mutter	7¼	6	10
69	Münchner Mädchen	7¾	5¾	10
70	Tyroler und Mädchen	7¾	5¾	10
71	Heilige Nacht	7¾	5¾	10
72	Schillers Denkmal	7¼	5⅝	10
73	Domino	7¼	6	10
76	Mutterliebe	7⅓	6	10
81	Wahrsagerin	7⅓	6	10
83	Badende Kinder	8½	6½	18
84	Sylvester-Abend	8½	6½	18
85	Verliebte Mädchen	7¼	6	10
93	Löwenburg	6¾	7½	12
94	Eggestersteine	6¾	7½	12
95	Betende Italienerin	7	5¾	10
96	Christus am Kreuz	6	5	6
97	Sklavin	6	7½	10
98	Drei Genien	8½	6¾	18
99	Zwei Kinder angelnd	5½	5½	6
100	Madonna	9½	5⅞	18
101	A Goldschmidts Töchterlein	8½	6½	18
102	B do. do.	8½	6½	18
103	Die beiden Brüder	8½	6½	18
107	Der Brautkranz	7¾	6½	12
108	Mutter mit Kind im Walde	8½	6¾	18
110	Lago di Como	6¾	8½	18
111	Die Bastey in der sächsischen Schweiz	6¾	8½	18
112	Waldlandschaft	6¾	8½	18
113	Der Messner und der Chorknabe	9½	7¾	25
117	Kind mit Katze	8	6½	18
118	Dom zu Cöln	6½	8½	18
119	Nonnenwerth	5	6⅜	8
120	Stolzenfels	5	6⅜	8
123	Elternliebe	8	6½	18
124	Weinschmecker	6½	8⅜	18
125	Rendezvous	5⅛	4⅜	6
126	Knabe mit Hund	5⅛	4⅜	6
127	Mädchen mit do.	5⅛	4⅜	6
128	Pilger und Bettlerin	5⅛	4	6
131	Kinder mit Traube	7¼	5⅜	10
132	Schiffbruch	6¾	8½	18
133	Mädchen im Negligé	7	5¾	10
134	Le Bonton de Rose	7	5¾	10
135	Vor der Trauung	7	6	10
136	Nach der Trauung	7	6	10
137	Mendelsohn Bartholdy	7	6	10
138	Abendmahl Christi	6½	8¼	18
140	Die Königin des Balles	7	6	10
141	Wunder der Rose	8¼	7	18
142	Kind im Walde	8¼	6½	18
143	Liebeserklärung	8¼	6¾	18
144	Flucht nach Egypten	6¾	5½	10
145	Jesus am Oelberg	8¼	6½	18

№.	Benennung.	Leipziger Zoll hoch.	breit.	Sgr.
146	Olga	6¾	6	10
147	Rosenstein	6¼	8½	18
151	Stuben-Kamrad	4	3½	4
157	Kuss der Mutter	3¾	3¼	4
158	Kuss der Geliebten	3¾	3¼	4
159	Kuss der Tochter	3¾	3¼	4
160	Kind mit Hund A	3¾	3¼	4
161	Kind mit Hund B	3¾	3¼	4
162	Havre	3¾	3¼	4
165	Regimentstochter	7	6	10
166	Damen Portrait, 2lei	4	2½	4
169	Helgoland	3¾	6	6
171	Schäfermädchen	7	5⅞	10
172	Paul und Virginie	7	5⅞	10
173	La Confiance et Protection	7	5½	10
174	Ezelin	6	7	10
175	Johannisberg	6	7	10
176	Die Lore Ley	7	6	10
177	Der Fischer nach Göthe	6¾	6	10
178	Ave Maria	5⅞	6¾	10
179	Jesus im Tempel	5½	4½	6
180	Jesus im Richthaus	5½	4½	6
181	Der Zinsgroschen	5½	4½	6
182	Christus am Oelberg	5½	4½	6
183	Daniel in der Löwengrube	5½	4½	6
184	Jacob und Rebecca	5½	4½	6
185	Das Wunder der Rose	5½	4½	6
186	Tyroler und sein Mädchen	5½	4½	6
187	Der sterbende Pilger	6¼	7¾	18
188	Hallelujah	8¼	6½	18
189	Bad Wittekind in Halle	8¼	8	18
191	Antigone	6½	8¼	18
192	Der Blinde mit einem Mädchen	8	6½	18
193	Imogene	5½	4¾	6
194	Beatrice	5½	4⅞	6
195	Der Alpenjäger	6⅞	5¾	10
196	Kinder mit Blumen	6¼	6½	10
197	Zopf und Schwert	6¾	8½	18
200	Schasemann überrascht seine Geliebte	6½	7	12
201	Hans und Gretchen	8¼	6½	18
203	Helena	5¼	4½	6
204	Margareth	5½	4½	6
205	Zwei Knaben mit Bilderbuch	5¾	6¾	10
207	Gustav Adolph	6½	8½	18
208	Madonna, klein	5½	4⅝	6
209	Knabe mit Hund und Reif	6	6¾	10
210	Mädchen mit Hund	6	6⅞	10
211	Lautenschlägerin	6¾	5⅞	10
212	Tabulet-Händler	6¾	5⅞	10
213	Romeo	8	6½	18
214	Julie	8	6½	18
220	Seeschlacht	6¼	8	18
221	Kindergruppe mit Hund	5¾	6¾	10
222	Wie der Verstand bei dem Mädchen kommt	8¼	6½	18
223	Mädchengruppe mit Hund	6⅝	6¾	10
224	Kinder, Ziegen weidend	5⅞	6¾	10
225	Knabe mit Hund, Portrait	3⅞	3¼	4
226	Desgleichen	3⅞	3¾	4
227	Mädchen mit Lamm	3⅞	3¾	4
228	Desgleichen mit Katze	3⅞	3¾	4

№.	Benennung.	Leipziger Zoll hoch.	breit.	Sgr.
229	Brautwerbung	6¾	6	10
230	Ditto Pendant	6¾	6	10
231	Das genesene Kind	8	6½	18
232	Anleitung zur Wohlthätigkeit	8	6½	18
233	Ankunft beim Vicar	6½	8½	18
234	Der Nachmittag	6½	8½	18
235	Pius IX.	6¾	5¾	10
236	Blindekuh spielend	6¾	5¾	10
237	Kinderwagen mit Hund	6	6¾	10
238	Gebet am Kreuz	8¼	6½	18
239	Esmeralda	7	6	10
240	Ditto tanzend	7	6	10
241	Zwei Bachantinnen	5¾	4¾	6
242	Die Auferstehung Maria	8¾	6	18
243	Die heilige Dreifaltigkeit	8¾	6	18
244	Vierländer	3⅞	3¼	4
245	Altenburger Mädchen	3⅞	3¼	4
246	Erntegruppe bei Gewitter	6¼	7½	18
247	Kindergruppe mit Hund	6½	5	8
248	Mädchen mit Hund	6½	5	8
249	Verliebte Mädchen	6½	5	8
250	Esmeralda tanzend	6½	5	8
251	Esmeralda Pendant	6½	5	8
252	Madonna dolorosa	8	6½	18
253	Joseph von seinen Brüdern verkauft	5½	4¾	6
254	Kind mit Katze	5½	4⅝	6
255	Kind mit Vogel	5½	4⅝	6
256	Anleitung zur Frömmigkeit	6½	8¼	18
257	Die Geschwister	8¼	6½	18
258	Champagnertrinker	8½	6½	18
260	Abschied Hectors von Andromache	6¼	5	8
261	Hectors Vorwürfe gegen seinen Bruder Paris	6¼	5	8
262	Urtheil des Paris	6¼	5	8
263	Venus führt Helena dem Paris zu	6¼	5	8
264	Das Morgengebet	6½	8½	18
265	Lachtaube	8¼	6⅝	18
266	Die Unschuld	8½	6⅝	18
267	Die Unschuld unter den Räubern	6½	8½	18
268	Der Spielkamrad	4	3½	4
269	Kinder mit Blumen	5¼	5½	6
271	La Sainte Vierge	9½	6½	25
272	Wunder der Rose	9	7½	25
273	Mädchen mit Taube	8½	6½	20
274	Mädchen spielend	8½	6½	20
275	Esmeralda	9⅞	7½	25
276	Coblenz	8¼	6½	18
277	Godesberg	8¼	6½	18
278	Bingen	8¼	6½	18
279	Brautkranz, gross	9	7¾	25
280	König von Preussen	6¾	5½	8
282	Königin von Preussen	6⅝	5½	8
284	Messner und Chorknabe	5½	4⅞	6
285	Der Frühling	8¾	7	20
286	Der Sommer	8½	6½	18
287	Christus am Oelberg	5½	4½	6
288	Mädchen mit Schwänen	8½	6½	18
290	Vier Knaben und Mädchen	7¾	6½	18
291	La Toilette	8½	6¾	18
292	Der Sommer	5½	4⅞	6
293	Grossvaters Liebling	6¾	5¼	10

№.	Benennung.	Leipziger Zoll hoch.	breit.	Sgr.
294	Erziehung Azors	6¼	5	8
295	Ems	3¾	5	5
296	Kurhaus in Ems	3½	5	5
297	Ems	3¾	5	5
298	Ems	3⅞	5	5
299	Erinnerung an Ems	7¼	10	30
301	Drachenfels	4¾	6½	8
302	Maria und Elisabeth	4½	3¼	4
303	Maria mit dem Kinde	4¾	3¼	4
304	Maria mit Engeln umgeben	4¾	3¼	4
305	Die Anbetung Maria	4¾	3¼	4
306	Tasso	6½	8¼	18
307	Neapolitaner Familie	6	7	10
308	Mitten durch's Land	6	7	18
309	Bei Gelegenheit	6½	8¼	18
310	4erlei Maria-Scenen	7¼	6½	18
311	Die Brieftaube	7¼	6¼	12
312	Kind mit Kaninchen	6½	8½	18
313	Der erste Ritt	6½	8½	18
314	Christus Portrait	8½	6¼	18
315	Tyroler Scene	6¾	5¼	8
316	Ditto	6¾	5¼	8
317	Lachtaube, klein	5½	4¼	6
318	Die Unschuld	5½	4¾	6
319	Milchmädchen	5½	4¾	6
320	Knabe, Spiegel küssend	6¼	6⅜	10
321	Mädchen mit Spiegel	6¾	6¼	10
322	Allein in der Welt	7	5½	10
323	Jesus tröstend	6½	8¼	18
325	Eilpost	7	6	10
326	Mädchen mit Hahn	7¼	6¼	12
327	Neuwied	6½	8½	18
328	Erhebung Maria's	8½	6¼	18
329	Mädchen mit Vogel	4	3¼	4
330	Mädchen mit Hase	4	3¼	4
331	Landschaft	4	3¼	4
332	Seeschiff	4	3¼	4
333	Bonn	4¾	6⅜	8
334	Die Pfalz	4¾	6¾	8
335	Fleur de Marie	8½	6½	18
336	St. Clothild	5¾	4¾	6
337	St. Anna	5¾	4¾	6
338	St. Madelaine	5¾	4¾	6
339	St. Therese	5¾	4¾	6
340	Luther mit Familie am Weihnachtsabend	6½	8¼	18
341	Heidelberg	5	6¾	8
342	Fr. W. Denkmal in Berlin	8½	6½	18
343	Vergiss mein nicht	5⅜	4¾	6
344	Betendes Mädchen	4	3¼	4
345	Betender Knabe	4	3¼	4
346	Das Glück der Kinder	4	3¼	4
347	Die Wohlthätigkeit	4	3¼	4
348	Die kleinen Fischer	4	3¼	4
349	Das Fest der Madonna	4	3¼	4
350	Die Ueberfahrt	6	7	10
351	Mutter mit betendem Kind	7	6	10
352	Brenda	7¾	6¼	12
353	La Belle des Belles	7¾	6¼	12
354	La Reine de la danse	7¾	6¼	12
355	Schwäbisch Mädchen mit Kind	7	6	10

№.	Benennung.	Leipziger Zoll hoch.	breit.	Sgr.
356	Vergiss mein nicht	8¼	6½	18
357	Willst du die Ruthe?	7¾	6¼	12
358	Der kleine Taugenichts	7¾	6¼	12
359	Das Milchmädchen	8¼	6½	18
360	Mütterliche Besorgniss	7	6	10
361	Aschenbrödel	7	6	10
362	Ländliche Kinderstube	7	6	10
363	Knabe mit Trommel	6½	5	8
364	Mädchen mit Blumen	6½	5	8
365	Spielende Kinder	7	6	10
366	Reinecke der Fuchs A	5¾	4¾	6
367	Reinecke der Fuchs B	5¾	4¾	6
370	Das Familienfest	3¾	3¼	4
371	Don Quizotte	3¾	3¼	4
372	Johannes	5¾	4¾	6
373	Das Kind Jesu	5¾	4¾	6
374	Gottvertrauen	4	3¼	4
375	Die fleissige Strickerin	4	3¼	4
377	Hoftheater in Dresden	4¾	5¾	6
378	Belvedere in do.	4¾	5¾	6
379	Schlossplatz in do.	6½	7¾	18
380	Die Erwartung	8½	6½	18
381	Betendes Mädchen	5¾	4¾	6
382	Betender Knabe	5¾	4¾	6
383	Das kranke Kind	5¾	4¾	6
384	Das fromme Kind	5¾	4¾	6
385	Neuwied Nro. 2.	5	6¾	8
386	Mädchen mit Reh	8½	6½	18
387	Mädchen mit Hund	8½	6½	18
388	Auf diesen Abend	7¾	6¼	12
389	Meine Seele ist stille zu Gott	6¾	5	10
390	Das Frühstück	6¾	5	8
391	Das Mittagsbrod	6¾	5	8
392	Bavaria	7½	9½	25
393	La petite Friponne	6¾	5¾	10
394	Das jüngste Brüderchen	6¾	5¾	10
395	Baden-Baden	6	7	10
396	Gleisweiler	6	7	10
397	Kaiser Joseph von Oesterreich	7½	6¾	12
398	Nürnberg	6	7	10
399	Sonntagsschnupfer	5¾	4¾	6
400	Der freigebige Schnupfer	5¾	4¾	6
401	Die Mohrenwäsche	6½	8¼	18
402	Tankred und Clorinde	7	6	10
403	Er liebt mich	5¾	5	6
404	Die Erwartung	5¾	4¾	6
405	Knabe Spiegel küssend	rund		6
406	Mädchen do. do.	rund		6
407	Kinder in Blumen	rund		6
408	Stuben-Kamrad	rund		5
409	Zwei Kinder angelnd	rund		5
410	Pepita	6½	5	8
411	Die Elfenkönigin	8½	6½	18
412	Die Schildwache	5½	4½	6
413	Der Sonntag-Nachmittag	7½	6	12
414	Schachspielergruppe	6½	8¼	18
415	Das Brautpaar	5¾	4¾	6
416	Der Reconvalescent	6½	5¾	10
417	Madonna	7⅞	6	12
419	Dame mit Pferd	6½	4¾	10

№.	Benennung.	Leipziger Zoll		Sgr.
		hoch.	breit.	
420	Die Sänger im Walde	8¼	6½	18
421	Flucht nach Egypten	5¼	4¾	6
422	Der Schläfer und die Maikäfer	8¼	6½	10
423	Der Frühling	3¾	3¼	4
424	Der Sommer	3¾	3¼	4
425	Der Herbst	3¾	3¼	4
426	Der Winter	3¾	3¼	4
427	Eva und Topsy	6½	4¾	8
428	Elisa und Henry	6½	4¾	8
429	Der Sturm	6¾	6	10
430	Kaiserin von Oestreich	7½	6	12
431	Die Büssende	7½	6¼	12
432	König von Baiern	6¾	5⅜	10
433	Egmonts letzte Stunde	6½	8	18
434	Madonna von Morillo	8	6½	18
435	do. do.	6½	4½	8
436	Weihnachtsabend	6¾	5¾	10
437	Villa des Kronprinzen von Würtemberg	6½	8¼	18
438	Schachspieler Schachmatt	6¼	8¼	18
439	Christus in Figur	5½	4½	6
440	Madonna do.	5½	4½	6
441	Columbus	6½	8½	18
442	Entenjagd	6¾	6	10
447	Hasenjagd	6¾	6	10
448	Der Freiersmann	6¼	7½	12
449	Hühnerjagd	4¾	6½	8
450	Das Abendgebet	3⅞	3¼	4
451	Der Küchenschrank	3⅞	3¼	4
452	Das Vesperbrod	3⅞	3¼	4
453	Der Unterricht	3⅞	3¼	4
454	Fuchsjagd	4¾	6½	8
455	Die Morgenstunde	6¾	6	10
456	Das gestörte Rendezvous	6¾	8½	18
457	Grossvaters Liebling	6⅞	5	8
458	Mutter mit betendem Kind	6⅞	5	8
459	Die Morgenstunde	6⅞	5	8
460	Das jüngste Brüderchen	6⅞	5	8
461	Badendes Mädchen	7¾	6½	12
462	Dergl. Pendant	7¾	6½	12
463	Amor und Psyche	7¾	6½	12
464	Savoyard	8¼	6¾	18
466	Der Judaskuss	8¼	6½	18
467	Der neckende Liebhaber	6¼	4⅞	8
468	Genoveva	6½	4¾	8
469	Bäckermädchen	7½	6¼	10
470	Vier Jahreszeiten	8	6¾	18
471	Vier Kinderscenen	8	6¾	18
472	Die Zuckerdüte	7	6	10
473	Die erste Lüge	7¾	6¼	12
474	Mutterliebe	6¾	5¾	10
475	Prosit! (Hasenclever die Weinprobe malend)	6½	4½	8
476	Thun in der Schweiz	6½	8¾	18
477	Christus das Kreuz tragend	5½	4¾	6
478	Die Büssende	5½	4⅝	6
479	Madonna von Langbein	7	6	10
480	Madonna mit Christus und Johannes	7	6	10
481	Geigenspieler	7	6	10
482	Das sprechende Bild	9¼	7½	25
483	Schlaf, Kindchen, schlaf!	9¼	7½	25
484	Biertrinker	4½	3½	4

№.	Benennung.	Leipziger Zoll		Sgr.
		hoch.	breit.	
485	Caffeeschwester	4	3½	4
486	Gebet am Abend	8⅝	6½	18
487	Gebet am Morgen	8⅝	6½	18
488	Pour lui	8¼	6½	18
489	C'est de lui	8¼	6½	18
490	Das erste Lächeln	9¼	7½	25
491	München	4¼	6¾	8
492	Die Findung Moses	7½	9⅝	25
493	Die erste Lüge	6⅞	5	8
494	Gebet am Morgen	7¼	6¼	10
495	Gebet am Abend	7¼	6¼	10
496	Pour lui	7¼	6¼	10
497	C'est de lui	7¼	6¼	10
498	Glyptothek	5	7	8
499	Maria von Kevelaer	5¾	4¾	6
500	Strassburger Münster	7½	5½	10
501	Chateau Chillion	5	6¾	8
502	Die Spinnerin	7	6	10
503	Der Gelehrte	7	6	10
504	Die Eierprobe	8½	6½	18
505	Denkmal des Marschall von Sachsen	8½	6½	18
506	Amor, Pfeil schärfend	6	7	10
507	Eiger, Mönch u. Jungfrau (Schweizer Landschaft)	8¼	6½	18
508	Der Grossmutter Liebling	6½	8½	18
509	Mutterschmerz	8¼	6½	18
510	Der Strick-Unterricht	8¼	6½	18
511	Der vom Blitz erschlagene Schäfer	6½	8¼	18
512	Tändelei	5¾	4¾	6
513	Die neuen Hausgenossen	5¾	4¾	6
514	Die Coquetten	7¾	6¼	12
515	Der Liebesbrief	7¾	6¼	12
516	Der kleine Gutschmecker	5¾	4¾	6
517	Der getäuschte Näscher	5¾	4¾	6
518	Hohenzollern	6¼	8¼	18
519	Holländische Winterlandschaft	7¾	6¼	12
520	Undine	7¾	6¼	12
521	Mädchenanstalt in Neuwied	6½	8¾	18
522	Nichts für den Wächter	5¾	4¾	6
523	Leyden	5¼	6¼	8
524	Amsterdam, Palais	5¼	6¼	8
525	Kind, Pferd fütternd	5¼	4¼	6
526	Reinhardtsbrunn	5	5¾	6
527	Wartburg	5	5¾	6
528	Des Hauses und des Feldes Segen	4	3½	4
529	Utrecht	5¼	6¼	8
530	Amsterdam	5½	6¼	8
531	Schreibunterricht	4	3½	4
532	Stickunterricht	4	3½	4
533	Fraternité	4	3½	4
534	Rheinfall bei Schaffhausen	6	7½	12
535	Frühling	5¾	4¾	6
536	Sommer	5¾	4¾	6
537	Herbst	5¾	4¾	6
538	Winter	5¾	4¾	6
539	Lidia Thompson	5¾	4¾	6
540	Berner Mädchen	7	6	10
541	Dies hat das Christkindlein gebracht	6½	8½	18
542	Madonna Sixtina	8¼	6½	18
543	Flucht nach Egypten	7½	9½	25
544	Des Farmers Liebling	7¾	6¼	12

№.	Benennung.	Leipziger Zoll		Sgr.
		hoch.	breit.	
545	Lindau am Bodensee	6½	8	12
546	Cadinella	7¾	6¼	12
547	Margarethe	5½	4½	6
548	Königs Denkmal in Lindau	7¾	6¼	12
549	Die schöne Schnitterin	8½	6½	18
550	Des Hauses und des Feldes Segen	8¼	6½	18
551	Mädchen am Brunnen	8¼	6½	18
552	Das Grab der Mutter	8¼	6½	18
553	Des Hauses und des Feldes Segen	5½	4½	6
554	Die Zuckerdüte	6½	5	8
555	Petersthal	6	7	10
556	Jacob bei Laban	5¾	4¼	6
557	Jacob und Rahel	5¾	4¾	6
558	Stick-Unterricht	5½	4½	6
561	Helgoland	4	3½	4
562	Luzern	6½	8½	18
563	Tells Capelle	6½	8½	18
564	Lausanne	6½	8½	18
565	Genf	6½	8½	18
566	Zu Tische	6½	5	8
567	Glückliche Zeit	6½	5	8
568	Festzug	6½	5	8
569	Herbstregen	6½	5	8
570				
571				
572	Rheinfall, zweite Ansicht	6½	8½	18
573	Die sorgsame Tochter	7	6	10
574	Der Ausgang aus der Kirche	7	6	10
575	Schiller- und Göthe-Gruppe	6¾	5	8
576	Der Frühling	7¼	5¼	12
577	Frankfurt a. M.	6½	8¼	18
578	Der Frühling	7¾	6¼	12
579	Der Sommer	7¾	6¼	12
580	Der Herbst	7¾	6¼	12
581	Der Winter	7¾	6¼	12
582	Schneewitchen	7¾	6¼	12
583	Hundefuhrwerk	4	3½	4
584	Hunde-Tanz	4	3½	4
585	Ophelia	5½	4½	6
586	Mopsa	5½	4½	6
587	Juliette	5½	4½	6
588	Römische Familie	4	3½	4
589	Habe Geduld	4	3¼	4
590	Mädchen mit Hund	6½	5	8
591	Schlotfeger und Maurer	7	6	10
592	Süsses Verlangen	6¾	5	8
593	Die kleine Eva	6½	5	8
594	Anna	5½	4½	6
595	Prinz und Prinzessin von Preussen (Royale)	7	6½	10
596	Jäger und Liebchen	6¾	5½	10
597	Dornröschen	7¾	6¼	12
598	Die Kartenschlägerin	7¾	6¼	12
599	Antoinette	7	6	10
600	Der Fischer, Pendant zu 178	5¾	6½	10
601	Das gefährdete Frühstück	6	4½	8
602	Stolzenfels	5	6¾	8
603	Oberwesel	5	6¾	8
604	Der Franzose	6½	5½	8
605	Schachmatt	6¾	5	8

№.	Benennung.	Leipziger Zoll		Sgr.
		hoch.	breit.	
606	Leonore	9¼	7½	25
607	Wartburg mit Eingang	5	6¾	8
608	do. Thal-Ansicht	5	6¾	8
609	Schachspieler	6½	5	8
610	Schachmatt	5¾	4¾	6
611	Die Abreise	7¼	9¼	25
612	Die Taufe	8½	6½	18
613	Heidelberg	5	6¾	8
614	Schachspieler	5¾	4¾	6
615	Heilige Nacht	8¾	6¾	20
616	Napoleon	7¾	6	12
617	Johannes	7	6	10
618	Erste Classe	7¼	9¼	25
619	Kommt her zu mir	7	6	10
620	Der Morgen	8½	6½	18
621	Johannes, klein	5½	4¾	6
622	Kind Jesu	5½	4¾	6
623	Das verirrte Kind	7½	6	12
624	Der neue Schüler	6½	8¼	18
625	Der verliebte Schuster	7½	6	12
626	Friedrich II.	7¾	6	12
627	Pferdestück	7¼	9¼	25
628	Der verliebte Schuster, klein	6½	4¾	8
629	Königin von Preussen	7	5¼	10
630	Das verirrte Kind	6½	4¾	8
631	Strom aufwärts	6½	8¼	18
632	Wohlthätigkeit	5¾	4¾	6
633	Bad Eigersburg	5	6½	8
634	Strom abwärts	6½	8¼	18
635	Strickunterricht	6¾	5	8
636	Der Naturforscher	5	4¼	6
637	Die Taufe	6	4½	8
638	Heilige Familie	5½	4½	6
639	Die Geduld-Probe	8¼	6½	18
640	Winzerfamilie	4	3¼	4
641	Sorgenlos, Kind mit Hund	4	3¼	4
642	Grossmutter und Enkel	4	3¼	4
643	Die beiden Wächter	4	3¼	4
644	Nur nicht geizig	7¾	6¼	12
645	Die Geduld-Probe	7	6	10
646	Das erste Almosen	7	6	10
647	Alle Neun	5½	4¾	6
648	Der Labetrunk	5½	4¾	6
649	Spazierritt	7	6	10
650	Königsbau in Stuttgart	6½	8½	18
651	Schreib-Unterricht	6½	6	10
652	Piccolomini	6¾	5	8
653	Wilhelm Tell	6¾	5	8
654	Carl Moor	6¾	5	8
655	Maria Stuart	6¾	5	8
656	Die reizende Silphide	3¾	3½	4
657	Hedwig, Tells Frau	6¾	5	8
658	Schiller	5¾	4¾	6
659	Schillers Frau	5¾	4¾	6
660	La Joe de la Maison	9	7½	25
661	Der Vergleich	9	7½	25
662	Grossmutters Enkel	5¾	4¾	6
663	Die beiden Wächter	5¾	4¾	6
664	Hohenschwangau	5¾	6½	8
665	Die Trauung aus der Glocke	6¾	5	8

№.	Benennung.	Leipziger Zoll hoch.	breit.	Sgr.
666	Ungarsche Pferde	6½	9¼	25
667	Die Taufe aus der Glocke	6¾	5	8
668	Dom zu Speyer	8¼	6½	18
669	Der Lauer See	4¼	6	8
670	Der Montblanc	4¼	6	8
671	Pferdestück	6	7¾	12
672	Ungarsche Pferde	5½	7	12
673	Astronomische Uhr in Strassburg	6¼	5	10
674	Der Brief	7½	6	12
675	Das Begräbniss aus der Glocke	6¾	5	8
676	Dom zu Speyer	7½	5¾	10
677	Das verunglückte Rendezvous	6¾	5	8
678	Das glückliche do.	6¾	5	8
679	Die Hausfrau aus der Glocke	6¾	5	8
680	Die Heimkehr	8½	6½	18
681	Die Antwort, Pendant zu 674.	7½	6	12
682	Die Abendstunde	8½	6½	18
683	Die Heimkehr	6½	5	8
685	Napoleon I. zu Pferd	7½	6	12
686	Laubach bei Coblenz	5	6¾	8
687	Apollinaris Kirche	5	6¾	8
688	Alle neune	4	3¼	4
689	Das gefährdete Frühstück	3¾	3¼	4
690	Genf	6½	8½	18
691	Die Abendstunde	7	6	10
692	Die Erwartung	7	6	10
693	Das Ebenbild	5¾	4¾	6
694	Des Hauses Freude	5¾	4¾	6
695	Die Mährchen-Erzählerin	7	6	10
696	Das Ebenbild	4	3¼	4
697	Des Hauses Freude	4	3¼	4
698	Der Weihnachtstraum	7	6	10
699	Madonna Sixt.	7	6	10
700	Die Weihnachtsgeschenke	7	6	10
701	La Vierge au Poisson	7	6	10
702	Johannes	5¾	4¾	6
703	Fliehende Christen	9	8	25
704	Erst beten	7	6	10
705	Der lustige Schornsteinfeger	6½	8½	18
706	Napoleon III.	7	5¾	10
707	Eugenie	7	5¾	10
708	Der Fasttag	6½	8½	18
709	Die Feierstunde	8¼	6¾	18
710	Der Clavierunterricht	7½	6	12
711	Der unterbrochene do.	7½	6	12
712	Die Feierstunde	7	5¾	10
713	Erst beten	5	4¼	6
714	Kind auf Hund reitend	7	6	10
715	Der gegenseitige Unterricht	8¼	6½	18
716	Familien-Andacht	8¼	6½	18

Anhang

zum

Preis-Courant über transparente Lichtschirme

von

C. G. SCHIERHOLZ & SOHN

in

Plaue bei Arnstadt.

№.	Benennung.	Leipziger Zoll hoch.	breit.	Sgr.
717	Kind auf Hund reitend	5½	4¾	6
718	Der Spazierritt	5½	4¾	6
719	Der Buchstabirunterricht	5½	4½	6
720	Der Hühnerkorb	5½	4½	6
721	Der Zinstag	6½	8½	18
722	Der verliebte Dorfschulze	6½	8¼	18
723	Der Hirtenknabe	6½	5	8
724	Drachenfels	5½	4½	6
725	Rheinstein	5½	4½	6
726	Seemanns Leben	5½	4½	6
727	Wasserfall	5½	4½	6
728	Das Lesecabinet	6½	8½	18
729	Die Rückkehr der Schnitter	6¼	8¼	18
730	Die Retourreise	6	7½	12
731	Herzog von Sachsen-Coburg-Gotha	6¾	4¾	8
732	Die Abreise	6	7½	12
733	Der Malerunterricht	4	3¼	4
734	Gesangübung	4	3¼	4
735	Bahnhof zu Hannover	6	7½	12
736	Die Unklugheit	3¼	3¼	4
737	un vilain trait de minet	4	3¼	4
738	Schlossplatz in Stuttgart	6½	8¼	18
739	Des Räubers Braut	6¾	5	8
740	Die Versöhnung	5½	4¾	6
741	Der Krieg	5½	4¾	6
742	„Baumwolle oder Seide?"	6½	5	8
743	Der grosse Bruder	3¾	3¼	4
744	Ein falscher Freund	3½	3	4
745	Die Schleichhändler	8½	6½	18
746	Mondwacht auf der Alp	8¼	6½	18
747	Amour maternel	7	5¼	12
748	Pendant dazu	7	5½	12
749	Seemanns Leben	7	9	25
750	„Schlag mal her!"	4	3¼	4
751	Die Versöhnung	4	3¼	4
752	Familiengruppe	7¼	6½	12
753	Christus am Kreuze	6½	4¾	8
754	Amour maternel	7	5¾	10
755	Pendant dazu	7	5¾	10

Endnotes

Introduction

[1]William Burton, *A General History of Porcelain* (London: Chatto, 1920), 154.

[2]Harold Newman, "Lithophane Plaques," *Antique Dealers and Collectors Guide*, August 1990, Statuscourt Ltd., London, pp. 33-35, 40.

[3]Correspondence from Robert A. Elder, Jr., to Mr. Cecil Zinkan at the Lightner Museum, dated March 29, 1959.

[4]Correspondence from Edmond Beroud to Mr. L. Newton Hayes, dated October 5, 1954.

[5]Undated 1965 correspondence from Laurel Blair to Amoret and Christopher Scott, dated July 21, 1965.

[6]Correspondence from Mr. Blair to Mrs. DeBow, dated February 13, 1967.

[7]Correspondence from Robert A. Elder, Jr. to Laurel Blair, dated August 14, 1964.

[8]Correspondence from *The Antique Collector*, Ltd. to Dr. Beroud, dated May 1, 1950.

Chapter 2

[1]Georg Lenz. "Lithophanien," in Kellers, Paul: *Monatsblätter/Die Bergstadt*, Heute Jahrgang 1920/21, Band. II, Leipzig/Breslau/Wien: Wilh. Gottl. Korn, 1920, p. 214.

[2]Elizabeth Baroody, "Lithophanes, A Surprise and Delight," *Hobbies*, vol. 90, no. 3, May 1985, p. 17; and G. Bernard and Therle Hughes, *After the Regency* (London: Lutterworth Press, 1952), p. 125.

[3]G.A.R. Goyle, "Lithophanes," *Antiques*, vol. XXIX, no. 4, April, 1936, p. 146.

[4]Parian ware or Parian porcelain is an unglazed biscuit porcelain introduced in 1846 at Copeland's in Stoke-on-Trent, and used extensively by other English and American manufacturers.

[5]According to http://www.booklocker.com/pdf/2358s.pdf "The Thirty Years War gave a deathblow to Germany's early patent system. Afterwards, German technology began to lag and it continued to do so until Bismarck's unification in 1871 brought about a rebirth of its patent system on a national basis, this time with two new procedures: opposition to the grant of a patent, and nullification of a patent already granted. These new procedures were in addition to the settled German practice of examination for novelty before the grant of a patent."

[6]Letter from D.H. Henson, Minton designer, to Laurel Blair, dated October 20, 1965.

[7]Paul Scott, *Ceramics and Print* (Philadelphia: University of Pennsylvania Press, 1995), p. 27.

[8]Rudolf Hainbach, *Pottery Decorating* (London: Scott, Greenwood & Son, 1924), pp. 143-147.

[9]Bichromate (ammonium or potassium) is a photosensitive chemical used in photographic emulsions and has been used in direct photo emulsions on ceramic surfaces. The bichromate turns to chrome oxide on firing, imparting color on photo-sensitized areas. It is a suspected carcinogen. Information from Paul Scott's *Ceramics and Print* (Philadelphia: University of Pennsylvania Press, 1995), p. 113.

[10]Paul Scott, *Ceramics and Print* (Philadelphia: University of Pennsylvania Press, 1995), p. 29.

[11]Walter E. Woodbury, *The Encyclopaedia of Photography* (1890), pp. 538-539.

[12]Email correspondence between Curtis Benzle and the author, dated February 21, 2007.

[13]James L. Murphy, "Ohio Features Ceramic Genius Walter D. Ford (1906-1988)," *Flash Point*, April-June 1991, vol. 4, no. 2, p. 16.

Chapter 3

[1]Correspondence from Laurel Blair to Mr. de Clairmont, dated July 21, 1967.

[2]Joseph Marryat, *A History of Pottery and Porcelain, Medieval and Modern* (London: J. Murray, 1857), p. 382.

[3]Bernard G. Hughes, *The Collector's Pocket Book of China* (London: Country Life, 1970), p. 178.

[4]Kirsten Dorothée Rather, *Lithophanien: Die Welt des Biedermeier im Porzellanbild* (Berlin: Kulturstiftung Schloss Britz, 2001), p. 5.

[5]Frick, *Geschichte der KPM*, p. 292.

[6]Ibid., p. 880.

[7]Geoffrey A. Godden, *Antique Glass and China* (New York: Castle Books, 1966), p. 35.

[8]Correspondence via email from Christine Davis to author, dated March 6, 2006.

[9]Correspondence from the E.G. Zimmermann company, to Bernard Rushton dated February 5, 1975.

[10]London Great Exhibition of the Works of All Nations, 1851, *Official Descriptive and Illustrated Catalogue* (London: Spicer Brothers, 1851), vol. III, p. 1060.

[11]Derek E. Ostergard, editor, *Along the Porcelain Road: Berlin and Potsdam in KPM Porcelain Painting 1815-1848* (New York: The Bard Graduate Center for Studies in the Decorative Arts, 1993), p. 83.

[12]Bärbel Kovalevski, "Georg Friedrich Kersting als Malervosteher an der Königlichsächsischen Porzellan Manufaktur Meissen von 1818-1847," *Keramik-Freunde der Schweiz*, no. 108, Dezember 1994, p. 61.

[13]Winfried Baer, *Berlin Porcelain* (Washington, D.C.: Smithsonian Institution Press,1980), p. 24.

[14]Derek E. Ostergard, editor, *Along the Porcelain Road: Berlin and Potsdam in KPM Porcelain Painting 1815-1848* (New York: The Bard Graduate Center for Studies in the Decorative Arts, 1993), p. 88.

[15]see illustration on page 136, Derek E. Ostergard, editor, *Along the Porcelain Road: Berlin and Potsdam in KPM Porcelain Painting 1815-1848* (New York: The Bard Graduate Center for Studies in the Decorative Arts, 1993).

[16]Derek E. Ostergard, editor, *Along the Porcelain Road: Berlin and Potsdam in KPM Porcelain Painting 1815-1848* (New York: The Bard Graduate Center for Studies in the Decorative Arts, 1993), pp. 168-169.

[17]Robert E. Röntgen, *The Book of Meissen* (Atglen, PA: Schiffer Publishing, 1996), p. 217.

[18]Hermann Jedding, *Meißener Porzellan des 19. und 20. Jahrhunderts 1800-1933* (München: Keyser, 1981), p. 175.

[19]London Great Exhibition of the Works of All Nations, 1851. *Official Descriptive and Illustrated Catalogue* (London: Spicer Brothers, 1851), vol. I, p. 1112.

[20]Robert E. Röntgen, *The Book of Meissen* (Atglen, PA: Schiffer Publishing, 1966), p. 217.

[21]Ibid., p. 218.

[22]Email correspondence from Helga Scheidt, Schloßmuseum Arnstadt, to author dated September 7, 2007.

[23]Schloßmuseum Arnstadt. *175 Jahre von Schierholz'sche Porzellanmanufaktur: Plauein Thüringen* (Förderverein Schloßmuseum Arnstadt, 1992), p. 28.

[24]Dorothée Kirsten Rather, *Lithophanien: Die Welt des Biedermeier im Porzellandbild* (Berlin: Kulturstiftung Schloss Britz, 2001), p. 5.

[25]Correspondence from Mr. Jean d'Albis from Haviland, to Mr. Blair, dated April 1, 1965.

[26]Ibid.

[27]Geoffrey Godden, *Godden's Guide to European Porcelain* (New York: Cross River Press, 1994), p. 205.

[28]Harold Newman, *Veilleuses: A Collector's Guide* (New York, London: Cornwall Books, 1987), p. 56.

[29]Chantal Meslin-Perrier, *La Lithophanie et Limoges – Musée National Adrien Dubouché* (Paris: Réunion des musées nationaux 49, rue Étienne-Marcel 75001 1992, pp. 10-11.

[30]Accession number 3371, donated by M. Bonnafair on June 22, 1969, from correspondence from Mademoiselle Jeanne Giacomotti to Laurel Blair, dated July 26, 1963.

[31]Email correspondence between author and Helga Scheidt, Schloßmuseum Arnstadt, dated October 6, 2007.

[32]Unpublished typescript from Harold Newman to Laurel Blair, sent with cover letter dated December 7, 1971.

[33]Chantal Meslin-Perrier, *La Lithophanie et Limoges* (Paris: Ed. de la Reunion des musees nationaux, 1992), p. 391.

[34]Alexandre Brongniart and D. Riocreaux, *Description méthodique du Musée Ceramique de la Manufacture Royale de Porcelaine de Sèvres* (Paris: A. Leleux, 1845), vol. 1, p. 289.

[35]Joseph Marryat, *Collections Towards A History of Pottery and Porcelain in the 15th, 16th, 17th, and 18th Centuries* (London: J. Murray, 1850), p. 264, and *A History of Pottery and Porcelain, Medieval and Modern* (London: J. Murray, 1857), p. 382.

[36]William Burton, *A General History of Porcelain* (London: Chatto, 1920), p. 154.

[37]Emanuel Poche, *Bohemian Porcelain* (Prague: Artia, 1957), p. 17.

[38]J. Folnesics and Dr. E. W. Braun, *Geschichte der K.K. Wiener Porzellan-Manufaktur.* (Wien: Druck und Verlag der K.K. Hof-und Staatsdruckerei, 1907), p. 138.

[39]Correspondence from Paul de la Roche in Soignies, to Laurel Blair, dated March 23, 1965.

[40]Correspondence from Harold Newman to Laurel Blair, dated March 14, 1983.

[41]Correspondence from Georges Licope, Conservateur, to Laurel Blair, dated April 13, 1967.

[42]Harold Newman, *Veilleuses 1750-1860* (South Brunswick, New Jersey: A.S. Barnes and Co., Inc., 1967), p. 180, and *Veilleuses: A Collector's Guide* (New York, London: Cornwall Books, 1987), p. 110.

[43]Harold Newman, *Veilleuses: A Collector's Guide* (New York: Cornwall Books, 1987), p. 104.

[44]Rüdiger Van Dyck, "Lithophanien. Transparente Porzellanbilder," *Sammler Journal*, 4, April 1987, p. 446.

[45]Ibid.

[46]Geoffrey Godden, *Antique China and Glass Under £5* (London: Arthur Barker Limited, 1966), p. 32.

[47]Ibid.

[48]Correspondence from Harold Newman to Laurel Blair, dated February 6, 1967.

[49]Rüdiger Van Dyck, "Lithophanien. Transparente Porzellanbilder," *Sammler Journal*, 4, April 1987, p. 446.

[50]Ibid.

[51]Correspondence from Bredo L. Grandjean, Curator, the Royal Copenhagen Porcelain Manufactory LTD., to Laurel Blair, dated April 20, 1965.

[52]*Pottery Gazette and Glass Trade Review.* "Translucent Embossments: Wax Modelling Method Used in Copenhagen," February 1951, p. 242.

[53]Geoffrey Bemrose, *Nineteenth Century English Pottery and Porcelain* (London: Faber and Faber, 1952), p. 43.

[54]see G. Bernard Hughes, *The Collector's Pocket Book of China* (London: Country Life, 1970), p. 179, and Geoffrey Bemrose, *Nineteenth Century English Pottery and Porcelain* (London: Faber and Faber, 1952), p. 43.

[55]G. Bernard Hughes, *The Collector's Pocket Book of China* (London: Country Life, 1970), pp. 178-179.

[56]Mellors & Kirk, *Antiques and Works of Art*, auction catalogue (Nottingham, February 8, 2007), p. 38, Lot 414.

[57]Correspondence from F.E. Ridgeway, Sales Manager at Coalport China Limited, to Laurel Blair, dated April 22, 1965.

[58]Correspondence from F.E. Ridgeway, Sales Manager at Coalport China Limited, to Laurel Blair, dated May 6, 1965.

[59]*Pottery Gazette and Glass Trade Review,* "Lithophane by Coalport," No. 80, December, 1955, p. 1859.

[60]Correspondence from Dr. Leonard Rakow to Laurel Blair, dated January 24, 1983.

[61]Correspondence from A.R. Mountford to Laurel Blair, dated May 6, 1963.

[62]Correspondence from W. Duckers to Laurel Blair, dated April 21, 1965.

[63]Marjories Cawley, "Antiques – Transparent Lithophanes," *South Wales Argus*, January 12, 1970, and Nicholas Pine, *The Concise Encyclopedia and Price Guide to Goss China*, n.d., n.p.

[64]*Blair Bulletin* No. 3, July 15, 1976, p. 2.

[65]According to G. Bernard Hughes, *The Country Life Pocket Book of China*, the cottages or pastille burners were containers for slow-burning smoldering cone-shaped pastilles composed of finely powdered willow wood charcoal with gum benzoin, powdered cinnamon, perfumed oils and other aromatics, p. 150-152.

[66]John Sandon, *The Dictionary of Worcester Porcelain, Volume I, 1751-1851* (Woodbridge: The Antique Collectors' Club, 1993), p. 222.

[67]Ibid., p. 221.

[68]Ibid., p. 222.

[69]Correspondence from Dr. Edmond Beroud to Mintons Limited, dated October 15, 1953.

[70]Correspondence from J. Steel to Dr. Edmond Beroud, dated October 27, 1953.

[71]Correspondence from A.R. Mountford to Laurel Blair, dated March 20, 1963.

[72]Geoffrey A. Godden, *Minton Pottery & Porcelain of the First Period 1793-1850* (London: Herbert Jenkins, 1968), p. 161.

[73]Ibid.

[74]Correspondence from Laurel Blair to Mr. D.H. Henson, Mintons, dated March 13, 1966.

[75]Correspondence from D.H. Henson to Laurel Blair, dated June 29, 1966.

[76]Correspondence from J.E. Johnson at Minton LTD. to Bernard Rushton, dated April 25, 1969.

[77]Geoffrey A. Godden, *Minton Pottery & Porcelain of the First Period 1793-1850* (London: Herbert Jenkins, 1968), p. 161.

[78]Correspondence from D.H. Henson, designer at Mintons to Laurel Blair, dated December 6, 1965.

[79]Correspondence from D.H. Henson to Laurel Blair, dated October 20, 1965.

[80]Ibid.

[81]Ibid.

[82]Correspondence from Anthony J. Wade, Chairman, Wade Potteries LTD to Laurel Blair, dated November 17, 1976, p. 1.

[83]Ibid.

[84]Ibid., p. 2.

[85]Correspondence from Laurel Blair to Anthony J. Wade, dated December 11, 1976.

[86]Leonard S. Rakow and Juliette K. Rakow, "Wedgwood Lithophanes," *Ars Ceramica*, Wedgwood Society of New York, 1985, No. 2, p. 11.

[87]Archival records from Research File, Josiah Wedgwood & Sons, Inc., New York City.

[88]Correspondence from Robert A. Elder, Jr., to Mrs. Annie Reese Wedgwood, dated October 23, 1953.

[89]Alexandre Brongniart, 1770-1847. *Traité des arts céramiques: ou des poteries, considérées dans leur histoire, leur pratique et leur théorie* (Paris: Passelin, Librairie de La Faculté de Médecine, 1877), vol. 1, p. 741.

[90]Correspondence from Robert A. Elder, Jr. to Laurel Blair, dated August 14, 1964, and correspondence from Robert A. Elder, Jr., to Mrs. Annie Reese Wedgwood, dated October 23, 1953.

[91]C. Boncz and K. Gink, *Herend China* (Budapest: Pannonia Press, 1962), p. 16.

[92]*Blair Museum of Lithophanes Bulletin* No. 16, dated September 19, 1978, p. 1.

[93]László Molnar, "Herendi litofan ablak," *Muvészettörténeti értesíto*, vol. XXVIII, no. 4, 1979, p. 243.

[94]Ibid.

[95]Ibid.

[96]Correspondence from Robert Grimm to Laurel Blair, dated July 13, 1978.

[97]Email correspondence from Steve Mattison to the author, dated March 26, 2007.

[98]Laurel Blair, *Blair Museum of Lithophanes & Carved Waxes, Lithophane Collectors' Club, Bulletin* No. 70, October 31, 1987, p. 6.

[99]Laurel Blair, *Blair Museum of Lithophanes & Carved Waxes, Lithophane Collectors' Club, Bulletin* No. 66, February 28, 1987, p. 3.

[100]Ibid., p. 2.

[101]Ibid.

[102]Harold Newman, "Lithophane Plaques," *Antique Dealers and Collectors Guide*, August, 1990, Statuscourt Ltd., London, p. 34.

[103]Correspondence via email between author and Oliva Rucellai, dated August 31, 2007.

[104]Correspondence via email between author and Filipa Quatorze of the Mvseu Histórico da Vista Alegre, dated August 6, 2007.

[105]Correspondence from Laurel Blair to Joaquim Pinto Basto, dated September 27, 1967.

[106]Tamara Kudrjawzewa, *Das Weisse Gold der Zaren* (Arnoldsche, 2000), cat. no. 76.

[107]Correspondence from Edmond Beroud to Laurel Blair, dated May 22, 1963.

[108]Correspondence from Dr. Rudolph Schnyder to Mr. Blair, dated August 18, 1965.

[109]Edwin A. Barber, "Historical Sketch of the Phoenixville Pottery," *The Clay Worker Magazine*, vol. 28, August 1897, p. 97.

[110]Ibid.

[111]Ibid.

[112]Ibid., p. 97-98.

[113]Martha Hill Hommel, "Some More About Lithophanes," *Hobbies*, July 1950, p. 77.

[114]Correspondence from Thomas U. Schock to Mrs. Martha Hummel, dated May 17, 1950.

[115]*Blair Bulletin No. 64*, October 31, 1986, p. 6, illustrated.

[116]*Blair Bulletin No. 65*, December 31, 1986, p. 4.

[117]Lithoplastics were an invention of Dr. Edmond Beroud.

[118]Blair *Bulletin* no. 22, October 15, 1979, p. 1.

[119]Dilys Jenkins, *Llanelly Pottery* (Swansea: Deb Books, 1968), p. 9.

[120]Gareth Hughes, *A Llanelli Chronicle* (Llanelli: Llanelli Borough Council, 1984), p. 331.

[121]Correspondence from Rollo Charles to Edmond Beroud, dated December 1, 1953.

[122]John Taylor, *The Complete Practical Potter, or a Comprehensive Collection of Receipts, for the Manufacture of China, Earthenware, Ironstone, &c. &c.* (Shelton: William White, 1847), p. 1.

[123]Isaac J. Williams, *A Guide to the Collection of Welsh Porcelain* (Cardiff: the National Museum of Wales, 1931), p. 10.

[124]Jelinger Symonds, "The Industrial Capacities of South Wales," *The Cambrian Journal*, vol. 1, 1854, p. 322.

[125]Dilys Jenkins, *Llanelly Pottery* (Swansea: Deb Books, 1968), p. 27.

[126]Derek E. Ostergard, editor, *Along the Porcelain Road: Berlin and Potsdam in KPM Porcelain and Painting 1815-1848* (New York: The Bard Graduate Center for Studies in the Decorative Arts, 1993), p. 83.

[127]Correspondence with attachments from the Staatliche Porzellan-Manufaktur Berlin to Laurel Blair, dated August 13, 1962.

[128]Quotation from *Official Report on the Industrial Exhibition of all nations at London in 1851*, Berlin, 1853, volume III, page 38 XXV classed burned goods.

[129]Bärbel Kovalevski, "Georg Friedrich Kersting als malervosteher an der Königlichsächsischen Porzellan Manufaktur Meissen von 1818 bis 1847, *Keramik-Freunde der Schweiz.* Mitteilungsblatt Nr. 108, Dezember 1994, p. 61. Her information was extracted from the Annual Reports of the Meissen Manufacture, Archiv der Staatlichen Porzellanmanufaktur Meißen, III G 2, "Gestaltung und Malerei," pages 210-215.

Chapter 4

[1]Correspondence from L. Newton Hayes to Edmond Beroud, dated October 1, 1954.

[2]R.L. Hobson, *Chinese Pottery and Porcelain*, vol. I (New York: Dover Publications, 1976), p. 50.

[3]Ibid., p. 51.

[4]R.L. Hobson, *Chinese Pottery and Porcelain*, vol. II (New York: Dover Publications, 1976), p. 4-5.

[5]Ibid., p. 5.

[6]Robert A. Elder, Jr., "Lithophanic Art," *Keramik-Freunde der Schweitz, Mitteilungsblatt*, no. 37, January 1957, p. 18.

[7]Ibid.

[8]Mrs. Willoughby Hodgson, *How to Identify Old Chinese Porcelain* (Chicago: A.C. McClurg & Co., 1907), pp. 19-20.

[9]Ibid., pp. 20-21.

[10]Ibid., p. 22.

[11]Ibid.

Chapter 5

[1]Andreas Blühm and Louise Lippincott, *Light! The Industrial Age 1750-1900: Art & Science, Technology and Society* (New York: Thames & Hudson, 2001), p. 96.

[2]Ibid.

[3]Carol Wax, *The Mezzotint: History and Technique* (New York: Harry N. Abrams, Inc., 1990), p. 117.

[4]Charles Thomas Jacobi, *The Printers' Handbook of Trade Recipes, Hints & Suggestions Relating to Letterpress and Lithographic Printing, Bookbinding Stationery, Engraving, etc.* (London: Chiswick Press, 1891), p. 289.

[5]Ibid., p. 290.

[6]Hans Meyer, *Böhmisches Porzellan und Steingut* (Leipzig: 1929), n.p.

[7]Heide L. Nichols, *The Fashioning of Middle-Class America* (New York: Peter Lang, 2004), p. 2.

[8]Ibid.

[9]Information supplied via email to the author, by Roger Norton, a Lincoln expert, on August 20, 2007.

[10]Edmond Beroud, "Lithophanes – What they are and Why they are a delightful item for collectors," *Spinning Wheel*, June 1951, p. 24.

[11]Correspondence between Laurel Blair and Frederick Voss, Research Historian at the National Portrait Gallery, Smithsonian Institution, dated June 8, 1977.

[12]Peter-Christian Wegner, "Literatur auf Porzellan: 'Paul et Virginie' also Meissner Lithophanie," *Keramos* (Bonn), vol. 177, July 2002, pp. 41-46, and "Literature auf Porzellan: Noch Einmal: 'Paul et Virginie' als Meissner Lithophanien," *Keramos* (Bonn), vol. 194, 2006, pp. 79-82.

[13]Hans Leichter, Berliner Lithophanien: eine fast vergessene Grafische Technik des Biedermeier," aus "Der Bär von Berlin," *Jahrbuch des Vereins für die Geschichte Berlins*, 23. Folge. Verlag, Berlin/Bonn: West Kreuz-Druckerei, 1974), p. 7.

[14]Derek Ostergard, editor, *Along the Porcelain Road: Berlin and Potsdam in KPM Porcelain and Painting 1815-1848* (New York: The Bard Graduate Center for Studies in the Decorative Arts, 1993), p. 83.

[15]Carol Wax, *The Mezzotint: History and Technique* (New York: Harry N. Abrams, Inc., 1990), p.117.

[16]Paul Hadley, "The Ancient Art of Lithophane," *Amateur Art and Camera*, March 1952, p. 46.

[17]Hans Rudolph Simmler, "Lithophanien leben vom Licht," p. 110.

Chapter 6

[1]*Hobbies*, "Smithsonian Report Traces Development of Lighting," January 1953, p. 67.

[2]Ibid.

[3]Hans Leichter, "Berliner Lithophanien: eine fast vergessene Grafische Technik des Biedermeier," *Der Bär von Berlin*, Jahr des Vereins für die Geschichte Berlins. 23. Folge. 1974, p. 10.

[4]Amoret and Christopher Scott, *Collecting Bygones* (New York: David McKay Company, Inc., 1964), p. 111.

[5]Ibid., p. 112.

[6]Ibid.

[7]Correspondence from C.M. Heffner to Dr. Edmond Beroud, dated January 11, 1951.

[8]Geoffrey Egan, "The London that records fail to show," *British Archaeology*, no. 16, July 1996.

[9]Ibid.

[10]Correspondence to Mr. Blair from M.J. Kuder, dated October 7, 1964.

[11]Correspondence to Bogue from Mr. Blair, dated 1976.

[12]Kirsten Dorothee Pliquet, *Lithophanien der KPM-Manufaktur Berlin (1828-1865)*, Magisterarbeit an der Universitat Hamburg, 1982, p. 51.

Chapter 7

[1]Ted Bartlett, *The Glen Iris Inn – Walking Tour Companion* (Letchworth State Park, Castile, New York, n.d.), p. 1.

[2]Ibid., p. 2.

[3]Sherman Peer, *A Sketch of William Pryor Letchworth and Glen Iris* (Letchworth State Park, Castile, New York: Genesee State Park Commission, 1956), n.p.

[4]Bartlett, p. 3.

[5]Bartlett, p. 4.

[6]A. Görling, B. Meyer, and A. Woltmann, *Art Treasures of Germany* (Boston: Samuel Walker & Company), p. 142.

[7]Herbert G. Houze, "Samuel Colt's Porcelain Transparencies," *The Magazine Antiques*, vol. 169, no. 4, April 2006, p. 111.

[8]Ibid., pp. 111-112.

[9]Ibid., p. 112.

[10]Ibid.

[11]One of the Colt lithophanes was sold at auction in Cincinnati, Ohio on June 6, 2007, for $5,500.

[12]Houze, p. 112.

[13]http://stlouis.missouri.org/chm accessed 2/20/06.

[14]*Blair Museum of Lithophanes Bulletin* No. 100, Winter Spring 2007, p. 2

[15]Ibid., p. 3.

[16]Ibid.

[17]Birgit Kümmel, "Fensterschmuck des Biedermeier – Die Lithophanien im Arolser Schloß," *Geschichtsblätter für Waldeck* Bd. 86, 1998, p. 118.

[18]Laszlo Molnar, "Herendi litofan ablak," *Muve'szetto¨rte'neti e'rtesi'to*, vol. XXVIII, no. 4, 1979, pp. 243. Translation was provided by Elizabeth Gulacsy

Chapter 9

[1]Louise Bruner, "Private Collectors – Toledoans who are at home with art," *Toledo Magazine*, Week of July 24-30, 1988, p. 12.

[2]Louise Bruner, "Lithophanes – an obscure art form resurrected," *The Blade Sunday Magazine*, March 28, 1965, p. 9.

[3]Laurel Blair, *Bulletin No. 1*, March 15, 1976, p. 1.

[4]Ibid.

[5]Ibid.

[6]Helen Wells, "The Magic Pictures," *The Miami Herald*, September 18, 1963, Section B, p. 1.

[7]Correspondence between Mr. Blair and Dr. Beroud conflicts with both Laurel Blair's report in his first *Bulletin No. 1*, dated March 15, 1976 and his unpublished, undated typescript preliminary book draft introduction. Because there is additional contradictory evidence in a *Toledo Blade* newspaper clipping dated March 3, 1965, one must assume that Mr. Blair's memory for exact dates had dimmed a bit by the time he issued his first newsletter a decade later. Unfortunately some of this misinformation was unwittingly repeated in *The Blair Museum of Lithophanes Bulletin No. 98*, published in the Spring 2005.

[8]Correspondence from Laurel Blair to Dr. and Mrs. Edmond Beroud, dated November 27, 1962.

[9]Ibid.

[10]Correspondence from Dr. Edmond Beroud to Laurel Blair, dated May 2, 1963.

[11]Laurel Blair, *Bulletin No. 1*, March 15, 1976, p. 2.

[12]Correspondence from Dr. Edmond Beroud to Laurel Blair, dated August 1, 1963.

[13]Ibid.

[14]Laurel Blair, *Bulletin No. 1*, March 15, 1976, p. 2

[15]Correspondence from George Blair to Laurel Blair, dated February 11, 1964.

[16]Louise Bruner, "Lighted Porcelain Art Form Proves Illuminating To Display Viewers," *Toledo Blade*, March 3, 1965, p. 33.

[17]Louise Bruner, "Lithophanes, Waxes Museum is Relocated," *The Blade*, October 11, 1972.

[18]Correspondence from Mr. Blair to Mr. W.D. John, dated February 13, 1967.

[19]Correspondence from William Hutton to Dr. Beroud, dated December 6, 1954.

[20]Kim Bates, "Lithophane Museum's Founder Concerned About City Takeover," *The Blade*, May 31, 1993.

[21]Blair *Bulletin* No. 42, February 28, 1983, p. 1.

[22]Ibid.

[23]Ibid., p. 2

[24]Correspondence from Adelaide Dember to Laurel Blair, dated November 29, 1967.

[25]Ibid.

[26]Correspondence from Adelaide Dember to Laurel Blair, dated December 11, 1967.

Chapter 10

[1]Amoret and Christopher Scott, "Lithophanes – A Neglected Branch of Victorian Ceramics," *Antique Dealer & Collector's Guide*, London, December 1966, p. 73.

[2]Francis Buckley, "In the Museums – Marine Lithophanes," *Antiques Magazine*, vol. 66, July 1954, p. 62.

[3]Ironically it was donated to the Mariner's Museum by Fred Hill, quite possibly the spouse of Mrs. Frederick F. Hill who wrote the inaccurate note about these pieces that became published in *Antiques Magazine* by Francis Buckley.

Chapter 11

[1]*Crockery & Glass Journal*, "Lithophanous Pictures, *Crockery & Glass Journal*, vol. 1, no. 12, March 27, 1875, p. 10.

[2]www.multiaxis.com/artcam/features/lithophanes.htm, accessed February 10, 2006, 7:41 p.m.

[3]Bessie M. Lindsey, *Lore of Our Land Pictured in Glass*, vol. II (Forsyth, Illinois: 1950), p, 291.

[4]Correspondence from John S. White to Mr. Blair, dated October 20, 1981.

[5]Correspondence from Edmond Beroud to Adrian Nagelvoort, dated April 26, 1957.

[6]Correspondence from Adrian Nagelvoort to Edmond Beroud, dated February 14, 1957.

[7]Email correspondence from Francis Dufort with the author, dated September 20, 2007.

[8]Ibid.

[9]Ibid.

[10]e-Business W@tch website accessed August 23, 2007.

[11]Email correspondence from Lisa Mann with the author, dated September 5, 2007.

Chapter 12

[1]Diana West, "Pictures in Porcelain," *Victorian Homes*, February 2000, p. 31.

[2]Ibid.

[3]The information about David Failing and Schmidt-Failing was supplied in an essay by Pat Schmidt and David Failing, with only a few changes by the author.

[4]Essay sent on disk by Curt Benzle to the author in March 2007. All information about Curt Benzle and his connection with lithophanes, is based on his own essay. All images were also provided by Mr. Benzle.

[5]Correspondence from Nicolai Klimaszewski to the author, dated August, 2007.

[6]Nicolai Klimaszewski, "Hand-Carving Lithophanes," *Ceramics Monthly*, October 2007, vol. 55, no. 8, p. 51.

[7]Correspondence from Nicolai Klimaszewski to author, dated August, 2007.

[8]All quotes by Marty Kubicki are from email correspondence in 2007.

Bibliography

Antique Doll Collector Magazine. "Auction Gallery – Preview: A Sale With

Lilliputian Dimensions," *Antique Doll Collector Magazine*, 4, no. 3 (April 2001): 16.

Antiques Journal. Classified ad for lithophanes (December 1965): 37.

Antiques Journal. Photograph of Ackerman lithophane collection (October 1989): 61.

Armour, John. Advertisement for "Transparent Porcelain Pictures," *Montreal Gazette*, no. 91 (June 16, 1853).

Art-Journal Advertiser, advertisement for E.G. Zimmermann, London, no. 189 (March 1854): n.p.

Art-Journal Advertiser, advertisement for E.G. Zimmermann, London (November 1854): iv.

Atterbury, Paul, ed. *The History of Porcelain*. New York: William Morrow and Company, Inc., 1982: 185-186.

Baer, Winfried. *Berlin Porcelain*. Washington, D.C.: Smithsonian Institution Press, 1980): 24, 91.

Barber, Edwin Atlee. *Marks of American Potters*. Philadelphia: Patterson & White Company, 1904: 28.

Barber, Edwin A. "Historical Sketch of the Phoenixville Pottery," *The Clay Worker Magazine*, 28 (August 1897): 96-9.

Barber, Edwin Atlee. *The Pottery and Porcelain of the United States*, 2nd Edition, G.P. Putnam's Sons, 1902: 267-270, 467-470.

Barnes, Jean. "Lithophanes Are Cast in Porcelain," *The Wichita Eagle and Beacon* (November 23, 1969): 4D.

Baroody, Elizabeth. "Lithophanes, A Surprise and Delight," *Hobbies*, 90, no. 3, (May 1985): 17-19.

Barth, Catherine. "Historic Lithophanes and Their Production," *Ceramics Monthly* (November 1978): 50-53.

Bartlett, Ted. *The Glen Iris Inn – Walking Tour Companion*. Letchworth State Park, Castile, New York, n.d.

Bates, Kim. "Lithophane Museum's Founder Concerned About City Takeover," *The Blade* (May 31, 1993).

Battie, David. *Sotheby's Concise Encyclopedia of Porcelain*. London: Chancellor Press, 1998: 159-160.

Bemrose, Geoffrey. *Nineteenth Century English Pottery and Porcelain*. London: Faber and Faber, 1952: 43.

Benson, Mildred. "Realtor Had Donated Lithophane Collection," *The Blade*, (September 28, 1993).

Berling, K. *Meissen China: An Illustrated History*. New York: Dover Publications, Inc., 1972: 83.

Bernasconi, J.R. *The Collector's Glossary of Antiques and Fine Arts* (London: The Estates Gazette Limited, 1967: 172.

Beroud, Edmond. "Lithophanes What They Are and Why They Are a Delightful Item for Collectors," *Spinning Wheel*, 7, no. 6 (June 1951): 22, 24, 27.

Bessin, Peter. "Bei Licht betrachtet -- Die Kunst der Lithophanie," *Weltkunst*, 72, no. 10 (October 2002): 1529-1532.

Bettinghaus Cay. "One Picture Is Worth a Thousand Words," *Opaque News*, 5, no. 3 (June 1990): 538.

Bettinghaus, Cay. "One Picture Is Worth a Thousand Words," *Opaque News*, 5, no. 4 (September 1990): 547.

Birmingham, Frederic. *Falstaff's Complete Beer Book*. New York: Universal-Award House, 1970: 92.

The Blade. "Laurel Blair Was Host," (March 4, 1965).

______. "The Blair Museum of Lithophanes," (March 5, 1965).

______. "Largest Collection of Lithophanes in the Country," (January 2, 1966).

______. "This French Bisque Veilleuse," (November 12, 1967).

______. "Rare Lithophanes, Waxes Displayed," (February 4, 1973): 22.

______. "Small Museum Owner Invited to Workshop," (April 21, 1974).

______. "Laurel Blair has returned from spending three weeks in England," (November 7, 1976).

______. "Waxes, Lithophanes in Unique Museum," (April 24, 1977): 2.

______. "Wanted: Eternal Custodian for Ethereal Artwork," (April 29, 1992).

______. "Blair Museum to be Open to the Public," (May 26, 1993).

______. "Blair Museum Board Nominations Made," (September 23, 1993).

______. "Suit Dropped to Block Move of Lithophanes," (October 13, 1995).

______. "Art of all types will be at Botanical Garden," (August 6, 2004): 21.

Blair, Laurel. Untitled essay about lithophanes, n.d.

Blair Museum of Lithophanes and Carved Waxes, Lithophan Collectors' Club Bulletins, March 15, 1976-1997. (approximately 97 issues.)

Blühm, Andreas and Louise Lippincott. *Light! The Industrial Age 1750-1900: Art & Science, Technology and Society*. New York: Thames & Hudson, 2001): 112-113.

Boger, Louise Ade. *The Dictionary of World Pottery and Porcelain*. New York: Charles Scribner's Sons, 1971: 200.

Boros, Ethel. "Antique Lore," *Better Living, Plain Dealer Home Magazine*, (November 25, 1972): 3, 4.

Bortner, Judy. "Our House For All Seasons," *Gallaudet Today*, Washington D.C.: Office of Alumni and Public Relations, 2, no. 3 (Spring 1972): 30-33.

Bristol, Olivia and Leslie Geddes-Brown. *Doll's Houses*. Mitchell Beazley/Reed International Books Limited, 1997): 86.

Brongniart, Alexandre. *Traité des arts céramiques: ou des poteries, considérées dans leur histoire, leur Pratique et Leur théorie*. 2 Bde u. Atlas, Paris: 1854, 2: 400-401.

Brongniart, Alexandre. *Traité des arts céramiques: ou des poteries, considérées dans leur histoire, leur pratique et leur théorie*. Paris: Passelin, Librairie De La Faculté De Médecine, 1877, 1: 41.

Brongniart, Alexander and Riocreaux, D. *Description méthodique du Musée Ceramique de la Manufacture Royale de Porcelaine de Sèvres*. Paris: A. Leleux, 1845, 1: 289, 290, 298.

Brosio, Valentino. *Porcellane e maioliche: italiane dell'Ottocento* (Milano:

Antonio Vallardi, 1964: 103.
Bruner, Louise. "Lighted Porcelain Art Form Proves Illuminating to Display Viewers," *The Blade* (March 3, 1965): 33.
______. "Lighted Porcelain Art Draws Praise," *The Blade* (March 3, 1965).
______. "Lithophanes – an obscure art form resurrected," *The Blade Sunday Magazine* (March 28, 1965): 9, 10.
______."Lithophane Waxes Museum is Relocated," *The Blade* (October 11, 1972).
______. "Curious About Lithophanes, Carved Waxes?," *The Blade* (October 15, 1972): 4.
______."Mr. Blair's Wax Museum," *The Blade Sunday Magazine* (April 8, 1973): 12-16, 18.
______. "Lithophanes," *Antiques*, 106, no. 1 (July 1974): 117-121.
______. "A Unique Toledo Museum Just Keeps On Growing," *The Blade* (April 17, 1977): 3.
______. "Private Collectors – Toledoans who are at home with art," *Toledo Magazine* (July 24-30, 1988): 2, 8-12.
Bucher, Bruno. *Geschichte der technischen künste*. Stuttgart: W. Spemann, 1875- 93, III: 547.
Buckley, Francis. "Lithophanes: A Forgotten Victorian Craze," *The Antique Collector*. London: National Magazine Co., 8 (July 17, 1937): 184-6.
______."Marine Lithophanes in the Mariners' Museum," *Antiques*, 66 (July 1954): 62.
Burton, William. *A General History of Porcelain*, II. London: Chatto, 1920: 153-4.
Buten, Harry M. *Wedgwood Rarities*. Merion, PA: Buten Museum of Wedgwood, 1969: 137.
Campo, Anne. "A la flamme des tisanières," *L'Estampille*, Sommaire, no. 46, n.d.: 29.
Capuzzo, Mike. "Gilded Age Trinkets are Today's 'Elegant Objects,'" *Miami Herald* (March 29, 1982): 1B.
Carney, Margaret. "Blair Museum of Lithophanes," *Toledo Botanical Garden Cultivation*, 4, no. 2 (April - June 2005): 13.
______. "Lithophanes and Asia: Translucent Translations," *Ceramic Monthly*, 55, no. 8 (October 2007): 48-51.
Cawley, Marjorie. "Antiques – Transparent Lithophanes," *South Wales Argus*, (January 12, 1970).
Ceramic Culture Innovation 1851-2000. Budapest, Lisbon, Limoges, Stoke-on-Trent, Faenza, Selb-Plößberg: Deutsches Porzellanmuseum, 2002: 164.
Chaffers, William. *Marks & Monograms on Pottery and Porcelain*, I. 1931: 500.
______. *Marks & Monograms on European & Oriental Pottery and Porcelain*. London: Reeves & Townes, 1932: 244.
Chatfield, Jayne C. "Lithophanes," *NEAA News*, 5, no. 10 (November, 1986): 1, 3.
Christie's. *Property From Two Ducal Collections at Woburn Abbey, Bedfordshire Sale 7013*, September 20-21, 2004, Christie's Auction, Sculpture Gallery, Bedfordshire, England.
Clements, Chase. "Fight Over Location for Blair Collection of Lithophanes Continues," *The Blade* (September 15, 1995).
Cole, Ann Kilborn. "Victorian Lithophanes," *The Philadelphia Inquirer Magazine* (November 16, 1958): 49.
Collard, Elizabeth. *19th Century Pottery and Porcelain in Canada*. Montreal: McGill-Queen's University Press, 1984: 194-195.
Country Life. "Lithophanic China," (April 9, 1948): 724-5.
Crockery & Glass Journal. "Lithophanous Pictures," *The Crockery & Glass Journal*, 1, no. 12 (March 27, 1875): 10.
Curmer, L. *L'Industrie Exposition des Produits de L'Industrie Francaise en 1844*. Paris, ca. 1844: 175.
Danckert, Ludwig. "Lithophanies," *Directory of European Porcelain*. London: Robert Hale, N.A.G. Press, 2004: 337-338.
DeAtley, Gertrude D. "About Antiques," *The Indianapolis Star* (May 2, 1965): 16.
______. "About Antiques," *The Indianapolis Star* (January 12, 1969): n.p.
Degenhardt, Richard K. *Belleek: The Complete Collector's Guide and Illustrated Reference*. Radnor, PA: Wallace-Homestead Book Company, 1993: 80, 82, 83, 177, 178.
Dente, Aldo. "Paesaggi," *Seducendo con l'arte, la collezione di ventagli dei Civici Musei di Storia ed Arte de trieste*. Civici Musei di Storia ed Arte, 2003: 138.
Drepperd, Carl. W. "Lithophanes," *A Dictionary of American Antiques*. Boston: Brantford, 1957: 224.
______."Transparencies," *First Reader for Antique Collectors*. Garden City, New York: Doubleday & Company, 1946: 128.
______."A Visit to Lithophania," *The Spinning Wheel* (November 1952) VIII, no. 11: 18, 20, 34.
Drew, James. "UT Accused of Lowering House Values," *The Blade* (May 12, 1993): 19.
Dreyfus, Camille. "Lithophanie," *La Grande encyclopédie, inventaire, raisonné des sciences, des lettres et des arts, par une société de savants et de gens de lettres*. Paris: H. Lamirault, 1886-1902: 335.
Elder, Robert A., Jr. "Lithophanic Art," *Keramik-Freunde der Schweiz*, Mitteilungsblatt, no. 37 (January 1957): 18-22, Tafel 1-VI.
Encyclopaedia Britannica, Inc. "Lithophanes," *Encyclopaedia Britannica*, 1992: 400.
Evans, Lyn. *Marks Shapes and Patterns of the Llanelly Pottery*, c. 1987, n.p.
Evenson, Rosemary Carter. "Lithophane Miniatures -- A New Art Form," *Miniature Gazette* (Fall 1984): 36-39.
Familien. P.P. svarer på spørsmål, *Familien*, no. 11, 1992: 68.
Fan Association of North America. "Lithophanes – Handscreens of Porcelain," *Fan Association of North America Quarterly* (Winter 1990-1991) IX, no. 3: 3-4.
Faÿ-Hallé, Antoinette and Barbara Mundt. *Porcelain of the Nineteenth Century*. New York: Rizzoli, 1983: 147-8, 275.
Farrell, Bill. "He's reviving a lost art," *The Sunday Observer-Dispatch*, n.d.
Fisher, Stanley W. *Worcester Porcelain*. London: Ward Lock & Co. Limited, n.d.): 24-25.
Fletcher, John Kyrle. "Llanelly Porcelain," *Connoisseur*, 84, no. 336 (August 1929): 87-88.
Fleming, John and Hugh Honour. *Dictionary of the Decorative Arts*. New York: Harper & Row Publishers, 1977: 475.
Folnesics, J. and Dr. E.W. Braun. *Geschichte der K.K. Wiener Porzellan-Manufaktur*. Hrsg. vom K.K. Österreichischen Museum für Kunst und Industrie. Wien: Druck und Verlag der K.K. Hof- und Staatsdruckerei, 1907: 138.
Ford, Walter D. "Application of Photography in Ceramics," *Bulletin of the American Ceramic Society*, 20, no. 1 (January 1941).
Frantz, Henri. *French Pottery and Porcelain*. London: G. Newnes, limited; New York: C. Scribner's sons, 1906: 114-115.
Freed, Frederick C. *Rare Porcelain Veilleuses Collection*. New York: The

Alectra Press, Inc., 1964: 37, 39, 55, 61, 83-85, 92.
Freeman, Larry. *New Light on Old Lamps*. Watkins Glen, New York: Century House, 1968: 113-114, 177-179.
Frick, G[eorg Friedrich Christoph]. "Geschichte der Königlichen Porzellanmanfaktur seit ihrer Entstehung: 1ter Theil bis zum Schluss des Jahres 1845." Excerts from manuscript copy made by an unknown co-worker in the factory. 1018 pages, with occasional corrections by Frick. Königliche Porzellan-Manufaktur, Berlin, Wegelystr.
_____. *Verhandlungen des Vereins zur Beförderung des Gewerbefleisses in Prussia*. 1827: 246.
Fricke, Erika. "Botanical Garden breaks mold with litohophane museum," *Toledo Blade*, n.d.
Frisk, William. "Chapter News – Toledo," *The Victorian Society in America Bulletin*, 5, no. 4 (April 1977): 4.
Gasnault, Paul and Edouard Garnier. *French Pottery*. London, 1884: 169.
Gaston, Mary Frank. *The Collector's Encyclopedia of Limoges Porcelain*. Paducah, Kentucky: Collector Books, 1991: 36.
Gilbert, Anne. "Lithophanes are valuable," *The Evening Bulletin* (October 27, 1978): 46B.
_____. "Lithophanes Will Light Up Your Life," *Collectors News*, 19, no. 7 (November 1978): 75-76.
Gilkyson, Phoebe H. "Were 'Lithophanes' Ever Made in Phoenixville," *Daily Republican* (June 8, 1964).
Godden, Geoffrey A. *Antique China and Glass Under £5*. London: Arthur Barker Limited, 1966: 27-33, plates 13-15.
_____. *Antique Glass and China*. South Brunswick and New York: A.S. Barnes and Company, 1966: 32-35, plates 13-15.
_____. *Godden's Guide to European Porcelain*. New York: Cross River Press, 1994: 146, 204-7, 252, 288, 311-314, plates 188, 189, 254-7, 332-33.
_____. *Minton Pottery & Porcelain of the First Period 1793-1850*. London: Herbert Jenkins, 1968: 53, 161.
_____. *Victorian Porcelain*. New York: Nelson, 1961: 195-196.
Good Housekeeping. "Paul Newman & Joanne Woodward's Lovely New York Home," (June 1978): 101-4.
Görling, A., B. Meyer, and A. Woltmann. *Art Treasures of Germany, A Collection of the Most Important Pictures of the Galleries of Dresden, Cassel, Brunswick, Berlin, Munich and Vienna*. Boston: Samuel Walker & Company, n.d.
Goyle, G.A.R. "Lithophanes," *The Magazine Antiques*, 29, no. 4 (April 1936): 146.
Graber, John. "Grounds include artisans, museum as well as flora," *The Courier* (July 24, 2004).
Greene, Vivien. *English Dolls' Houses of the Eighteenth and Nineteenth Centuries*. London: B.T. Batsford Ltd., 1955: 68, 196, 68.
Greene, Vivien and Margaret Towner. *The Vivien Greene Dolls' House Collection*. Woodstock, New York: The Overlook Press, 1995: 179.
Hadley, Paul. "The Ancient Art of Lithophane," *Amateur Art and Camera* (March 1952): 12-15, 46.
Haggar, Reginald G. *The Concise Encyclopedia of Continental Pottery and Porcelain*. New York: Hawthorn Books, Inc., 1960: 269.
Hainbach, Rudolf. *Pottery Decorating*. London: Scott, Greenwood & Son, 1924: 143-147.
Hamilton, Grant. "Lithophanes Come to Life with Light," *The New York-Pennsylvania Collector* (September 2007): 1B, 7B.
Hannover, Emil and Bernard Rackham. *Pottery & Porcelain: A Handbook for Collectors, III. European Porcelain*. London: Ernest Benn Limited, 1925: 104, 542.
Hansen, Harald. *Transparente Steine Optische Kästen*. Monchengladbach: Museum Schloss Reydt, 2003. Exhibition catalogue December 14, 2003 – February 29, 2004.
Hardy, Ruth Howard. "Lithoplastics – A New Art Developed By This Bywood Dentist," *Upper Darby News* (April 10, 1952): 19.
Harper, George W., Editor. "Lithophane," *Antique Collector's Guide and Reference Handbook*. New York: George W. Harper, 1939: 39.
Historisches Museum Murten. *Lithophanien: Romantische Zeugen des 19. Jahrhunderts*. Murten: Historisches Museum Murten, 1987. Exhibition catalogue October 24, 1987-April 4, 1988.
Hively, Sue. "Enlightening Hobby Enjoyed by Mrs. Owings," *Sandusky Register*, (December 31, 1969): 9-10.
Hobson, R.L. *Chinese Pottery and Porcelain*, I, II. New York: Dover Publications, 1976.
Hodgson, Mrs. Willoughby. *How to Identify Old Chinese Porcelain*. Chicago: A.C. McClurg & Co., 1907: 19-22.
Hommel, Martha Hill. "Some more about Lithophanes," *Hobbies* (July 1950): 76, 77.
_____. "Lithophanes – Again?," *Hobbies – The Magazine for Collectors* (July 1951): 78-80.
_____. "Lithophanes inspired by Thorvaldsen," *Hobbies* (July 1955): 74, 76.
Hommel, Rudolf. "Lithophanes," *Hobbies* (August 1949): 80-81.
_____. "Lithophane Addenda," *Hobbies* (January 1950): 57.
Honey, William Bower. *German Porcelain*. London: Faber and Faber, 1947: 31-32.
Houze, Herbert G. "Samuel Colt's Porcelain Transparencies," *The Magazine Antiques*, 169, no. 4 (April 2006): 106-115.
_____. Edited by Elizabeth Mankin Kornhauser. *Samuel Colt: Arms, Art, and Invention*. New Haven: Yale University Press; Hartford, Conn.: Wadsworth Atheneum Museum of Art, 2006: 232.
Hughes, G. Bernard. "Lithophane Pictures in Porcelain," *Country Life*, 110, (August 31, 1951): 648-649.
_____. *Victorian Pottery and Porcelain*. London: Spring Books, 1959: 89-92.
_____. *The Collector's Pocket Book of China*. London: Country Life, 1970: 178-179, 256-258.
Hughes, G. Bernard and Therle. *After the Regency*. London: Lutterworth Press, 1952: 124-125.
Hughes, Gareth. *A Llanelli Chronicle*. Llanelli: Llanelli Borough Council, 1984: 29, 51, 143-144, 255, 331, 354, illus. 334.
Hughes, Gareth and Robert Pugh. *Llanelly Pottery*. Llanelli: Llanelli Borough Council, 1990: 2-4, pl. 1-4.
Jacobi, Charles Thomas. *The Printers' Handbook of Trade Recipes, Hints & Suggestions Relating to Letterpress and Lithographic Printing, Bookbinding Stationery, Engraving, etc.* London: Chiswick Press, 2nd ed., 1891: 289-90.
Jacobs, David. "Council to Take Final Vote on Apartments," *The Blade* (February 19, 1996).
James, Arthur E. *Potters and Potteries of Chester County, Pennsylvania*. Chester County Historical Society, 1945: 70-73.
Janviers, Catherine. *Practical Keramics for Students*. London: Chatte & Mindus, 1880: 95.
Jedding, Hermann et al. *Hohe Kunst zwischen Biedermeier und Jugend-*

stil: Historismus in Hamburg und Norddeutschland. Katalog zur Ausstellung im Museum für Kunst und Gewerbe, Hamburg, June 23 – August 14, 1977: 276-280.

Jedding, Hermann. *Meißener Porzellan des 19. und 20. Jahrhunderts 1800-1933.* München: Keyser, 1981: 58, 175.

Jenkins, Dilys. *Llanelly Pottery.* Swansea: Deb Books, 1968: 10, 26-28.

Jervis, William Percival. *The Encyclopedia of Ceramics.* New York, 1902: 447.

Johnson, Ruth Louise. "Lithophanes add luster to your life," *The Antiques Journal* (March 1960): 37.

Jones, Mike. "Lithophane collection could move to Sylvania," *The Blade* (July 14, 1992): 9.

Karmarsch, Karl. *Geschichte der Technologie seit der Mitte der achtzehnten Jahrhunderts.* München: R. Oldenbourg, 1872: 503.

Kent County News. "2nd Annual Antique Show Oct. 21-22-23," *Kent County News,* VII, no. 38, Chestertown, Maryland (October 17, 1952): 1.

Kerr, Rose and John Ayers. *Blanc De Chine: Porcelain from Dehua.* Chicago: Art Media Resources, Ltd., 2002.

Kinsey Institute for Research in Sex, Gender, and Reproduction. *The Art of Desire: Erotic Treasures From the Kinsey Institute.* Bloomington, Indiana: School of Fine Arts Gallery, Indiana University, Bloomington, 1997: 103.

Klamkin, Marian. *Collectibles: A Compendium.* Garden City, New York: Dolphin Books, 1981: 151-152.

Kolbe, Georg. *Geschichte der Königlichen Porzellanmanufactur zu Berlin...in Veran-lassung des hundertjährigen Bestehens der Königl.-Manufactur.* Berlin: 1863.

Köllmann, Erich. *Berliner Porzellan 1763-1963.* Braunschweig: Klinkhardt & Biermann, 1966, I: 80, 141, 185-86, 208, 249, 268, and II: Tafel 230, 231.

Koontz, Paul. "High-Tech Lithophanes," *Tech Directions,* 62, no. 7 (February 2003): 26-27.

Kovalevski, Bärbel. "Georg Friedrich Kersting als malervosteher an der Königlichsächsischen Porzellan Manufaktur Meissen von 1818 bis 1847," *Keramik-Freunde der Schweiz,* Mitteilungsblatt no. 108 (December 1994): 3-88.

Kovel, Ralph and Terry. *The Kovel's Antiques Price List.* New York: Crown Publishers, 1980: 372-373.

______. *Kovels' Know Your Collectibles.* New York: Three Rivers Press, 1981: 175.

______. "Old Lithophane molds spark curiosity about originals," *The Ann Arbor News* (February 27, 1983): G3.

Kudrjawzewa, Tamara. *Das Weisse Gold Der Zaren.* Arnoldsche Art Publishers, 2000: 140, 186.

Kümmel, Birgit. "Fensterschmuck des Biedermeier – Die Lithophanien im Arolser Schloß," *Geschichtsblätter für Waldeck,* 86 (1998): 116-140.

Kunstgewerbemuseum der Stadt Köln. *Berliner Porzellan 1751-1954.* Köln Eigelsteintorburg: Kunstgewerbemuseum der Stadt Köln, 1954: 69, 71. Exhibition catalogue July 17 – September 12, 1954.

Kunze, Joachim. "Lithophanien der Meissner Porzellanmanufaktur," *Keramos Köln,* no. 92 (April 1981): 3-10.

Lane, Tahree. "Lithophane Museum hires its first curator," *The Blade* (June 23, 2004): D3.

______. "Form & Function: From 'wearable art' to political cartoons, from glass and pastels to lithophanes, area galleries are alive with creativity," *The Blade* (September 16, 2007): 4H.

Lattes, Wanda. "Le meraviglie della cera," *La Nazione,* Firenze, Mercoledi (March 4, 1975): 9.

Leichter, Hans. "Berliner Lithophanien: eine fast vergessene Grafische Technik des Biedermeier," aus "Der Bär von Berlin," *Jahrbuch des Vereins für die Geschichte Berlins,* 23. Folge. Berlin/Bonn: West Kreuz-Druckerei, 1974.

Lenz, Georg. "Lithophanien," in Kellers, Paul: *Monatsblätter/Die Bergstadt,* Heute Jahrgang 1920/21, II. Leipzig/Breslau/Wien: Wilh. Gottl. Korn, 1920: 213-220.

Lewis, Holden. "Council to Rub Out Old Law on Massages," *The Blade* (May 10, 1993): 11.

______. "Art patron goes begging for home for collection," *The Blade,* 1993, n.p.

Lindsey, Bessie M. *Lore of Our Land Pictured in Glass,* vol. II. Forsyth, Illinois: 1950: frontispiece, 291.

London Great Exhibition of the Works of All Nations, 1851. *Official Descriptive and Illustrated Catalogue.* London: Spicer Brothers, 1851, I: 1xxv, III: 1060, 1112, 1197.

London Telegram. "Antiques for Everyman," *London Telegram* (February 9, 1966).

Lühning, Frauke. "'Der Pastor am Fenster,' Eine Lithophanie im Museum Kellinghusen," *Nordelbingen,* 56 (1987): 63-67.

Mackay, James. *An Encyclopedia of Small Antiques.* New York: Harper & Row, 1975: 151.

MacSwiggan, Amelia E. *Fairy Lamps.* New York: Fountainhead Publishers, 1962: 74.

Mann, Charles C. "Antiques in the Chinese Taste: the Wondrous Ornamentation of Table Screens," *Architectural Digest,* 41 (June 1984): 84-9.

Manusov, Eugene V. *Encyclopedia of Character Steins.* Des Moines: Wallace-Homestead Book Co., 1976: 7-8, 11, 45, 67, 83, 85-86, 90, 110, 126, 140, 148, 159-160, 162-164, 166-167, 174, 179, 186, 199, 203-205.

______. "The Light at the End of the Tunnel – Lithophanes," *Prosit,* The Quarterly Bulletin of the Stein Collectors International, no. 58 (December 1979): 622.

Manusov, Eugene V. and Mike Wald. *Character Steins: A Collector's Guide.* New York, Toronto, London: Cornwall Books, 1987: 44, 64-66.

Marryat, Joseph. *Collections Towards A History of Pottery and Porcelain in the 15th, 16th, 17th, and 18th Centuries.* London: J. Murray, 1850: 264.

______. *A History of Pottery and Porcelain, Medieval and Modern.* London: J. Murray, 1857: 264, 382.

Marsh, Betty. "Society – The Blair Museum of Lithophanes," *The Toledo Times* (March 5, 1965): 6.

Maust, Don. "Fabulous Lithophanes and Their New Home," *The Antiques Journal,* 21, no. 11 (November 1966): 6-13, 16.

McCaslin, Mary J. *Royal Bayreuth: A Collector's Guide Book II.* Marietta, Ohio: Antique Publications, 2000: 20.

McClelland, Ann Samonial. "Light on Lithophanes," *Canadian Antiques Collector,* I, no. 7 (December 1966): 17-19.

McClinton, Katharine Morrison. "Lithophanes," *A Handbook of Popular Antiques.* New York: Bonanza Books, 1966: 225-228.

McMillen, Dorothy. "The Gentle Glow of Long Ago," *American Collector* (September 1977): 18, 19, 29.

Meeson, Graham B. The Life and Works of Mr. G.C. Cartlidge are discussed with regard to his role as the main practitioner of a photo-ceramic technique afte1895. Typewritten thesis, n.d.

Mellors & Kirk. *Antiques and Works of Art*, auction catalogue, Nottingham (February 8, 2007: 37-39, lots 410-423.

Meslin-Perrier, Chantal. *La Lithophanie et Limoges*. Paris: Ed. de la Réunion des musées nationaux, 1992. Exhibition at Musée National Adrien Dubouché, September 24, 1992- January 4, 1993.

______."Le Retour de la Lithophanie," *L'industrie Céramique & Verrière*, no. 894 (June 1994): 390-391.

Meyer, Hans. *Böhmisches Porzellan und Steingut*. Leipzig, 1927: 24, 69-70 + Tafel XXVI.

Meyer, Joseph. *Meyers Konversationslexikon*, Verlag des Bibliographischen Instituts, 10. Leipzig und Wien: Vierte Auflage, 1885-1892: 837.

Michelman, Dorothea S. "Pictures in Porcelain," *The Antiques Journal* (July 1964): 21-25.

Miller, Judith. *The Illustrated Dictionary of Antiques & Collectibles*. Boston, New York, London: Bulfinch Press/Little Brown & Co., 2001: 239.

Molnar, László. "Herendi litofan ablak," *Muvészettörténeti értesíto*, 28, no. 4 (1979): 243-252.

Morrin, Marianne. "The Old West End," *Toledo Metropolitan* (June 1986): 10-13, 18, 20.

Murphy, James. "Ohio Features Ceramic Genius Walter D. Ford (1906-1988)," *Flash Point*, 4, no. 2 (April-June 1991): 1, 16.

Museum News. "A Collection of Once-Popular Lithophanes Is Looking for a Home," 70 (September October 1991): 8.

Museum Update. "Blair Museum of Lithophanes and Waxes," Newsletter of the Ohio Museums Association, 10, no. 5 (September October 1989): 3.

New Encyclopaedia Britannica. "Lithophane." Chicago: Encyclopaedia Britannica, Inc., 2002: 400.

Newman, Harold. "Lithophane Plaques," *Antique Dealers and Collectors Guide*. London: Statuscourt Ltd., August 1990: 33-35, 40.

Newman, Harold. *Veilleuses 1750-1860*. South Brunswick, New Jersey: A.S. Barnes and co., Inc., 1967: 23, 101, 103-108, 248-249.

______. *Veilleuses: A Collector's Guide*. New York, London: Cornwall Books, 1987: 17, 69-72, 162, 168-169.

Nichols, Heidi L. *The Fashioning of Middle-Class America: Sartain's Union Magazine of Literature and Art and Antebellum Culture*. New York: Peter Lang, 2004.

Oakes, Gertrude. "Lithophanes," *Popular Ceramics* (November 1965): 12-15.

Orme, Edward. *An Essay on Transparent Prints and on Transparencies in General*, 1807.

Ostergard, Derek E., editor. *Along the Porcelain Road: Berlin and Potsdam in KPM Porcelain and Painting 1815-1848*. New York: The Bard Graduate Center for Studies in the Decorative Arts, 1993: 83, 88, 137, 168, 170.

Page, Peggy. "Lithophanes: an art form that wouldn't stay dead," *The Ann Arbor News* (April 15, 1984): E1-2.

Pazaurek, Gustav. *Gläser der Empire –und Biedermeierzeit*. Leipzig: Klinkhardt & Biermann, 1923: 66-68. – Überarbeitere Auflage, Eugen von Philippovich, ed., Brausschweig: Klinkhardt & Biermann, 1976.

Peer, Sherman. *A Sketch of William Pryor Letchworth and Glen Iris*. Letchworth State Park, Castile, New York: Genesee State Park Commission, 1956.

Philadelphia Inquirer Magazine. "An Island of Her Own," *The Philadelphia Inquirer Magazine* (April 19, 1953).

Phillips, Son & Neale. *English and Continental Ceramics and Glass*, auction October 6, 1976, Sale No. 20,899, London: 22-23.

Plinval de Guillebon, Régine de. *Porcelain of Paris 1770-1850*. New York: Walker and Company, 1972: 120, 128.

Pliquet, Kirsten Dorothée. *Lithophanien der KPM-Manufaktur Berlin (1828-1865)*, Magisterarbeit an der Universität Hamburg, 1982.

Poche, Emanuel. *Bohemian Porcelain*. Prague: Artia, 1957: 59.

Porzellanmanufactur Plaue. *Lithophanien: Leuchten für Sammler*. Thüringen: Porzellanmanufactur Plaue, 1998.

Pottery Gazette and Glass Trade Review. "Lithophane by Coalport," no. 80, (December 1955)1859.

______. "Translucent Embossments: Wax Modelling Method Used in Copenhagen." (February 1951): 242-243.

______. "Translucent Embossments Rediscovered." (October 1950): 1504-1507.

______. "Translucent Embossments: Letters from Correspondents Summarized," (December 1950): 1818.

Préaud, Tamara, Derek Ostergard, et al. *The Sèvres Porcelain Manufactory: Alexander Brongniart and the Triumph of Art and Industry, 1800-1847*. New Haven, Connecticut: Bard Graduate Center for Studies in the Decorative Arts, New York, 1997: 133.

Prime, William. C. *Pottery & Porcelain of All Times and Nations*. New York: Harper & Brothers, 1878: 296-297.

Rakow, Leonard S. and Juliette K. "Wedgwood Lithophanes," *Ars Ceramica*, Wedgwood Society of New York, no. 2 (1985): 10-12.

Random House. *The Random House Collector's Encyclopedia Victoriana to Art Deco*. New York: Random House, 1974: 174.

Rather-Pliquet, Kirsten Dorothée. *Die Lithophanien der KPM Berlin* (1828-1865), *Ein Beitrag zur Porzellangeschichte des 19. Jahrhunderts*. Universität Hamburg, Hamburg 1993. Dissertation.

Rather, Kirsten Dorothée. *Lithophanien: Die Welt des Biedermeier im Porzellanbild*. Berlin: Kulturstiftung Schloss Britz, 2001.

Rawding, Amelia E. "Lithophanes Art of the Victorian Era," *Hobbies* (July 1958): 66-67.

Realtor's Headlines. "Realtor's Interest In Nearly-Lost Art Form Leads To World's Largest Collection of Lithophanes," *Realtor's Headlines*, 34, no. 14 (April 3, 1967): 4, 6.

Robinson, David. "Lithophanic Porcelain – Collecting Wisely," *London Financial Times* (April 15, 1972): n.p.

Röntgen, Robert E. *The Book of Meissen*. Atglen, PA: Schiffer Publishing, 1996: 217-218, 319-321.

Rozin, Alfred. Lithophane: ploché barevne¬ vrstvené a ryté sklo z let 1850 – 1890 od K. Pfola z Kamenického S±enova. Kamenické S±enove¬: Muzeum skla, 1979. 6 panel folder.

Ruf, Bob and Pat. *Fairy Lamps -- Elegance in Candle Lighting*. Atglen, PA: Schiffer Publishing, 1996: 129-138.

Sandon, John. *The Dictionary of Worcester Porcelain, Volume I, 1751-1851*. Woodbridge: The Antique Collectors' Club, 1993: 221-222.

Sandon, Henry and John. *Grainger's Worcester Porcelain*. London: Barrie & Jenkins, 1989: 146-147.

Savage, George. *Porcelain Through the Ages*. Baltimore, Maryland: Penguin Books, 1963: 141.

______."Lithophanes," *Dictionary of Antiques*. New York: Mayflower Books, 1978: 244.

______."Lithophanes," *Dictionary of 19th Century Antiques and Later Objets d'Art*. Barrie Jenkins, 1978.

Savage, George and Harold Newman. *An Illustrated Dictionary of Ceramics*. New York: Thames and Hudson, 1985: 180-81.

Scheffler, Wolfgang. *Berlin im Porzellanbild seiner Manufaktur*. Berlin: Bruno Hessling, 1963: 31.

Scherf, Helmut. *Thüringer Porzellan: Unter Besonderer Berücksichtigung Der Erzeugnisse Des 18. Und Frühen 19. Jahrhunderts*. Wiesbaden: Ebeling Verlag, 1980: 43, 48, plate 52.

Schinck, Sheila. "David Failing," *Collectors Mart* (July August 1989): 56.

Schloßmuseum Arnstadt. *175 Jahre von Schierholz'sche Porzellanmanufaktur: Plaue in Thüringen*. Förderverein Schloßmuseum Arnstadt, 1992: 27-28, 30, 44-45, 54-55, 70-71, 78.

Schmidt, Pat. "David Failing's Unique Porcelain Lithophane Lamp Art," *Handmade Accents: the Buyer's Guide to American Artisans*, no. 12 (Fall 1989): 29-31.

Schmidt, W. "Lithophanien: Partner des Lichts." *Volkskunst. Zeitschrift für Volkstümliche Sachkultur*, München, 7, no. 2, 1984: 46-49.

Schock, Thomas U. "Lithophanes Are Worth Collecting; Porcelain Pictures on Display," (unknown newspaper),(n.d.): n.p.

______."Illustrations Showing a Group of Rare Lithophanes," flyer for *The Rocking Chair Antique Shop*, c. April 1948.

______."Lithophanes Are Worth Collecting," *American Antiques Journal* (May 1949): 16-17, 27.

______."Lithophanes," *Chester County Day* (October 6, 1951): 3.

Schöldl, Aug. "Verfahren zur Herstellung von Bildern auf keramischen Erzeugnisen auf photographischem Wege," *Keramische Rundschau*, 33 Jahrgang, no. 44, 1925: 751.

Scott, Amoret and Christopher. "Lithophanes – A Neglected Branch of Victorian Ceramics," *Antique Dealer & Collectors' Guide*. London, December 1966: 72-73.

______. *Collecting Bygones*. New York: David McKay Company, Inc., 1964: 111-112, 119-120.

______. "Collecting: See-Through Beauty," *Weekly Telegraph* (March 19, 1971).

Scott, Connie. "The Blair Lithophane Museum," *Fairy Lamps – Elegance in Candle Lighting*, no. XXX (February 2004): 5-8.

Scott, Paul. *Ceramics and Print*. Philadelphia: University of Pennsylvania Press, 1995: 26-27.

Scott, Rebekah. "Perseverance, Man's Charity Finally Pay Off," and " Quirky lithophane art museum set to open in July," *The Blade* (June 5, 2002): B 1-2.

______. "Red Tape Keeping Art Under Wraps," *The Blade* (September 29, 2001): 1-2.

Searles, Susan Claire. "Toledo museum displays world's largest collection of lithophanes," *The Herald* (July 23, 2003): 6.

Shinn, Charles and Dorrie. *The Illustrated Guide to Victorian Parian China*. London: Barrie & Jenkins, 1971: 105.

Shull, Thelma. "Notes on Chinese Porcelain," *Hobbies Magazine* (October 1949): 77.

______. *Victorian Antiques*. Rutland, Vermont: Charles E. Tuttle Company, 1963: 229-230.

Sigov, Mike. "Collection of Lithophanes Slated for Move to Garden," *The Blade* (August 14, 1995).

Simmler, Hans. "Lithophanien – Romantische Zeugen des 19. Jahrhunderts," *Keramik-Freunde Der Schweiz*, no. 32 (November 1987): 7-9, 12-13, plates 5, 6.

______. "Lithophanien: Ein beinahe vergessenes Kuntsgewerbe des 19. Jahrhunderts," *Magazin Sammeln 4* (April 1987) Druckerei Bruhin AG Freienbach: 22-27.

Society of Men of Letters. *La Grande Encyclopédie inventaire, raisonné des science, des lettres et des arts, par une société de savants et de gens de lettres*, 22. Paris: H. Lamirault, 1886-1902: 335.

Solis-Cohen, Lita and Bob Schwabach. "And Once You Find Out What It Is..." *Philadelphia Inquirer* (1974/1975).

Stafford, Barbara Maria and Frances Terpak. *Devices of Wonder: From the World in a Box to Images on a Screen*. Los Angeles: Getty Research Institute, 2001: 390.

Steckelings, KH. W. "Leuchtender Stein -- Über den Werdegang der Lithophanie," *Photo Antiquaria*. Mitteilungen des Clubs Daguerre, Sonderdruck, 1994.

______.Steckelings, KH. W. "Lithophanie: Leuchtender Stein," *Camera Obscura: Museum zur Vorgeschichte des Films*. Essen: Klartext, 2006: 62-63.

Stembridge, J. & Co. "Bijou Transparencies," advertisement, 1888.

Streichert, Hubert and Geneviève. "Faiences de Rubelles," *Rubelles 1982-83*: 14-15.

______. *Rubelles 1842-1992 Exposition du 8 au 17 Mai 1992*. Rubelles: 1992.

Symons, Jelinger. "The Industrial Capacities of South Wales," *The Cambrian Journal*, I, 1854: 321-22.

Tarjanyi, Judy. "Home to enhance Blair lithophanes," *The Blade* (June 19, 1996): 1, 4.

Tarter, Jabe. "Antiques Queries," *The Blade* (February 21, 1977): n.p.

Taylor, John. *The Complete Practical Potter or A Comprehensive Collection of Receipts, for the Manufacture of China, Earthenware, Ironstone, etc. etc.* Shelton: William White, 1847: 1

The Times Herald. "Exhibit Rare Lithophanes At Antique Show Next Week," Norristown, Pennsylvania (September 13, 1952): 4.

Tri-State Trader. "Question Box." (September 11, 1976): 2

Truesdell, Bill. *Directory of Unique Museums*. Kalamazoo, Michigan: Oryx Press, 1985: entry no. 202.

Urban, Stanislav. "La Parabole des Lithophanes, (A Parable of Lithophanies)" *[Tchecoslovaque] Revue due verre*, 36, no. 7 (1971): 200-205.

Vallongo, Sally. "Rare treasure trove goes begging," *The Blade* (May 12, 1991): 1-2.

______. "Toledo Top Stop for Swiss Pair Seeking 19th Century Art Form," *The Blade* (September 6, 1993).

van Dyck, Rüdiger. 'Lithophanien der Meissner Porzellanmanufaktur: Eine Ergänzung zum gleichlautenden Beitrag von Joachim Kunze." *Keramos*, no. 109 (July 1985): 17-22.

______."Lithophanien. Transparente Porzellanbilder," *Sammler Journal*, 4 (April 1987): 442-446.

Warman, Edwin G. *The Sixth Antiques and Their Current Prices*. Uniontown, Pennsylvania, 1960: 245-246.

______. *Warman's Ninth Antiques and Their Current Prices*. Uniontown, Pennsylvania: E.G. Warman Publishing Inc., 1968: 268-269.

Webster's Dictionary. "Lithophane." The World Publishing Company, 1962: 434.

Wegner, Peter-Christian. "Literatur auf Porzellan: 'Paul et Virginie' als Meissner Lithophanie," *Keramos* (Bonn), 177 (July 2002): 41-46.

______. "Literatur auf Porzellan: Noch Einmal: 'Paul et Virginie' als Meissener Lithophanien," *Keramos* (Bonn), 194 (2006): 79-82.

Wells, Helen. "'The Magic Pictures,'" *The Miami Herald* (September 18, 1963): 1-B.

West, Diana. "Pictures in Porcelain," *Victorian Homes* (February 2000): 29-31.

Williams, Isaac J. *A Guide to the Collection of Welsh Porcelain*. Cardiff: The National Museum of Wales, 1931: 10, plate XLI.

Williams, Laurence W. *Collector's Guide to Souvenir China* (Paducah, Kentucky: Collector Books, Schroeder Publishing Co., Inc., 1998: 100-101, 129.

Winder, Judith. "Toledo's Lithophane Museum an Enlightening Experience," *Old West End Magazine*, 2, no. 7 (July 2006): 22-23.

Wirtler, Ulrike. *Lampen, Lauchter and Lanterns: Die Bestände des Kölnischen Stadtmuseums*. Köln: 1991:115-121, color plates 38-39, plates 252-254.

Wood, Violet. *Victoriana: A Collector's Guide*. New York: MacMillan Co., 1961.

Woodbury, Walter E. *The Encyclopaedia of Photography*. London: Iliffe, 1890: 538.

Wykes-Jones, Max. *7,000 Years of Pottery and Porcelain*. New York: Philosophical Library, 1958: 156.

Zanger, Horst. "Lithophanie, das leuchtende Porzellanbild: eine faszinierde Technik fand unter Georg Friedrich Kersting Eingang in die Produktion der Porzellanmanufaktur Meissen," *Heimatzeitschrift fur Landsleute und Freunde Mecklenburgs*, 43, no. 12 (2001): 7.

Zinn, Rachel. "Toledo to tout porcelain art," *The Blade* (February 19, 2004).

Index